BARAKAMON

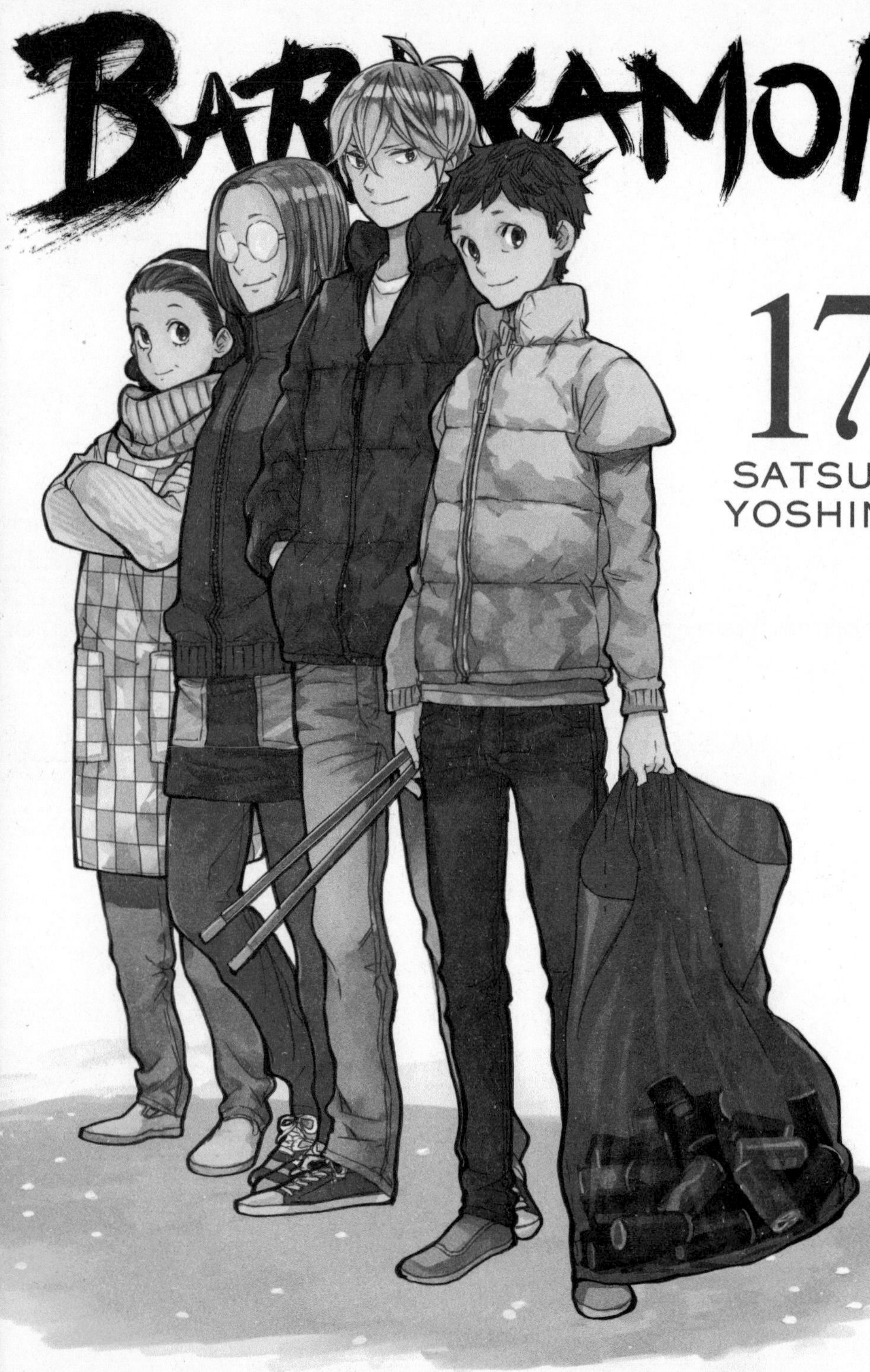

17

SATSUKI
YOSHINO

Contents

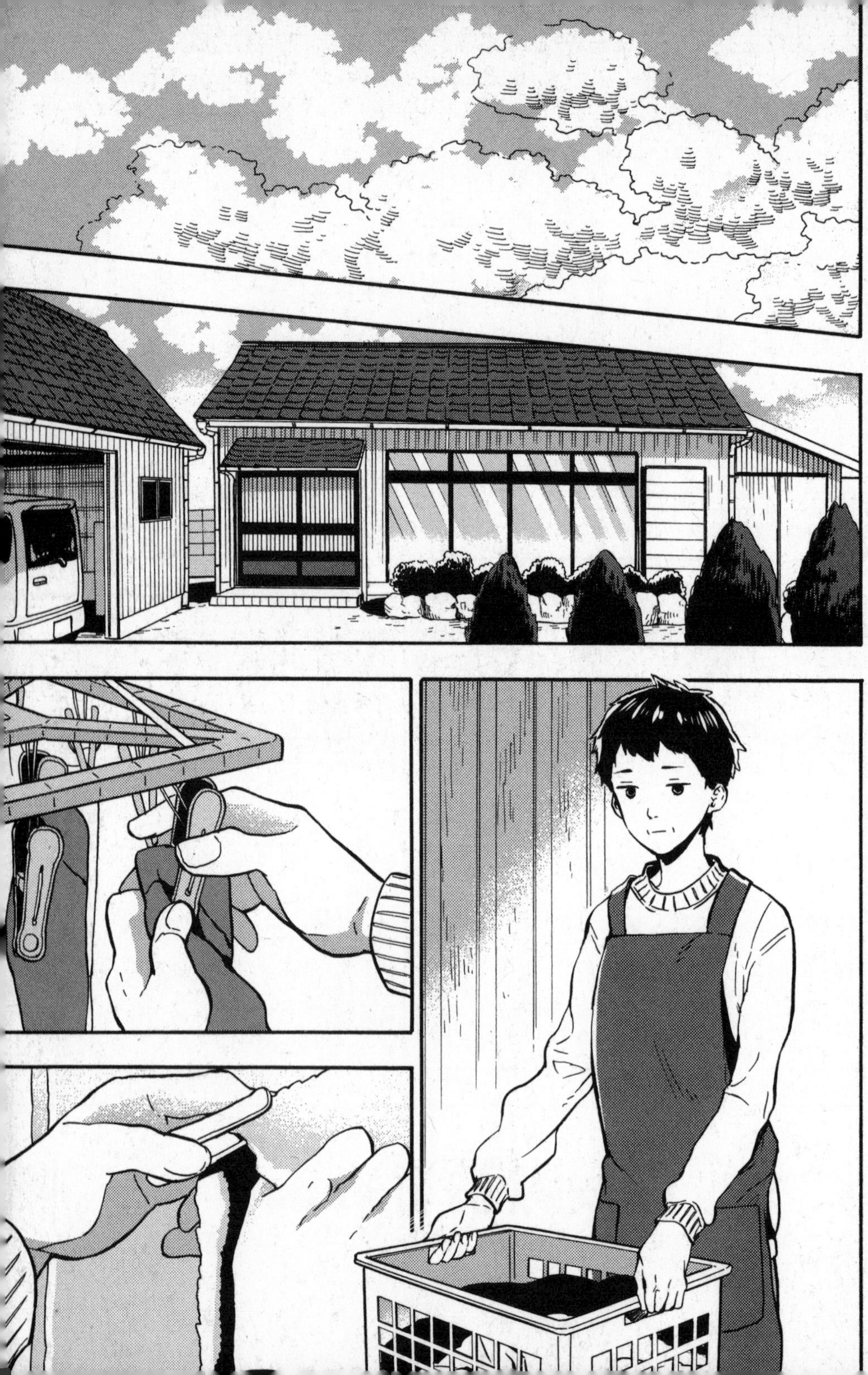

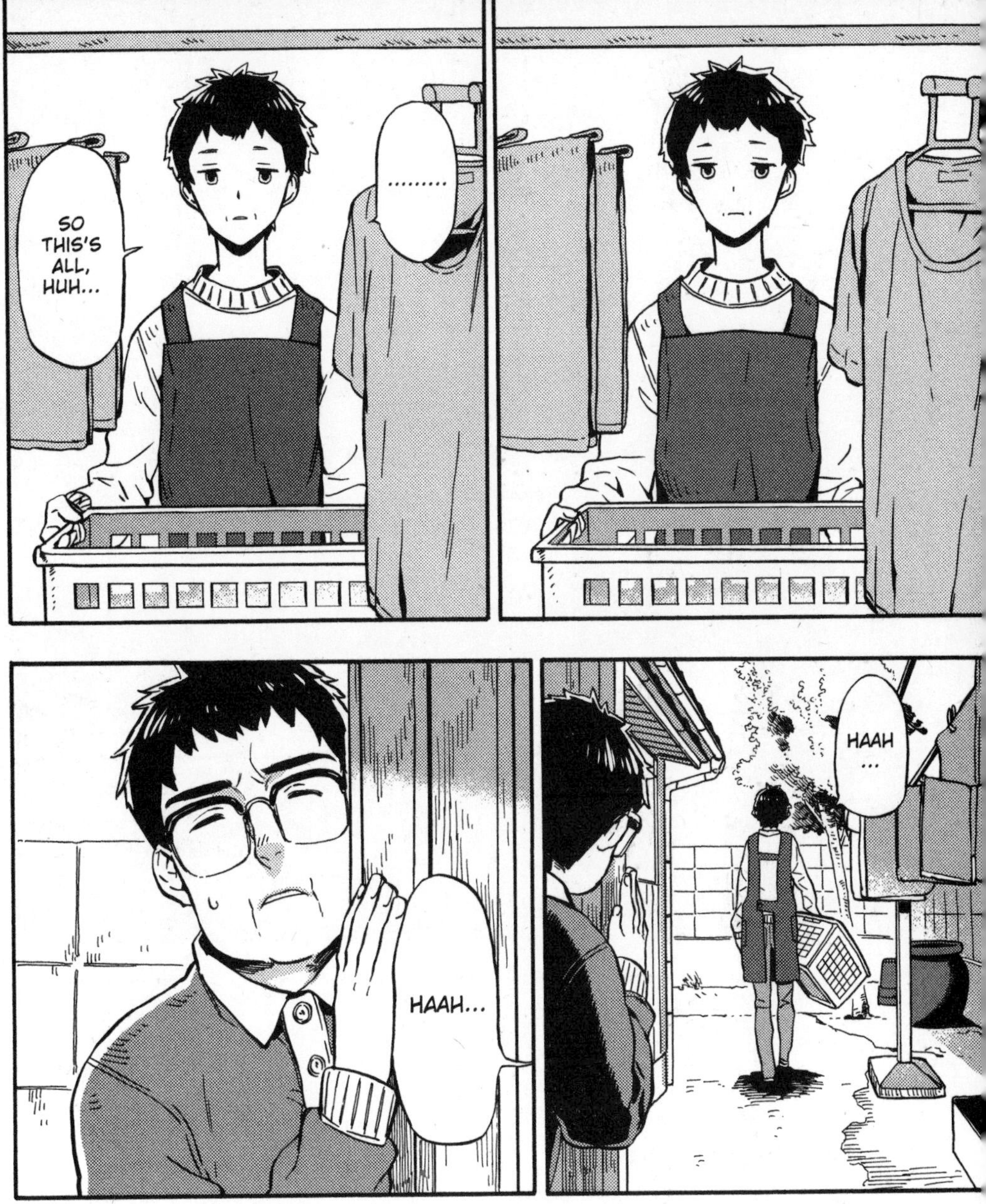
....
SO THIS'S ALL, HUH...
HAAH ...
HAAH...

Act.122
SEWA DE SEWA DE
(Translation: Worried Sick)

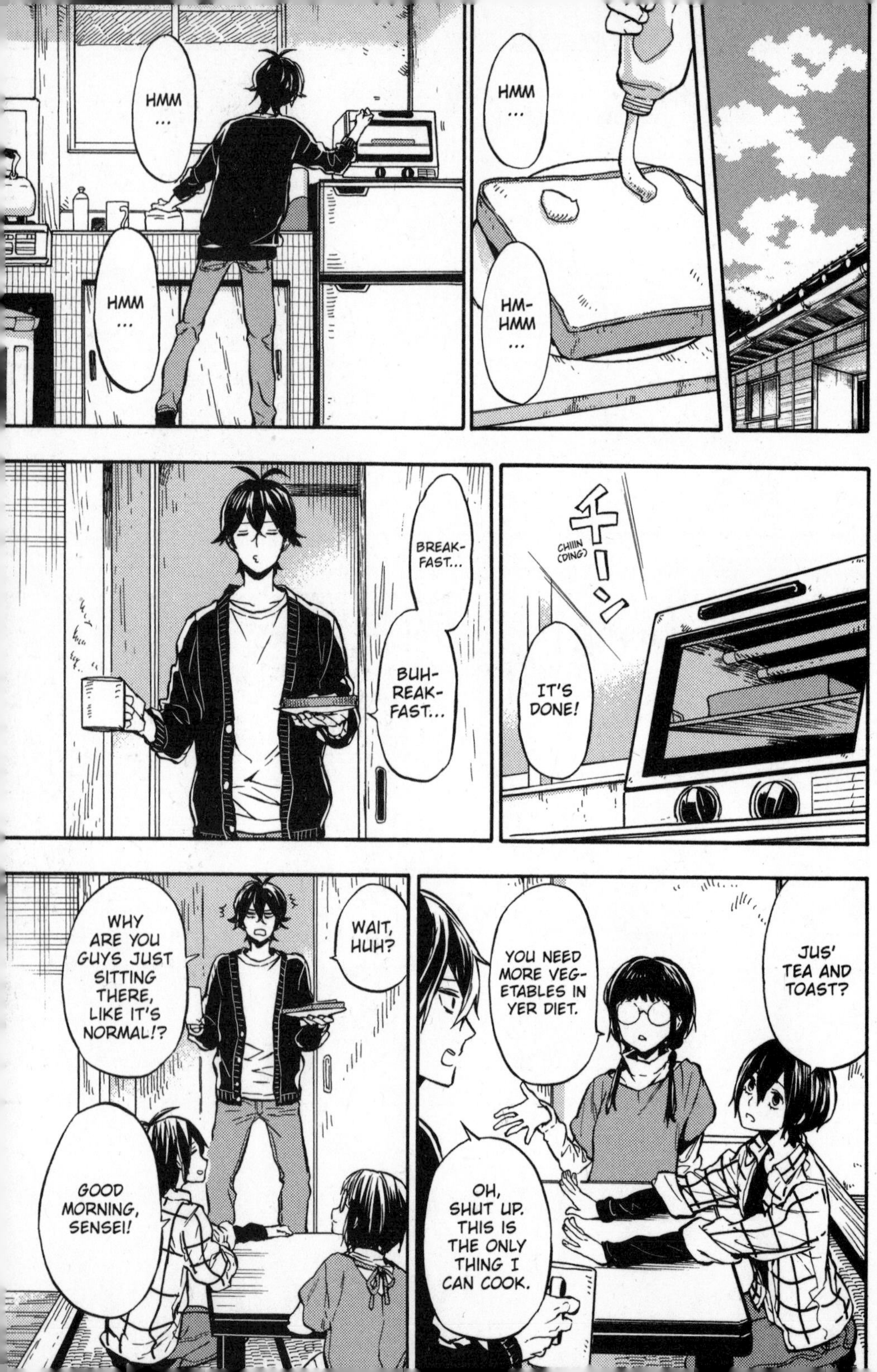
HMM...
HM-HMM...
HMM...
HMM...
チーン
CHIIIN (DING)
IT'S DONE!
BREAK-FAST...
BUH-REAK-FAST...
JUS' TEA AND TOAST?
YOU NEED MORE VEG-ETABLES IN YER DIET.
OH, SHUT UP. THIS IS THE ONLY THING I CAN COOK.
WAIT, HUH?
WHY ARE YOU GUYS JUST SITTING THERE, LIKE IT'S NORMAL!?
GOOD MORNING, SENSEI!

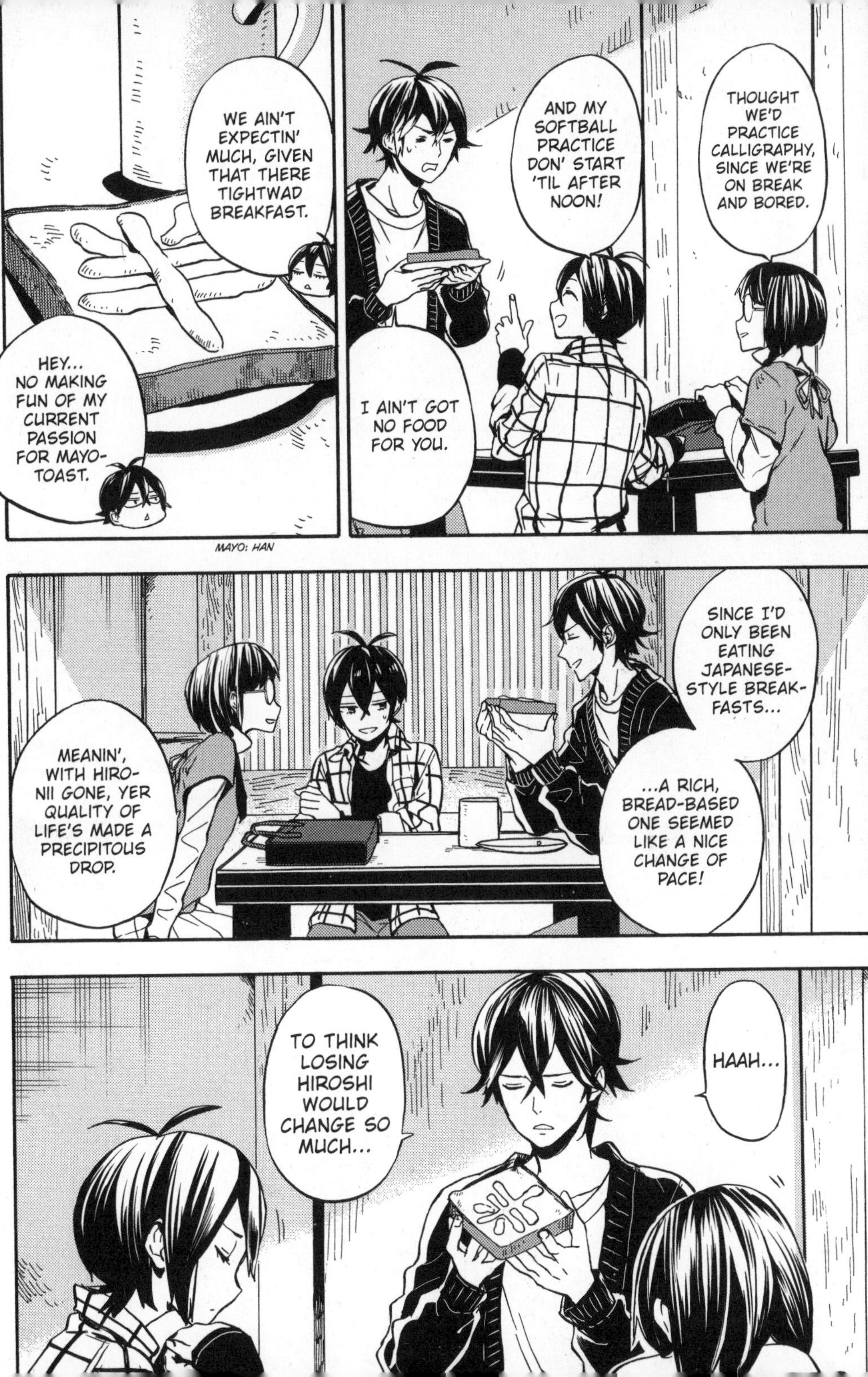
THOUGHT WE'D PRACTICE CALLIGRAPHY, SINCE WE'RE ON BREAK AND BORED.
AND MY SOFTBALL PRACTICE DON' START 'TIL AFTER NOON!
I AIN'T GOT NO FOOD FOR YOU.
WE AIN'T EXPECTIN' MUCH, GIVEN THAT THERE TIGHTWAD BREAKFAST.
HEY... NO MAKING FUN OF MY CURRENT PASSION FOR MAYO-TOAST.
MAYO: HAN
SINCE I'D ONLY BEEN EATING JAPANESE-STYLE BREAK-FASTS...
...A RICH, BREAD-BASED ONE SEEMED LIKE A NICE CHANGE OF PACE!
MEANIN', WITH HIRO-NII GONE, YER QUALITY OF LIFE'S MADE A PRECIPITOUS DROP.
HAAH...
TO THINK LOSING HIROSHI WOULD CHANGE SO MUCH...

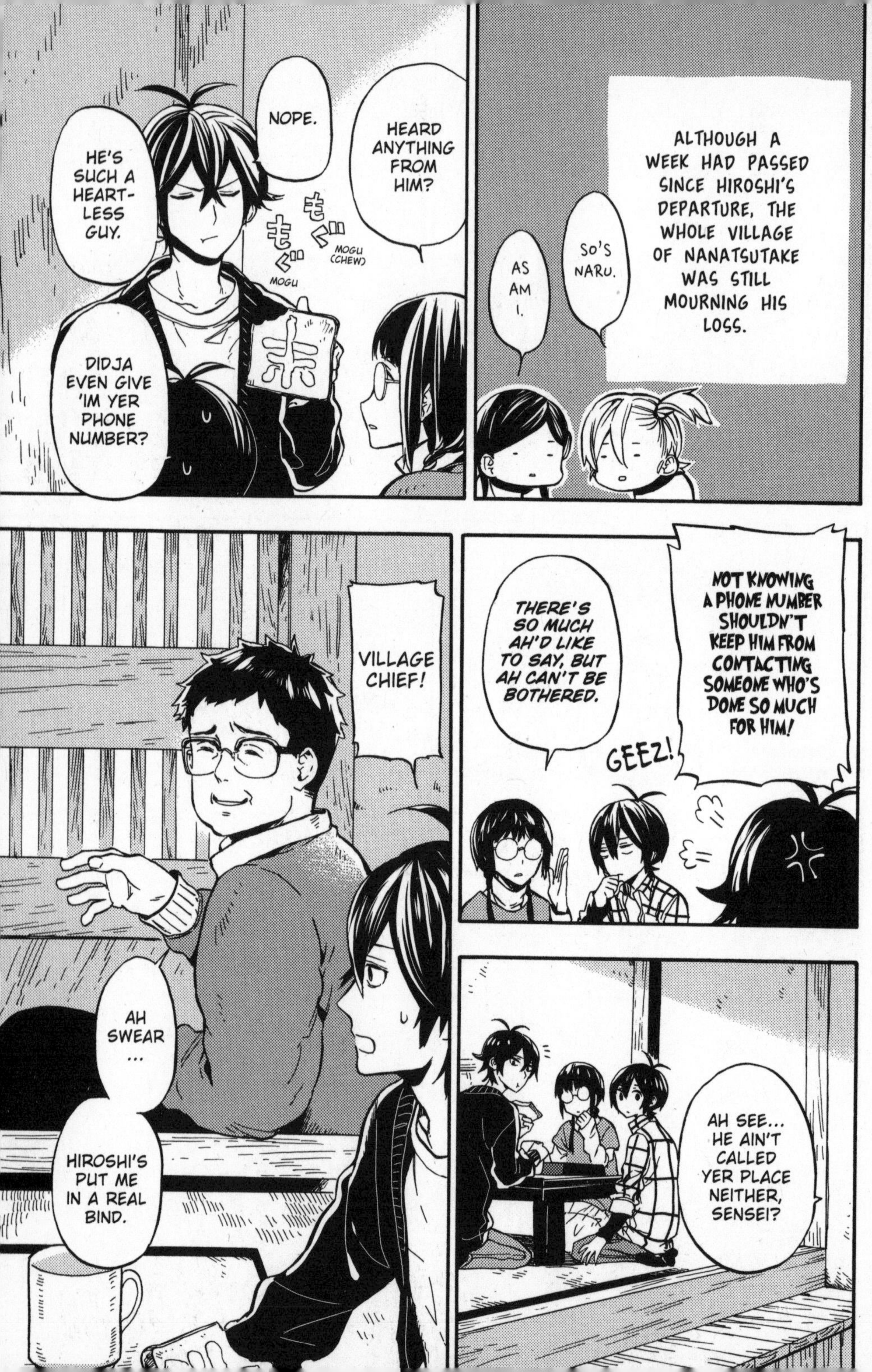
ALTHOUGH A WEEK HAD PASSED SINCE HIROSHI'S DEPARTURE, THE WHOLE VILLAGE OF NANATSUTAKE WAS STILL MOURNING HIS LOSS.
SO'S NARU.
AS AM I.
HEARD ANYTHING FROM HIM?
NOPE.
HE'S SUCH A HEARTLESS GUY.
MOGU (CHEW)
MOGU
DIDJA EVEN GIVE 'IM YER PHONE NUMBER?
NOT KNOWING A PHONE NUMBER SHOULDN'T KEEP HIM FROM CONTACTING SOMEONE WHO'S DONE SO MUCH FOR HIM!
GEEZ!
THERE'S SO MUCH AH'D LIKE TO SAY, BUT AH CAN'T BE BOTHERED.
AH SEE... HE AIN'T CALLED YER PLACE NEITHER, SENSEI?
VILLAGE CHIEF!
AH SWEAR...
HIROSHI'S PUT ME IN A REAL BIND.

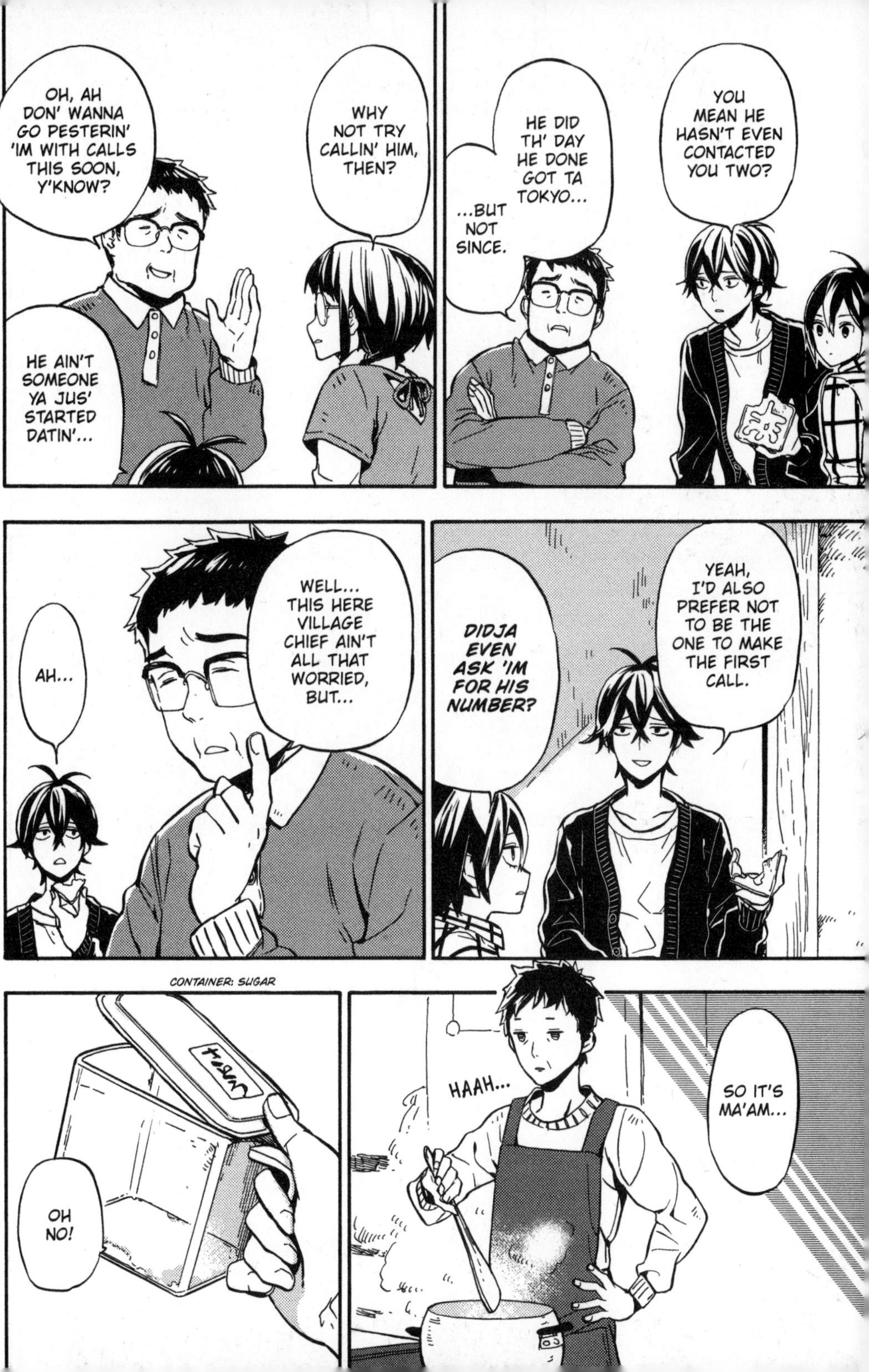
YOU MEAN HE HASN'T EVEN CONTACTED YOU TWO?
HE DID TH' DAY HE DONE GOT TA TOKYO...
...BUT NOT SINCE.
WHY NOT TRY CALLIN' HIM, THEN?
OH, AH DON' WANNA GO PESTERIN' 'IM WITH CALLS THIS SOON, Y'KNOW?
HE AIN'T SOMEONE YA JUS' STARTED DATIN'...
YEAH, I'D ALSO PREFER NOT TO BE THE ONE TO MAKE THE FIRST CALL.
DIDJA EVEN ASK 'IM FOR HIS NUMBER?
WELL... THIS HERE VILLAGE CHIEF AIN'T ALL THAT WORRIED, BUT...
AH...
SO IT'S MA'AM...
HAAH...
CONTAINER: SUGAR
OH NO!

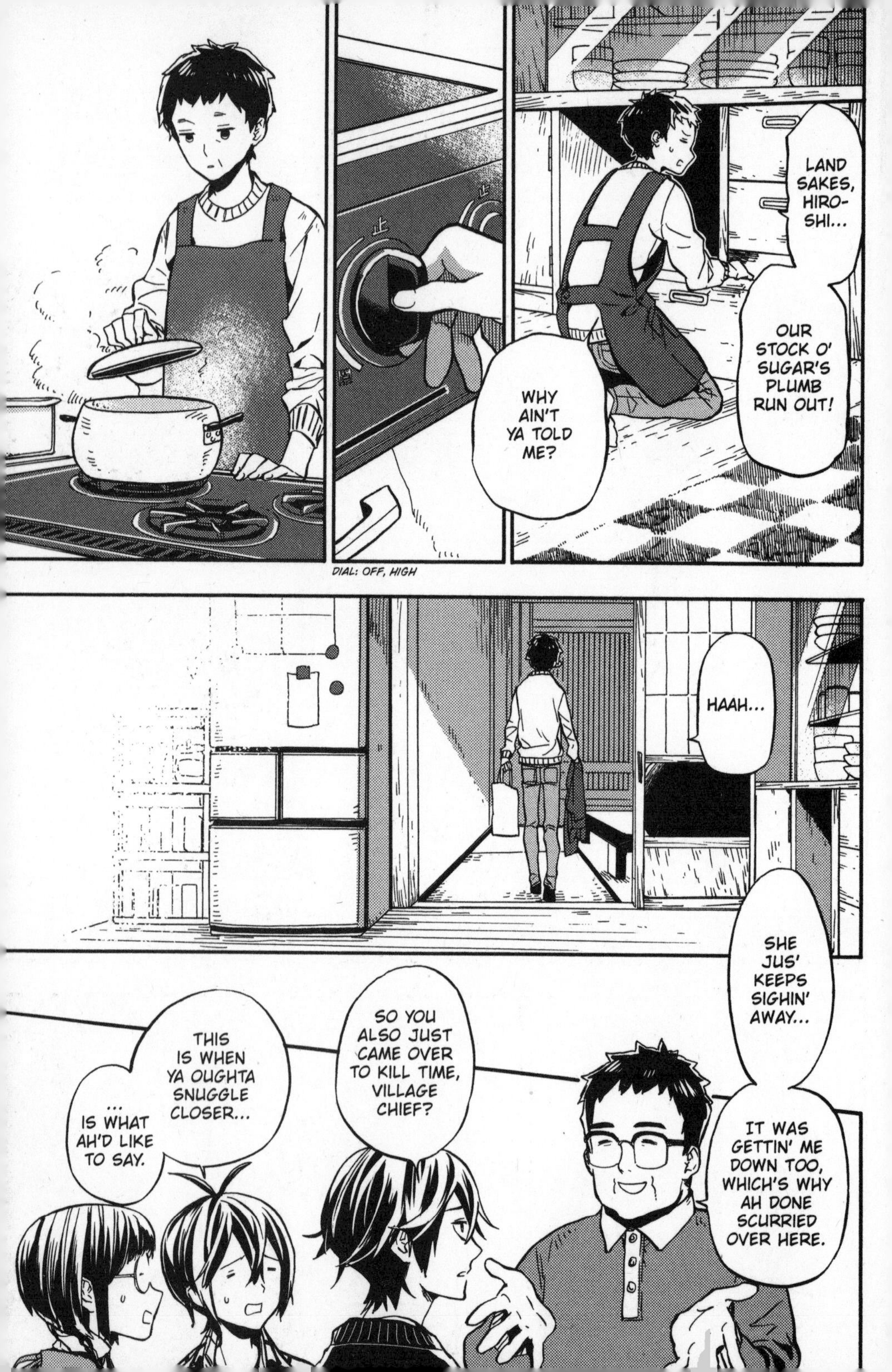
LAND SAKES, HIRO-SHI...
OUR STOCK O' SUGAR'S PLUMB RUN OUT!
WHY AIN'T YA TOLD ME?
DIAL: OFF, HIGH
HAAH...
SHE JUS' KEEPS SIGHIN' AWAY...
IT WAS GETTIN' ME DOWN TOO, WHICH'S WHY AH DONE SCURRIED OVER HERE.
SO YOU ALSO JUST CAME OVER TO KILL TIME, VILLAGE CHIEF?
THIS IS WHEN YA OUGHTA SNUGGLE CLOSER...
...IS WHAT AH'D LIKE TO SAY.

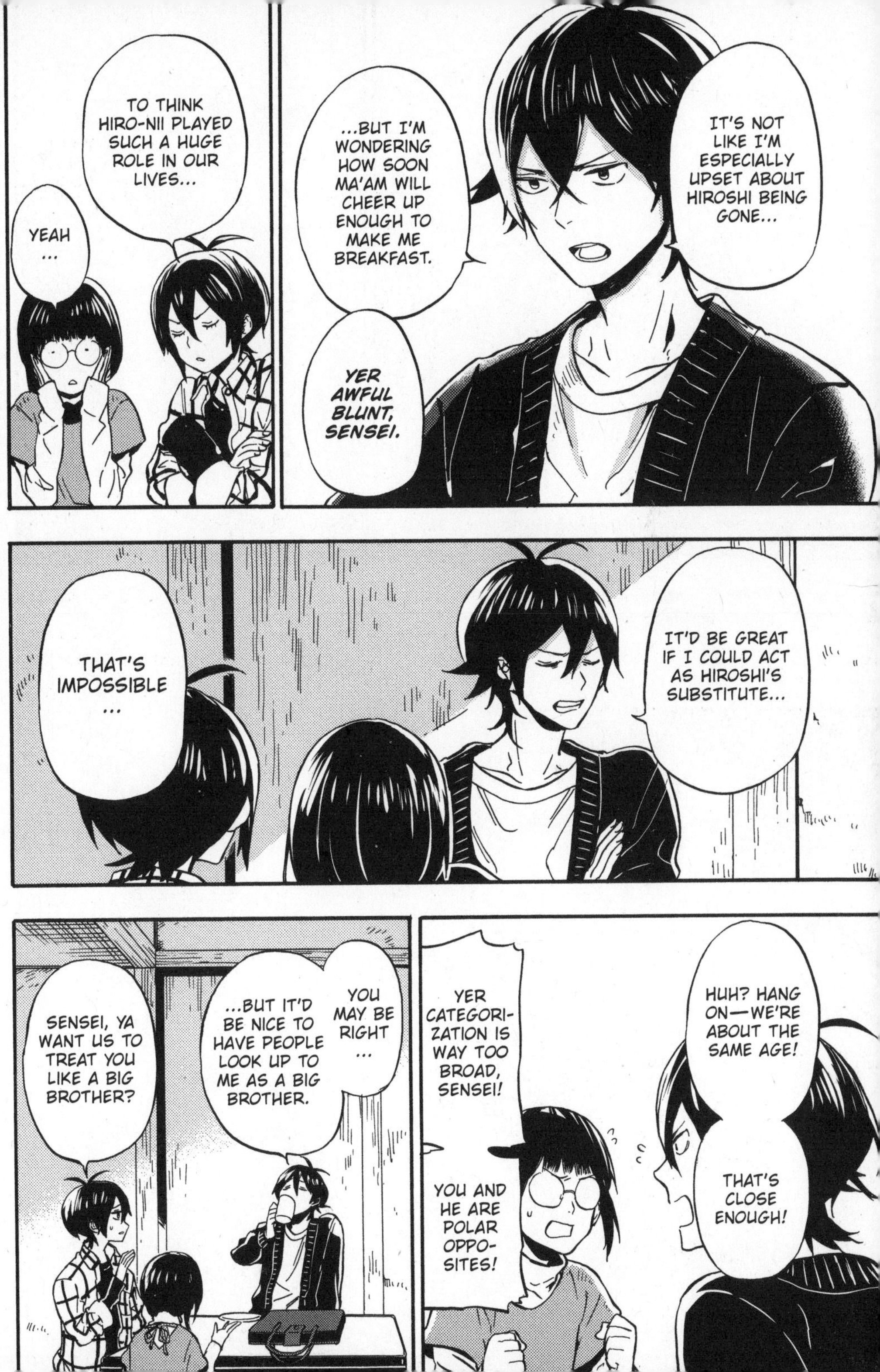
IT'S NOT LIKE I'M ESPECIALLY UPSET ABOUT HIROSHI BEING GONE...
...BUT I'M WONDERING HOW SOON MA'AM WILL CHEER UP ENOUGH TO MAKE ME BREAKFAST.
YER AWFUL BLUNT, SENSEI.
TO THINK HIRO-NII PLAYED SUCH A HUGE ROLE IN OUR LIVES...
YEAH ...
IT'D BE GREAT IF I COULD ACT AS HIROSHI'S SUBSTITUTE...
THAT'S IMPOSSIBLE ...
HUH? HANG ON—WE'RE ABOUT THE SAME AGE!
YER CATEGORIZATION IS WAY TOO BROAD, SENSEI!
THAT'S CLOSE ENOUGH!
YOU AND HE ARE POLAR OPPOSITES!
YOU MAY BE RIGHT ...
...BUT IT'D BE NICE TO HAVE PEOPLE LOOK UP TO ME AS A BIG BROTHER.
SENSEI, YA WANT US TO TREAT YOU LIKE A BIG BROTHER?

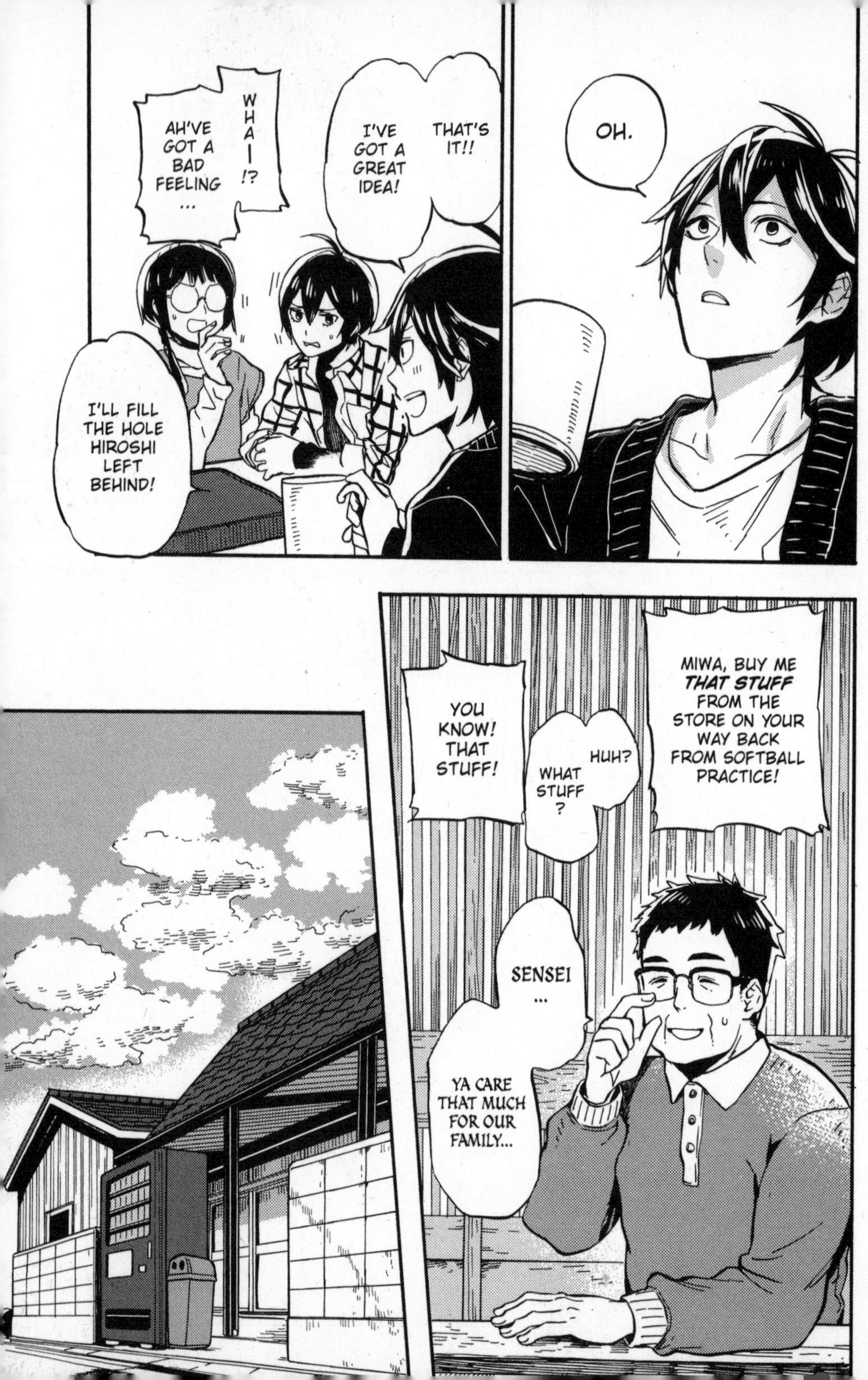
OH.
THAT'S IT!!
I'VE GOT A GREAT IDEA!
WHA-!?
AH'VE GOT A BAD FEELING...
I'LL FILL THE HOLE HIROSHI LEFT BEHIND!
MIWA, BUY ME THAT STUFF FROM THE STORE ON YOUR WAY BACK FROM SOFTBALL PRACTICE!
HUH?
WHAT STUFF?
YOU KNOW! THAT STUFF!
SENSEI...
YA CARE THAT MUCH FOR OUR FAMILY...

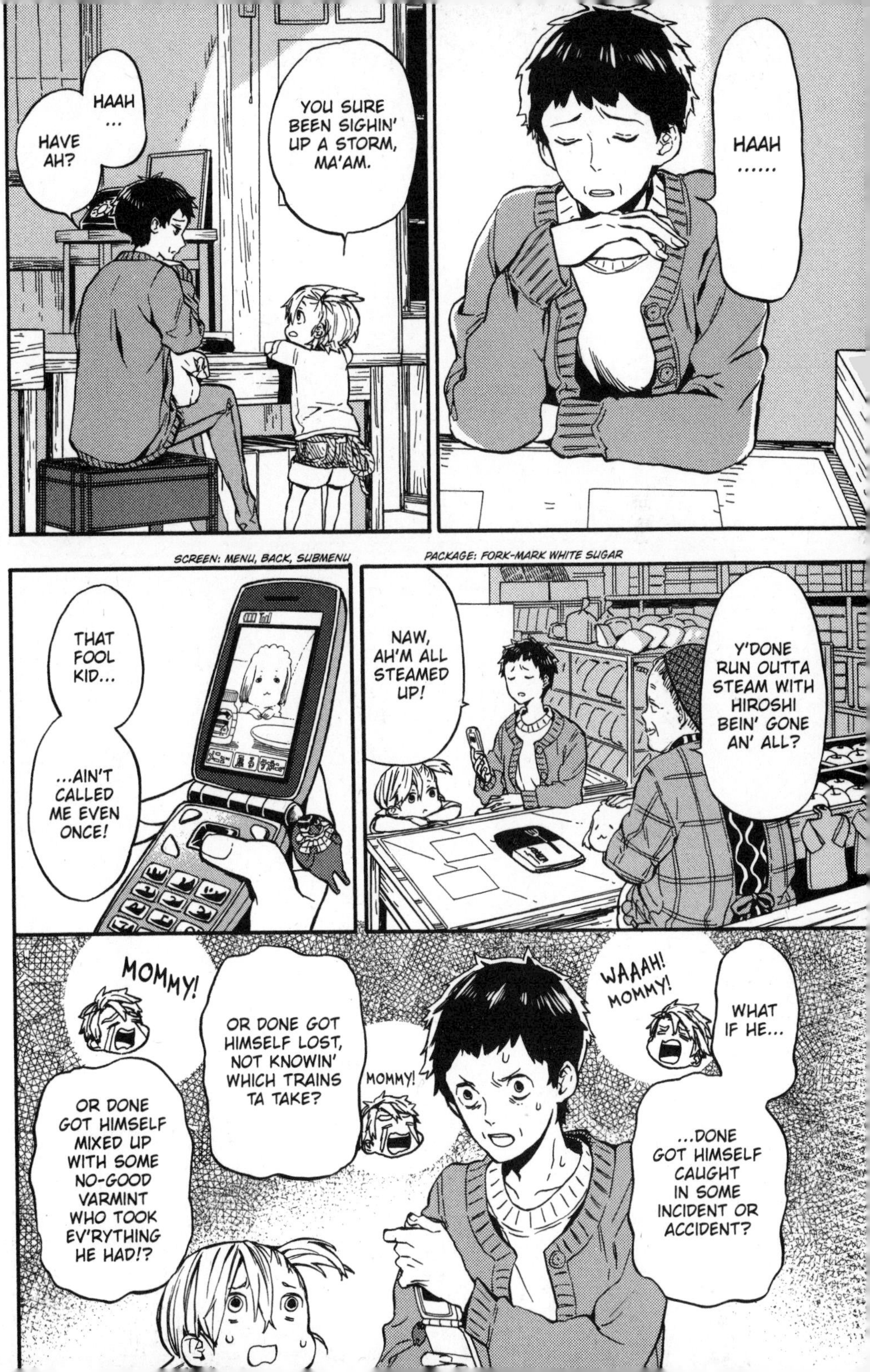
HAAH ......
YOU SURE BEEN SIGHIN' UP A STORM, MA'AM.
HAAH ... HAVE AH?
PACKAGE: FORK-MARK WHITE SUGAR
Y'DONE RUN OUTTA STEAM WITH HIROSHI BEIN' GONE AN' ALL?
NAW, AH'M ALL STEAMED UP!
SCREEN: MENU, BACK, SUBMENU
THAT FOOL KID...
...AIN'T CALLED ME EVEN ONCE!
WAAAH! MOMMY!
WHAT IF HE...
...DONE GOT HIMSELF CAUGHT IN SOME INCIDENT OR ACCIDENT?
MOMMY!
OR DONE GOT HIMSELF LOST, NOT KNOWIN' WHICH TRAINS TA TAKE?
MOMMY!
OR DONE GOT HIMSELF MIXED UP WITH SOME NO-GOOD VARMINT WHO TOOK EV'RYTHING HE HAD!?

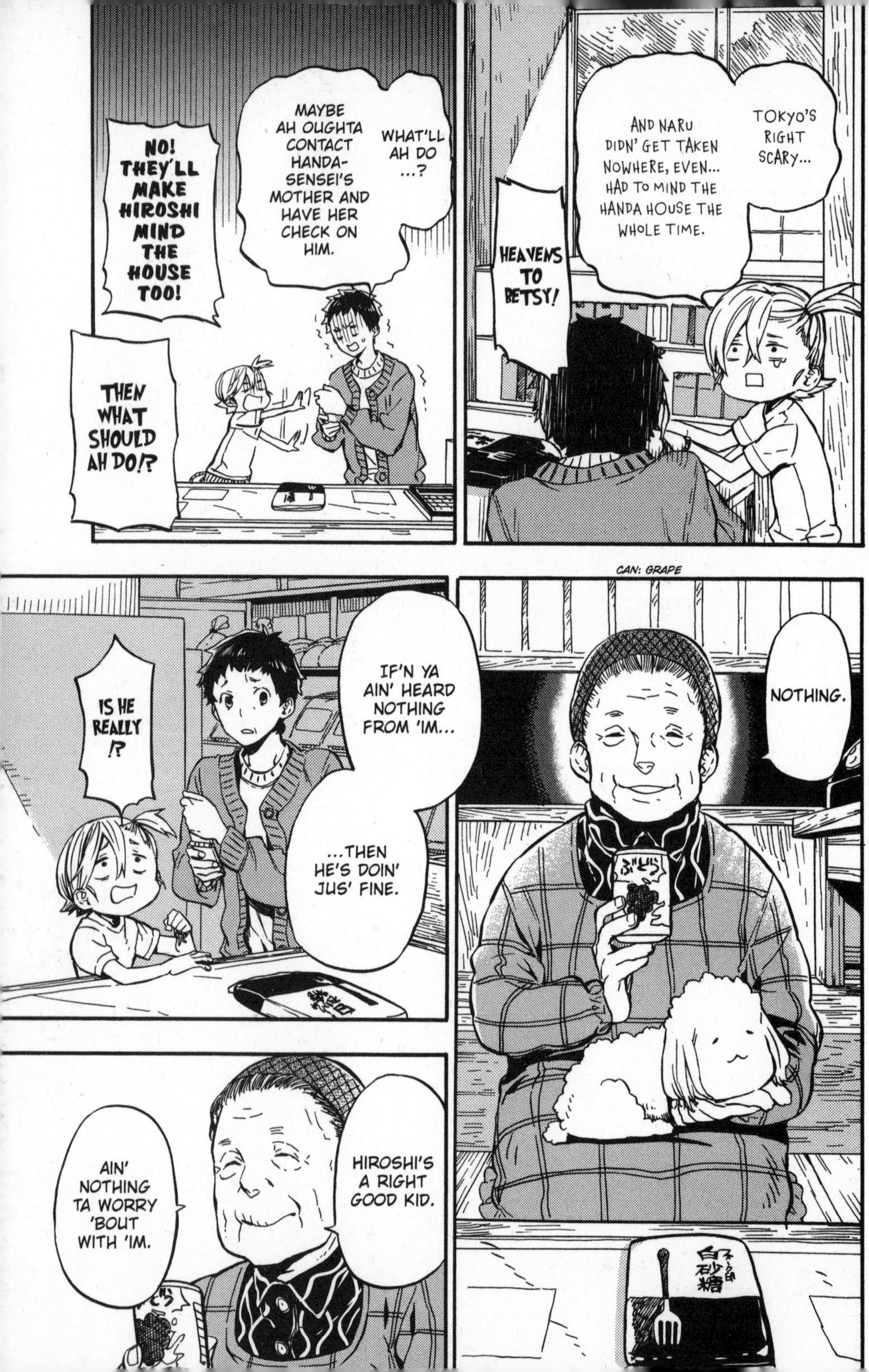
TOKYO'S RIGHT SCARY...
AND NARU DIDN' GET TAKEN NOWHERE, EVEN... HAD TO MIND THE HANDA HOUSE THE WHOLE TIME.
HEAVENS TO BETSY!
WHAT'LL AH DO ...?
MAYBE AH OUGHTA CONTACT HANDA-SENSEI'S MOTHER AND HAVE HER CHECK ON HIM.
NO! THEY'LL MAKE HIROSHI MIND THE HOUSE TOO!
THEN WHAT SHOULD AH DO!?
CAN: GRAPE
NOTHING.
IF'N YA AIN' HEARD NOTHING FROM 'IM...
...THEN HE'S DOIN' JUS' FINE.
IS HE REALLY !?
HIROSHI'S A RIGHT GOOD KID.
AIN' NOTHING TA WORRY 'BOUT WITH 'IM.

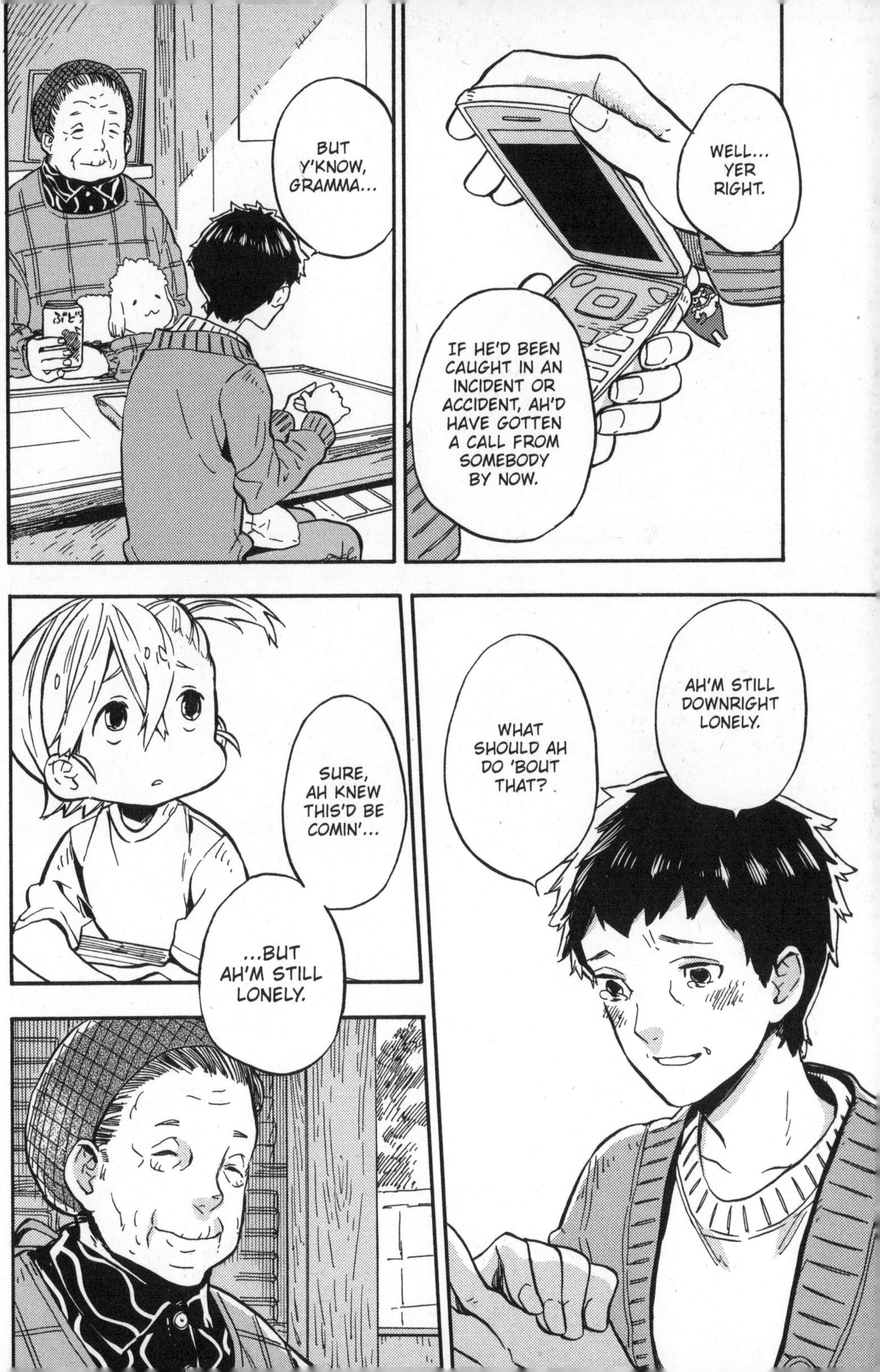
WELL... YER RIGHT.
IF HE'D BEEN CAUGHT IN AN INCIDENT OR ACCIDENT, AH'D HAVE GOTTEN A CALL FROM SOMEBODY BY NOW.
BUT Y'KNOW, GRAMMA...
AH'M STILL DOWNRIGHT LONELY.
WHAT SHOULD AH DO 'BOUT THAT?
SURE, AH KNEW THIS'D BE COMIN'...
...BUT AH'M STILL LONELY.

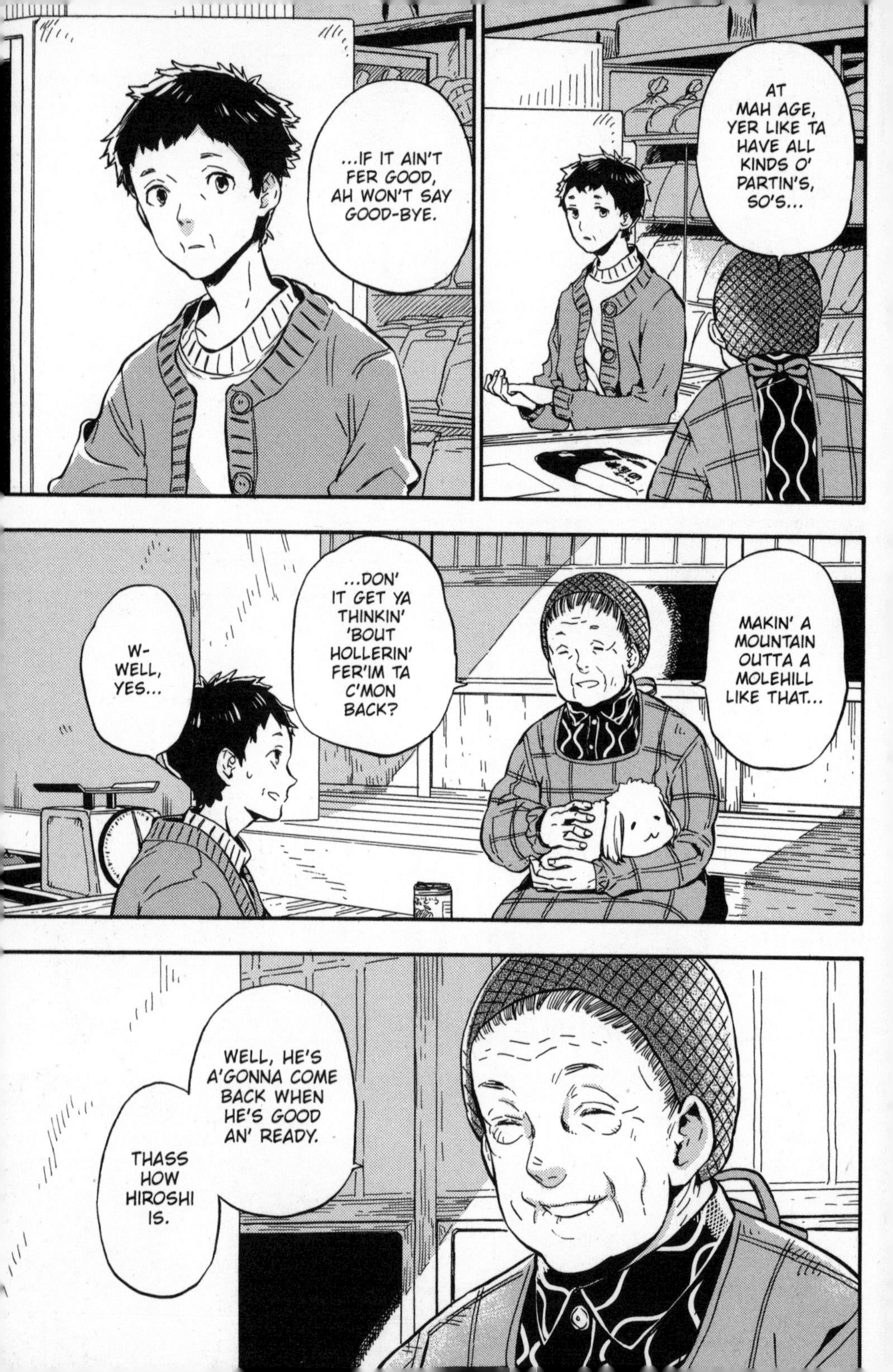
AT MAH AGE, YER LIKE TA HAVE ALL KINDS O' PARTIN'S, SO'S...
...IF IT AIN'T FER GOOD, AH WON'T SAY GOOD-BYE.
MAKIN' A MOUNTAIN OUTTA A MOLEHILL LIKE THAT...
...DON' IT GET YA THINKIN' 'BOUT HOLLERIN' FER'IM TA C'MON BACK?
W-WELL, YES...
WELL, HE'S A'GONNA COME BACK WHEN HE'S GOOD AN' READY.
THASS HOW HIROSHI IS.

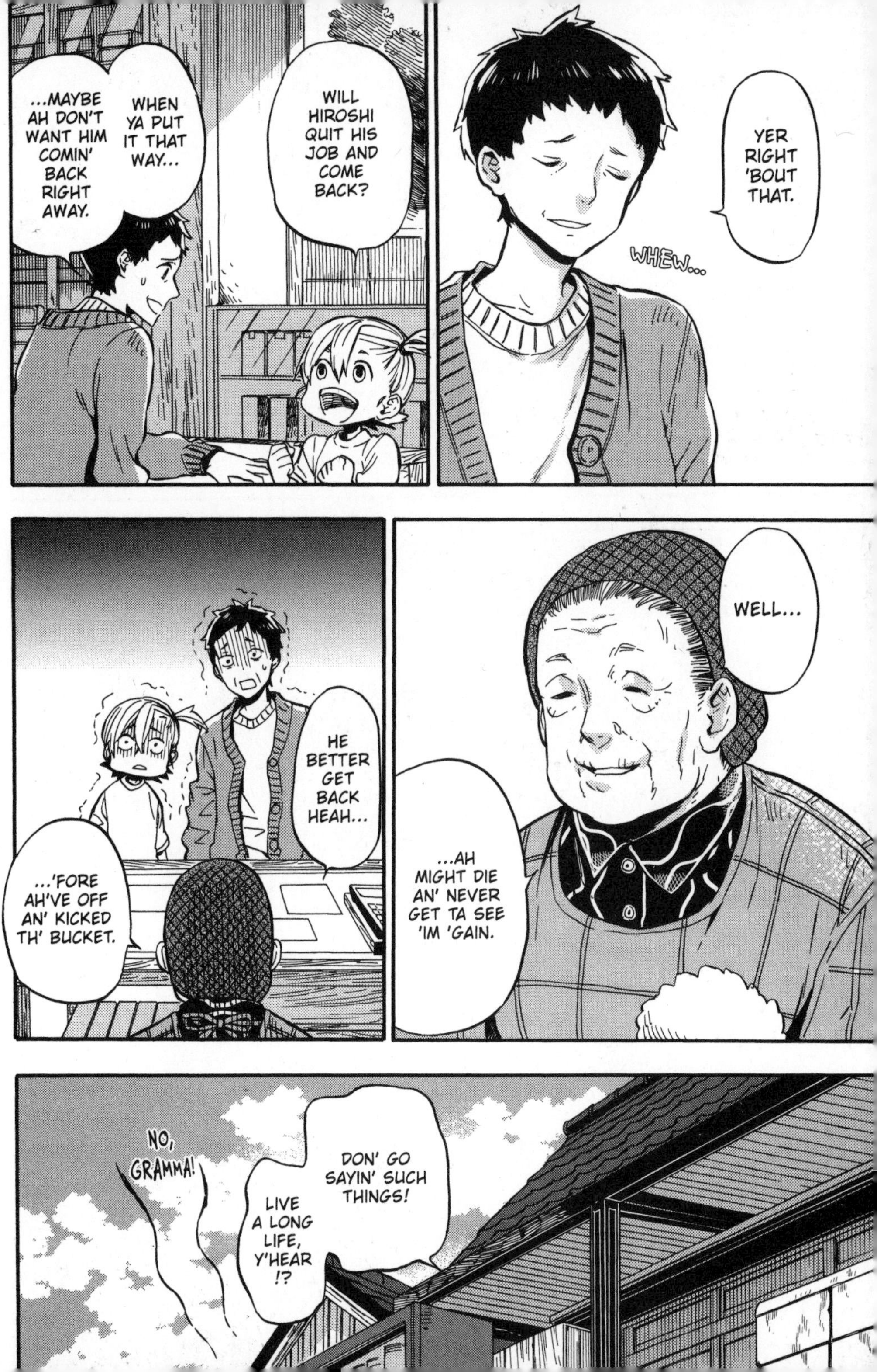
YER RIGHT 'BOUT THAT.
WHEW...
WILL HIROSHI QUIT HIS JOB AND COME BACK?
WHEN YA PUT IT THAT WAY...
...MAYBE AH DON'T WANT HIM COMIN' BACK RIGHT AWAY.
WELL...
...AH MIGHT DIE AN' NEVER GET TA SEE 'IM 'GAIN.
HE BETTER GET BACK HEAH...
...'FORE AH'VE OFF AN' KICKED TH' BUCKET.
DON' GO SAYIN' SUCH THINGS!
LIVE A LONG LIFE, Y'HEAR!?
NO, GRAMMA!

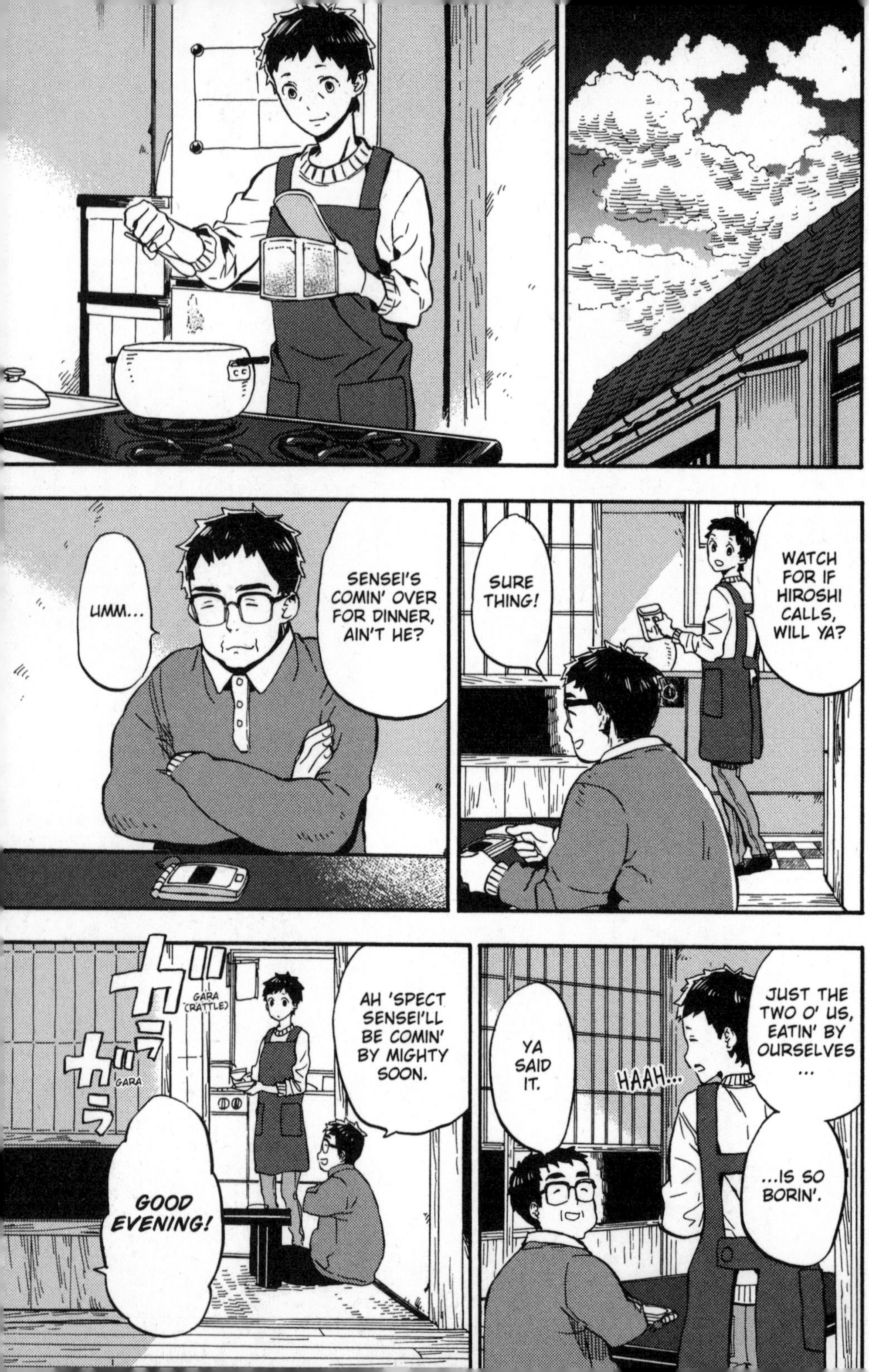
WATCH FOR IF HIROSHI CALLS, WILL YA?
SURE THING!
SENSEI'S COMIN' OVER FOR DINNER, AIN'T HE?
UMM...
JUST THE TWO O' US, EATIN' BY OURSELVES ...
HAAH...
...IS SO BORIN'.
YA SAID IT.
AH 'SPECT SENSEI'LL BE COMIN' BY MIGHTY SOON.
ガラ GARA (RATTLE)
ガラ GARA
GOOD EVENING!

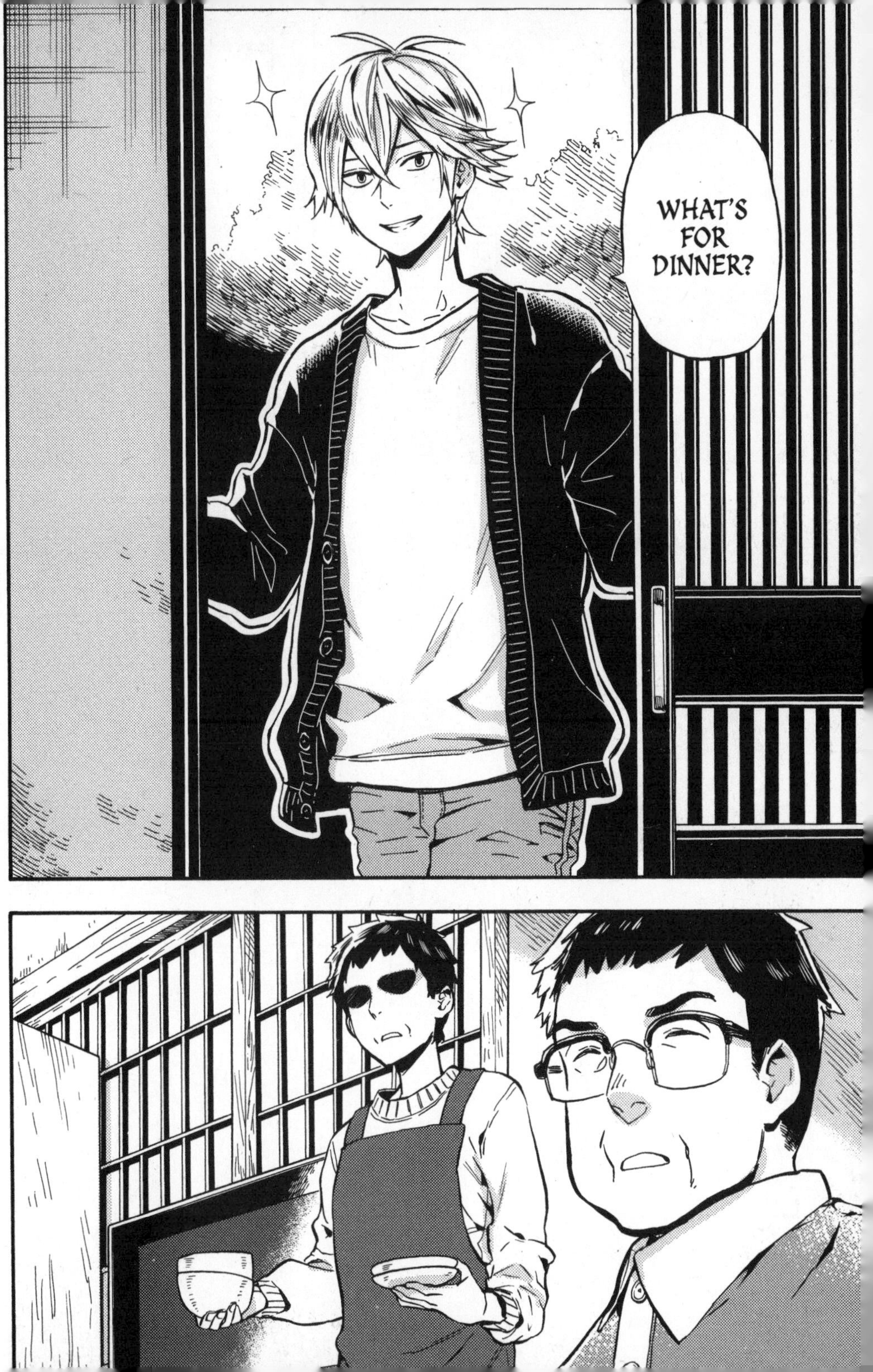
WHAT'S FOR DINNER?

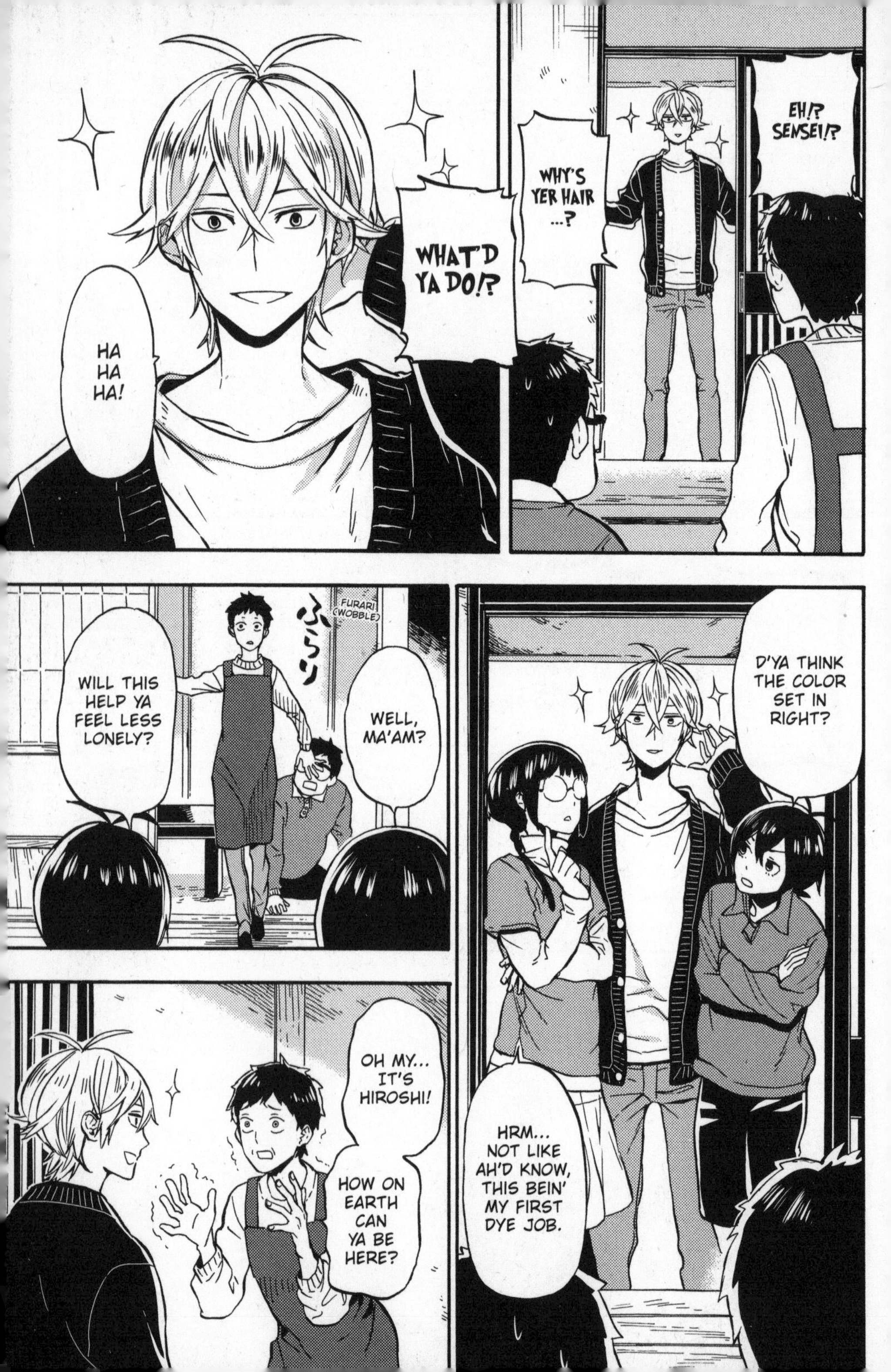
EH!? SENSEI!?
WHY'S YER HAIR ...?
WHAT'D YA DO!?
HA HA HA!
D'YA THINK THE COLOR SET IN RIGHT?
HRM... NOT LIKE AH'D KNOW, THIS BEIN' MY FIRST DYE JOB.
WELL, MA'AM?
ふらり
FURARI (WOBBLE)
WILL THIS HELP YA FEEL LESS LONELY?
OH MY... IT'S HIROSHI!
HOW ON EARTH CAN YA BE HERE?

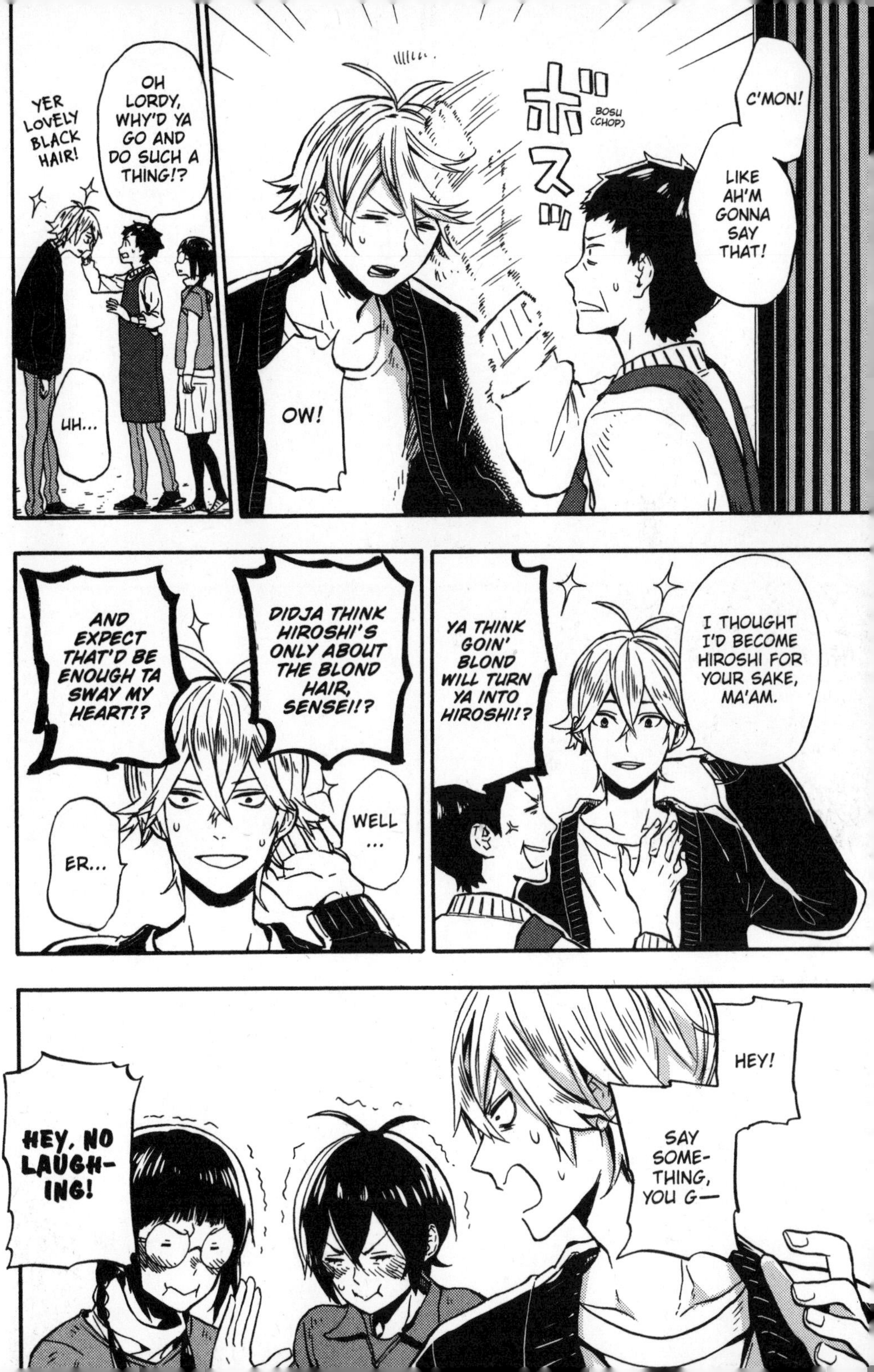
C'MON!
LIKE AH'M GONNA SAY THAT!
BOSU (CHOP)
OW!
OH LORDY, WHY'D YA GO AND DO SUCH A THING!?
YER LOVELY BLACK HAIR!
UH...
I THOUGHT I'D BECOME HIROSHI FOR YOUR SAKE, MA'AM.
YA THINK GOIN' BLOND WILL TURN YA INTO HIROSHI!?
DIDJA THINK HIROSHI'S ONLY ABOUT THE BLOND HAIR, SENSEI!?
AND EXPECT THAT'D BE ENOUGH TA SWAY MY HEART!?
WELL...
ER...
HEY!
SAY SOME-THING, YOU G—
HEY, NO LAUGH-ING!

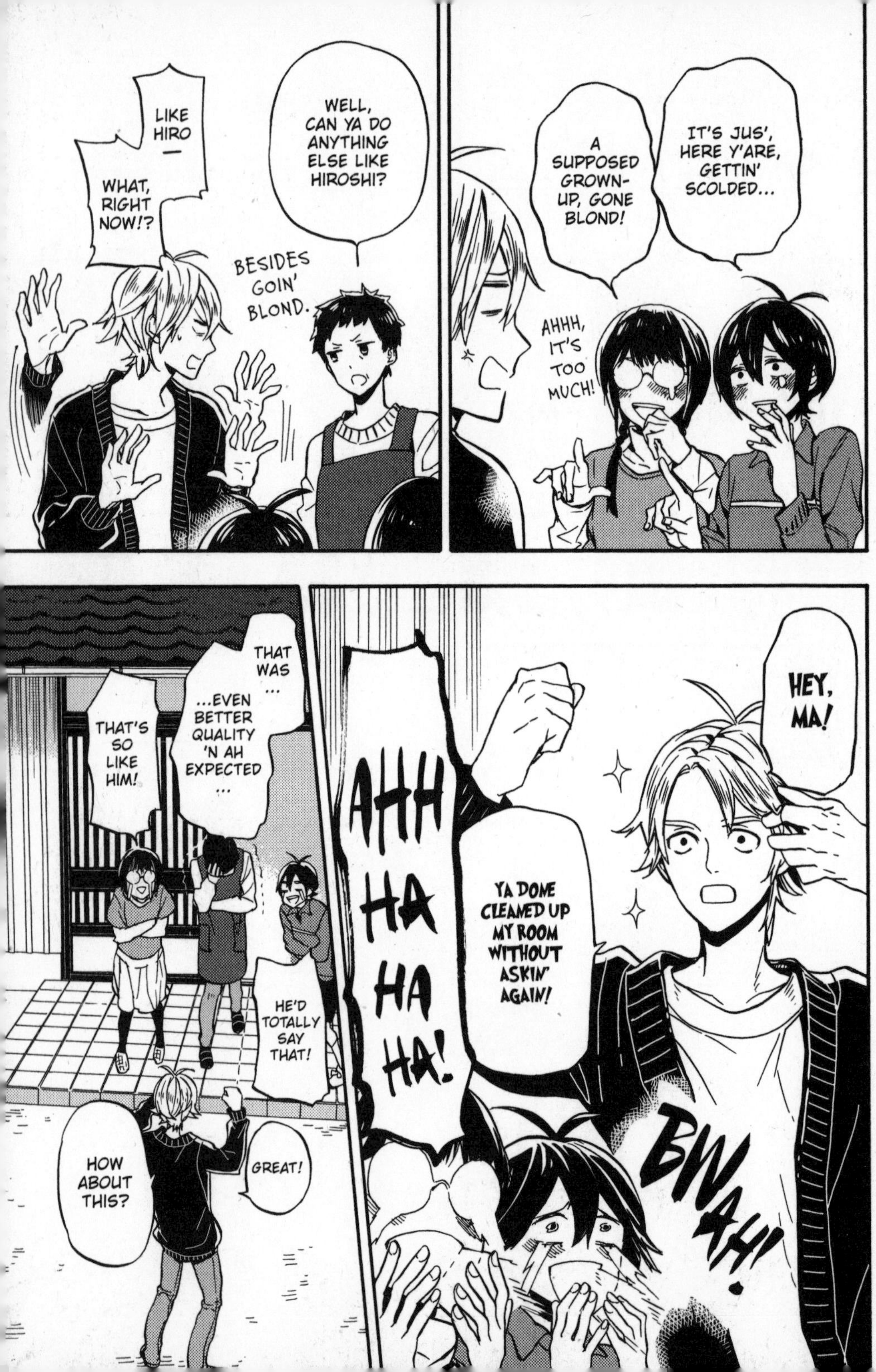
IT'S JUS', HERE Y'ARE, GETTIN' SCOLDED...
A SUPPOSED GROWN-UP, GONE BLOND!
AHHH, IT'S TOO MUCH!
WELL, CAN YA DO ANYTHING ELSE LIKE HIROSHI?
BESIDES GOIN' BLOND.
LIKE HIRO—
WHAT, RIGHT NOW!?
HEY, MA!
YA DONE CLEANED UP MY ROOM WITHOUT ASKIN' AGAIN!
AHH HA HA HA!
BWAH!
THAT WAS...
...EVEN BETTER QUALITY 'N AH EXPECTED...
THAT'S SO LIKE HIM!
HE'D TOTALLY SAY THAT!
GREAT!
HOW ABOUT THIS?

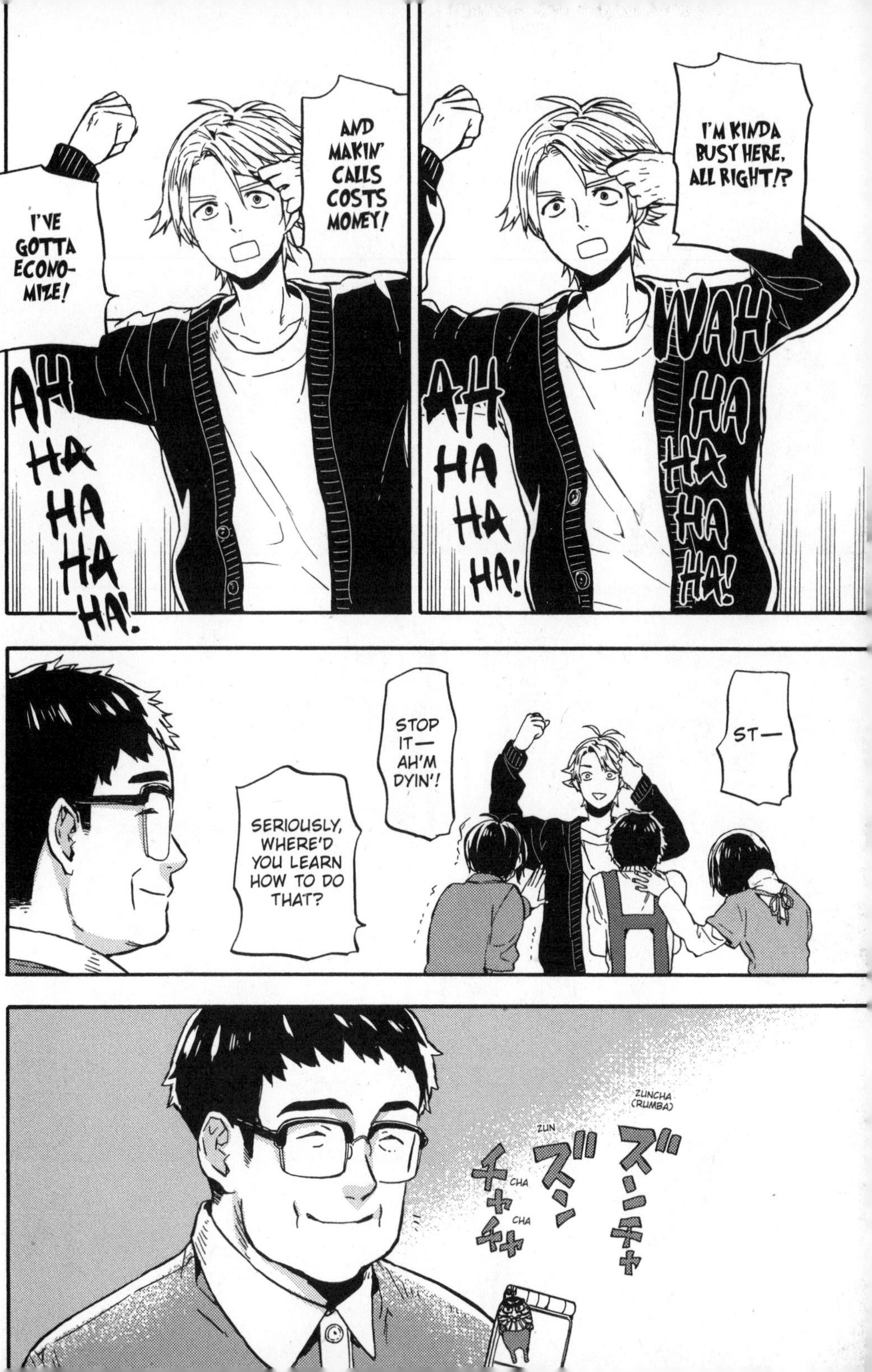
I'M KINDA BUSY HERE, ALL RIGHT!?
WAH HA HA HA HA HA!
AH HA HA HA HA!
AND MAKIN' CALLS COSTS MONEY!
I'VE GOTTA ECONO-MIZE!
AH HA HA HA HA HA!
ST—
STOP IT— AH'M DYIN'!
SERIOUSLY, WHERE'D YOU LEARN HOW TO DO THAT?
ズンチャ
ZUNCHA (RUMBA)
ズン
ZUN
チャ
CHA
チャ
CHA

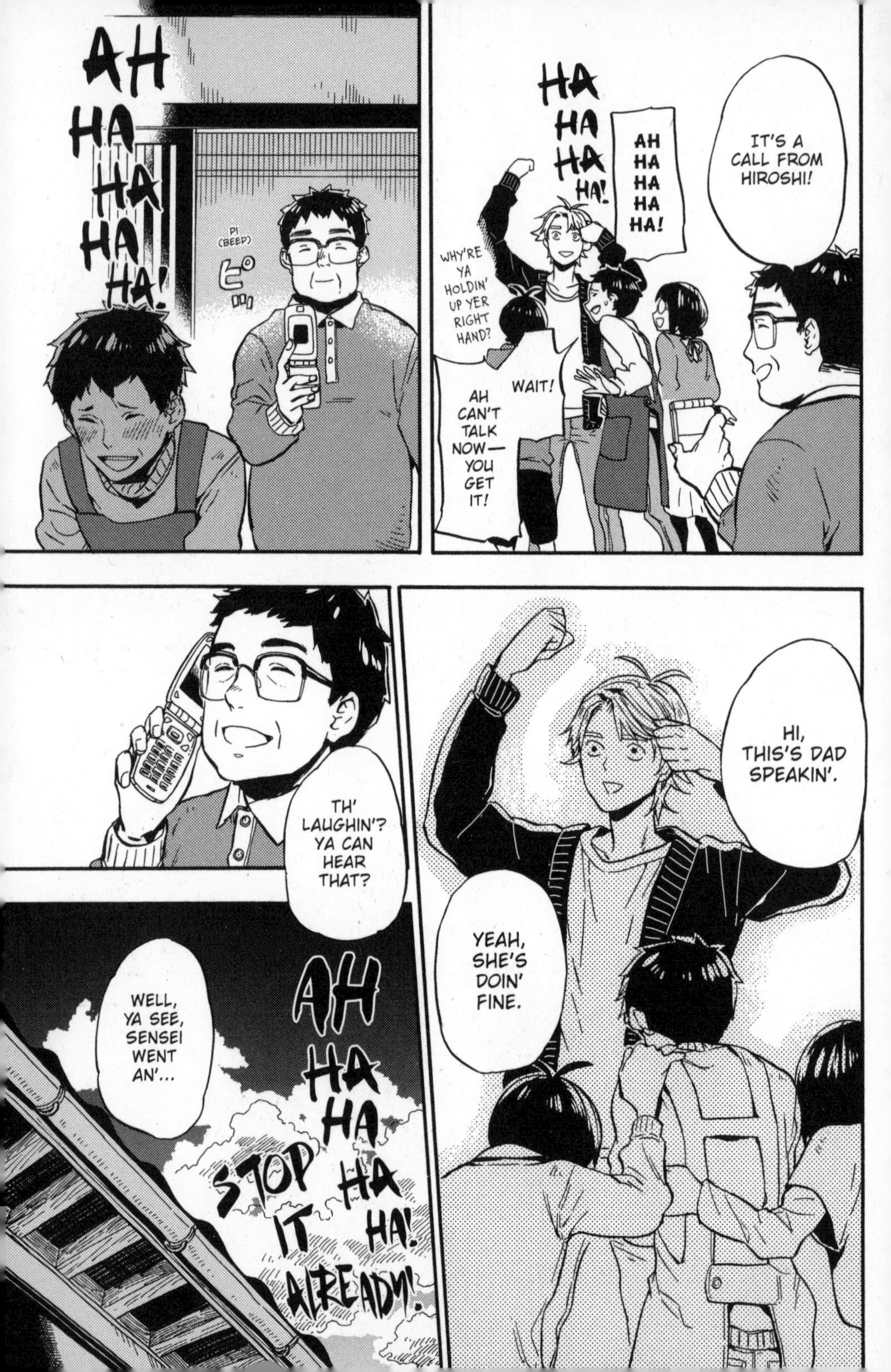
IT'S A CALL FROM HIROSHI!
HA HA HA HA!
AH HA HA HA HA HA!
WHY'RE YA HOLDIN' UP YER RIGHT HAND?
WAIT!
AH CAN'T TALK NOW— YOU GET IT!
AH HA HA HA HA HA!
PI (BEEP)
ピ
HI, THIS'S DAD SPEAKIN'.
YEAH, SHE'S DOIN' FINE.
TH' LAUGHIN'? YA CAN HEAR THAT?
AH HA HA HA HA!
STOP IT ALREADY!
WELL, YA SEE, SENSEI WENT AN'...

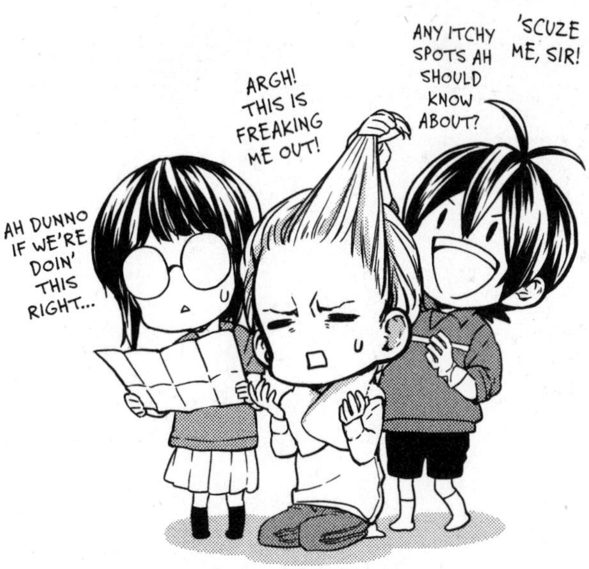
'SCUZE ME, SIR!
ANY ITCHY SPOTS AH SHOULD KNOW ABOUT?
ARGH! THIS IS FREAKING ME OUT!
AH DUNNO IF WE'RE DOIN' THIS RIGHT...

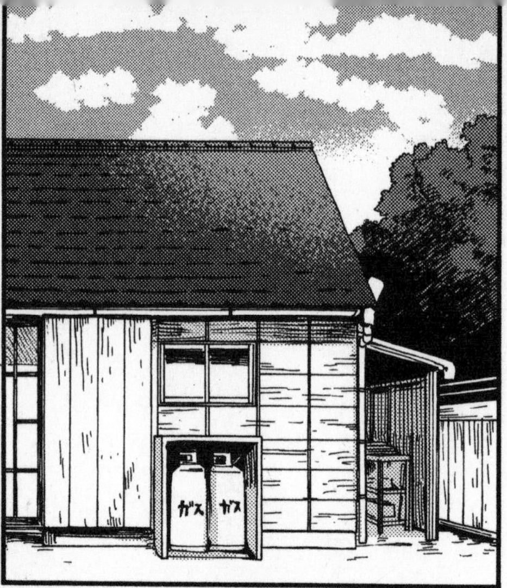
ガス
ガス

TANKS: GAS

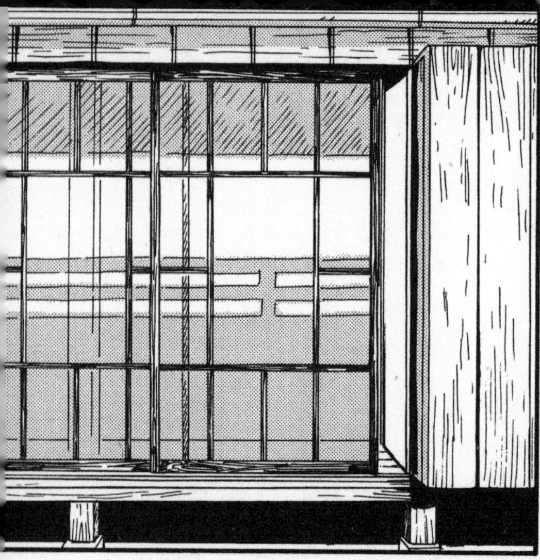

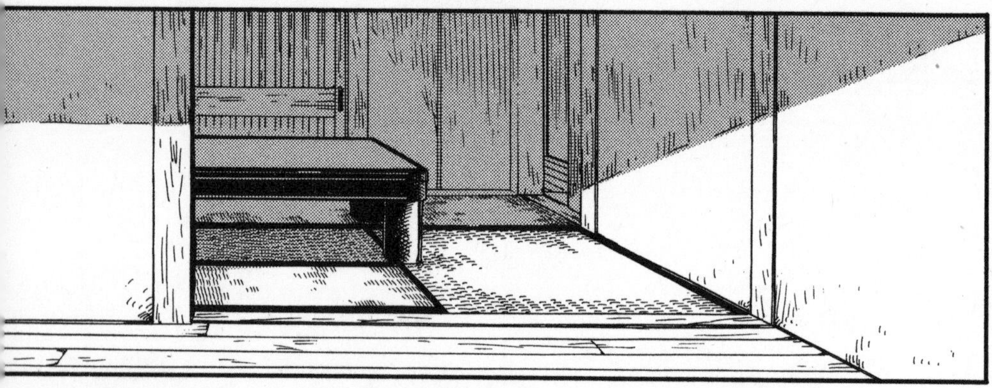

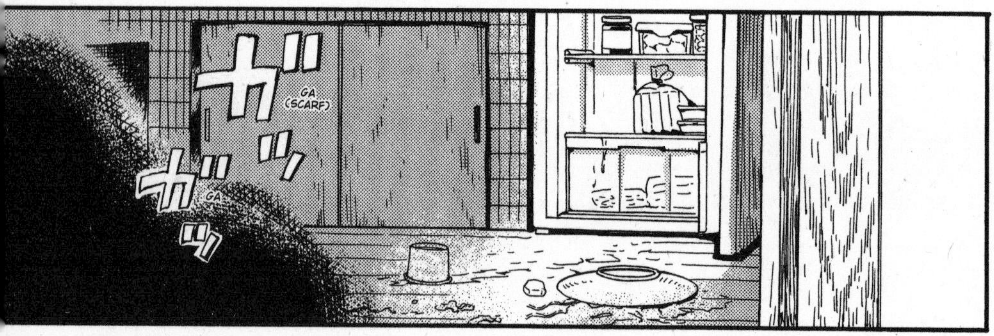
ガッ
GA (SCARF)
ガッ
GA

Act. 123
ATESU
(Translation: Playing Pranks)

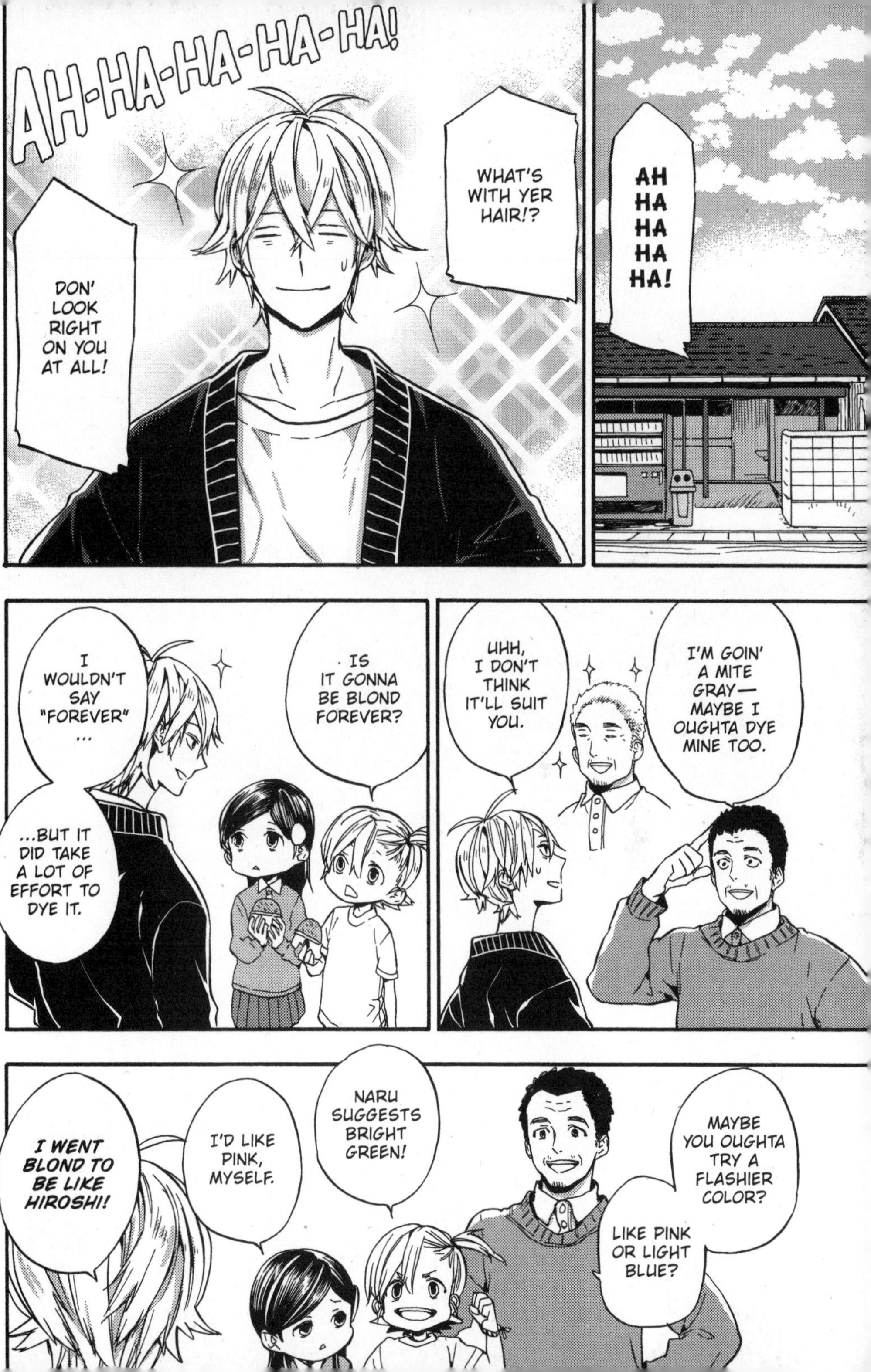
AH HA HA HA HA!
AH-HA-HA-HA-HA!
WHAT'S WITH YER HAIR!?
DON' LOOK RIGHT ON YOU AT ALL!
I'M GOIN' A MITE GRAY— MAYBE I OUGHTA DYE MINE TOO.
UHH, I DON'T THINK IT'LL SUIT YOU.
IS IT GONNA BE BLOND FOREVER?
I WOULDN'T SAY "FOREVER" ...
...BUT IT DID TAKE A LOT OF EFFORT TO DYE IT.
MAYBE YOU OUGHTA TRY A FLASHIER COLOR?
LIKE PINK OR LIGHT BLUE?
NARU SUGGESTS BRIGHT GREEN!
I'D LIKE PINK, MYSELF.
I WENT BLOND TO BE LIKE HIROSHI!

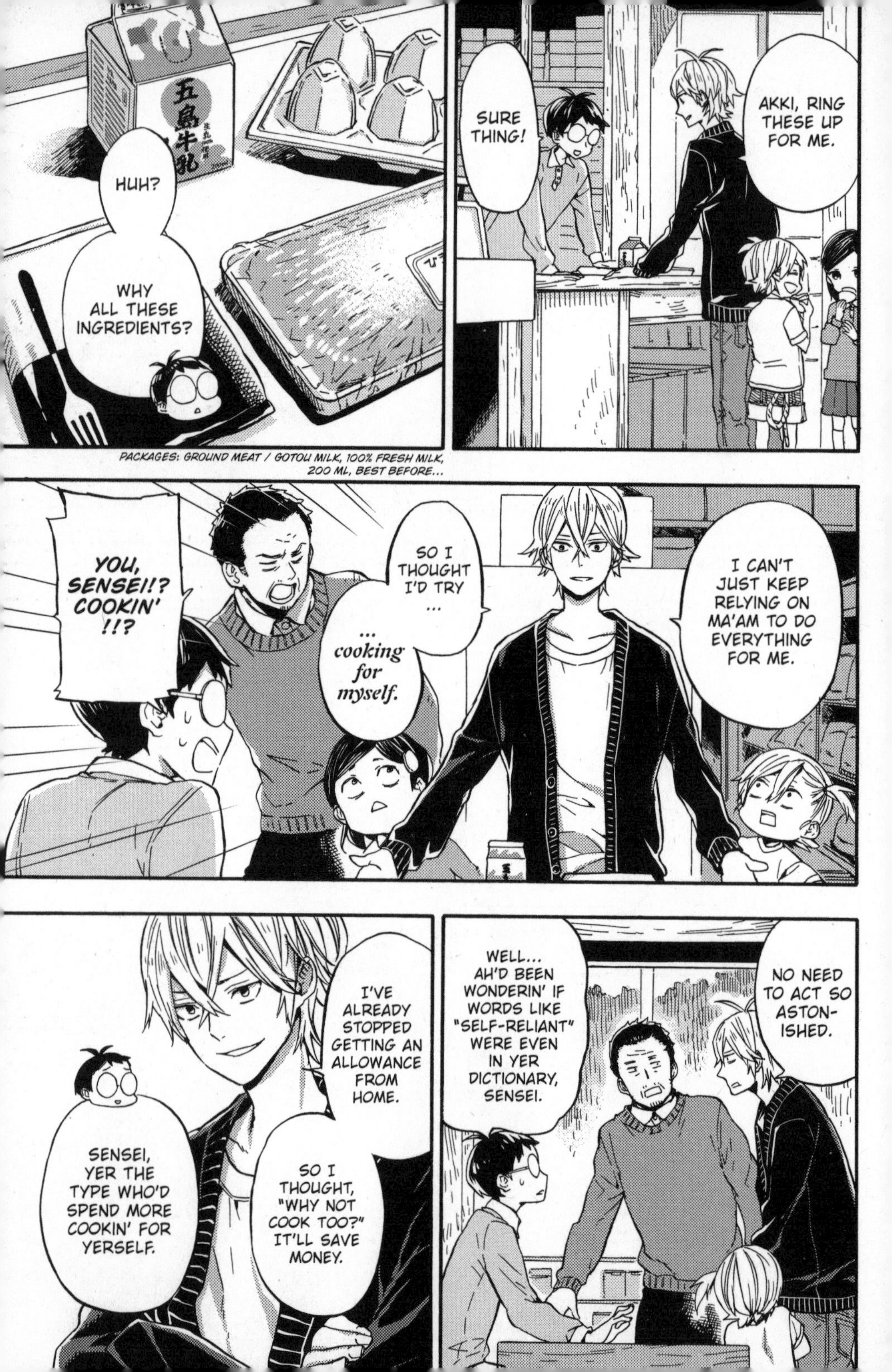
AKKI, RING THESE UP FOR ME.
SURE THING!
五島牛乳
HUH?
WHY ALL THESE INGREDIENTS?
PACKAGES: GROUND MEAT / GOTOU MILK, 100% FRESH MILK, 200 ML, BEST BEFORE...
I CAN'T JUST KEEP RELYING ON MA'AM TO DO EVERYTHING FOR ME.
SO I THOUGHT I'D TRY ...
... *cooking for myself.*
YOU, SENSEI!? COOKIN' !!?
NO NEED TO ACT SO ASTON-ISHED.
WELL... AH'D BEEN WONDERIN' IF WORDS LIKE "SELF-RELIANT" WERE EVEN IN YER DICTIONARY, SENSEI.
I'VE ALREADY STOPPED GETTING AN ALLOWANCE FROM HOME.
SO I THOUGHT, "WHY NOT COOK TOO?" IT'LL SAVE MONEY.
SENSEI, YER THE TYPE WHO'D SPEND MORE COOKIN' FOR YERSELF.

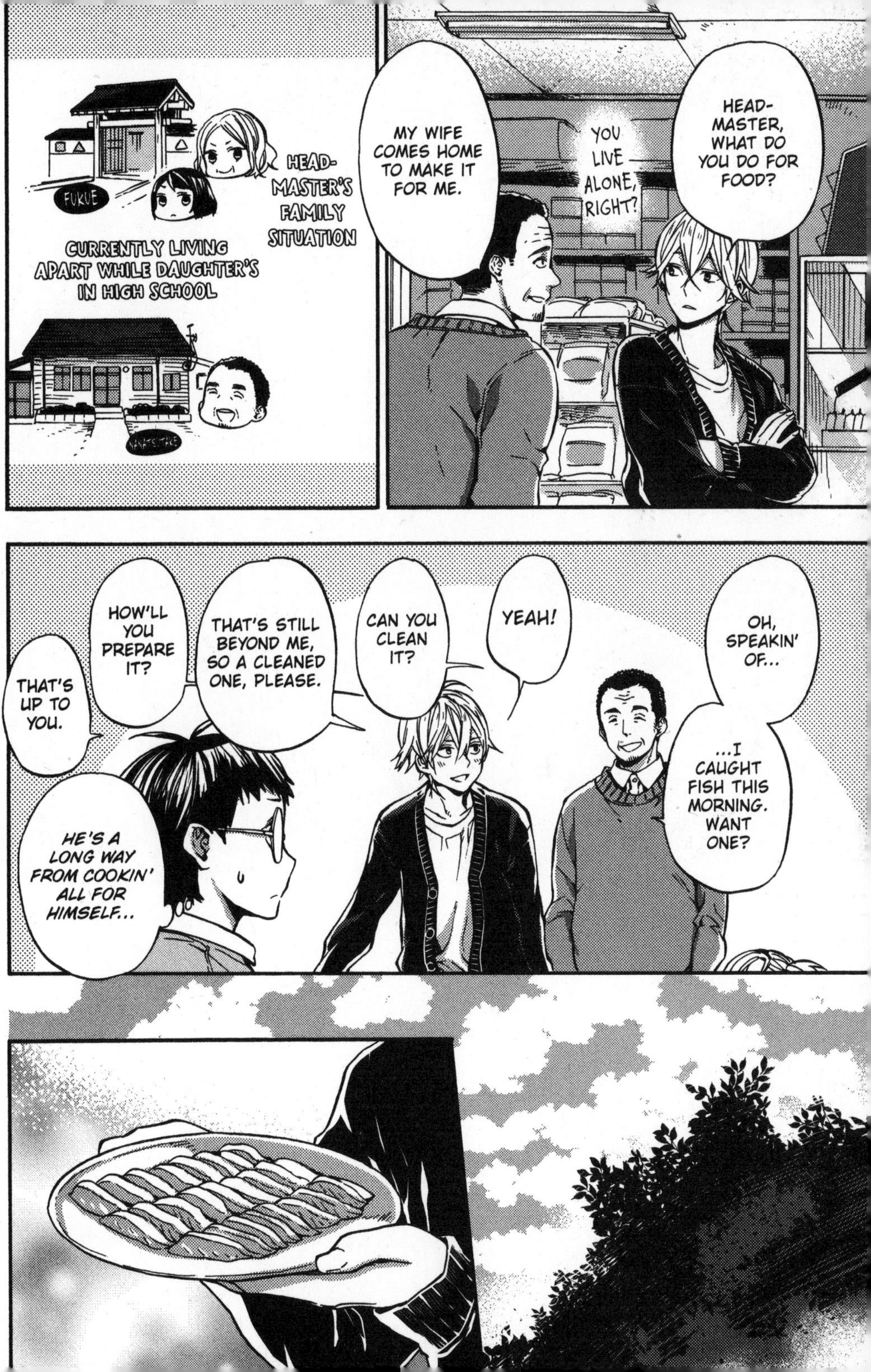
HEAD-MASTER, WHAT DO YOU DO FOR FOOD?
YOU LIVE ALONE, RIGHT?
MY WIFE COMES HOME TO MAKE IT FOR ME.
HEAD-MASTER'S FAMILY SITUATION
FUKUE
CURRENTLY LIVING APART WHILE DAUGHTER'S IN HIGH SCHOOL
NANATSUTAKE
OH, SPEAKIN' OF...
...I CAUGHT FISH THIS MORNING. WANT ONE?
YEAH!
CAN YOU CLEAN IT?
THAT'S STILL BEYOND ME, SO A CLEANED ONE, PLEASE.
HOW'LL YOU PREPARE IT?
THAT'S UP TO YOU.
HE'S A LONG WAY FROM COOKIN' ALL FOR HIMSELF...

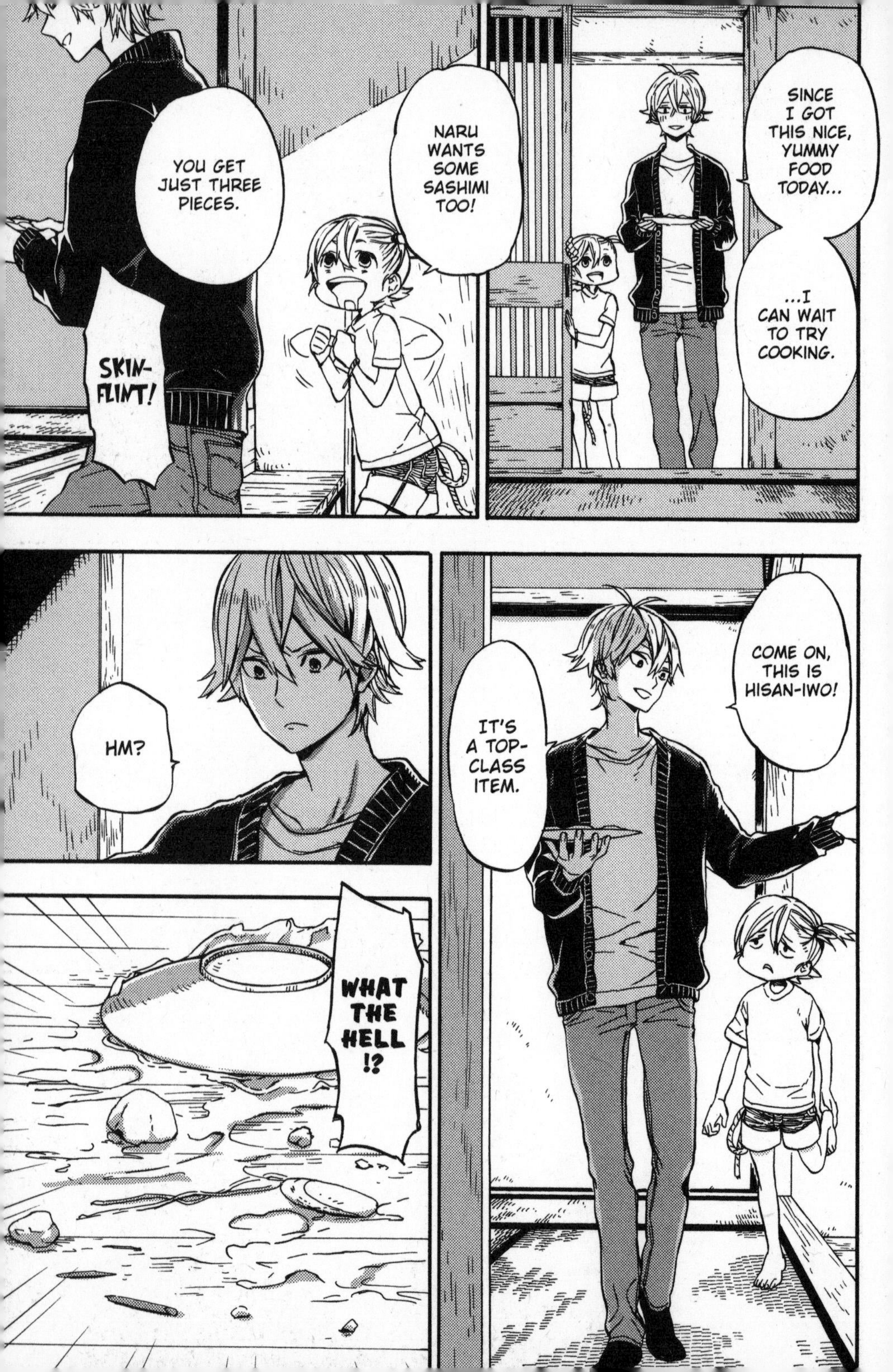
SINCE I GOT THIS NICE, YUMMY FOOD TODAY...
...I CAN WAIT TO TRY COOKING.
NARU WANTS SOME SASHIMI TOO!
YOU GET JUST THREE PIECES.
SKIN-FLINT!
COME ON, THIS IS HISAN-IWO!
IT'S A TOP-CLASS ITEM.
HM?
WHAT THE HELL !?

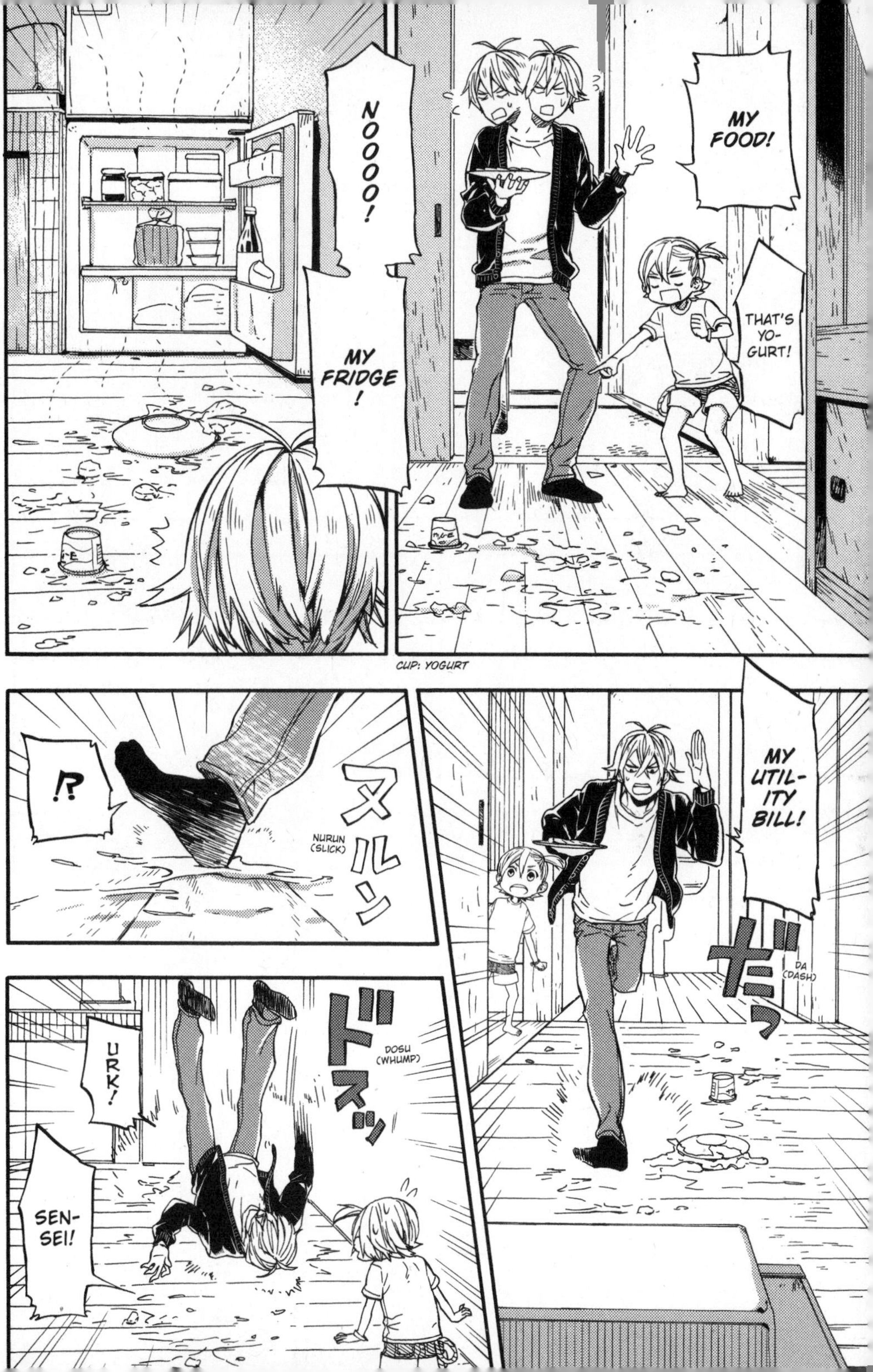
MY FOOD!
THAT'S YO-GURT!
NOOOOO!
MY FRIDGE!
CUP: YOGURT
MY UTIL-ITY BILL!
DA (DASH)
!?
NURUN (SLICK)
DOSU (WHUMP)
URK!
SEN-SEI!

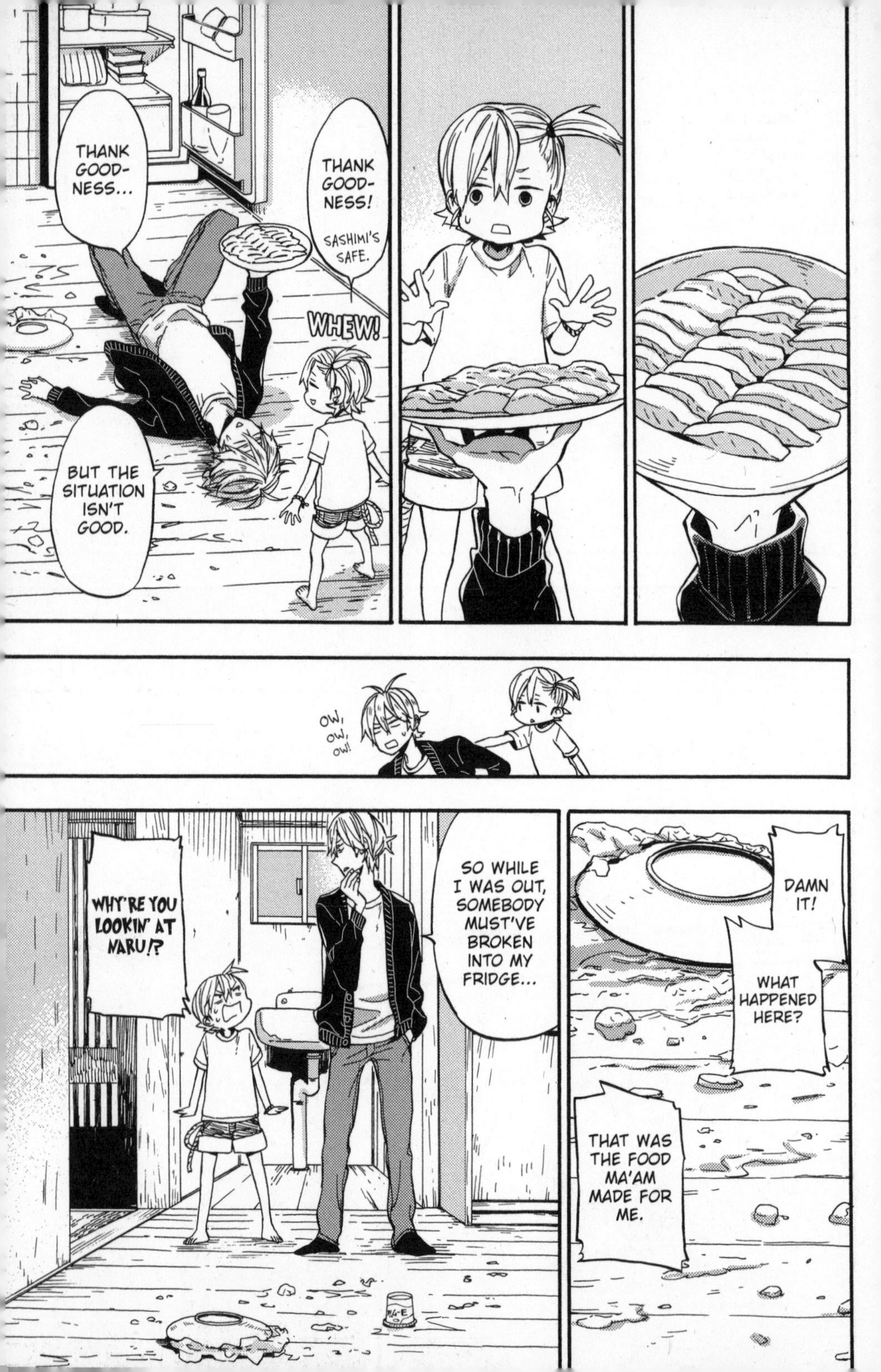
THANK GOODNESS! SASHIMI'S SAFE.
WHEW!
THANK GOODNESS...
BUT THE SITUATION ISN'T GOOD.
OW, OW, OW!
DAMN IT!
WHAT HAPPENED HERE?
THAT WAS THE FOOD MA'AM MADE FOR ME.
SO WHILE I WAS OUT, SOMEBODY MUST'VE BROKEN INTO MY FRIDGE...
WHY'RE YOU LOOKIN' AT NARU!?

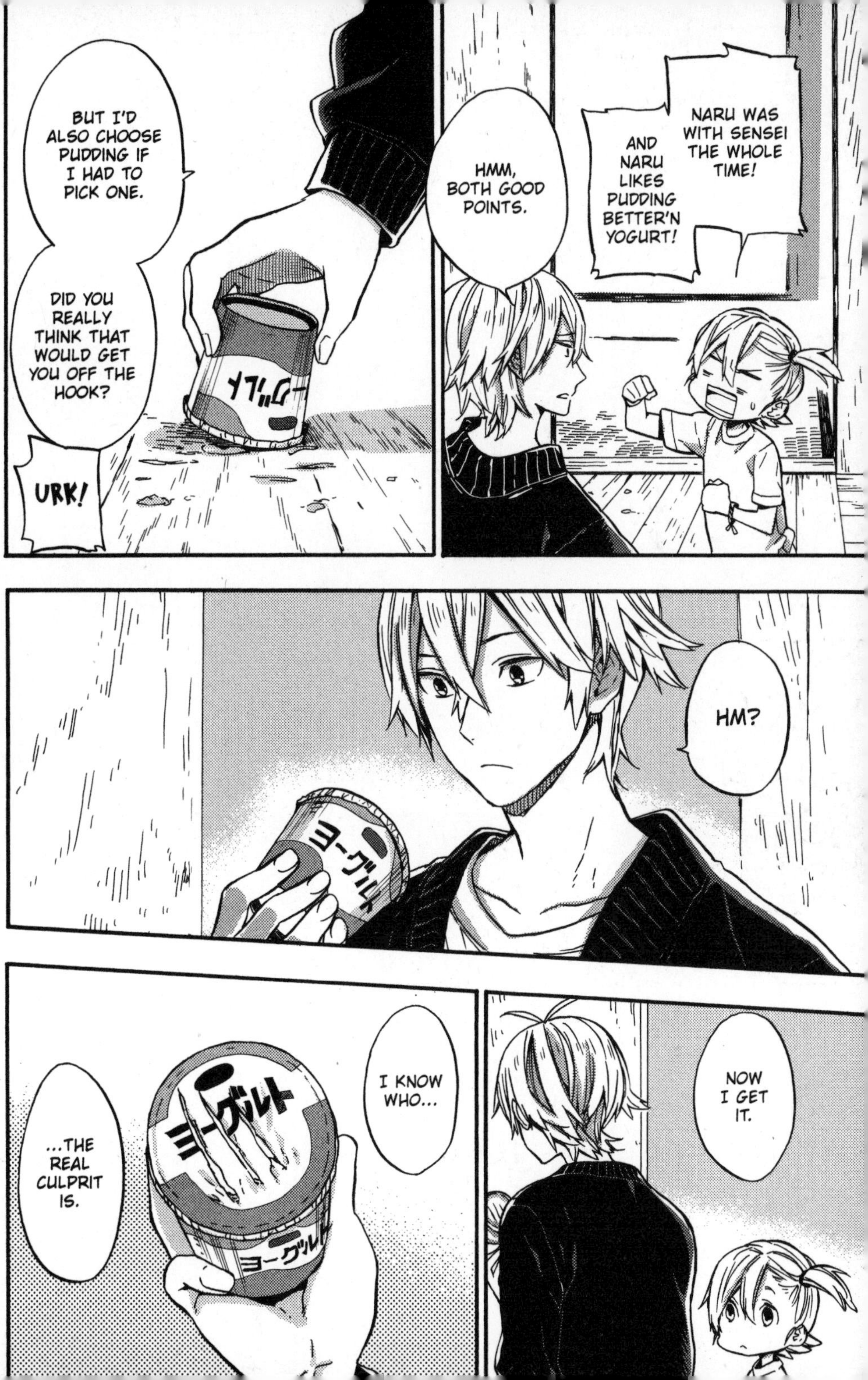
NARU WAS WITH SENSEI THE WHOLE TIME!
AND NARU LIKES PUDDING BETTER'N YOGURT!
HMM, BOTH GOOD POINTS.
BUT I'D ALSO CHOOSE PUDDING IF I HAD TO PICK ONE.
DID YOU REALLY THINK THAT WOULD GET YOU OFF THE HOOK?
URK!
HM?
ヨーグルト
NOW I GET IT.
I KNOW WHO...
...THE REAL CULPRIT IS.
ヨーグルト
ヨーグルト

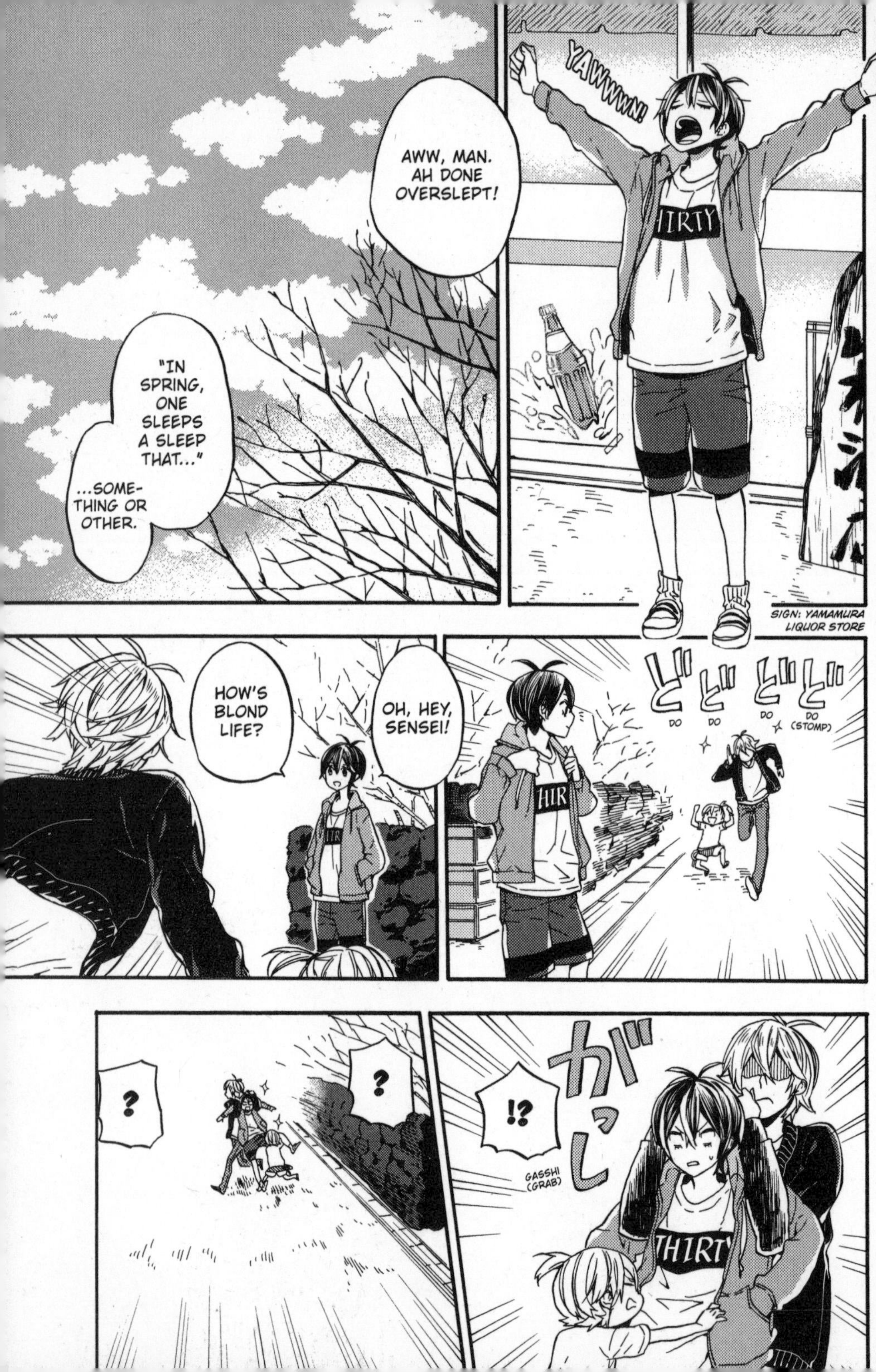
YAWWWN!
AWW, MAN. AH DONE OVERSLEPT!
SIGN: YAMAMURA LIQUOR STORE
"IN SPRING, ONE SLEEPS A SLEEP THAT..."
...SOME-THING OR OTHER.
どどどど
DO DO DO DO (STOMP)
OH, HEY, SENSEI!
HOW'S BLOND LIFE?
がっし
GASSHI (GRAB)
!?
?
?

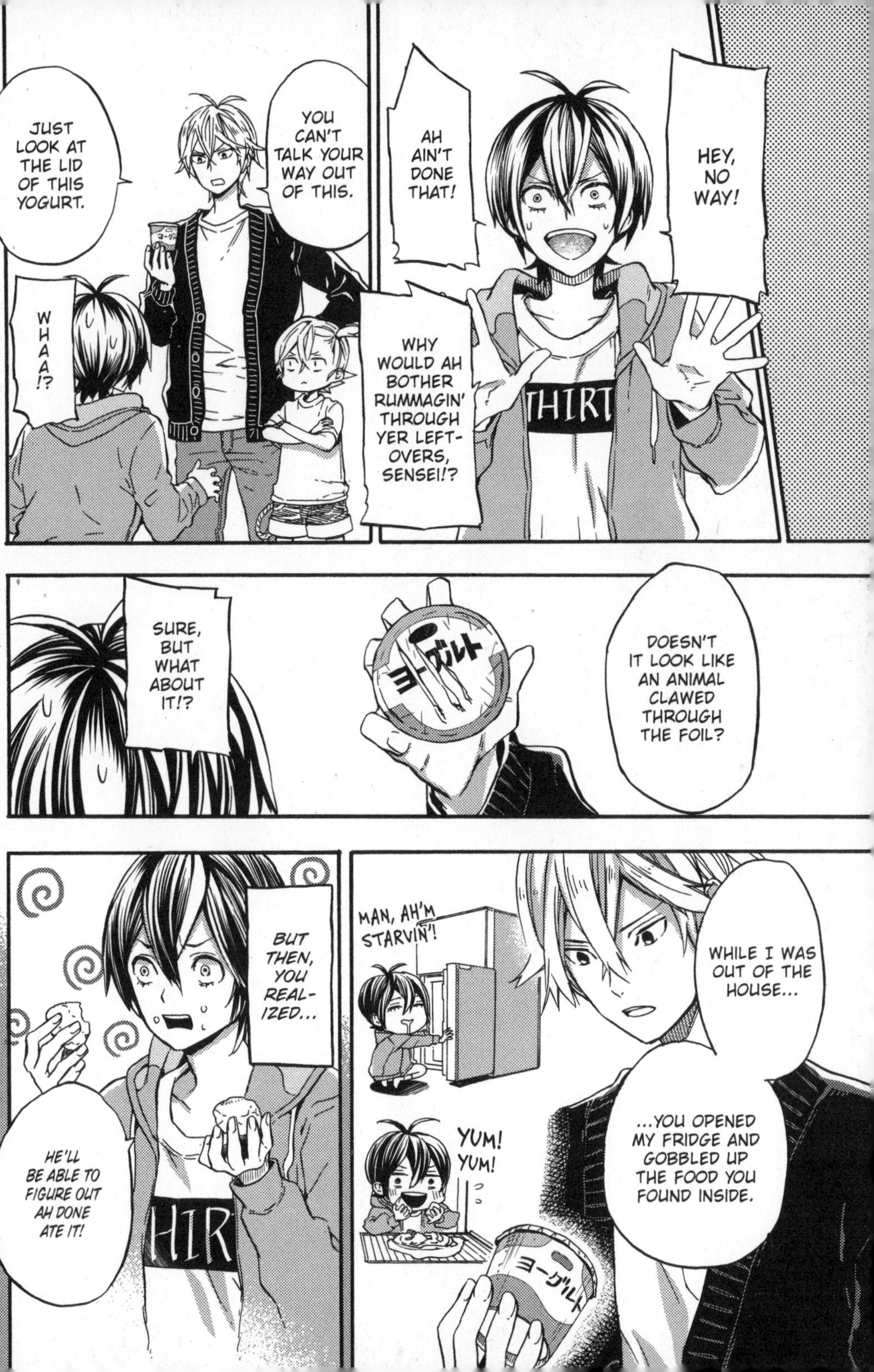
HEY, NO WAY!
AH AIN'T DONE THAT!
WHY WOULD AH BOTHER RUMMAGIN' THROUGH YER LEFT-OVERS, SENSEI!?
YOU CAN'T TALK YOUR WAY OUT OF THIS.
JUST LOOK AT THE LID OF THIS YOGURT.
WHAAA!?
DOESN'T IT LOOK LIKE AN ANIMAL CLAWED THROUGH THE FOIL?
ヨーグルト
SURE, BUT WHAT ABOUT IT!?
WHILE I WAS OUT OF THE HOUSE...
MAN, AH'M STARVIN'!
...YOU OPENED MY FRIDGE AND GOBBLED UP THE FOOD YOU FOUND INSIDE.
YUM! YUM!
BUT THEN, YOU REALIZED...
HE'LL BE ABLE TO FIGURE OUT AH DONE ATE IT!

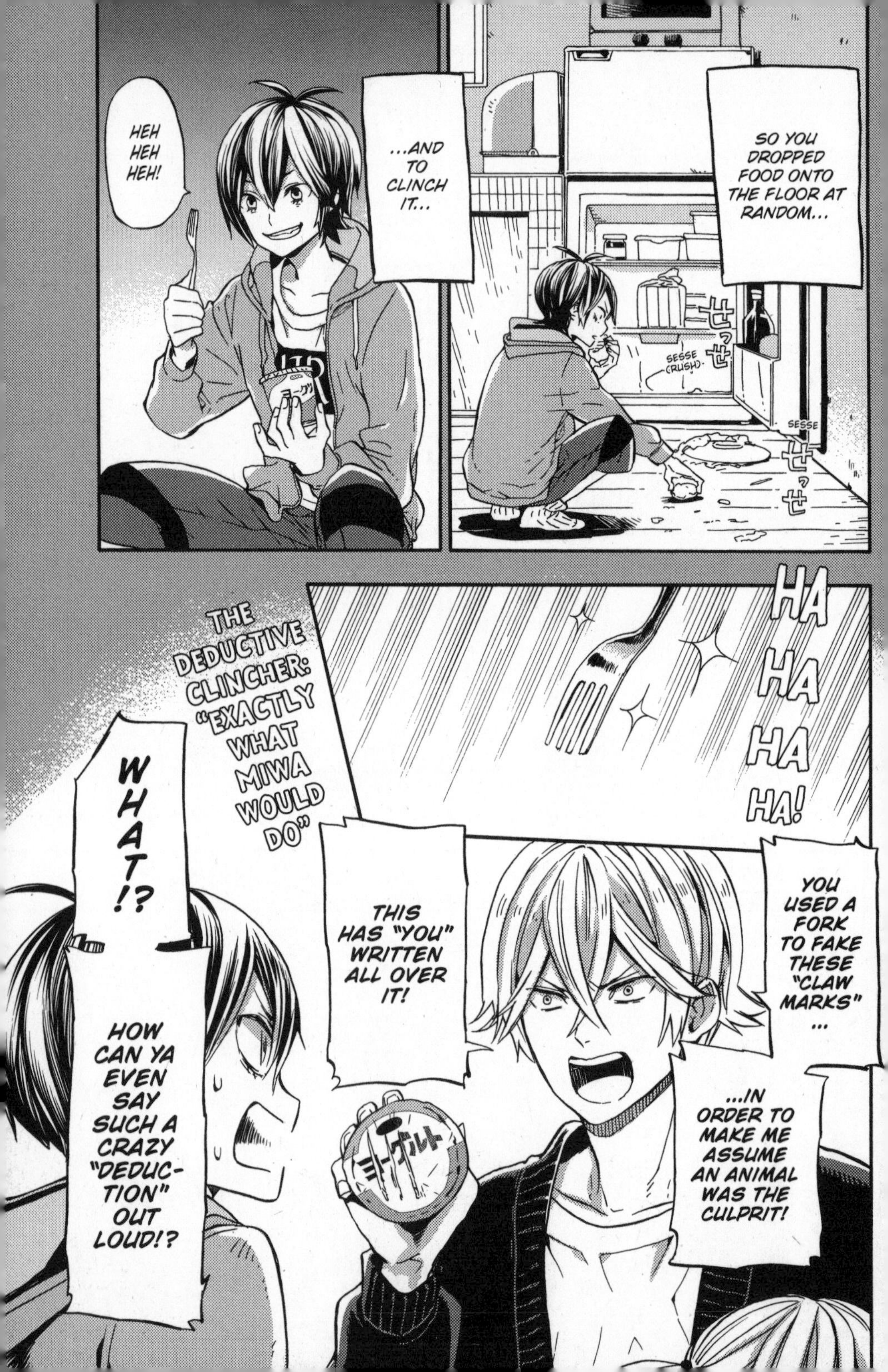
SO YOU DROPPED FOOD ONTO THE FLOOR AT RANDOM...
せっせ
SESSE (RUSH)
SESSE
せっせ
...AND TO CLINCH IT...
HEH HEH HEH!
HA HA HA HA HA!
THE DEDUCTIVE CLINCHER: "EXACTLY WHAT MIWA WOULD DO"
YOU USED A FORK TO FAKE THESE "CLAW MARKS"...
...IN ORDER TO MAKE ME ASSUME AN ANIMAL WAS THE CULPRIT!
THIS HAS "YOU" WRITTEN ALL OVER IT!
ヨーグルト
WHAT!?
HOW CAN YA EVEN SAY SUCH A CRAZY "DEDUCTION" OUT LOUD!?

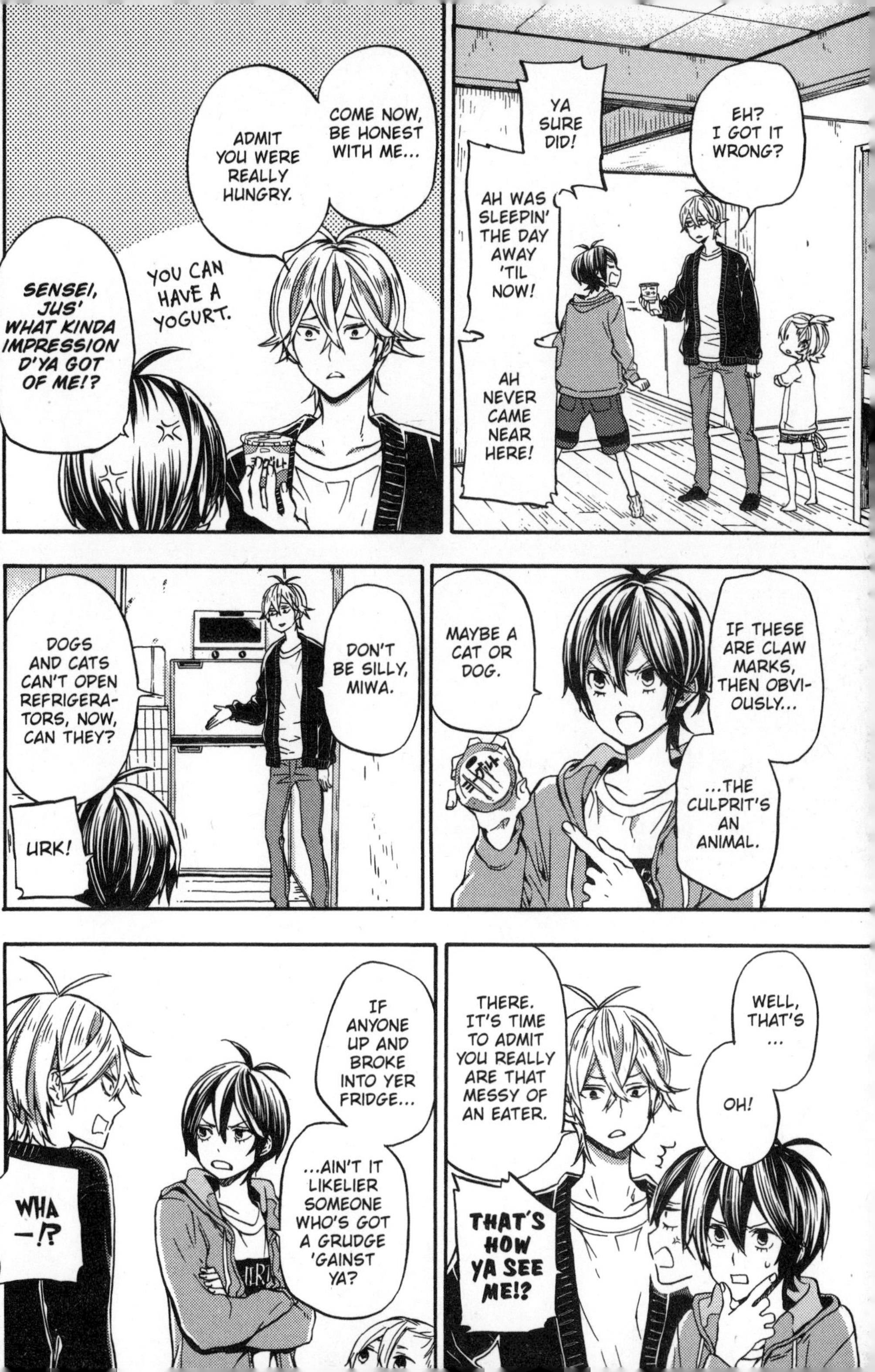
EH? I GOT IT WRONG?
YA SURE DID!
AH WAS SLEEPIN' THE DAY AWAY 'TIL NOW!
AH NEVER CAME NEAR HERE!
COME NOW, BE HONEST WITH ME...
ADMIT YOU WERE REALLY HUNGRY.
YOU CAN HAVE A YOGURT.
SENSEI, JUS' WHAT KINDA IMPRESSION D'YA GOT OF ME!?
IF THESE ARE CLAW MARKS, THEN OBVIOUSLY...
...THE CULPRIT'S AN ANIMAL.
MAYBE A CAT OR DOG.
DON'T BE SILLY, MIWA.
DOGS AND CATS CAN'T OPEN REFRIGERATORS, NOW, CAN THEY?
URK!
WELL, THAT'S ...
OH!
THERE. IT'S TIME TO ADMIT YOU REALLY ARE THAT MESSY OF AN EATER.
THAT'S HOW YA SEE ME!?
IF ANYONE UP AND BROKE INTO YER FRIDGE...
...AIN'T IT LIKELIER SOMEONE WHO'S GOT A GRUDGE 'GAINST YA?
WHA—!?

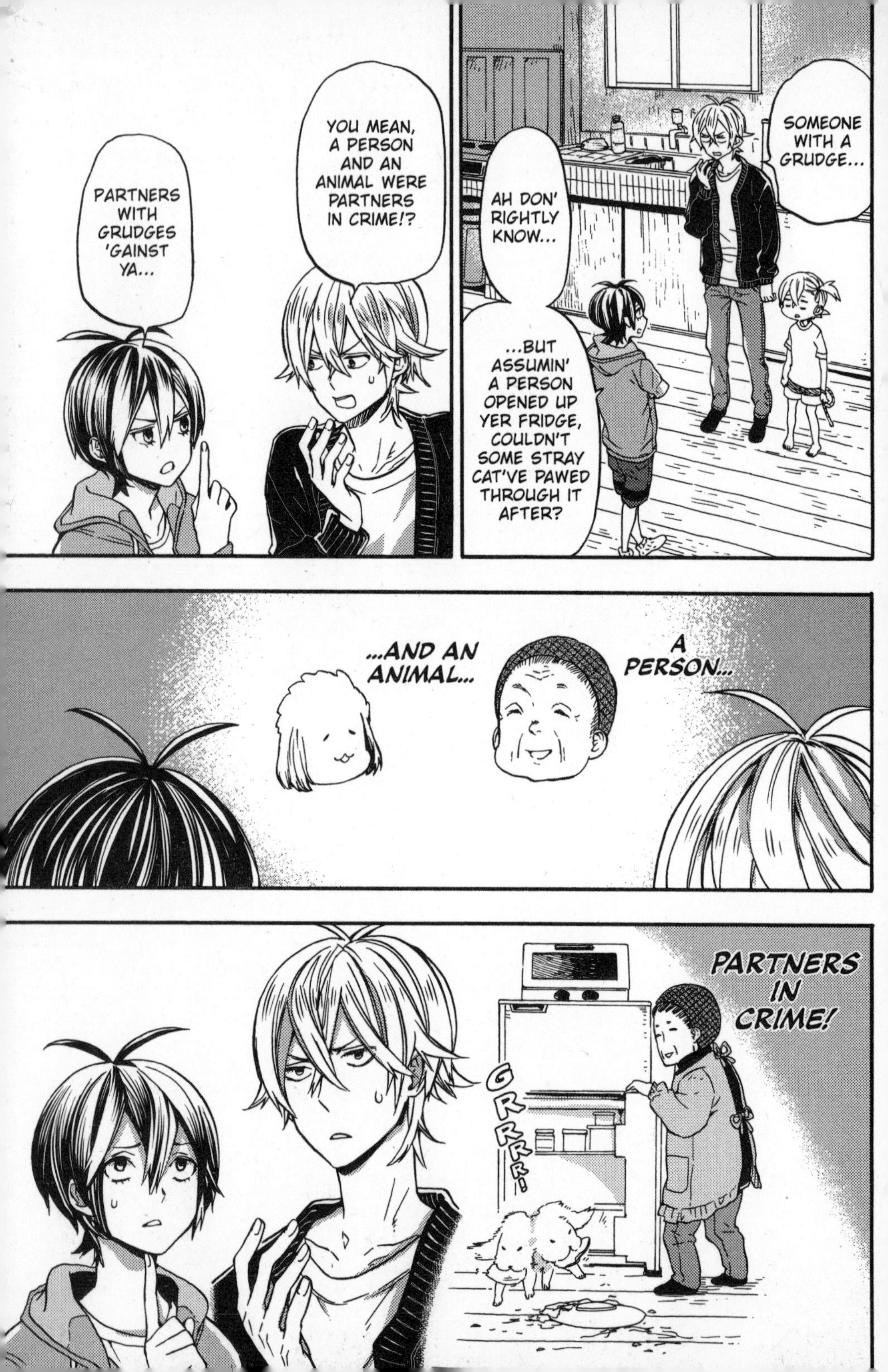
SOMEONE WITH A GRUDGE...
AH DON' RIGHTLY KNOW...
...BUT ASSUMIN' A PERSON OPENED UP YER FRIDGE, COULDN'T SOME STRAY CAT'VE PAWED THROUGH IT AFTER?
YOU MEAN, A PERSON AND AN ANIMAL WERE PARTNERS IN CRIME!?
PARTNERS WITH GRUDGES 'GAINST YA...
A PERSON...
...AND AN ANIMAL...
PARTNERS IN CRIME!
GRRRR!

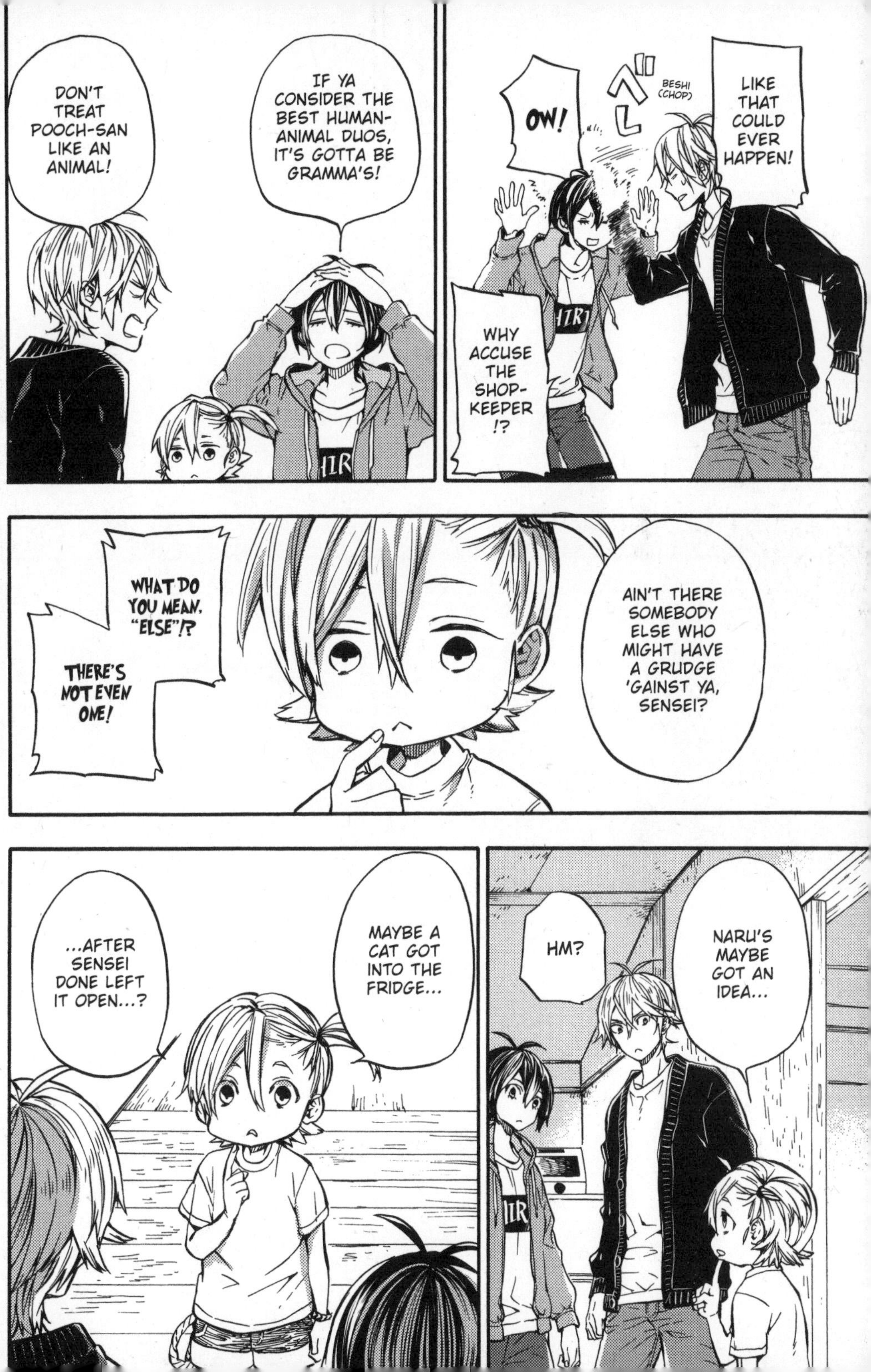
LIKE THAT COULD EVER HAPPEN!
BESHI (CHOP)
OW!
WHY ACCUSE THE SHOPKEEPER!?
IF YA CONSIDER THE BEST HUMAN-ANIMAL DUOS, IT'S GOTTA BE GRAMMA'S!
DON'T TREAT POOCH-SAN LIKE AN ANIMAL!
AIN'T THERE SOMEBODY ELSE WHO MIGHT HAVE A GRUDGE 'GAINST YA, SENSEI?
WHAT DO YOU MEAN, "ELSE"!?
THERE'S NOT EVEN ONE!
NARU'S MAYBE GOT AN IDEA...
HM?
MAYBE A CAT GOT INTO THE FRIDGE...
...AFTER SENSEI DONE LEFT IT OPEN...?

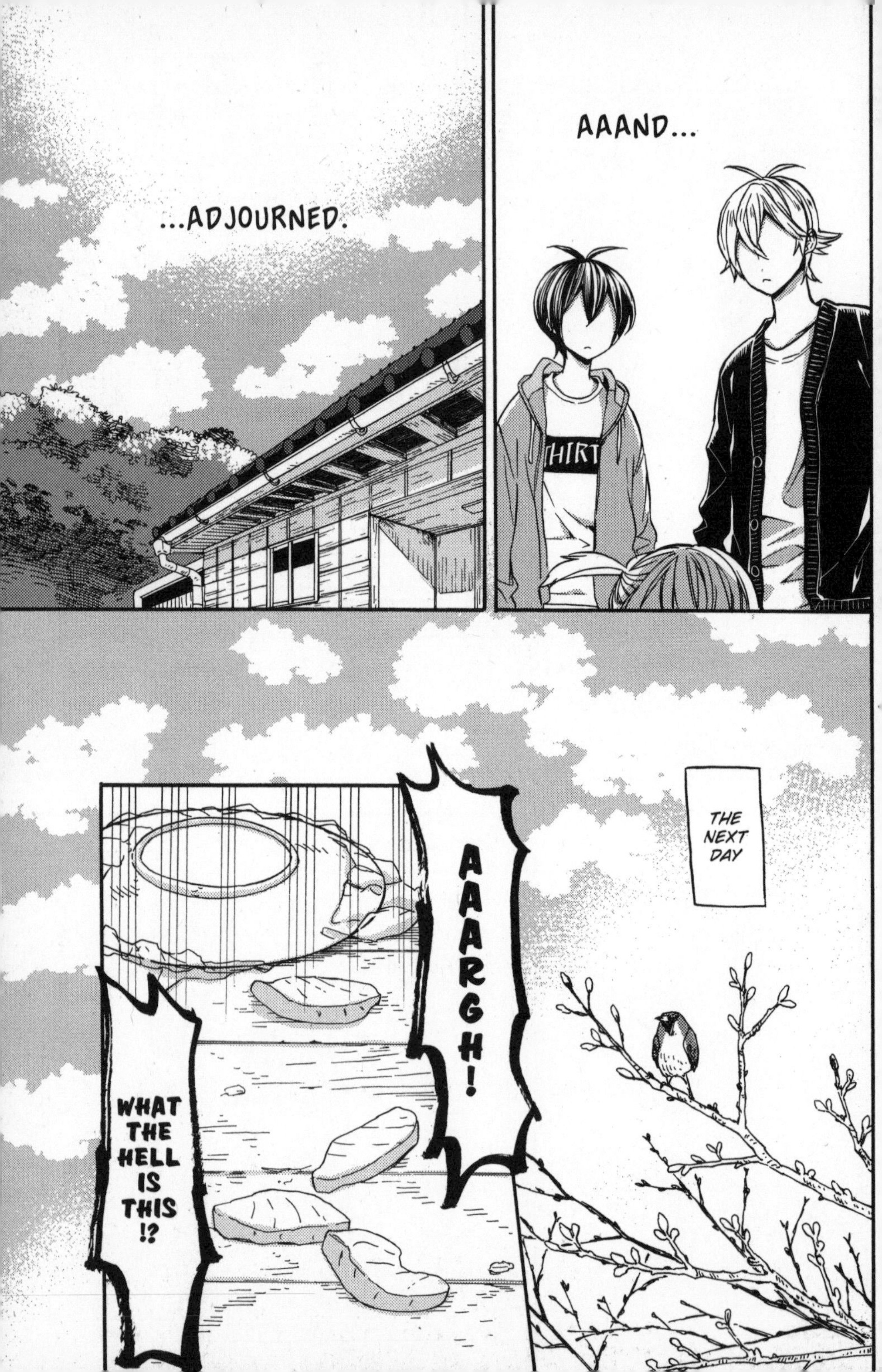
AAAND...
...ADJOURNED.
THE NEXT DAY
AAAARGH!
WHAT THE HELL IS THIS!?

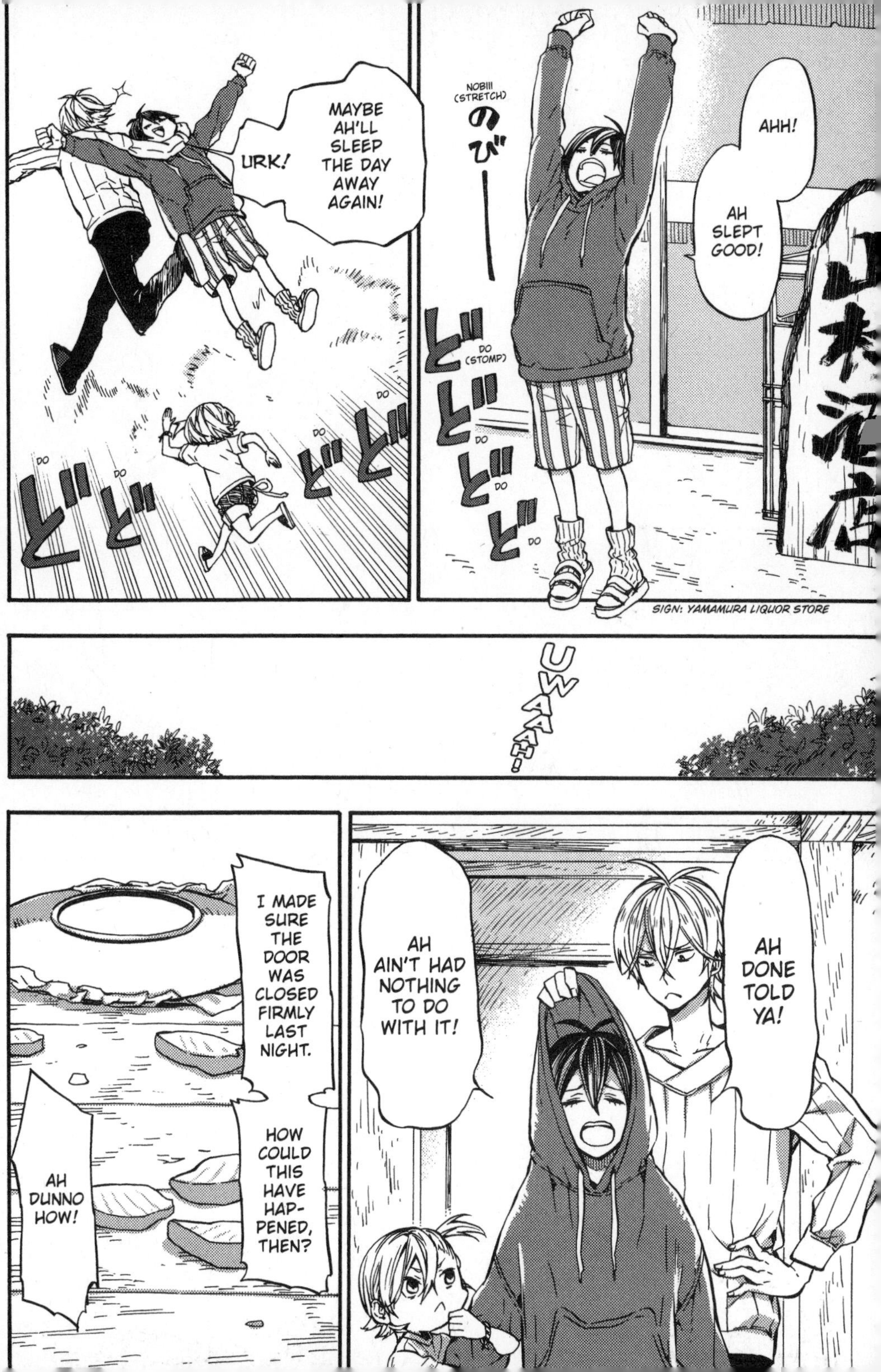
NOBIII (STRETCH)
のびー
AHH!
AH SLEPT GOOD!
DO (STOMP)
DO
DO
DO
SIGN: YAMAMURA LIQUOR STORE
MAYBE AH'LL SLEEP THE DAY AWAY AGAIN!
URK!
DO
DO
DO
DO
UWAAAAH!
AH DONE TOLD YA!
AH AIN'T HAD NOTHING TO DO WITH IT!
I MADE SURE THE DOOR WAS CLOSED FIRMLY LAST NIGHT.
HOW COULD THIS HAVE HAPPENED, THEN?
AH DUNNO HOW!

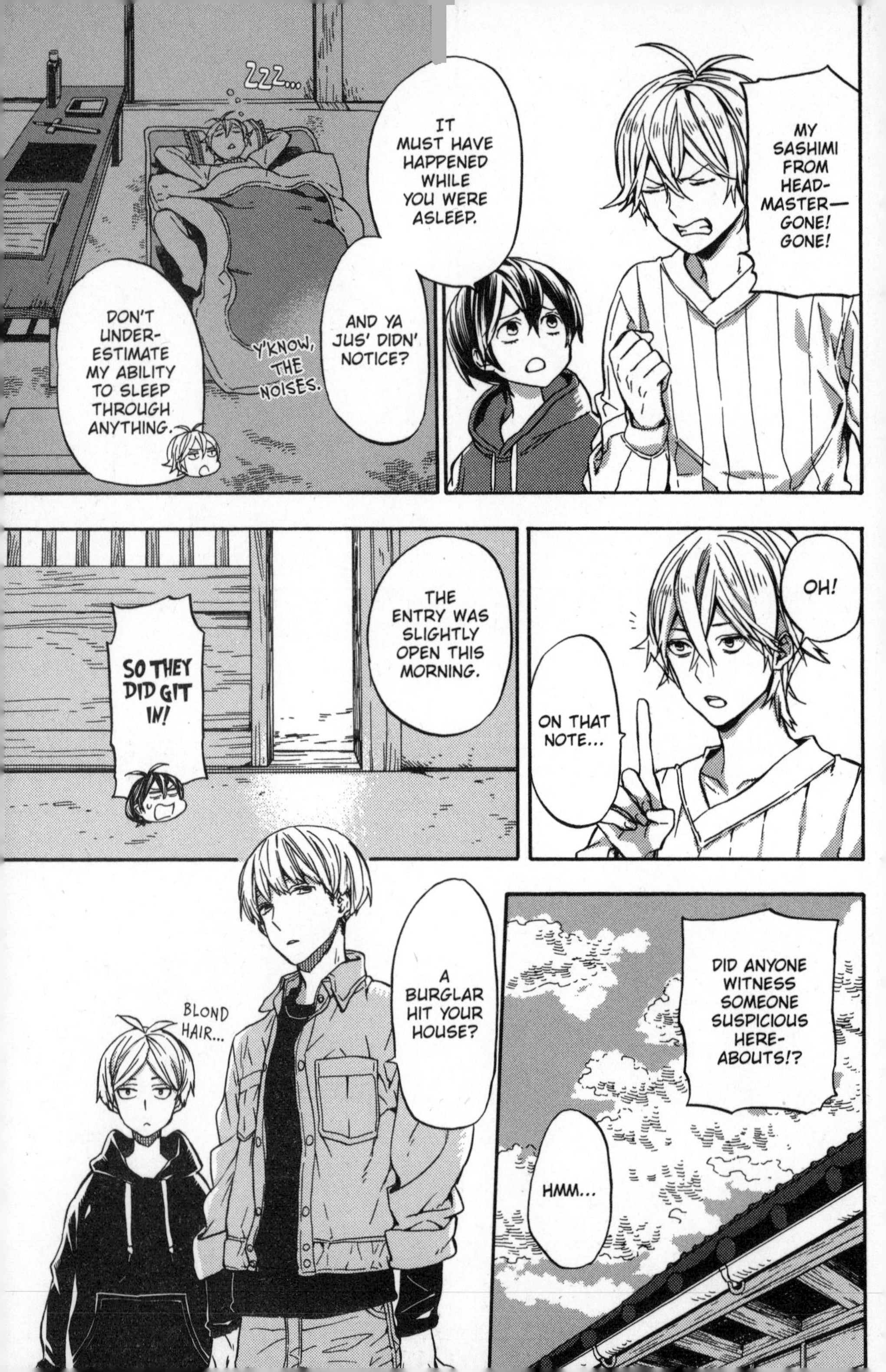
MY SASHIMI FROM HEAD-MASTER— GONE! GONE!
IT MUST HAVE HAPPENED WHILE YOU WERE ASLEEP.
ZZZ...
AND YA JUS' DIDN' NOTICE?
Y'KNOW, THE NOISES.
DON'T UNDER-ESTIMATE MY ABILITY TO SLEEP THROUGH ANYTHING.
OH!
ON THAT NOTE...
THE ENTRY WAS SLIGHTLY OPEN THIS MORNING.
SO THEY DID GIT IN!
DID ANYONE WITNESS SOMEONE SUSPICIOUS HERE-ABOUTS!?
HMM...
A BURGLAR HIT YOUR HOUSE?
BLOND HAIR...

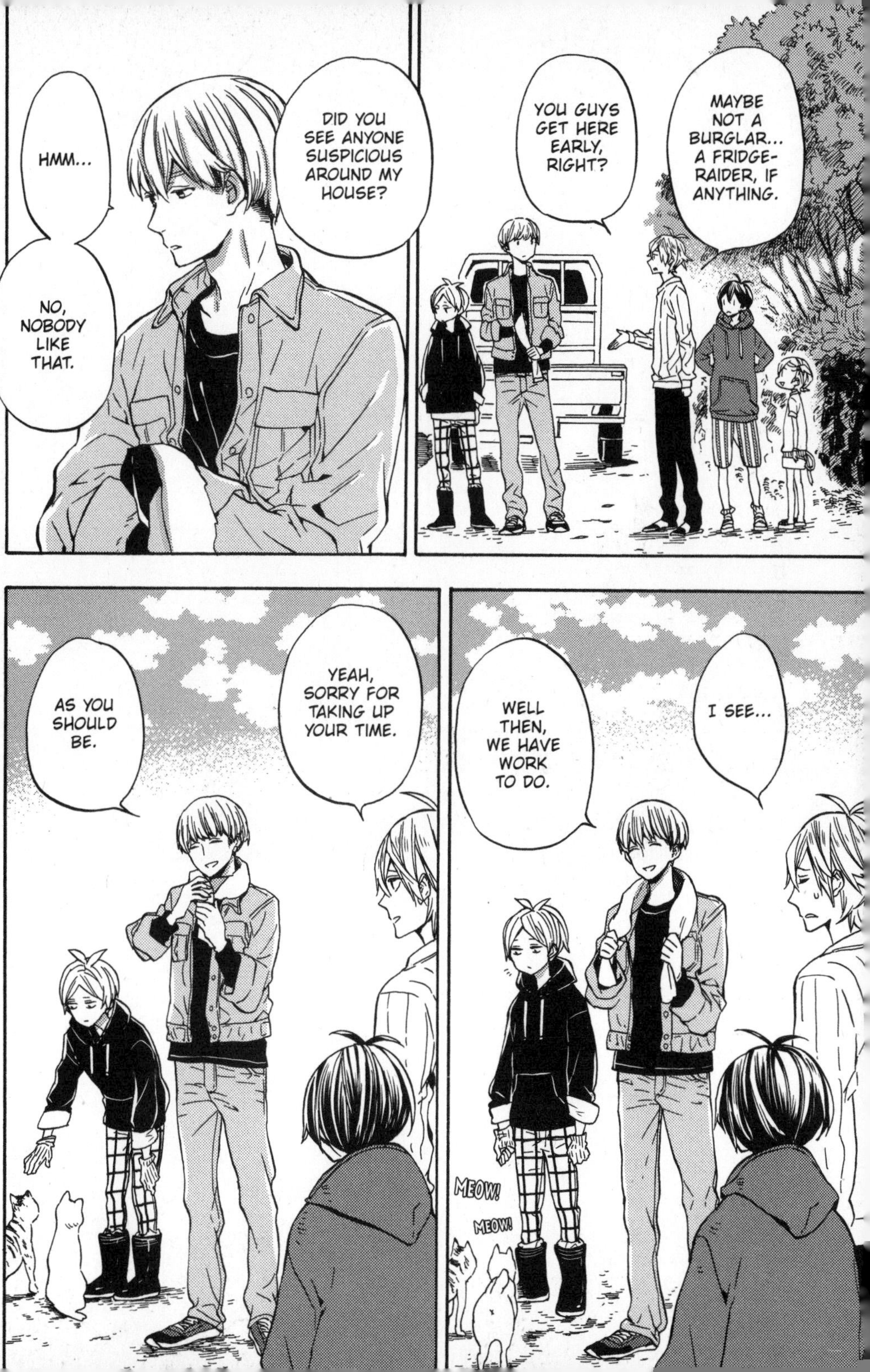
MAYBE NOT A BURGLAR... A FRIDGE-RAIDER, IF ANYTHING.
YOU GUYS GET HERE EARLY, RIGHT?
DID YOU SEE ANYONE SUSPICIOUS AROUND MY HOUSE?
HMM...
NO, NOBODY LIKE THAT.
I SEE...
WELL THEN, WE HAVE WORK TO DO.
MEOW!
MEOW!
YEAH, SORRY FOR TAKING UP YOUR TIME.
AS YOU SHOULD BE.

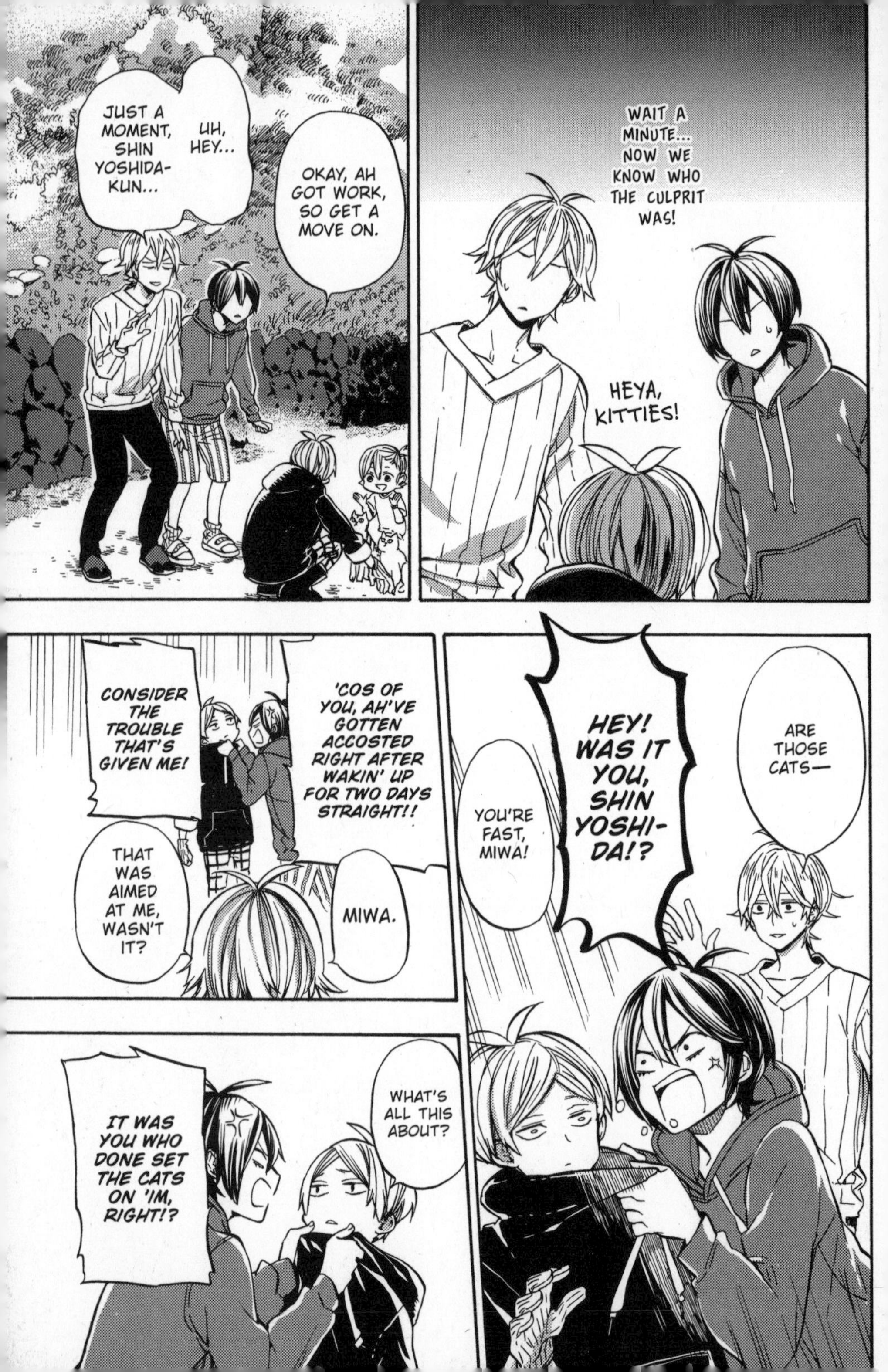
WAIT A MINUTE... NOW WE KNOW WHO THE CULPRIT WAS!
HEYA, KITTIES!
OKAY, AH GOT WORK, SO GET A MOVE ON.
UH, HEY...
JUST A MOMENT, SHIN YOSHIDA-KUN...
ARE THOSE CATS—
HEY! WAS IT YOU, SHIN YOSHIDA!?
YOU'RE FAST, MIWA!
'COS OF YOU, AH'VE GOTTEN ACCOSTED RIGHT AFTER WAKIN' UP FOR TWO DAYS STRAIGHT!!
CONSIDER THE TROUBLE THAT'S GIVEN ME!
MIWA.
THAT WAS AIMED AT ME, WASN'T IT?
WHAT'S ALL THIS ABOUT?
IT WAS YOU WHO DONE SET THE CATS ON 'IM, RIGHT!?

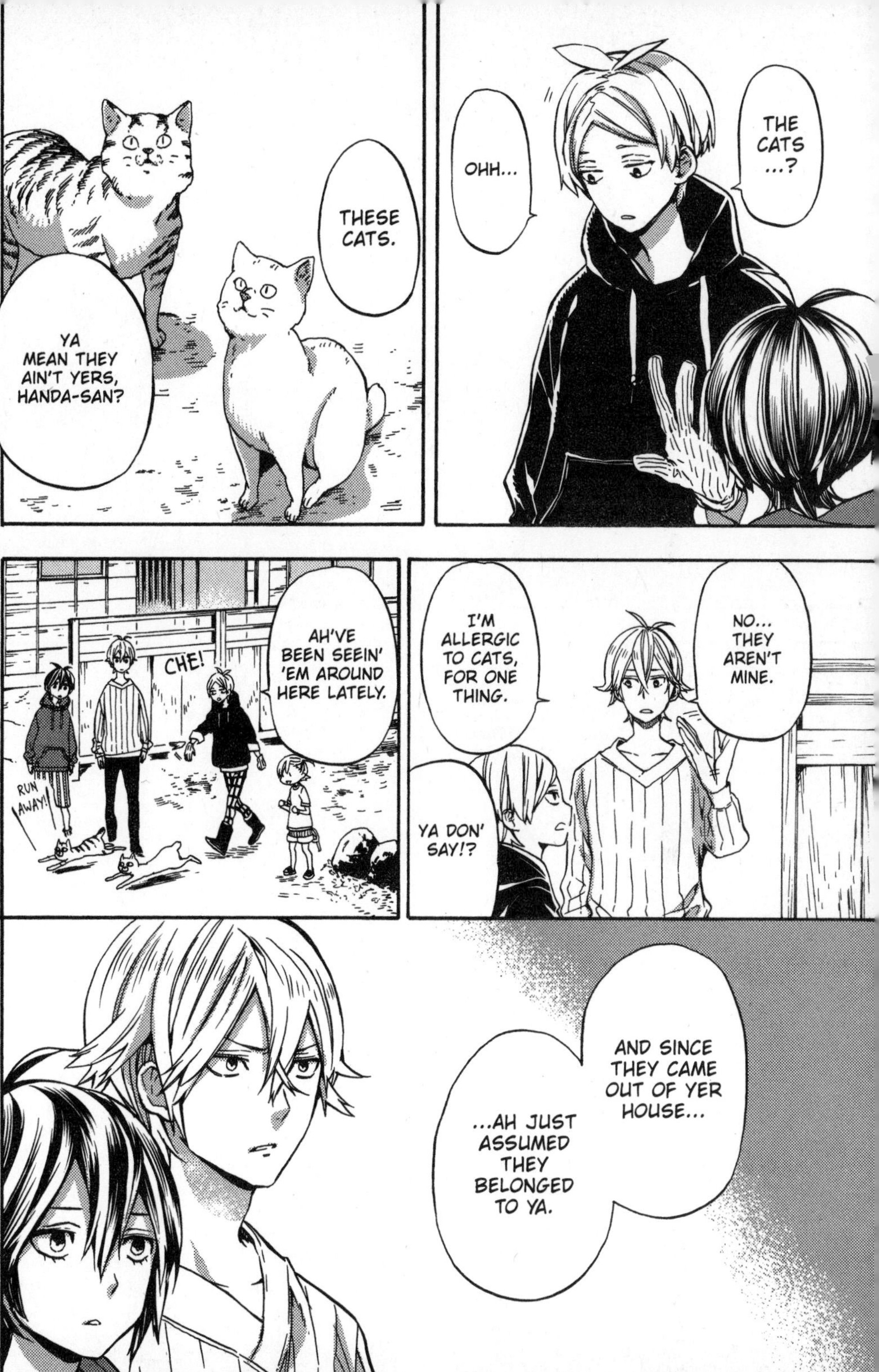
THE CATS ...?
OHH...
THESE CATS.
YA MEAN THEY AIN'T YERS, HANDA-SAN?
NO... THEY AREN'T MINE.
I'M ALLERGIC TO CATS, FOR ONE THING.
YA DON' SAY!?
AH'VE BEEN SEEIN' 'EM AROUND HERE LATELY.
CHE!
RUN AWAY!
AND SINCE THEY CAME OUT OF YER HOUSE...
...AH JUST ASSUMED THEY BELONGED TO YA.

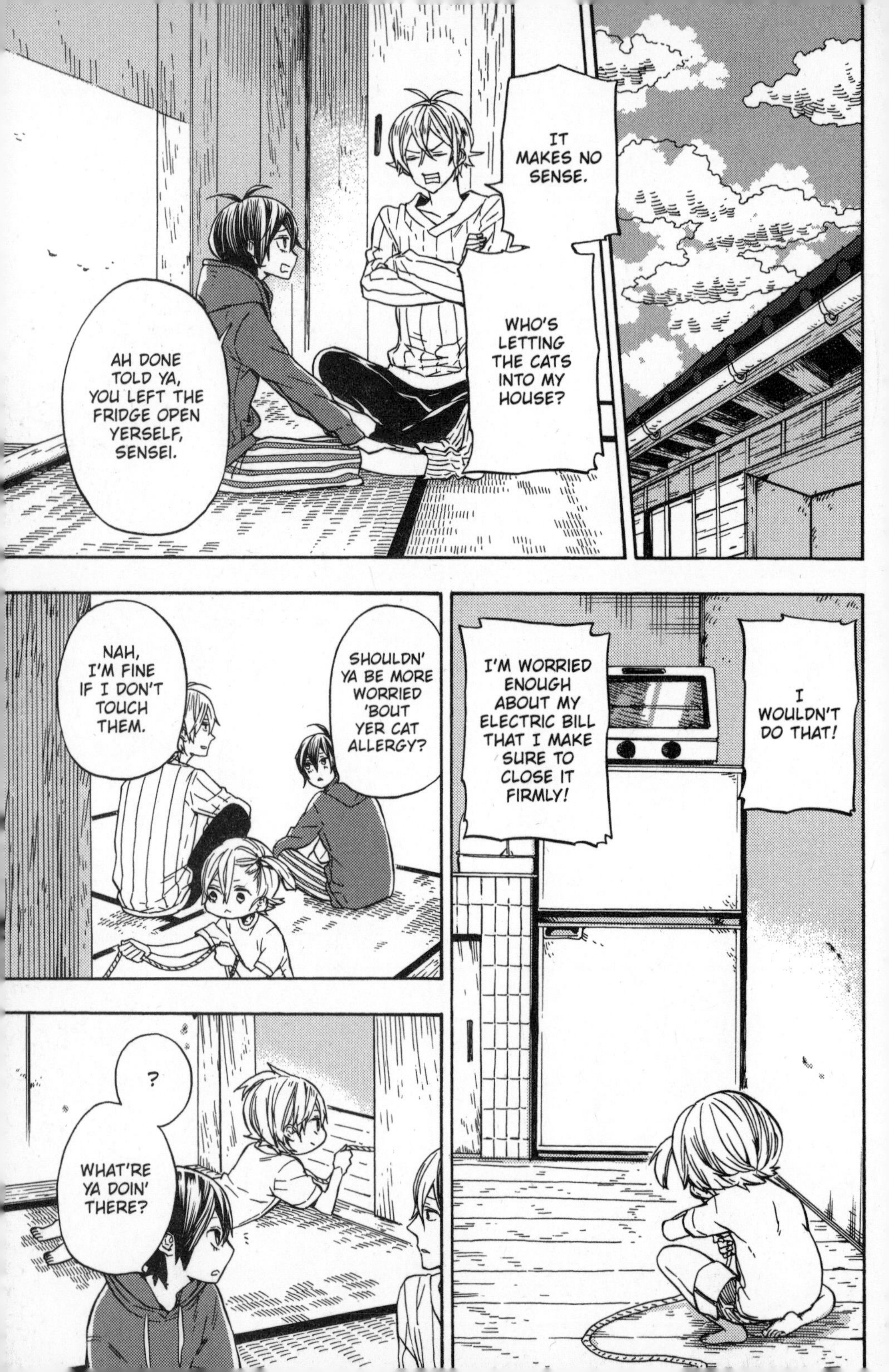
IT MAKES NO SENSE.
WHO'S LETTING THE CATS INTO MY HOUSE?
AH DONE TOLD YA, YOU LEFT THE FRIDGE OPEN YERSELF, SENSEI.
I WOULDN'T DO THAT!
I'M WORRIED ENOUGH ABOUT MY ELECTRIC BILL THAT I MAKE SURE TO CLOSE IT FIRMLY!
SHOULDN' YA BE MORE WORRIED 'BOUT YER CAT ALLERGY?
NAH, I'M FINE IF I DON'T TOUCH THEM.
?
WHAT'RE YA DOIN' THERE?

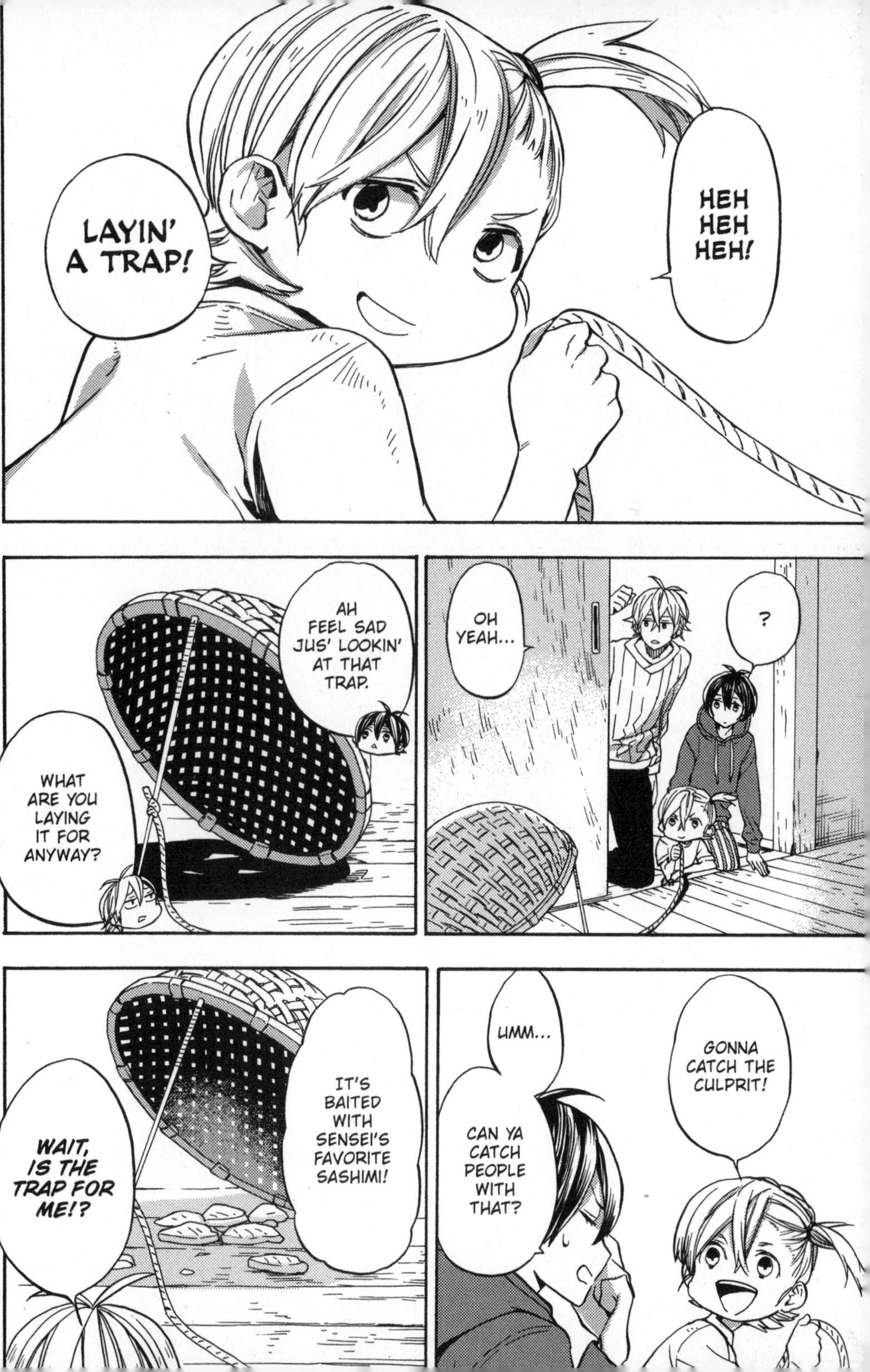
HEH HEH HEH!
LAYIN' A TRAP!
?
OH YEAH...
AH FEEL SAD JUS' LOOKIN' AT THAT TRAP.
WHAT ARE YOU LAYING IT FOR ANYWAY?
GONNA CATCH THE CULPRIT!
UMM...
CAN YA CATCH PEOPLE WITH THAT?
IT'S BAITED WITH SENSEI'S FAVORITE SASHIMI!
WAIT, IS THE TRAP FOR ME!?

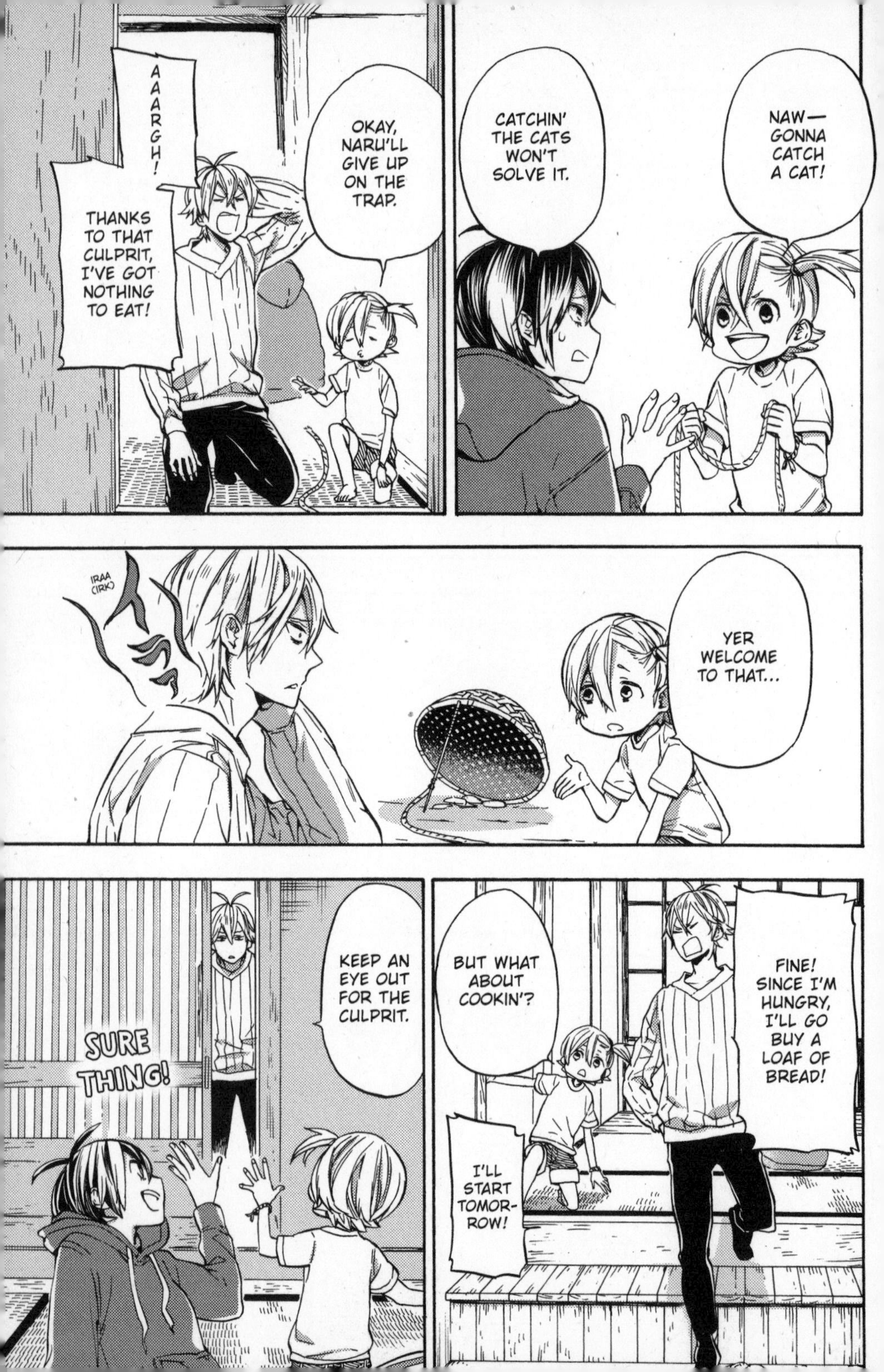
NAW— GONNA CATCH A CAT!
CATCHIN' THE CATS WON'T SOLVE IT.
OKAY, NARU'LL GIVE UP ON THE TRAP.
AAAARGH!
THANKS TO THAT CULPRIT, I'VE GOT NOTHING TO EAT!
YER WELCOME TO THAT...
IRAA (IRK)
FINE! SINCE I'M HUNGRY, I'LL GO BUY A LOAF OF BREAD!
BUT WHAT ABOUT COOKIN'?
I'LL START TOMORROW!
KEEP AN EYE OUT FOR THE CULPRIT.
SURE THING!

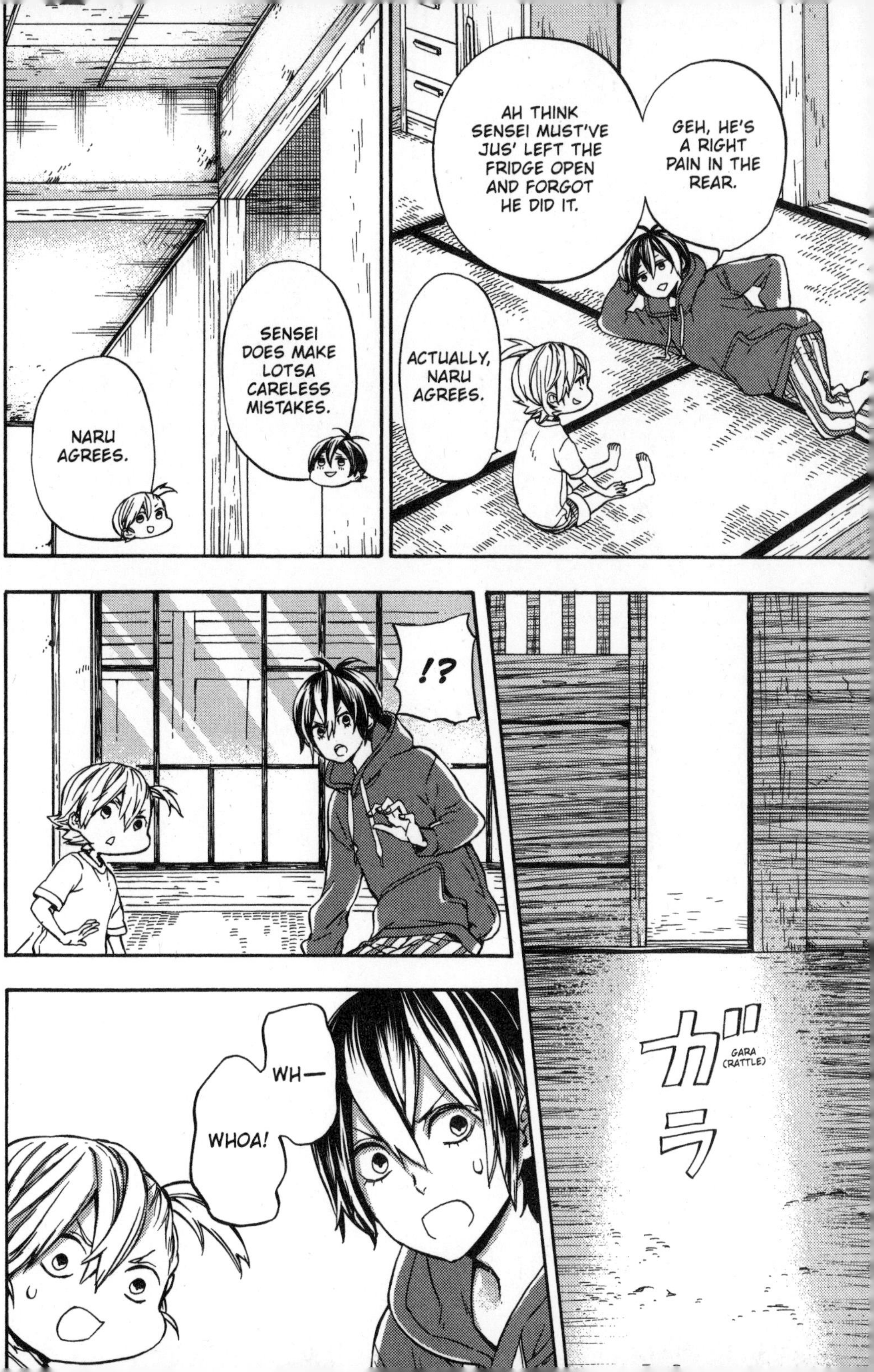
GEH, HE'S A RIGHT PAIN IN THE REAR.
AH THINK SENSEI MUST'VE JUS' LEFT THE FRIDGE OPEN AND FORGOT HE DID IT.
ACTUALLY, NARU AGREES.
SENSEI DOES MAKE LOTSA CARELESS MISTAKES.
NARU AGREES.
ガラ
GARA (RATTLE)
!?
WH—
WHOA!

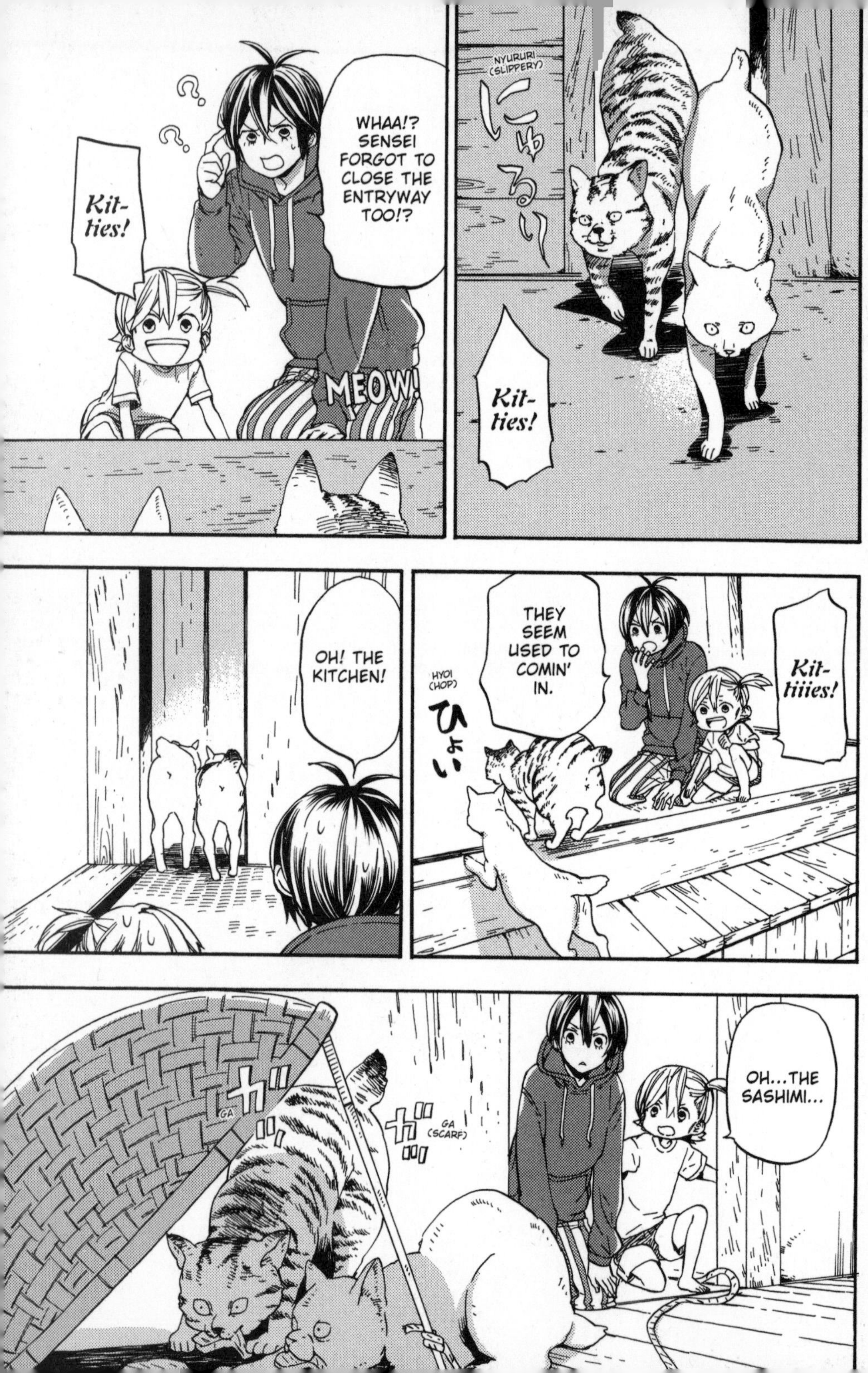

NYURURI (SLIPPERY)
にゅるい
Kit-ties!
WHAA!? SENSEI FORGOT TO CLOSE THE ENTRYWAY TOO!?
Kit-ties!
MEOW!
Kit-tiiies!
THEY SEEM USED TO COMIN' IN.
HYOI (HOP)
ひょい
OH! THE KITCHEN!
OH...THE SASHIMI...
GA (SCARF)
ガッ
GA
ガッ

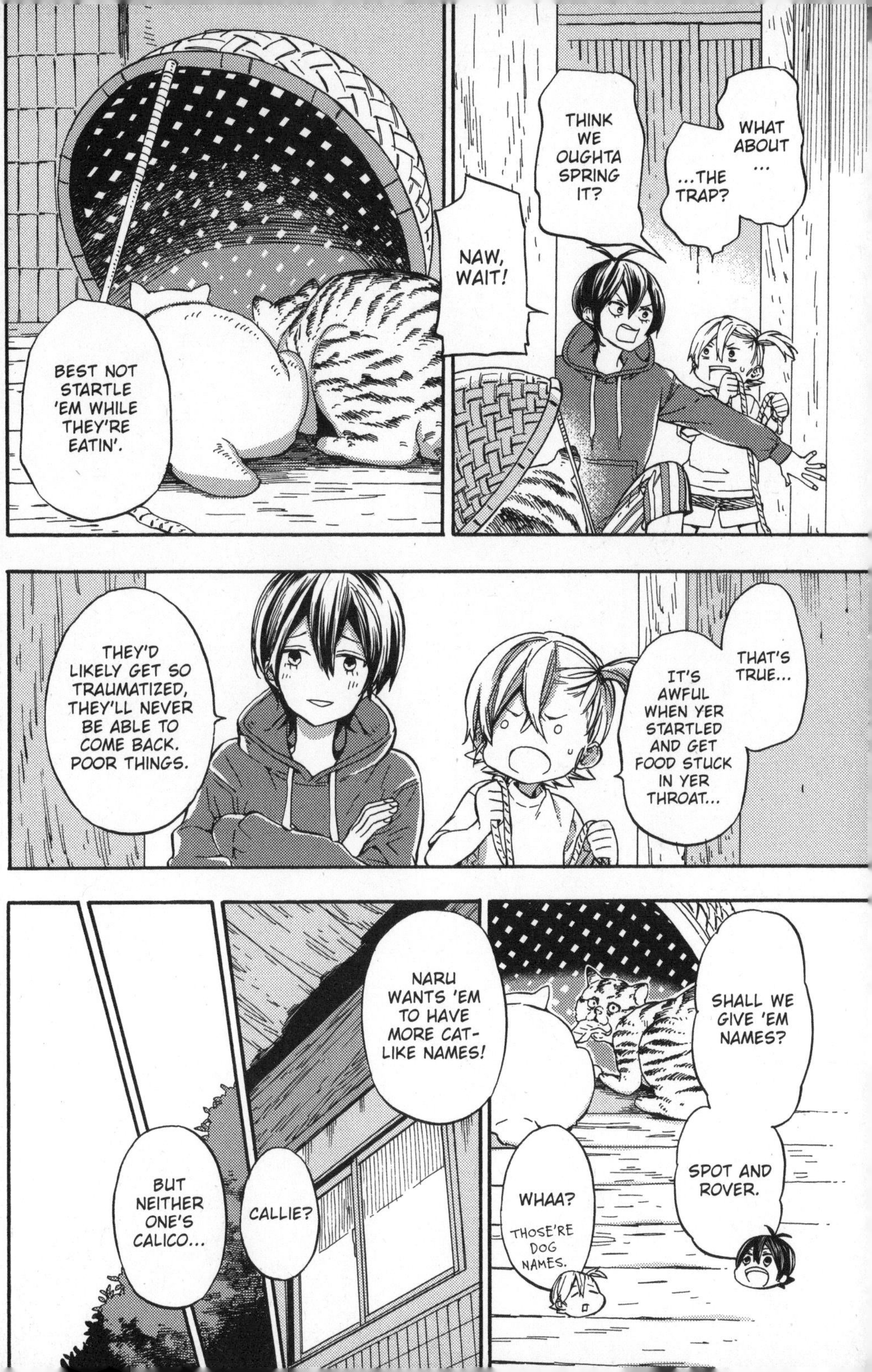
WHAT ABOUT ...
...THE TRAP?
THINK WE OUGHTA SPRING IT?
NAW, WAIT!
BEST NOT STARTLE 'EM WHILE THEY'RE EATIN'.
THAT'S TRUE...
IT'S AWFUL WHEN YER STARTLED AND GET FOOD STUCK IN YER THROAT...
THEY'D LIKELY GET SO TRAUMATIZED, THEY'LL NEVER BE ABLE TO COME BACK. POOR THINGS.
SHALL WE GIVE 'EM NAMES?
SPOT AND ROVER.
WHAA?
THOSE'RE DOG NAMES.
NARU WANTS 'EM TO HAVE MORE CAT-LIKE NAMES!
CALLIE?
BUT NEITHER ONE'S CALICO...

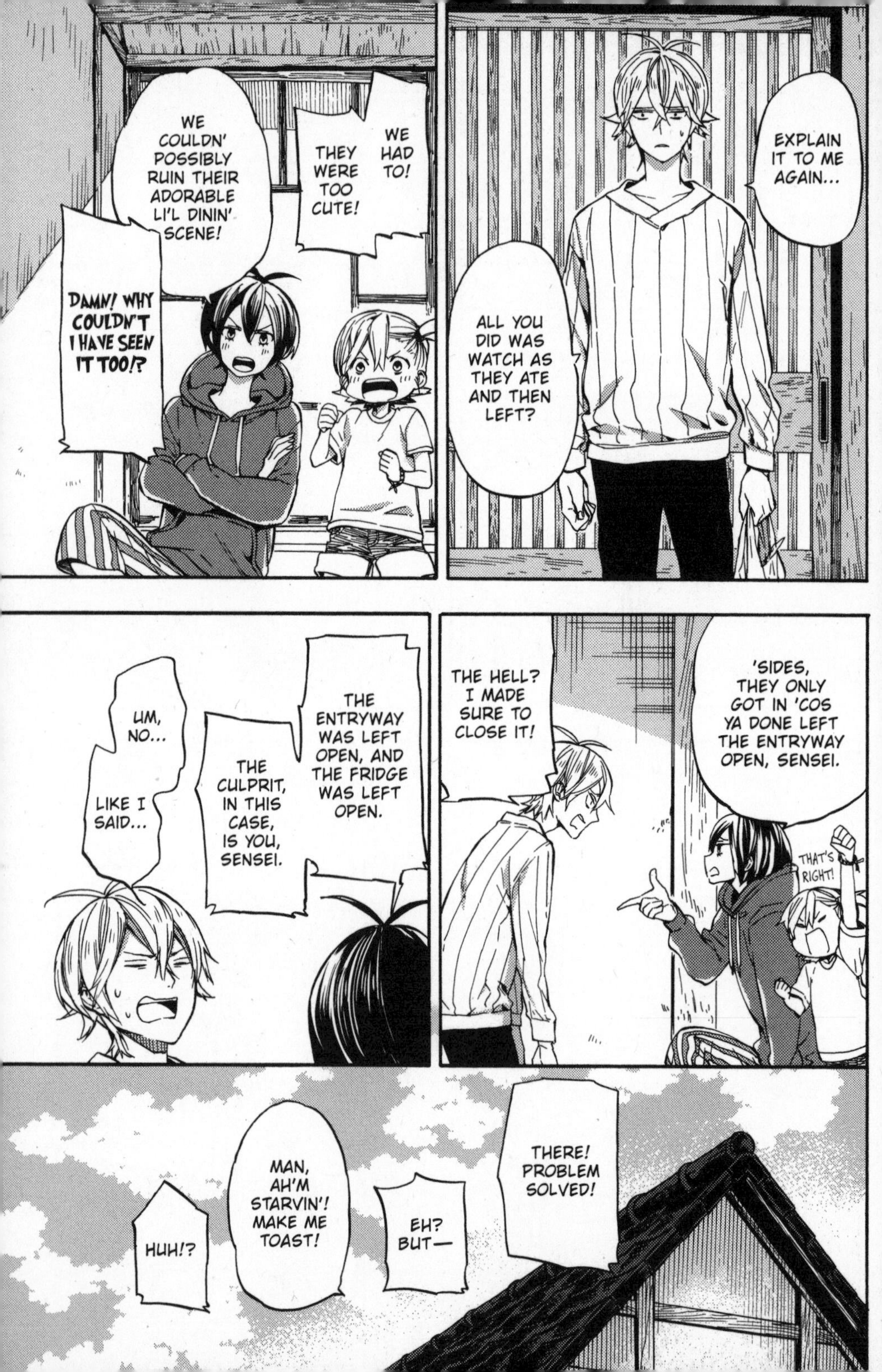
EXPLAIN IT TO ME AGAIN...
ALL YOU DID WAS WATCH AS THEY ATE AND THEN LEFT?
WE HAD TO!
THEY WERE TOO CUTE!
WE COULDN' POSSIBLY RUIN THEIR ADORABLE LI'L DININ' SCENE!
DAMN! WHY COULDN'T I HAVE SEEN IT TOO!?
'SIDES, THEY ONLY GOT IN 'COS YA DONE LEFT THE ENTRYWAY OPEN, SENSEI.
THE HELL? I MADE SURE TO CLOSE IT!
THAT'S RIGHT!
THE ENTRYWAY WAS LEFT OPEN, AND THE FRIDGE WAS LEFT OPEN.
THE CULPRIT, IN THIS CASE, IS YOU, SENSEI.
UM, NO...
LIKE I SAID...
THERE! PROBLEM SOLVED!
EH? BUT—
MAN, AH'M STARVIN'! MAKE ME TOAST!
HUH!?

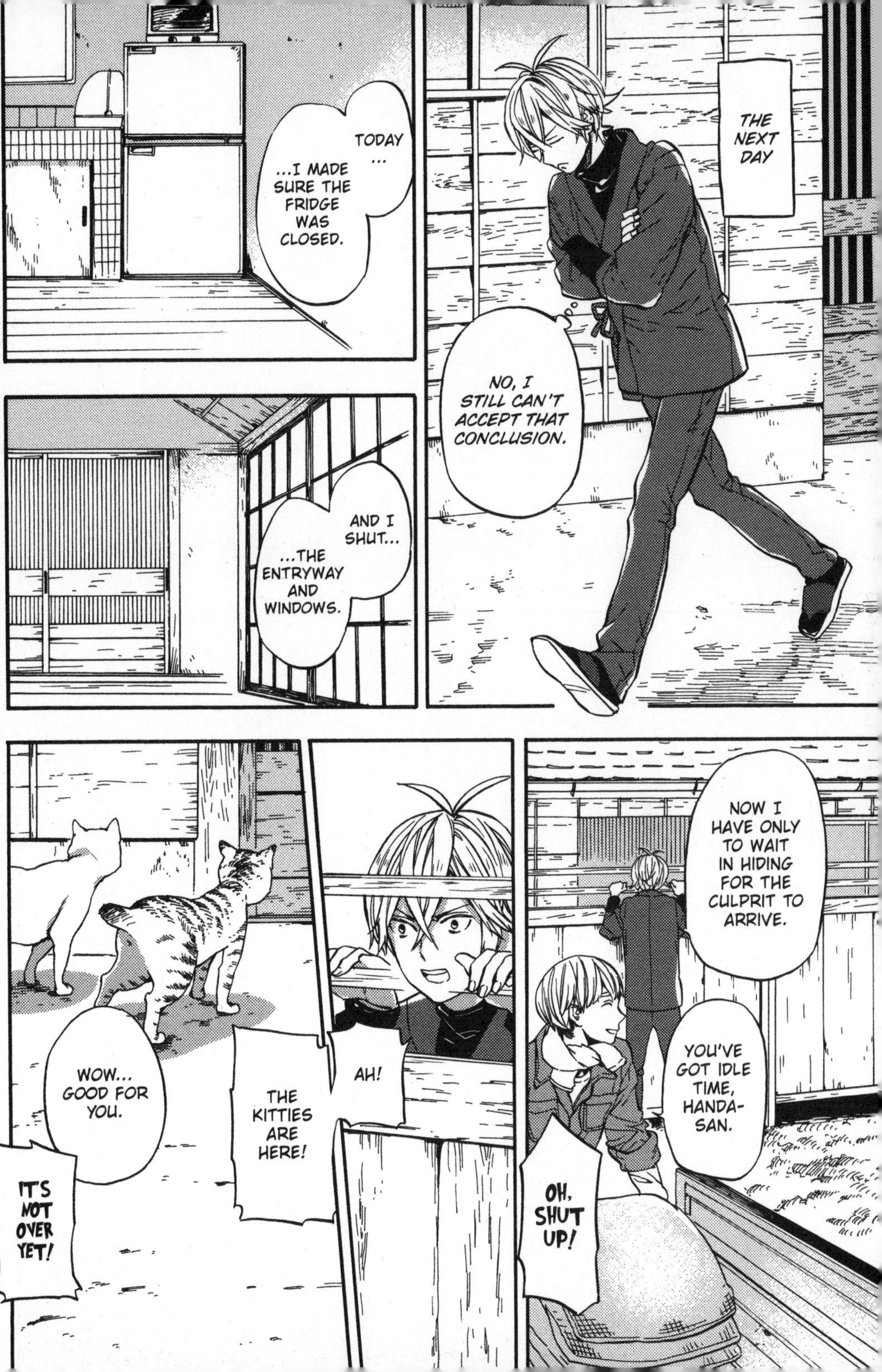
THE NEXT DAY
NO, I STILL CAN'T ACCEPT THAT CONCLUSION.
TODAY ...
...I MADE SURE THE FRIDGE WAS CLOSED.
AND I SHUT...
...THE ENTRYWAY AND WINDOWS.
NOW I HAVE ONLY TO WAIT IN HIDING FOR THE CULPRIT TO ARRIVE.
YOU'VE GOT IDLE TIME, HANDA-SAN.
OH, SHUT UP!
AH!
THE KITTIES ARE HERE!
WOW... GOOD FOR YOU.
IT'S NOT OVER YET!

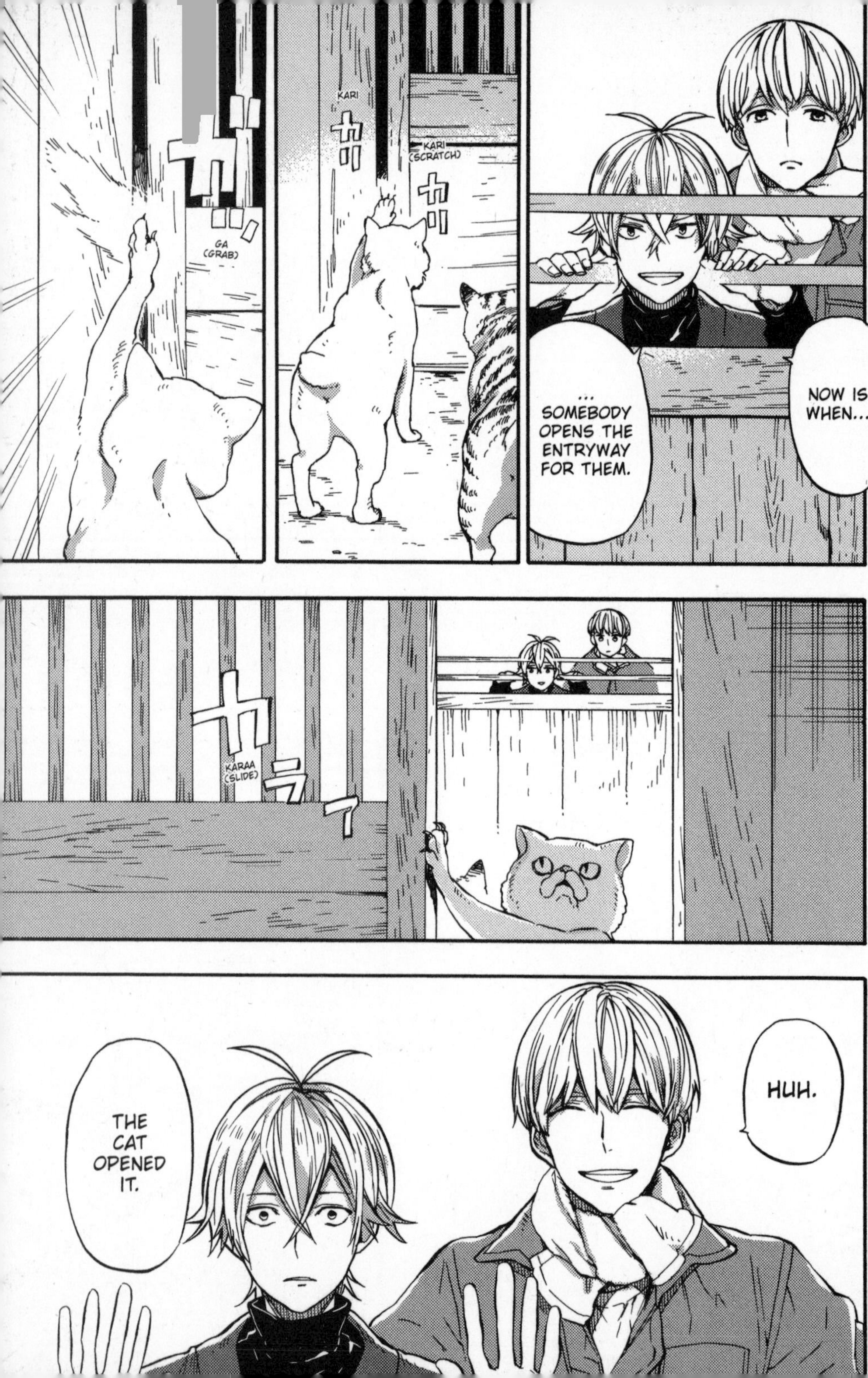
NOW IS WHEN...
...SOMEBODY OPENS THE ENTRYWAY FOR THEM.
カリ
KARI
カリ
KARI (SCRATCH)
ガッ
GA (GRAB)
カラァ
KARAA (SLIDE)
HUH.
THE CAT OPENED IT.

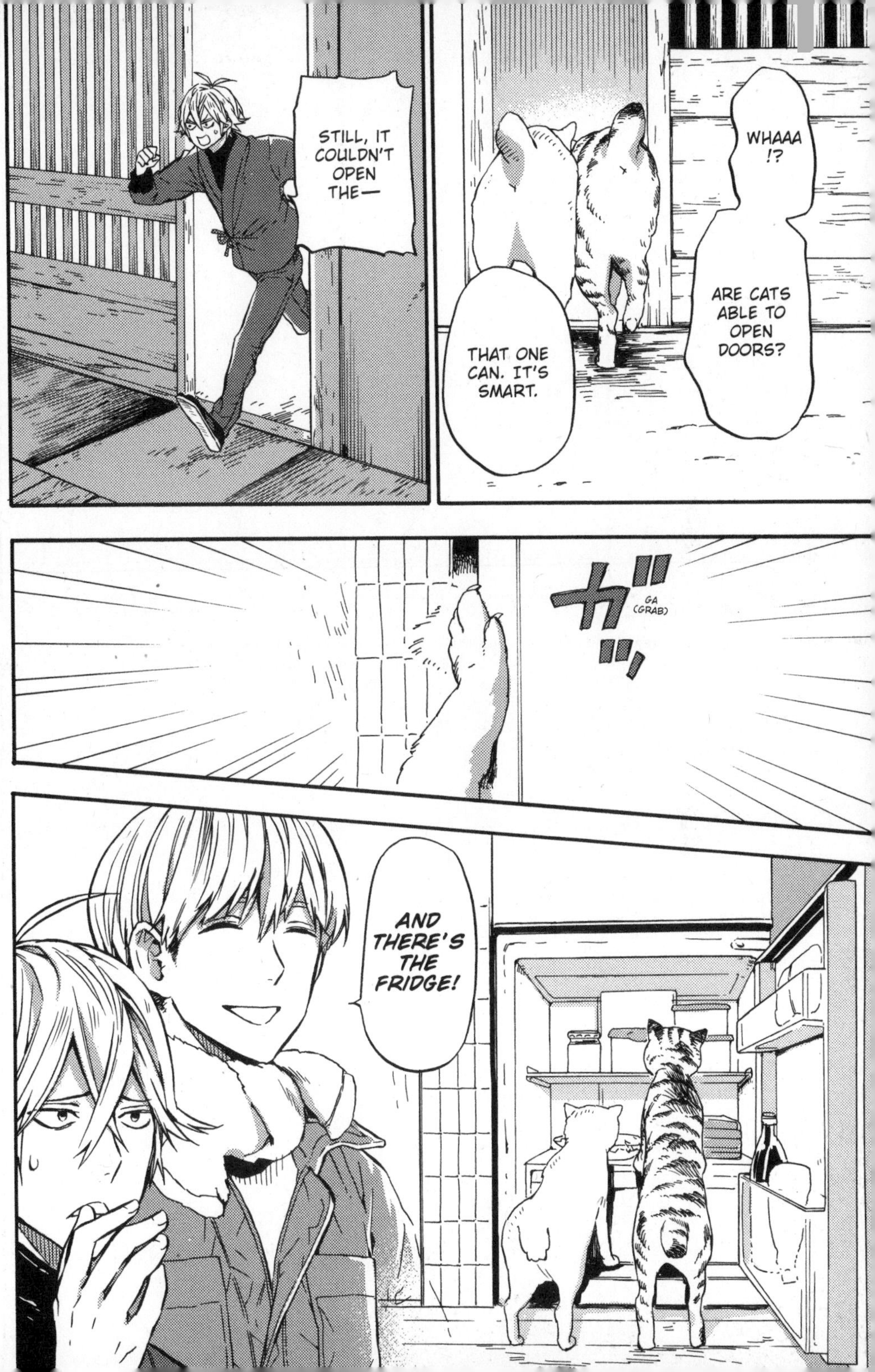
WHAAA!?
ARE CATS ABLE TO OPEN DOORS?
THAT ONE CAN. IT'S SMART.
STILL, IT COULDN'T OPEN THE—
GA (GRAB)
AND THERE'S THE FRIDGE!

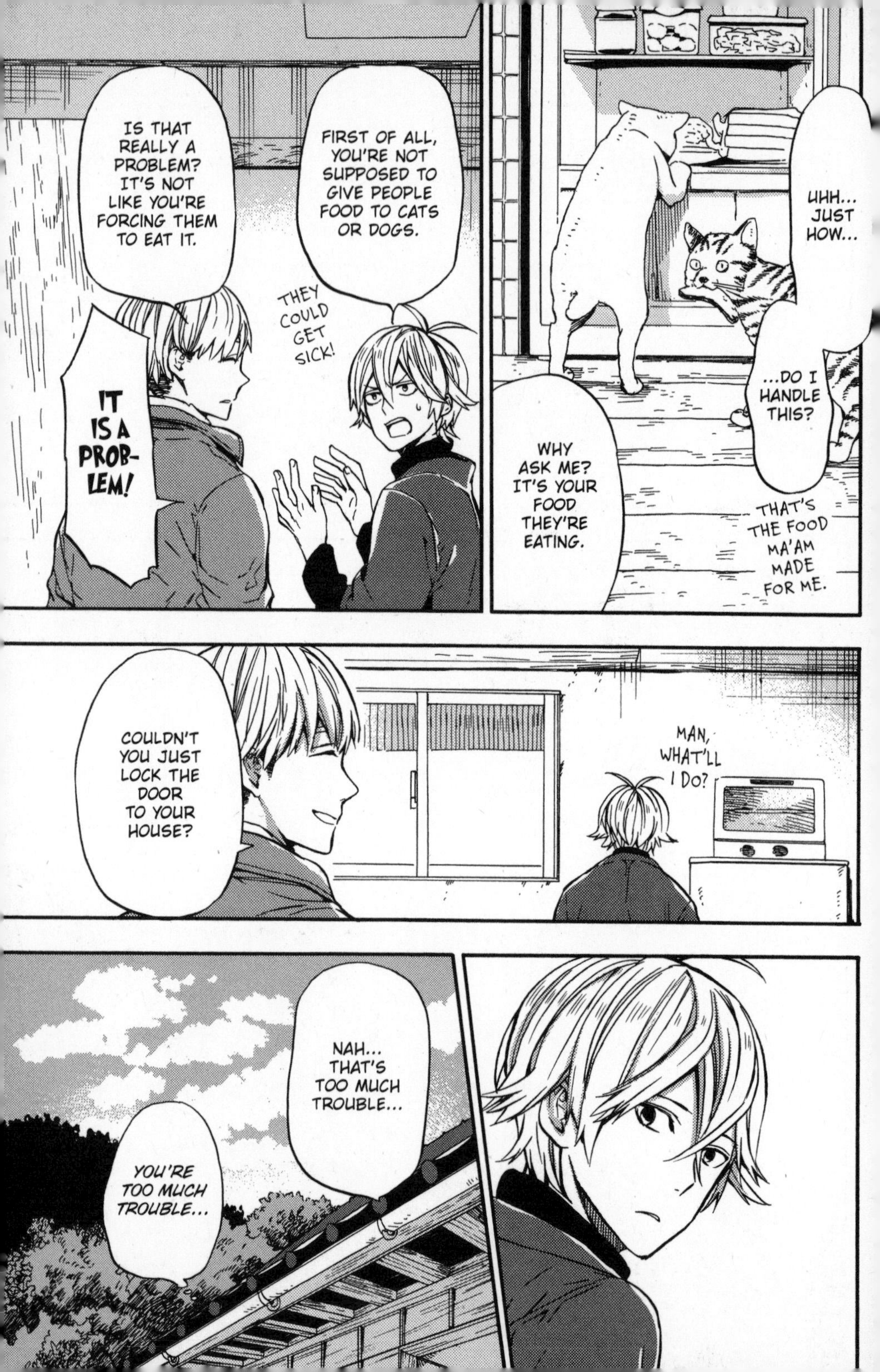
UHH... JUST HOW...
...DO I HANDLE THIS?
WHY ASK ME? IT'S YOUR FOOD THEY'RE EATING.
THAT'S THE FOOD MA'AM MADE FOR ME.
FIRST OF ALL, YOU'RE NOT SUPPOSED TO GIVE PEOPLE FOOD TO CATS OR DOGS.
THEY COULD GET SICK!
IS THAT REALLY A PROBLEM? IT'S NOT LIKE YOU'RE FORCING THEM TO EAT IT.
IT IS A PROB-LEM!
MAN, WHAT'LL I DO?
COULDN'T YOU JUST LOCK THE DOOR TO YOUR HOUSE?
NAH... THAT'S TOO MUCH TROUBLE...
YOU'RE TOO MUCH TROUBLE...

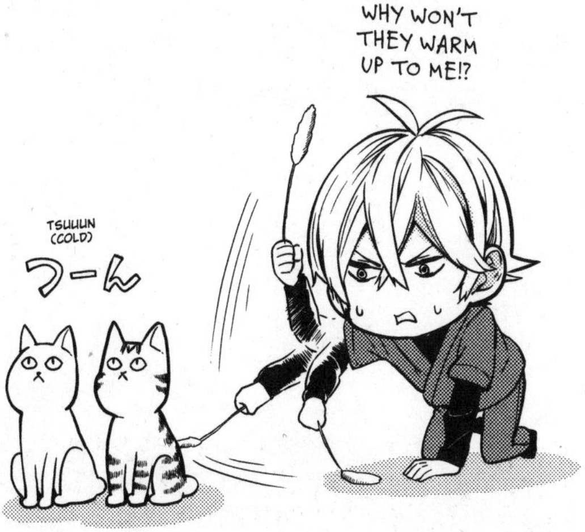
WHY WON'T THEY WARM UP TO ME!?
TSUUUN (COLD)
つーん

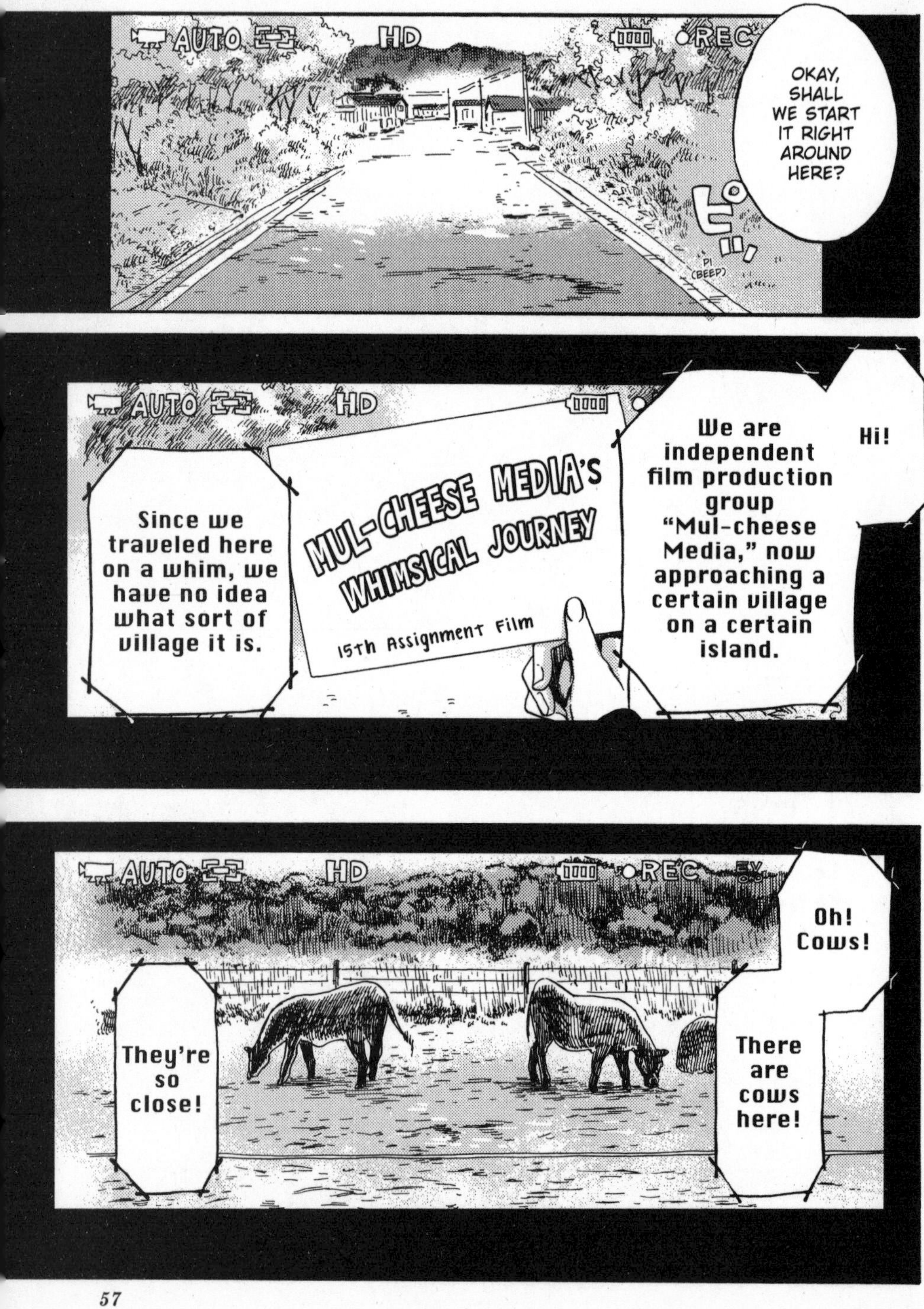
AUTO HD REC
OKAY, SHALL WE START IT RIGHT AROUND HERE?
PI (BEEP)
AUTO HD
Hi!
We are independent film production group "Mul-cheese Media," now approaching a certain village on a certain island.
MUL-CHEESE MEDIA'S WHIMSICAL JOURNEY
15th Assignment Film
Since we traveled here on a whim, we have no idea what sort of village it is.
AUTO HD REC
Oh! Cows!
There are cows here!
They're so close!

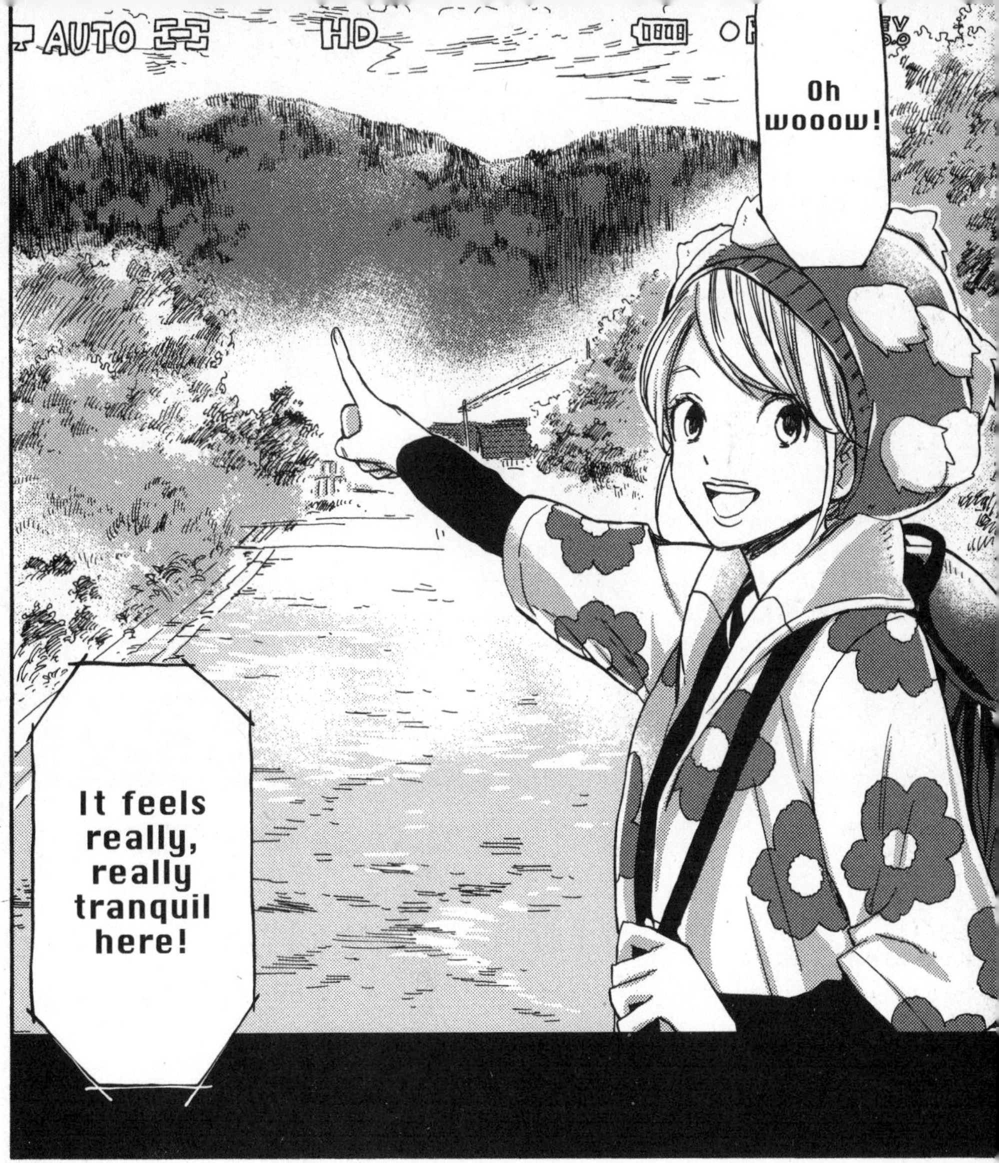
AUTO
HD
Oh wooow!
It feels really, really tranquil here!

Act. 124
BANBE
(Translation: Monster)

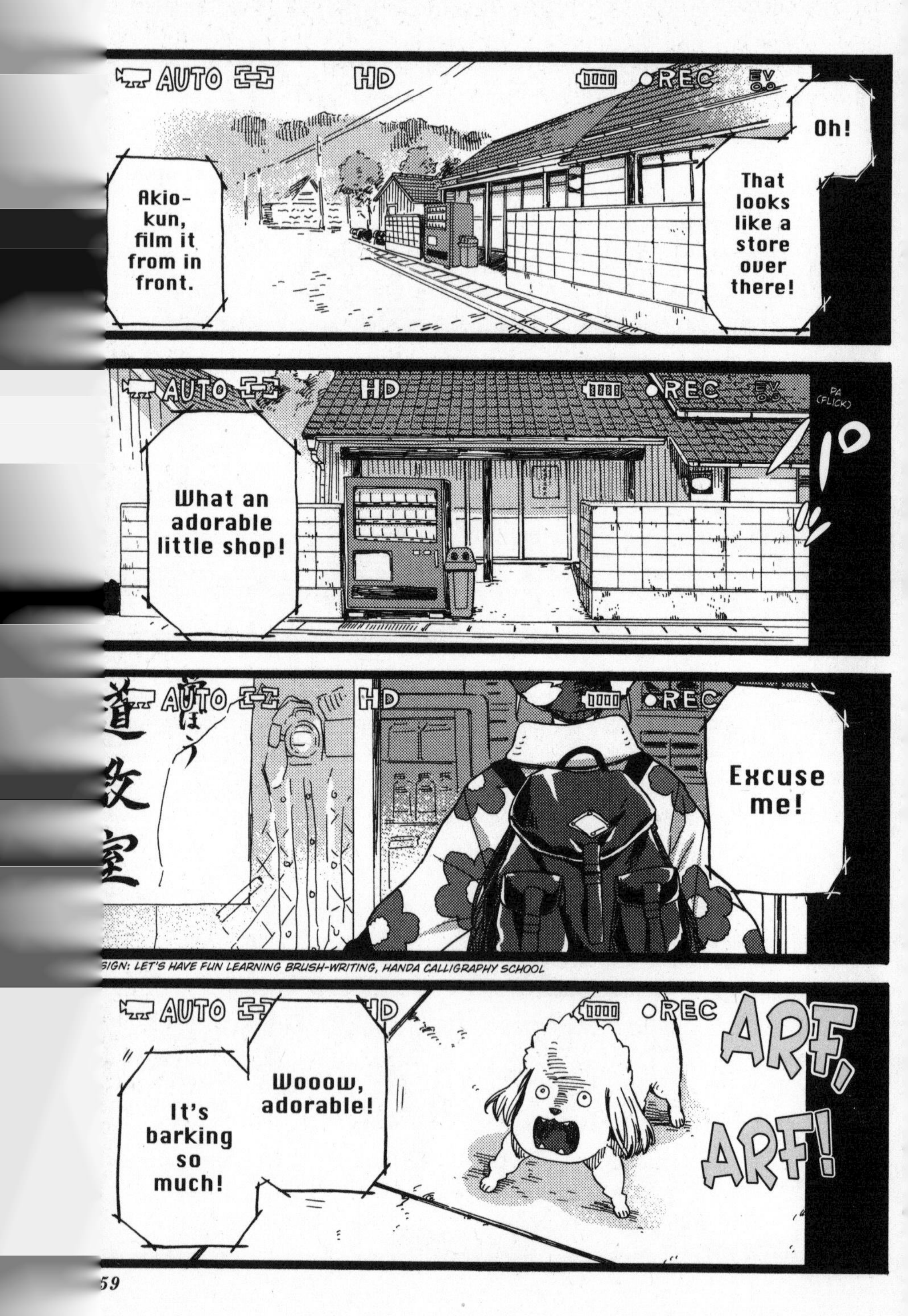
Oh!
That looks like a store over there!
Akio-kun, film it from in front.
PA (FLICK)
What an adorable little shop!
Excuse me!
SIGN: LET'S HAVE FUN LEARNING BRUSH-WRITING, HANDA CALLIGRAPHY SCHOOL
ARF, ARF!
Wooow, adorable!
It's barking so much!

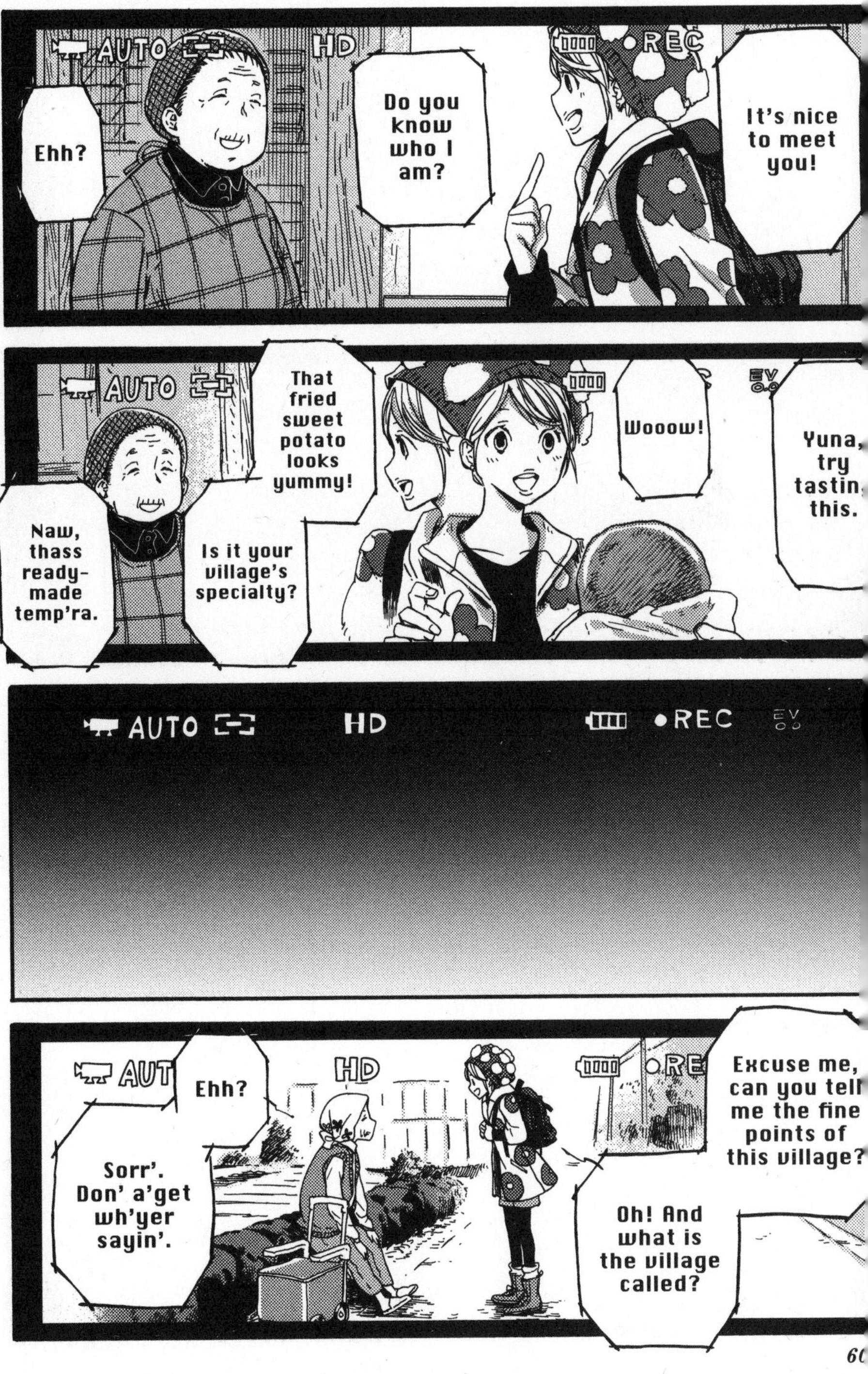
It's nice to meet you!
Do you know who I am?
Ehh?
Yuna, try tastin this.
Wooow!
That fried sweet potato looks yummy!
Is it your village's specialty?
Naw, thass ready-made temp'ra.
AUTO HD REC
Excuse me, can you tell me the fine points of this village?
Oh! And what is the village called?
Ehh?
Sorr'. Don' a'get wh'yer sayin'.

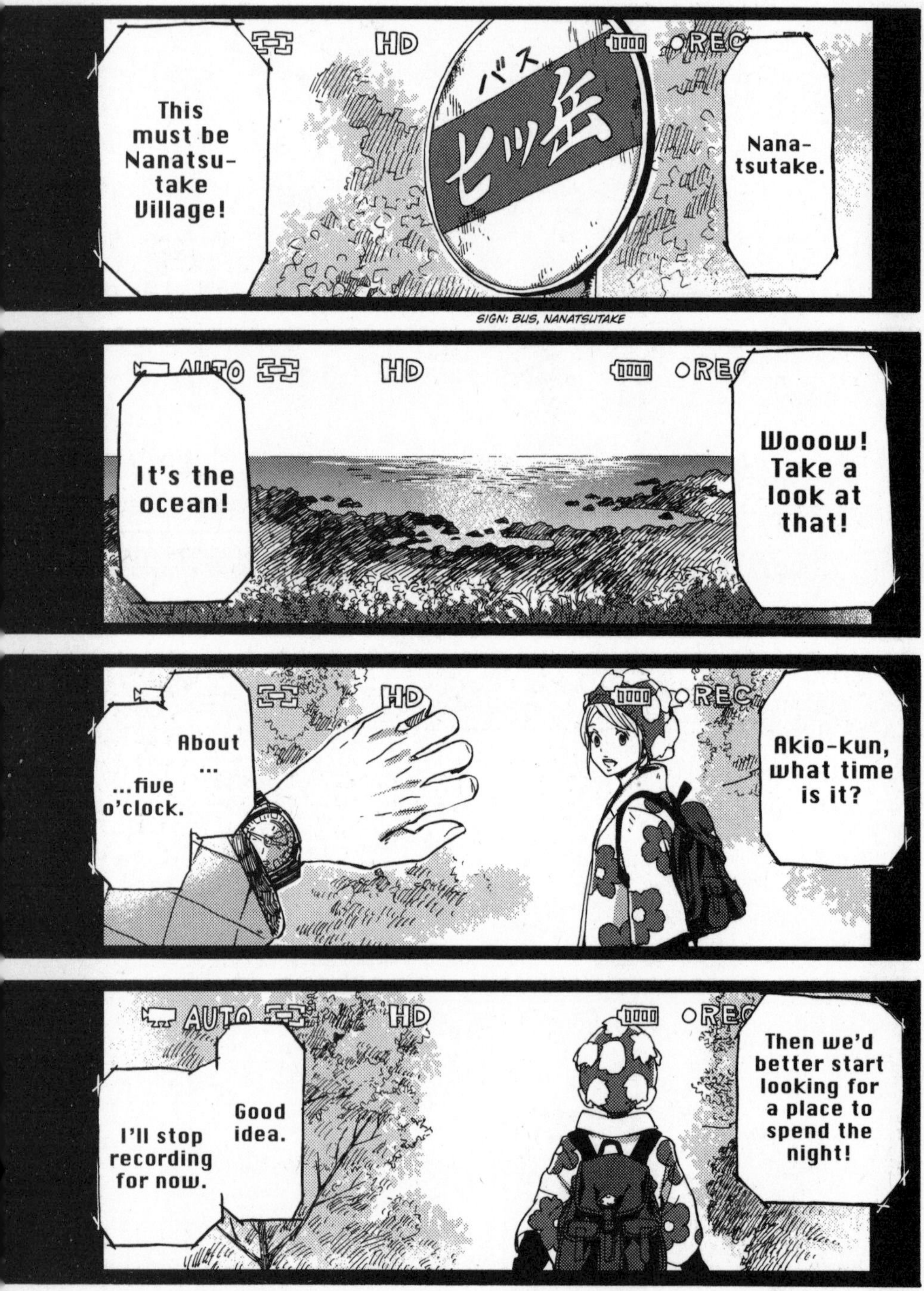
Nana-tsutake.
This must be Nanatsu-take Village!
バス
七ツ岳
SIGN: BUS, NANATSUTAKE
Wooow! Take a look at that!
It's the ocean!
Akio-kun, what time is it?
About ...
...five o'clock.
Then we'd better start looking for a place to spend the night!
Good idea.
I'll stop recording for now.

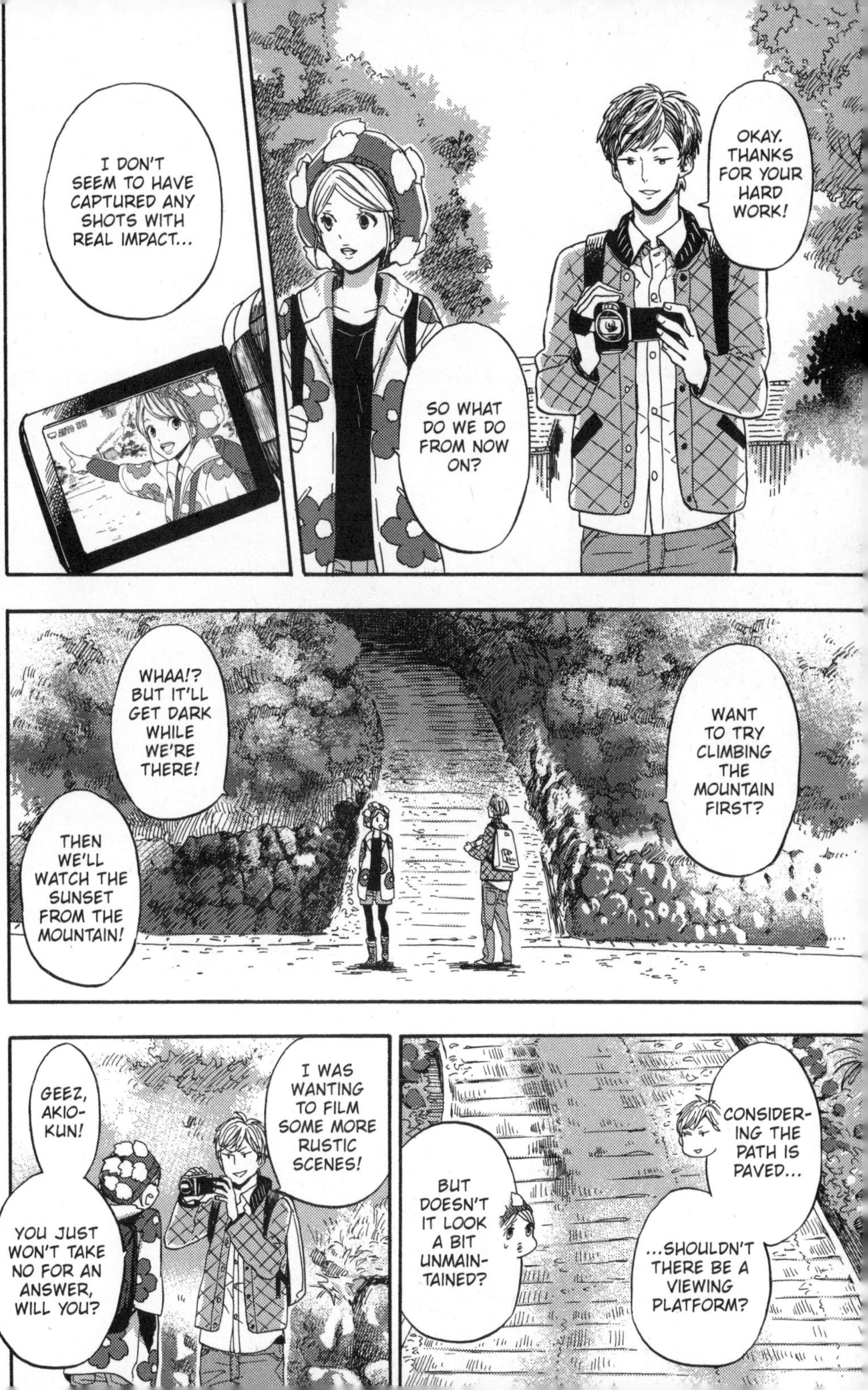
OKAY. THANKS FOR YOUR HARD WORK!
SO WHAT DO WE DO FROM NOW ON?
I DON'T SEEM TO HAVE CAPTURED ANY SHOTS WITH REAL IMPACT...
WANT TO TRY CLIMBING THE MOUNTAIN FIRST?
WHAA!? BUT IT'LL GET DARK WHILE WE'RE THERE!
THEN WE'LL WATCH THE SUNSET FROM THE MOUNTAIN!
CONSIDERING THE PATH IS PAVED...
...SHOULDN'T THERE BE A VIEWING PLATFORM?
BUT DOESN'T IT LOOK A BIT UNMAINTAINED?
I WAS WANTING TO FILM SOME MORE RUSTIC SCENES!
GEEZ, AKIO-KUN!
YOU JUST WON'T TAKE NO FOR AN ANSWER, WILL YOU?

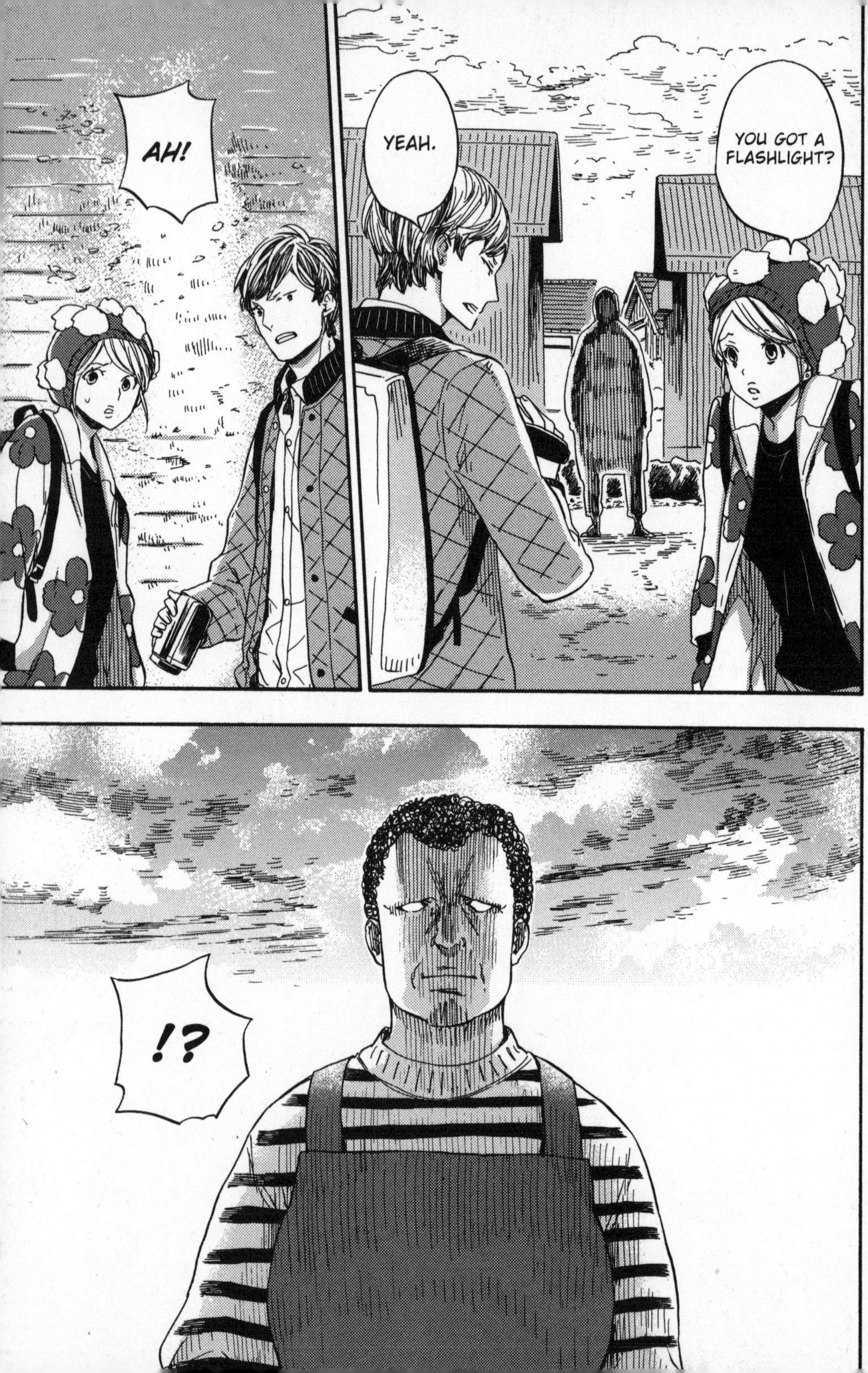
YOU GOT A FLASHLIGHT?
YEAH.
AH!
!?

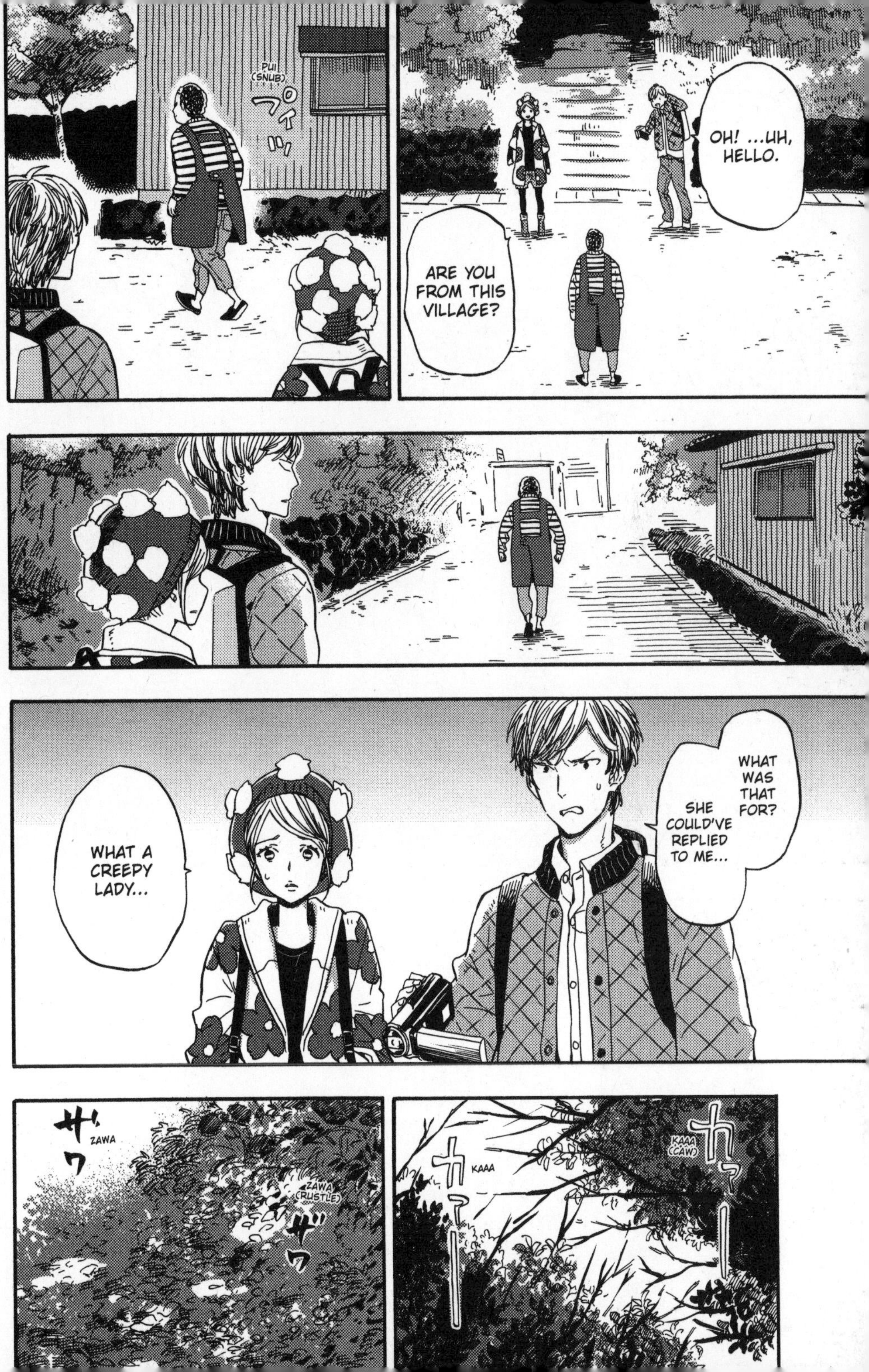
OH! ...UH, HELLO.
ARE YOU FROM THIS VILLAGE?
PUI (SNUB)
フイッ
WHAT WAS THAT FOR?
SHE COULD'VE REPLIED TO ME...
WHAT A CREEPY LADY...
KAAA (CAW)
カァー
KAAA
カァー
ザワ
ZAWA
ZAWA (RUSTLE)
ザワ

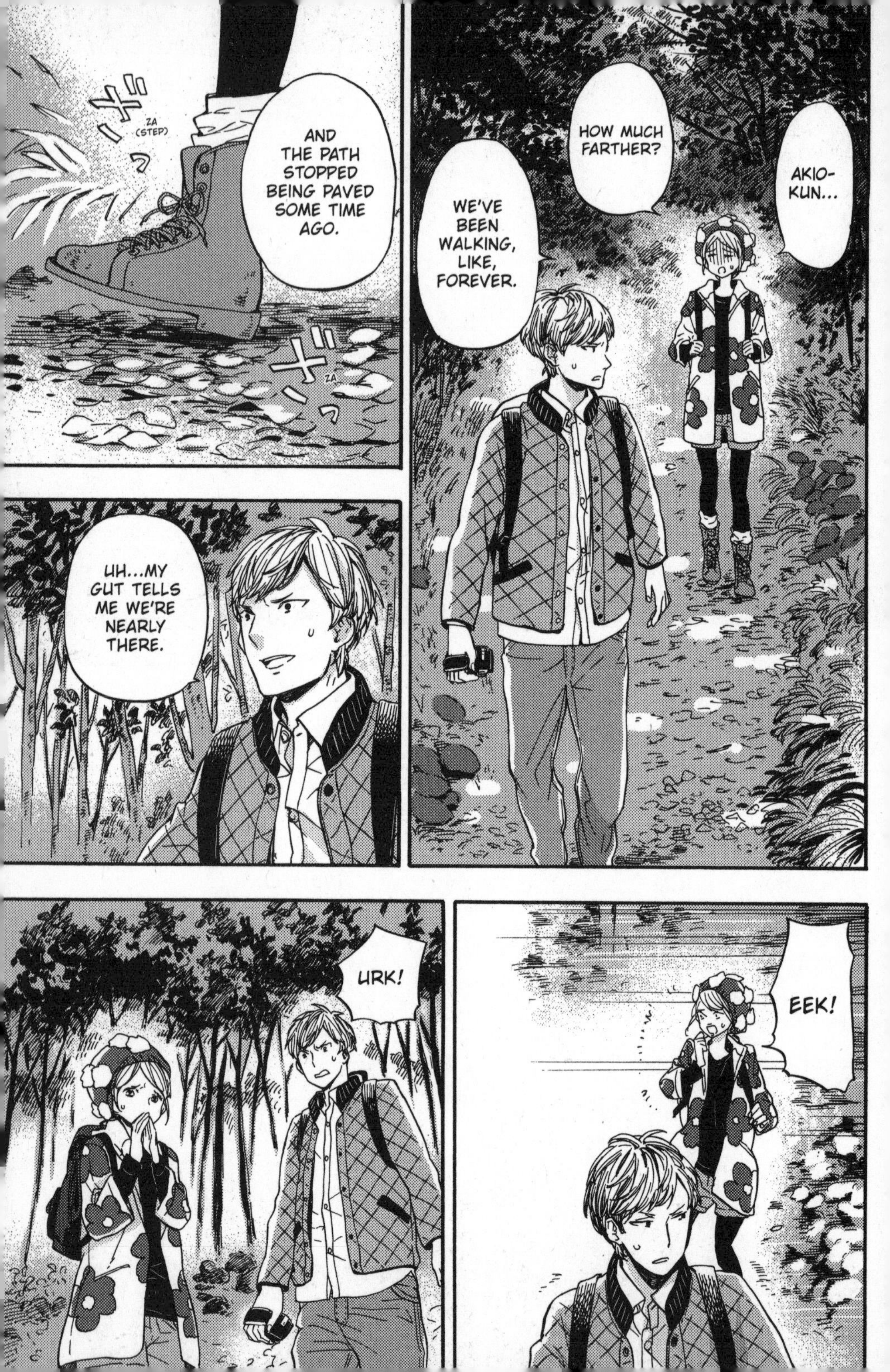
AKIO-KUN...
HOW MUCH FARTHER?
WE'VE BEEN WALKING, LIKE, FOREVER.
ZA (STEP)
AND THE PATH STOPPED BEING PAVED SOME TIME AGO.
ZA
UH...MY GUT TELLS ME WE'RE NEARLY THERE.
EEK!
URK!

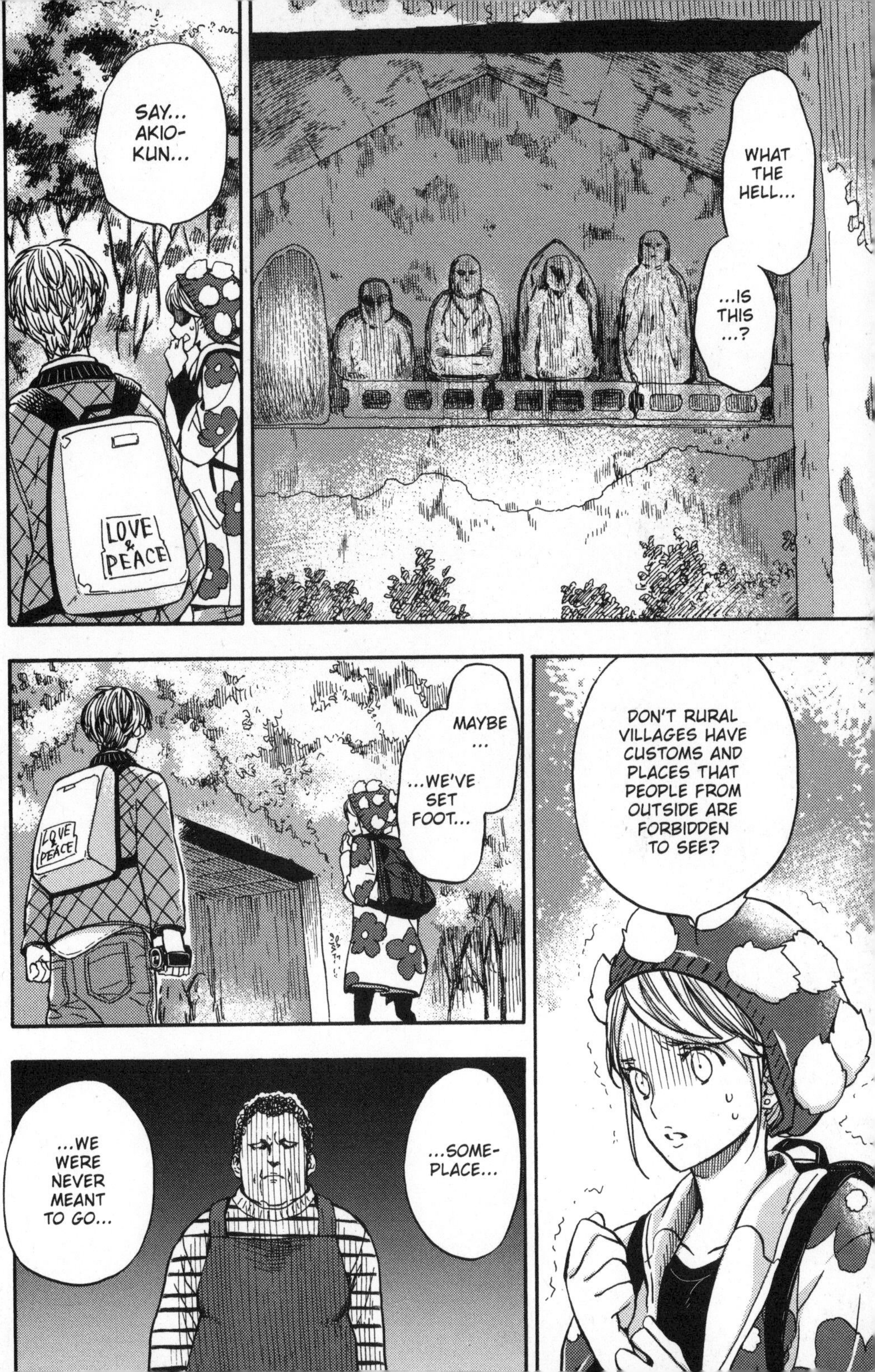
WHAT THE HELL...
...IS THIS ...?
SAY... AKIO-KUN...
LOVE & PEACE
DON'T RURAL VILLAGES HAVE CUSTOMS AND PLACES THAT PEOPLE FROM OUTSIDE ARE FORBIDDEN TO SEE?
MAYBE ...
...WE'VE SET FOOT...
LOVE & PEACE
...SOME-PLACE...
...WE WERE NEVER MEANT TO GO...

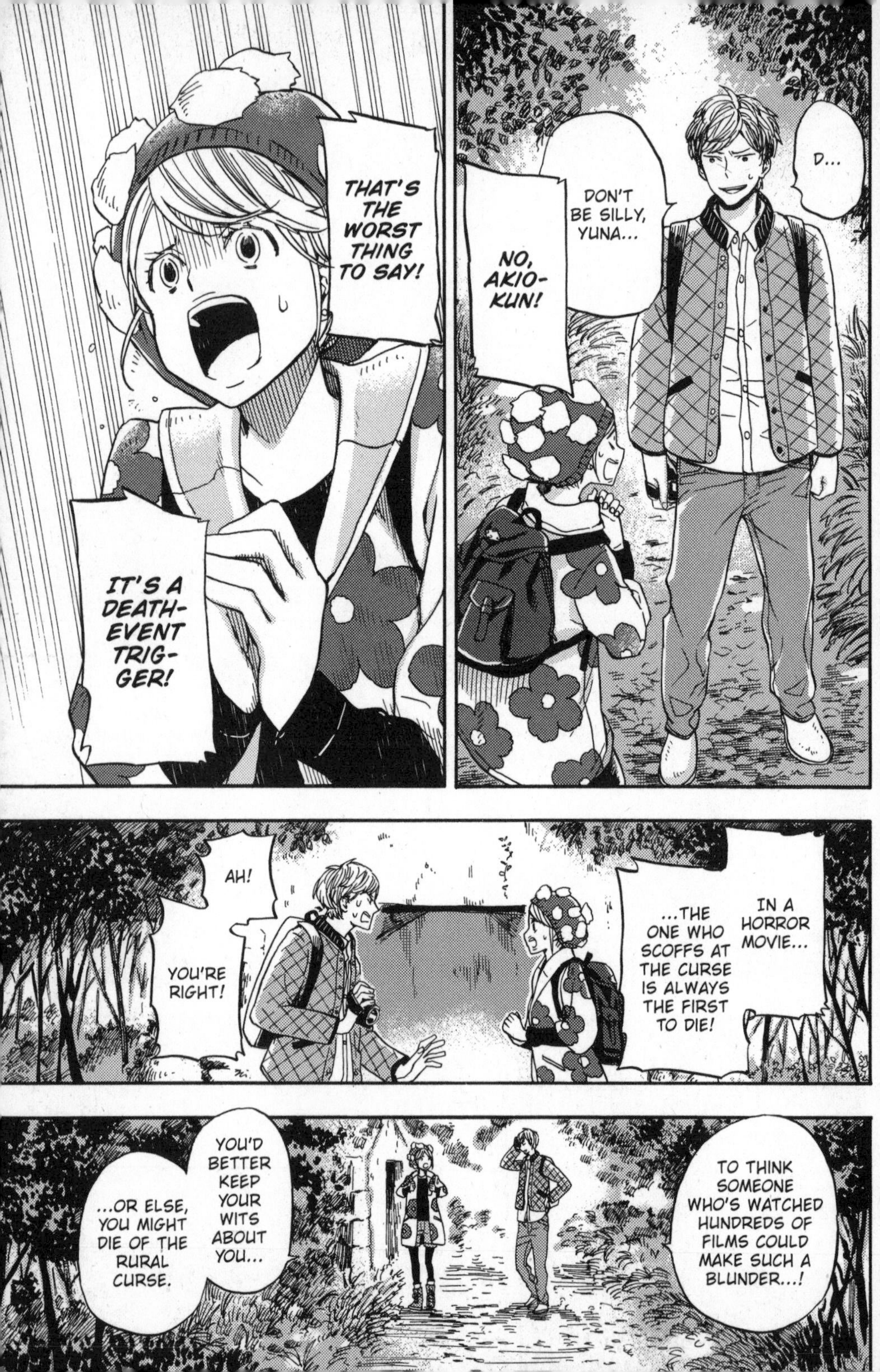
D...
DON'T BE SILLY, YUNA...
NO, AKIO-KUN!
THAT'S THE WORST THING TO SAY!
IT'S A DEATH-EVENT TRIGGER!
IN A HORROR MOVIE...
...THE ONE WHO SCOFFS AT THE CURSE IS ALWAYS THE FIRST TO DIE!
AH!
YOU'RE RIGHT!
TO THINK SOMEONE WHO'S WATCHED HUNDREDS OF FILMS COULD MAKE SUCH A BLUNDER...!
YOU'D BETTER KEEP YOUR WITS ABOUT YOU...
...OR ELSE, YOU MIGHT DIE OF THE RURAL CURSE.

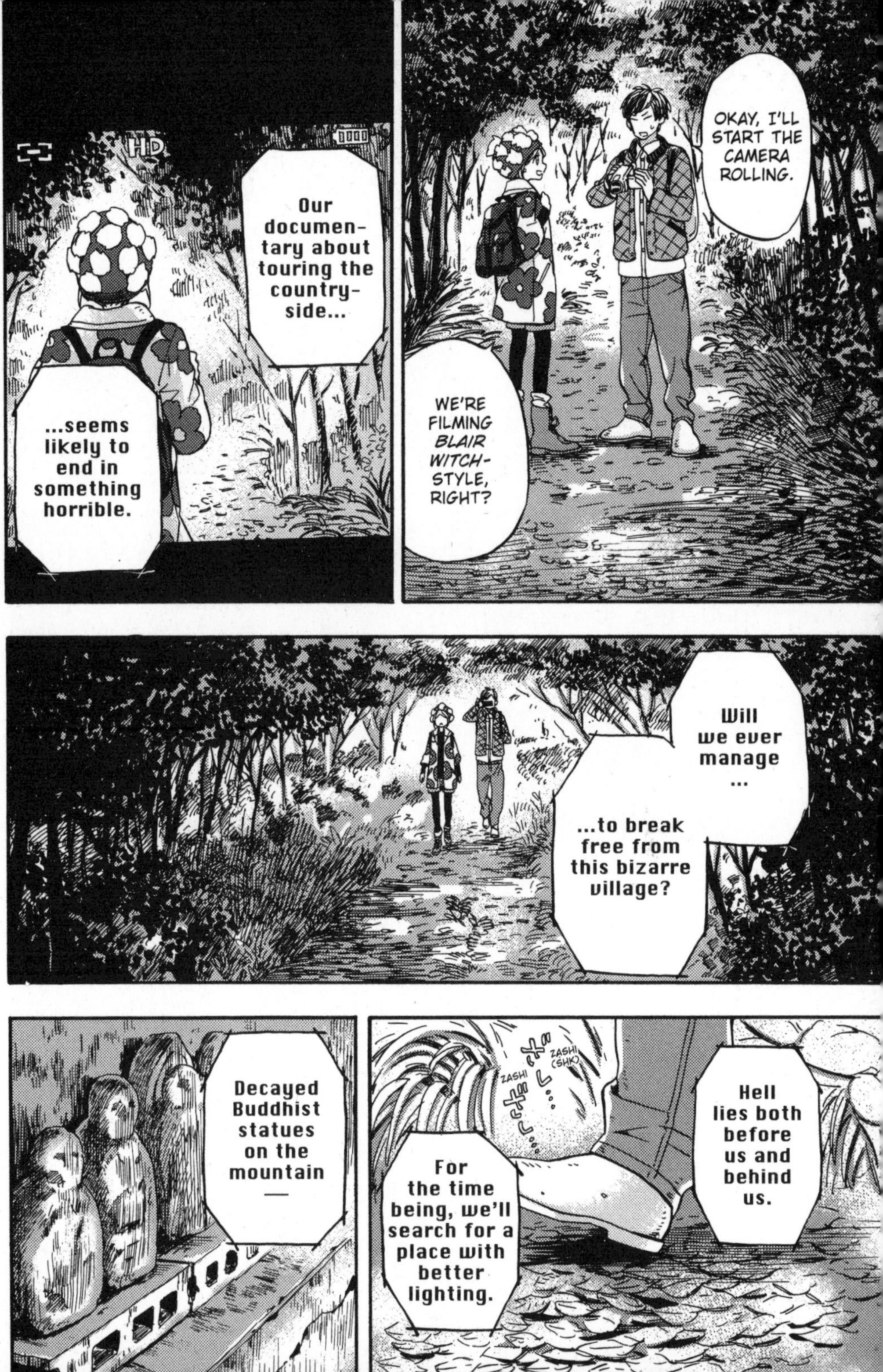

OKAY, I'LL START THE CAMERA ROLLING.
WE'RE FILMING *BLAIR WITCH*-STYLE, RIGHT?
HD
Our documentary about touring the countryside...
...seems likely to end in something horrible.
Will we ever manage ...
...to break free from this bizarre village?
Hell lies both before us and behind us.
ZASHI (SHK)
ZASHI
For the time being, we'll search for a place with better lighting.
Decayed Buddhist statues on the mountain —

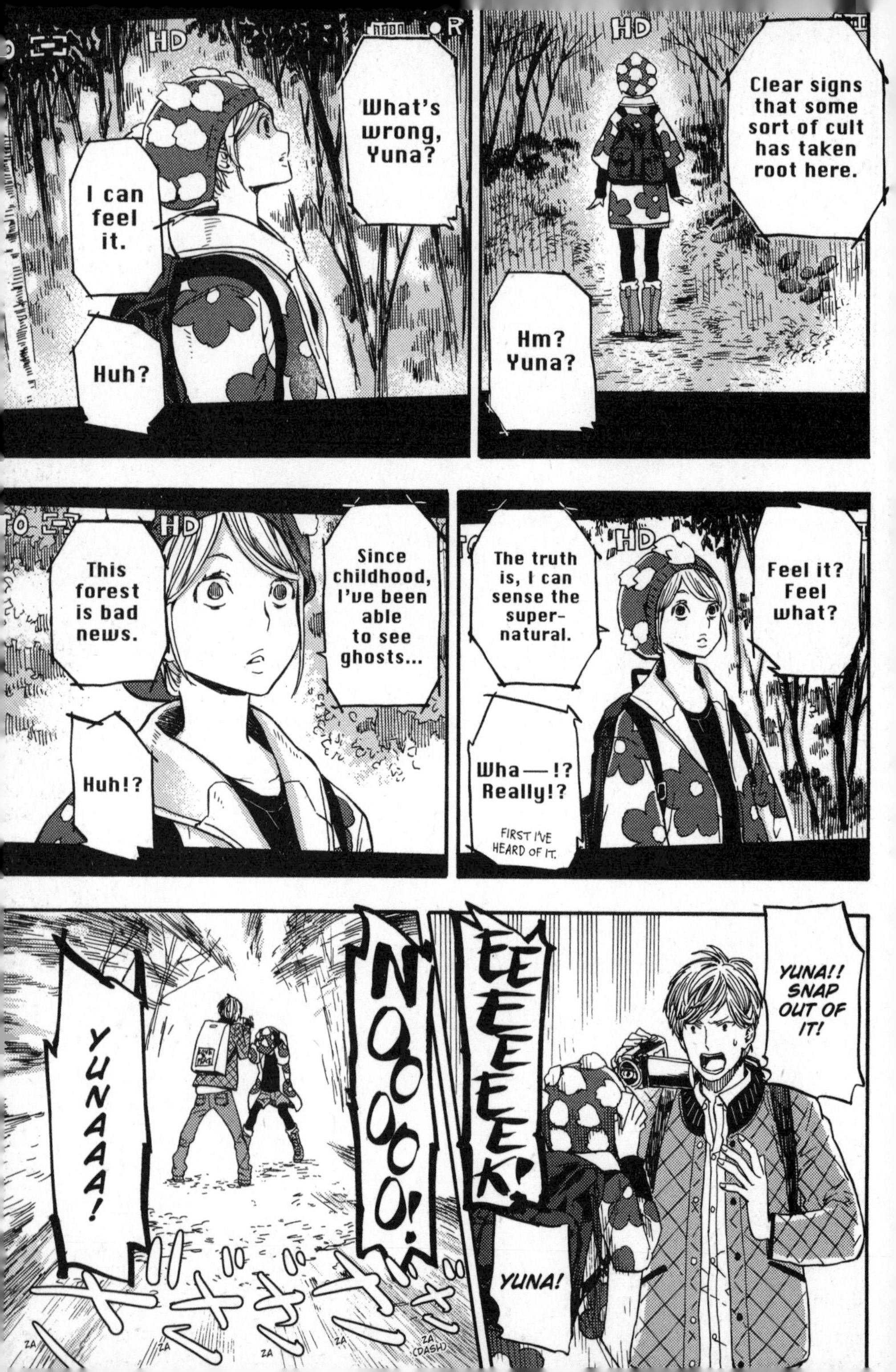

Clear signs that some sort of cult has taken root here.
Hm? Yuna?
What's wrong, Yuna?
I can feel it.
Huh?
Feel it? Feel what?
The truth is, I can sense the super-natural.
Wha—!? Really!?
FIRST I'VE HEARD OF IT.
Since childhood, I've been able to see ghosts...
This forest is bad news.
Huh!?
YUNA!! SNAP OUT OF IT!
EEEEEEEK!
YUNA!
NOOOOOO!
YUNAAAA!
ZA ZA ZA ZA (DASH)

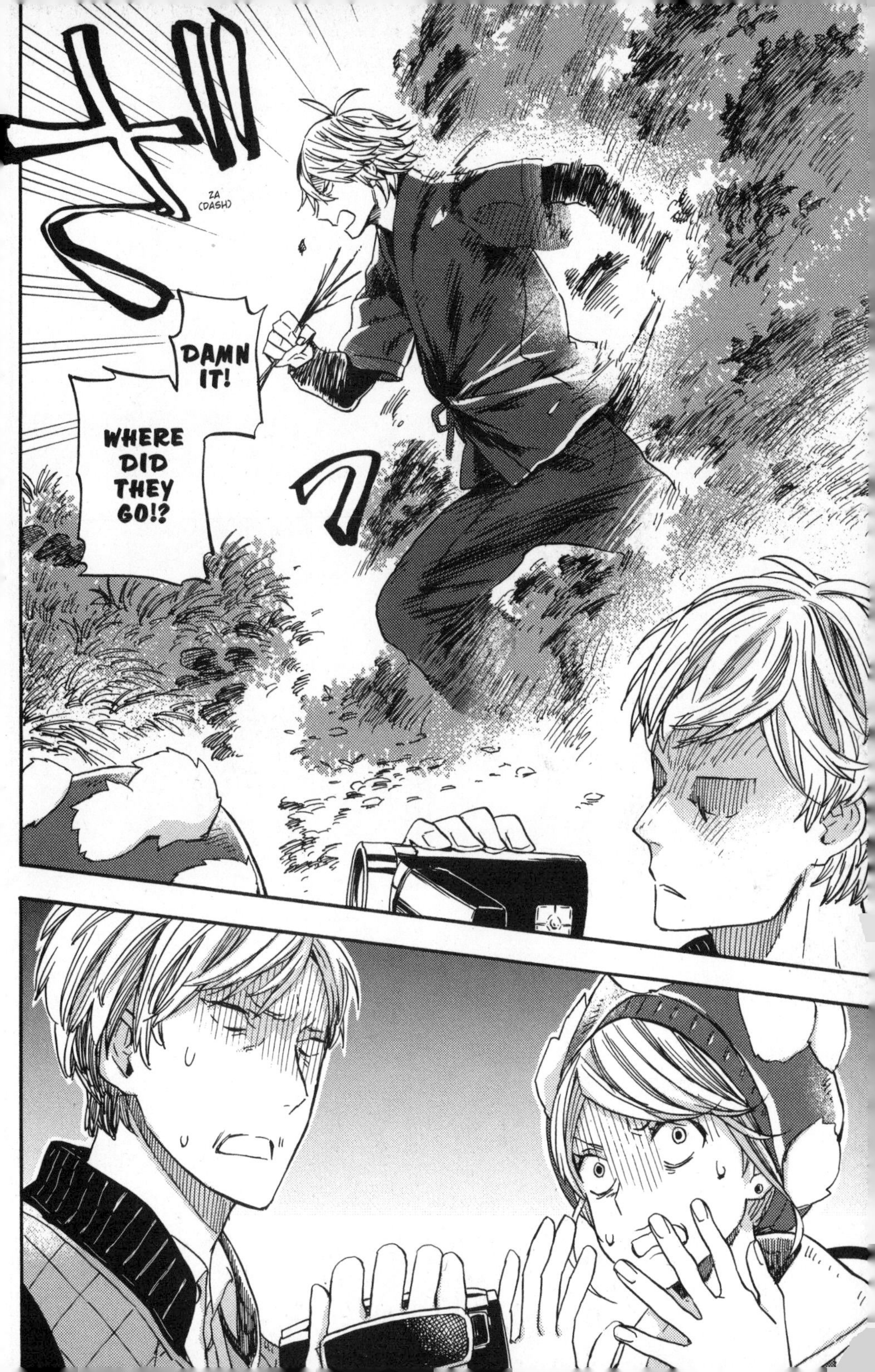
ZA (DASH)
DAMN IT!
WHERE DID THEY GO!?

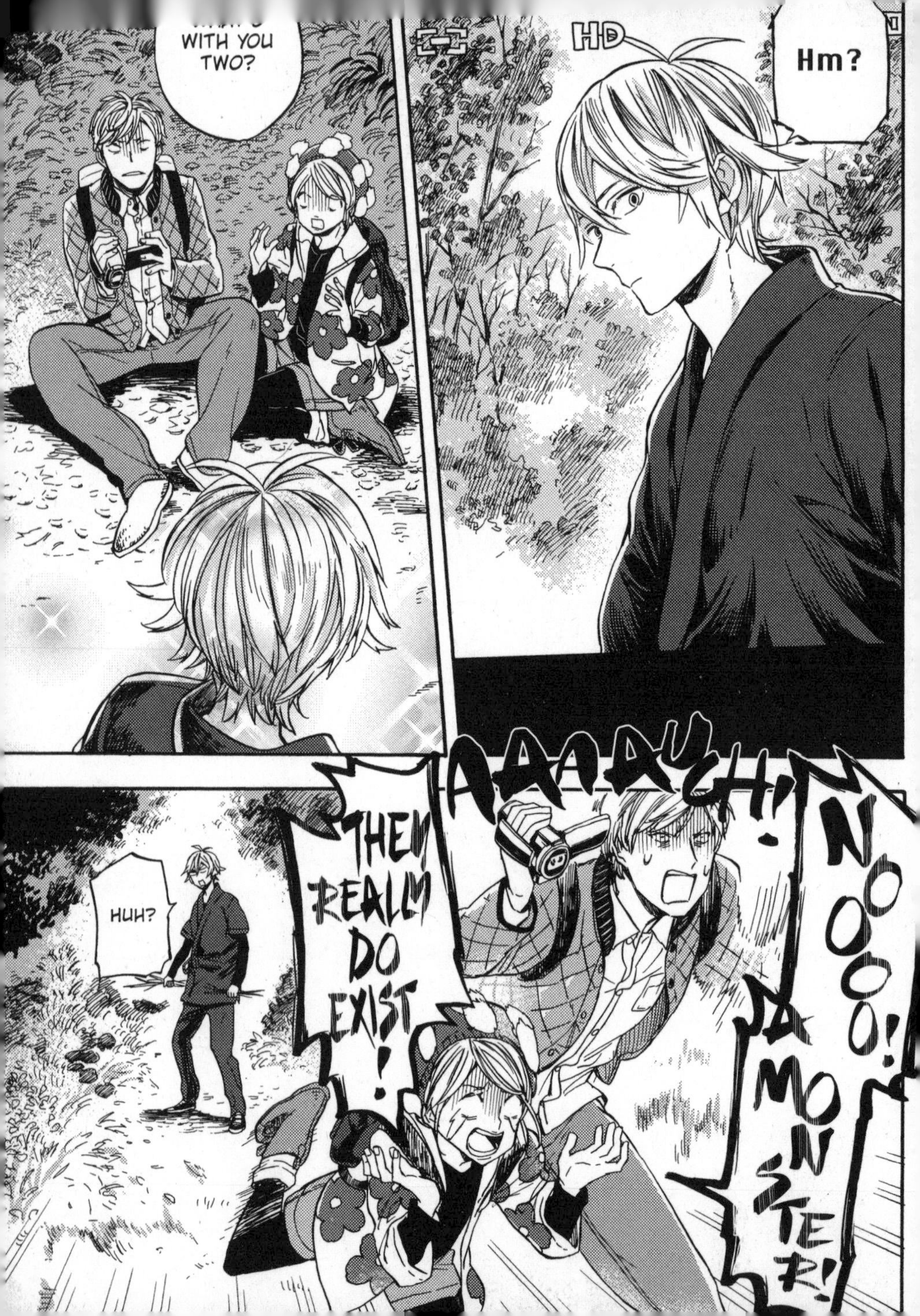
HD
Hm?
WITH YOU TWO?
NOOOO! A MONSTER!
AAAAUGH!
THEY REALLY DO EXIST!
HUH?

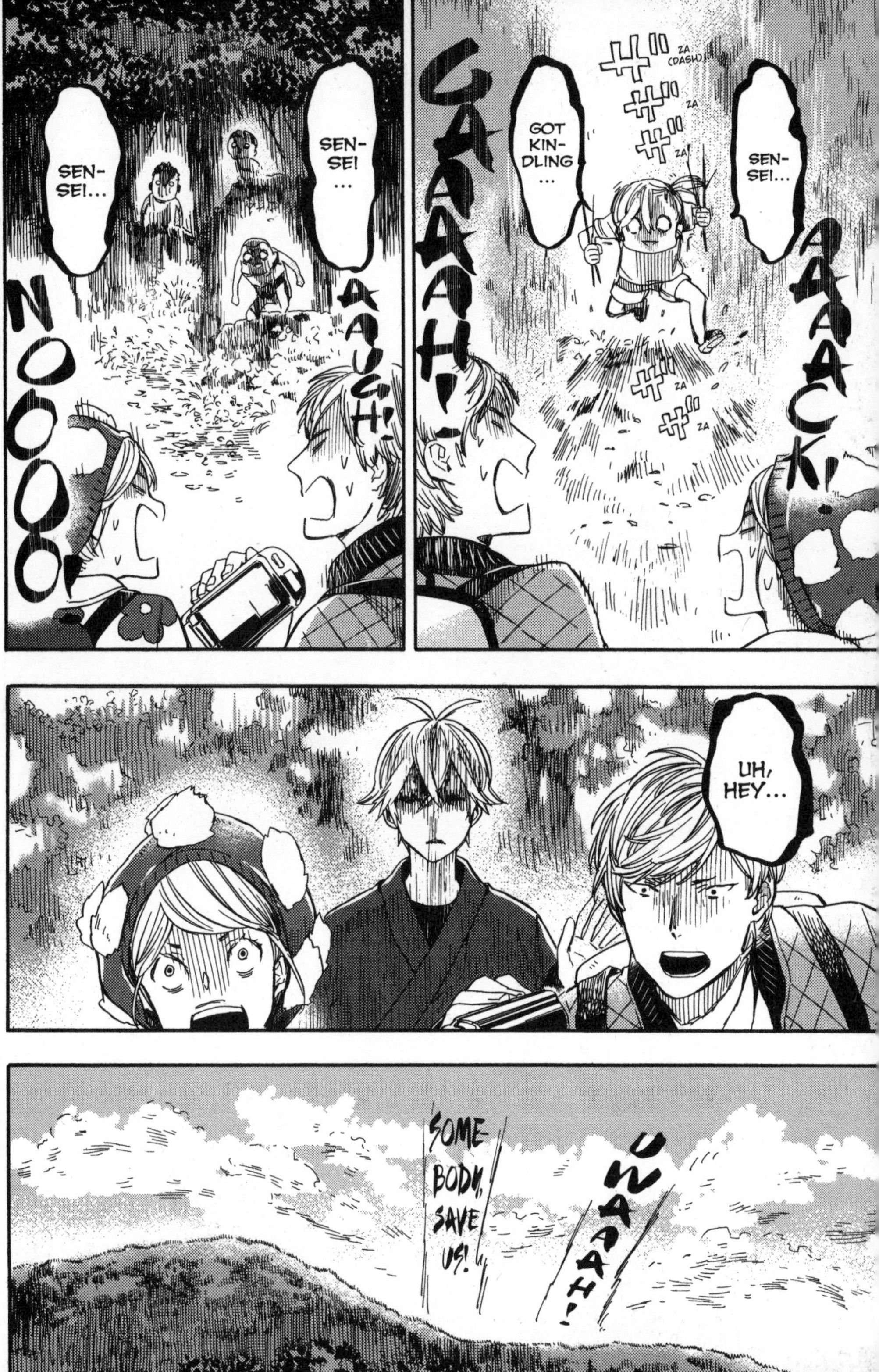
SEN-SEI!...
ZA (DASH)
ZA
ZA
GOT KIN-DLING...
AAACK!
ZA
ZA
GAAAAH!
SEN-SEI! ...
AAUGH!
SEN-SEI!...
NOOOO!
UH, HEY...
UWAAAH!
SOME-BODY, SAVE US!

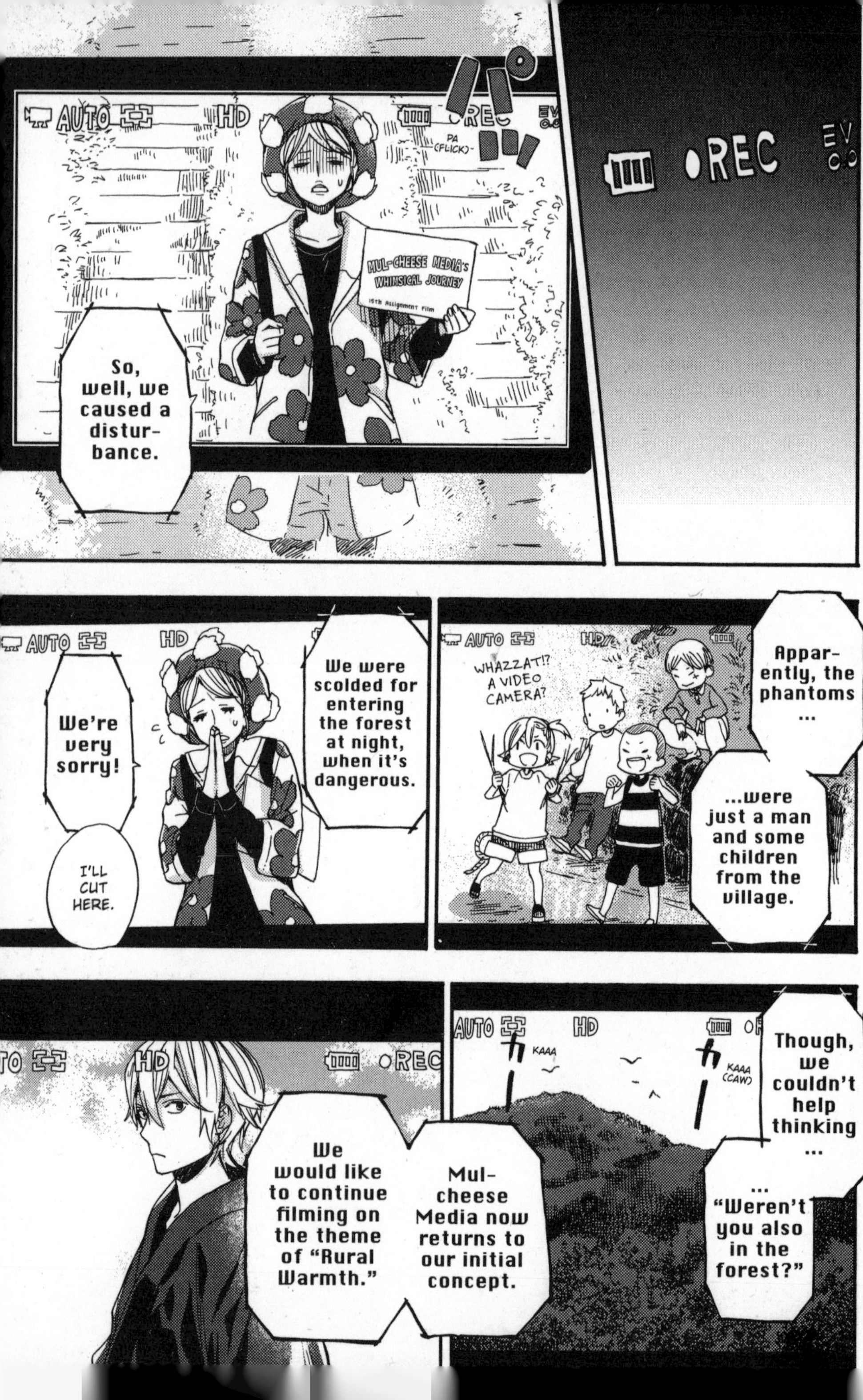

REC
PA (FLICK)
MUL-CHEESE MEDIA's WHIMSICAL JOURNEY
15th Assignment Film
So, well, we caused a disturbance.
Apparently, the phantoms ...
...were just a man and some children from the village.
WHAZZAT!? A VIDEO CAMERA?
We were scolded for entering the forest at night, when it's dangerous.
We're very sorry!
I'LL CUT HERE.
KAAA
KAAA (CAW)
Though, we couldn't help thinking ...
... "Weren't you also in the forest?"
Mul-cheese Media now returns to our initial concept.
We would like to continue filming on the theme of "Rural Warmth."

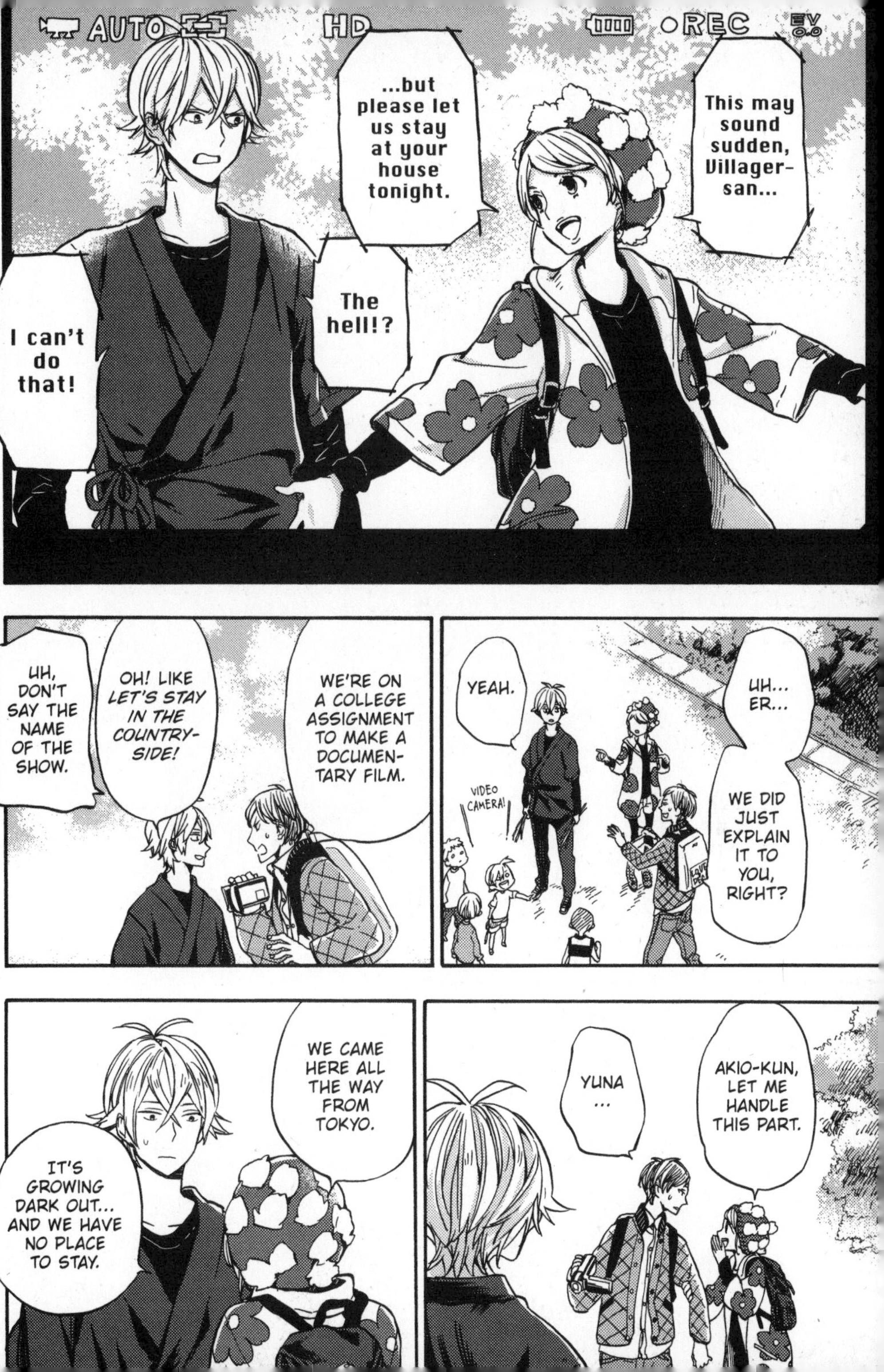
This may sound sudden, Villager-san...
...but please let us stay at your house tonight.
The hell!?
I can't do that!
UH... ER...
YEAH.
WE DID JUST EXPLAIN IT TO YOU, RIGHT?
VIDEO CAMERA!
WE'RE ON A COLLEGE ASSIGNMENT TO MAKE A DOCUMENTARY FILM.
OH! LIKE *LET'S STAY IN THE COUNTRYSIDE!*
UH, DON'T SAY THE NAME OF THE SHOW.
AKIO-KUN, LET ME HANDLE THIS PART.
YUNA...
WE CAME HERE ALL THE WAY FROM TOKYO.
IT'S GROWING DARK OUT... AND WE HAVE NO PLACE TO STAY.

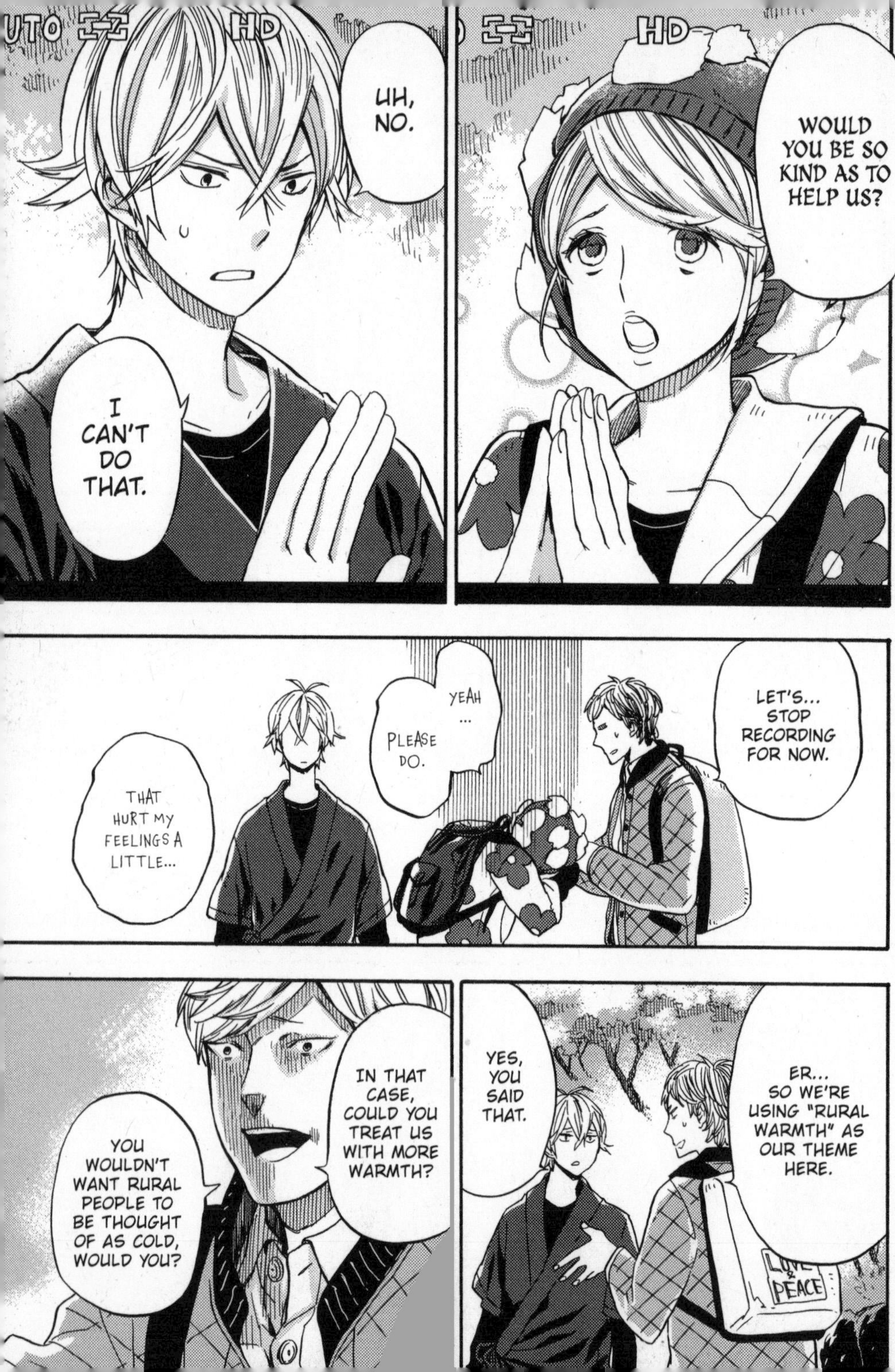
HD
WOULD YOU BE SO KIND AS TO HELP US?
HD
UH, NO.
I CAN'T DO THAT.
LET'S... STOP RECORDING FOR NOW.
YEAH ... PLEASE DO.
THAT HURT MY FEELINGS A LITTLE...
ER... SO WE'RE USING "RURAL WARMTH" AS OUR THEME HERE.
YES, YOU SAID THAT.
LOVE & PEACE
IN THAT CASE, COULD YOU TREAT US WITH MORE WARMTH?
YOU WOULDN'T WANT RURAL PEOPLE TO BE THOUGHT OF AS COLD, WOULD YOU?

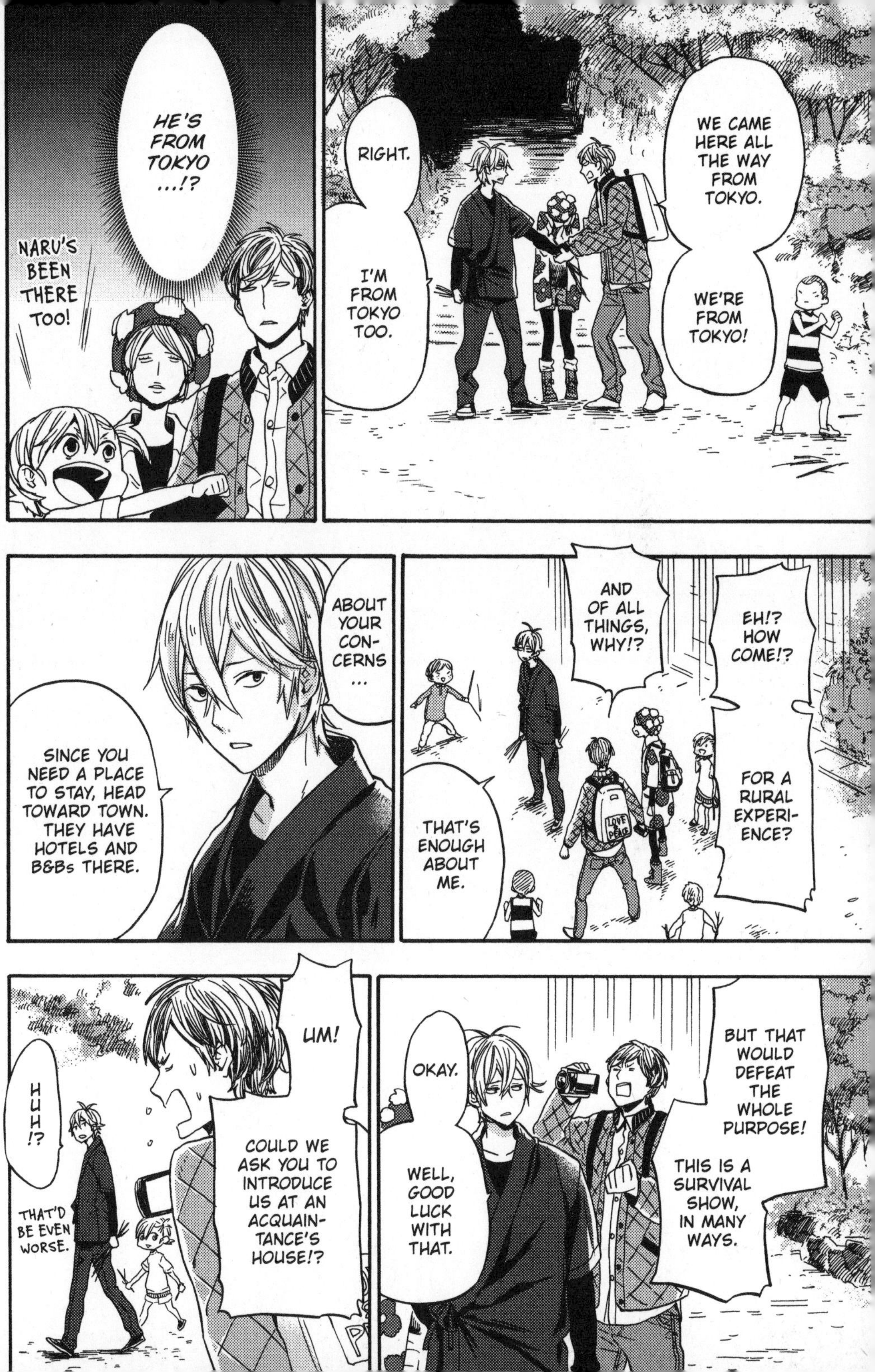
WE CAME HERE ALL THE WAY FROM TOKYO.
WE'RE FROM TOKYO!
RIGHT.
I'M FROM TOKYO TOO.
HE'S FROM TOKYO ...!?
NARU'S BEEN THERE TOO!
EH!? HOW COME!?
FOR A RURAL EXPERIENCE?
AND OF ALL THINGS, WHY!?
THAT'S ENOUGH ABOUT ME.
ABOUT YOUR CON-CERNS ...
SINCE YOU NEED A PLACE TO STAY, HEAD TOWARD TOWN. THEY HAVE HOTELS AND B&Bs THERE.
BUT THAT WOULD DEFEAT THE WHOLE PURPOSE!
THIS IS A SURVIVAL SHOW, IN MANY WAYS.
OKAY.
WELL, GOOD LUCK WITH THAT.
UM!
COULD WE ASK YOU TO INTRODUCE US AT AN ACQUAIN-TANCE'S HOUSE!?
HUH!?
THAT'D BE EVEN WORSE.

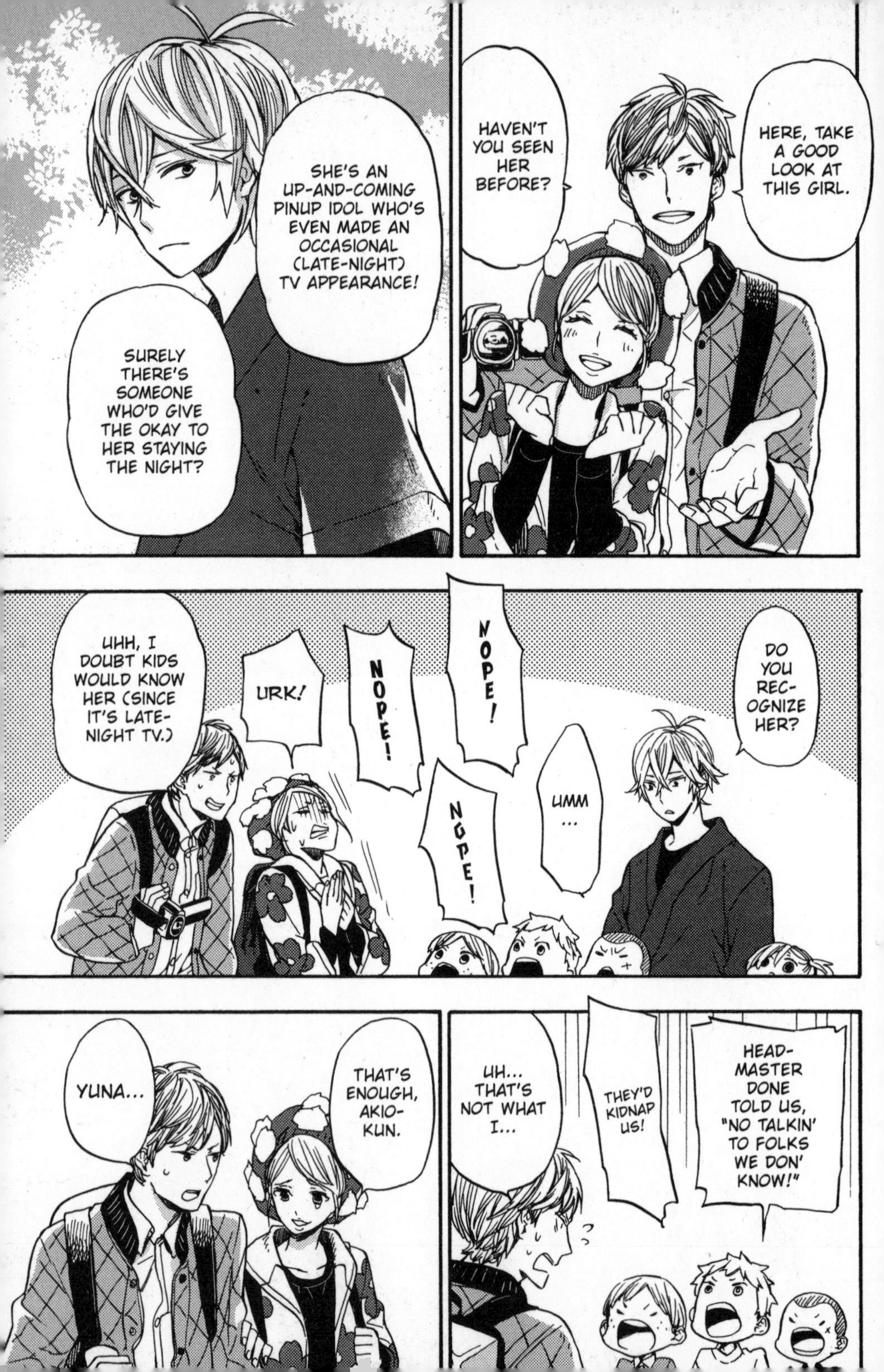
HERE, TAKE A GOOD LOOK AT THIS GIRL.
HAVEN'T YOU SEEN HER BEFORE?
SHE'S AN UP-AND-COMING PINUP IDOL WHO'S EVEN MADE AN OCCASIONAL (LATE-NIGHT) TV APPEARANCE!
SURELY THERE'S SOMEONE WHO'D GIVE THE OKAY TO HER STAYING THE NIGHT?
DO YOU RECOGNIZE HER?
NOPE!
UMM...
NOPE!
NOPE!
URK!
UHH, I DOUBT KIDS WOULD KNOW HER (SINCE IT'S LATE-NIGHT TV.)
HEAD-MASTER DONE TOLD US, "NO TALKIN' TO FOLKS WE DON' KNOW!"
THEY'D KIDNAP US!
UH... THAT'S NOT WHAT I...
THAT'S ENOUGH, AKIO-KUN.
YUNA...

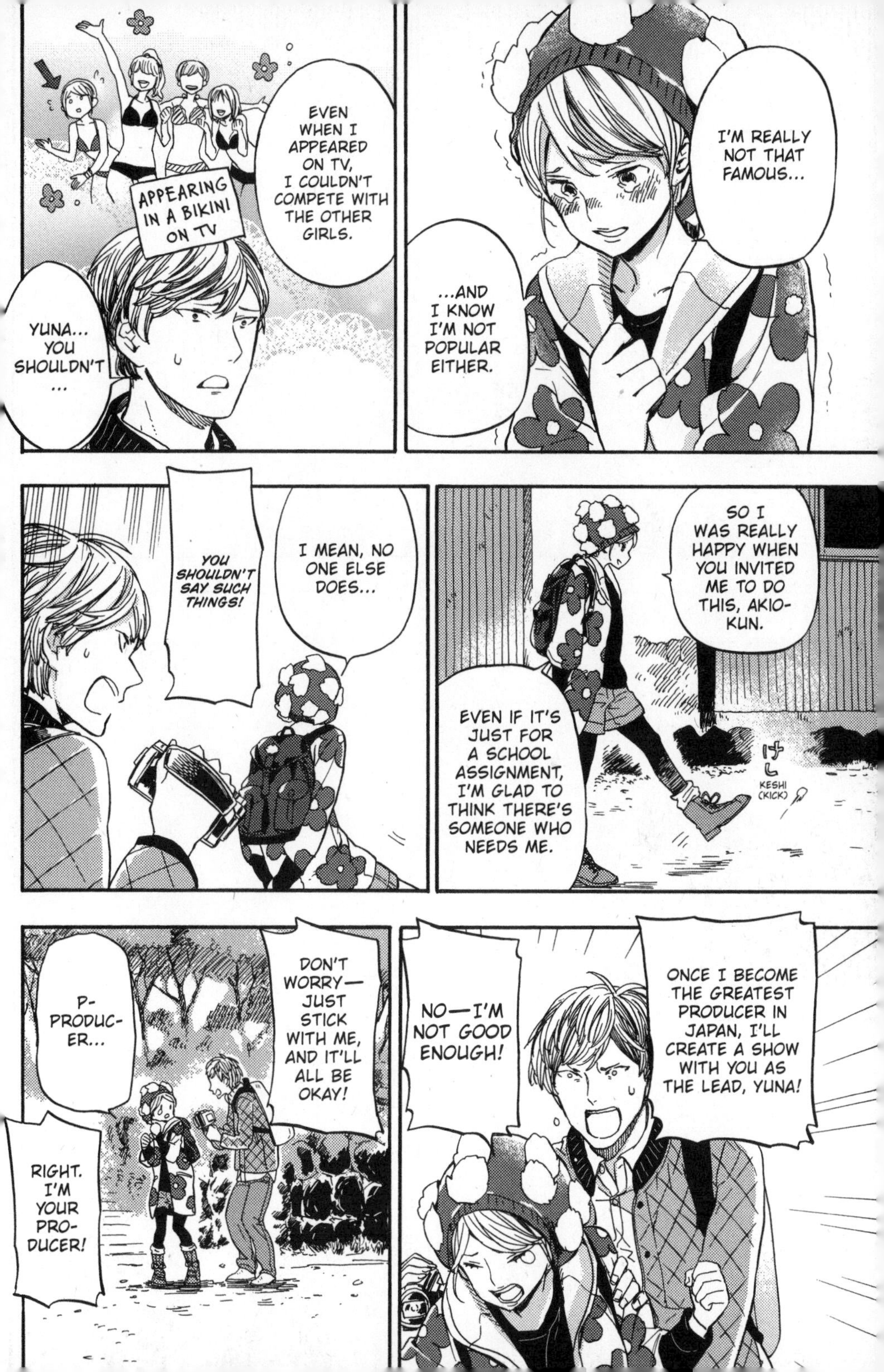
I'M REALLY NOT THAT FAMOUS...
...AND I KNOW I'M NOT POPULAR EITHER.
EVEN WHEN I APPEARED ON TV, I COULDN'T COMPETE WITH THE OTHER GIRLS.
APPEARING IN A BIKINI ON TV
YUNA... YOU SHOULDN'T ...
SO I WAS REALLY HAPPY WHEN YOU INVITED ME TO DO THIS, AKIO-KUN.
EVEN IF IT'S JUST FOR A SCHOOL ASSIGNMENT, I'M GLAD TO THINK THERE'S SOMEONE WHO NEEDS ME.
KESHI (KICK)
I MEAN, NO ONE ELSE DOES...
YOU SHOULDN'T SAY SUCH THINGS!
ONCE I BECOME THE GREATEST PRODUCER IN JAPAN, I'LL CREATE A SHOW WITH YOU AS THE LEAD, YUNA!
NO—I'M NOT GOOD ENOUGH!
DON'T WORRY—JUST STICK WITH ME, AND IT'LL ALL BE OKAY!
P-PRODUCER...
RIGHT. I'M YOUR PRODUCER!

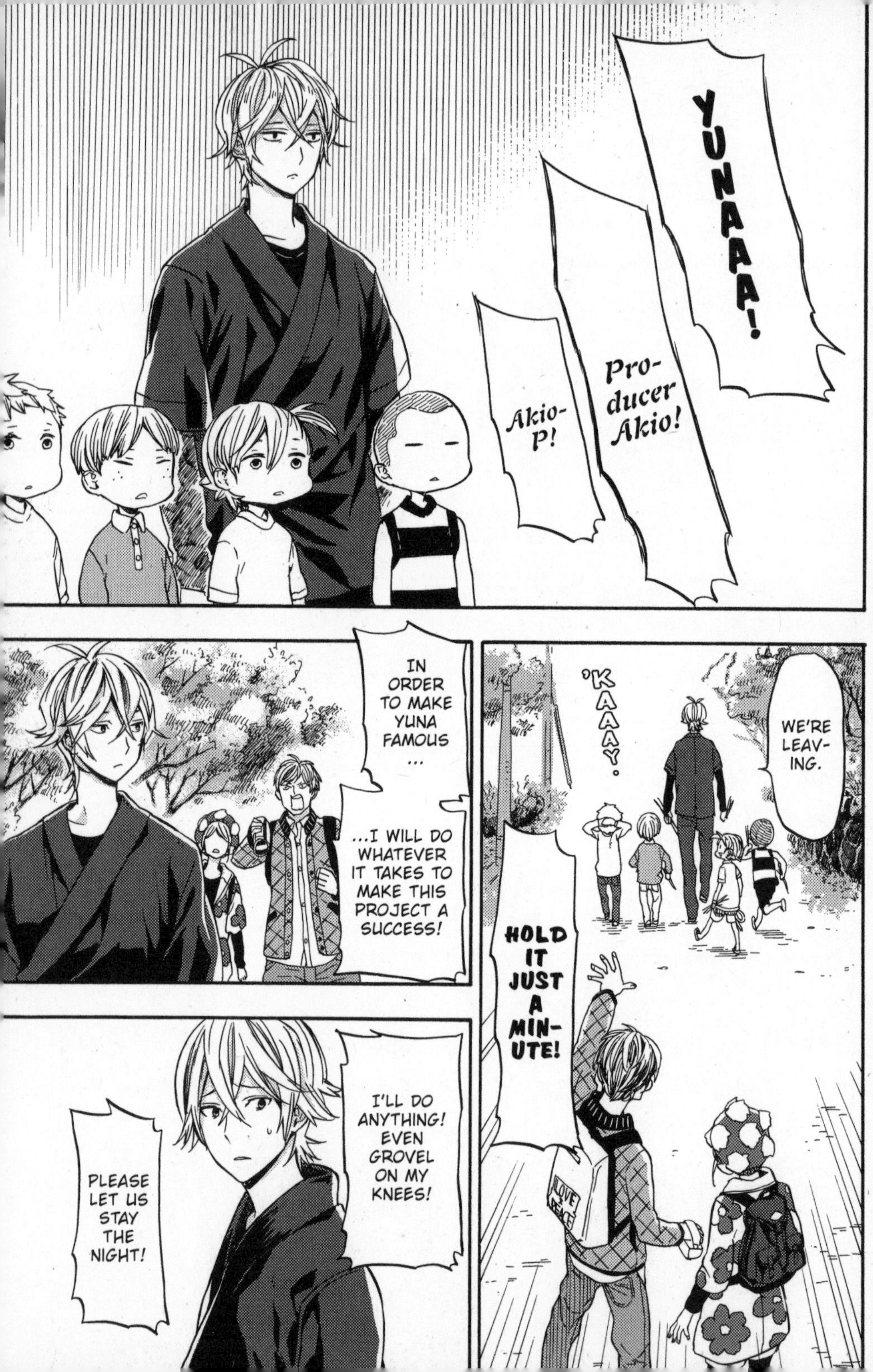
YUNAAA!
Pro-ducer Akio!
Akio-P!
WE'RE LEAV-ING.
'KAAAAY.
HOLD IT JUST A MIN-UTE!
IN ORDER TO MAKE YUNA FAMOUS ...
...I WILL DO WHATEVER IT TAKES TO MAKE THIS PROJECT A SUCCESS!
I'LL DO ANYTHING! EVEN GROVEL ON MY KNEES!
PLEASE LET US STAY THE NIGHT!

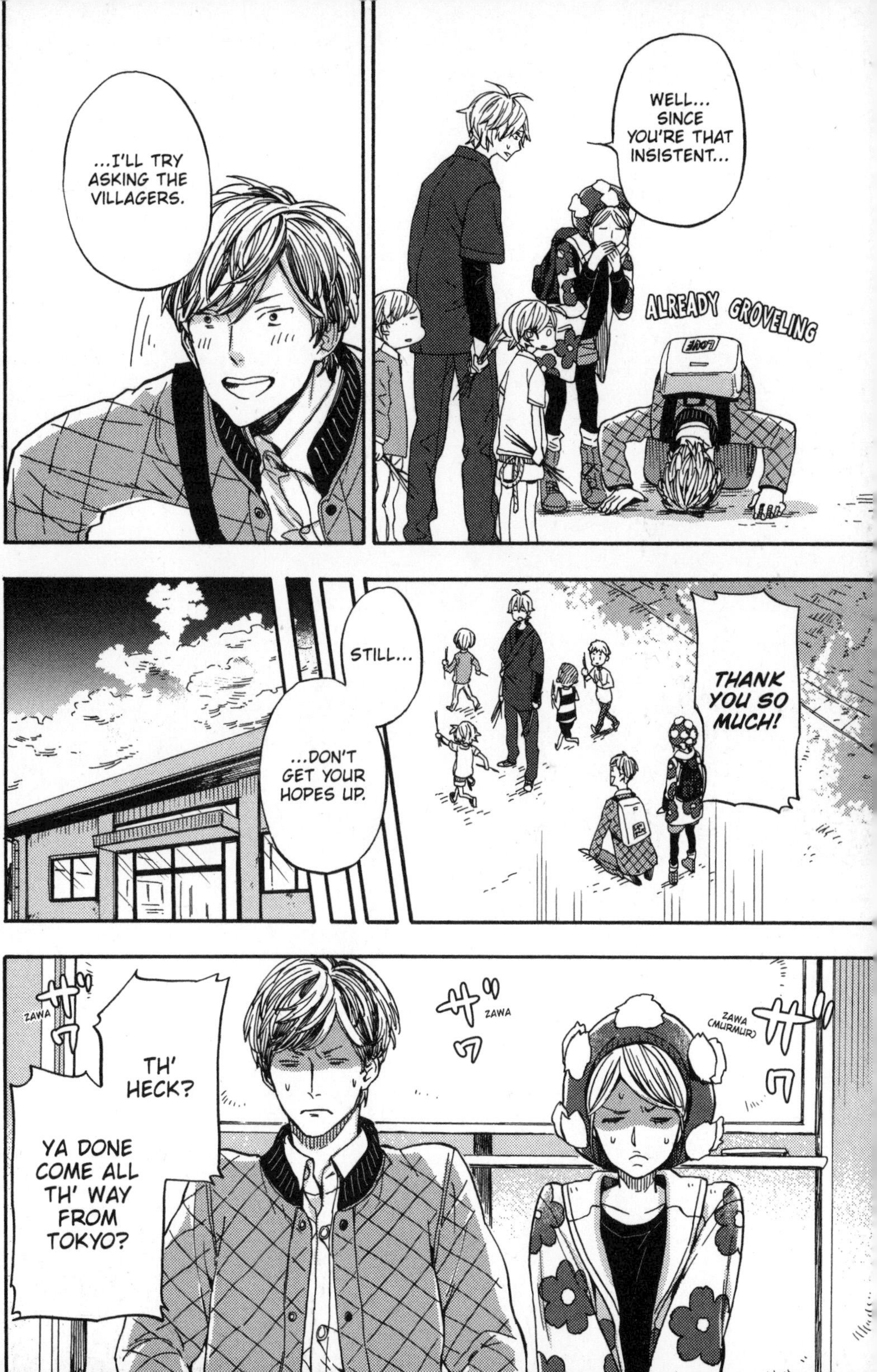
WELL... SINCE YOU'RE THAT INSISTENT...
ALREADY GROVELING
...I'LL TRY ASKING THE VILLAGERS.
THANK YOU SO MUCH!
STILL...
...DON'T GET YOUR HOPES UP.
ZAWA (MURMUR)
ZAWA
TH' HECK?
YA DONE COME ALL TH' WAY FROM TOKYO?
ZAWA

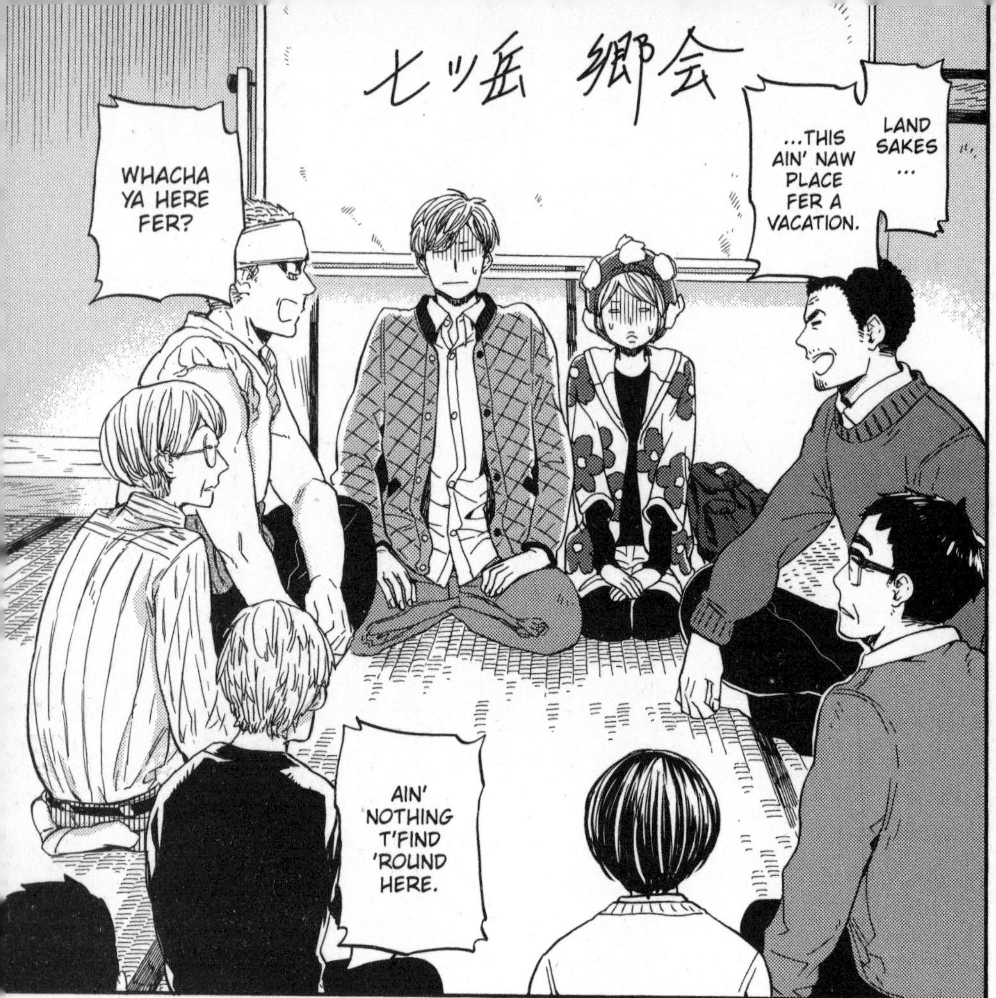
七ッ岳 郷会
LAND SAKES ...
...THIS AIN' NAW PLACE FER A VACATION.
WHACHA YA HERE FER?
AIN' NOTHING T'FIND 'ROUND HERE.

BOARD: NANATSUTAKE VILLAGE MEETING

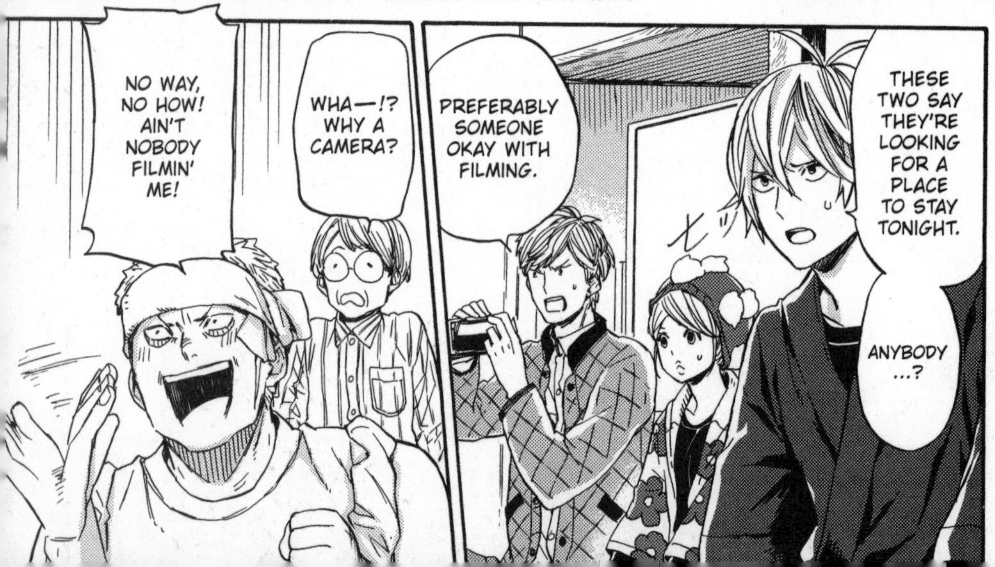
THESE TWO SAY THEY'RE LOOKING FOR A PLACE TO STAY TONIGHT.
ANYBODY ...?
PREFERABLY SOMEONE OKAY WITH FILMING.
WHA—!? WHY A CAMERA?
NO WAY, NO HOW! AIN'T NOBODY FILMIN' ME!

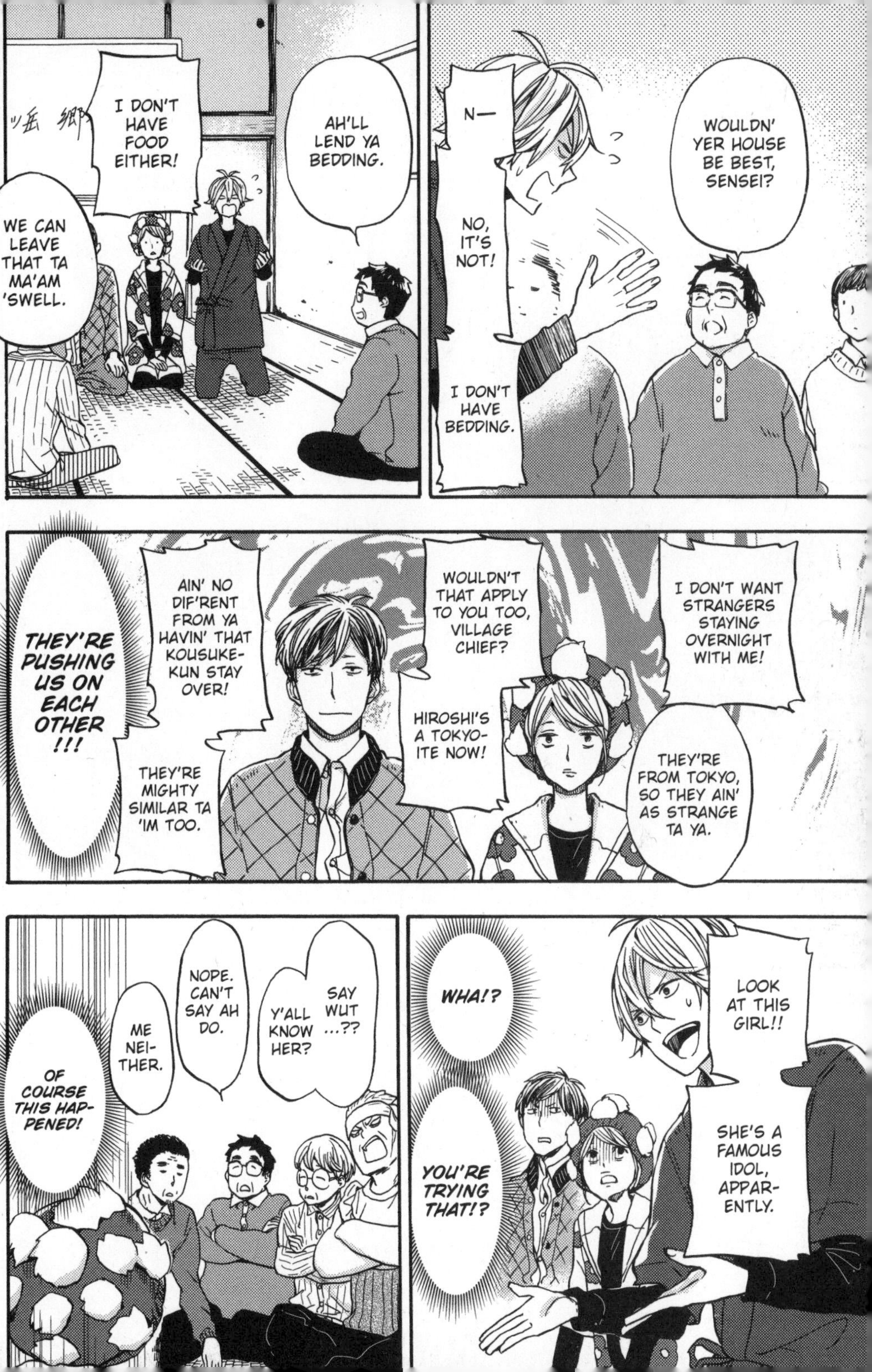
WOULDN' YER HOUSE BE BEST, SENSEI?
N—
NO, IT'S NOT!
I DON'T HAVE BEDDING.
AH'LL LEND YA BEDDING.
I DON'T HAVE FOOD EITHER!
WE CAN LEAVE THAT TA MA'AM 'SWELL.
I DON'T WANT STRANGERS STAYING OVERNIGHT WITH ME!
THEY'RE FROM TOKYO, SO THEY AIN' AS STRANGE TA YA.
WOULDN'T THAT APPLY TO YOU TOO, VILLAGE CHIEF?
HIROSHI'S A TOKYO-ITE NOW!
AIN' NO DIF'RENT FROM YA HAVIN' THAT KOUSUKE-KUN STAY OVER!
THEY'RE MIGHTY SIMILAR TA 'IM TOO.
THEY'RE PUSHING US ON EACH OTHER!!!
LOOK AT THIS GIRL!!
SHE'S A FAMOUS IDOL, APPARENTLY.
WHA!?
YOU'RE TRYING THAT!?
SAY WUT ...??
Y'ALL KNOW HER?
NOPE. CAN'T SAY AH DO.
ME NEITHER.
OF COURSE THIS HAPPENED!

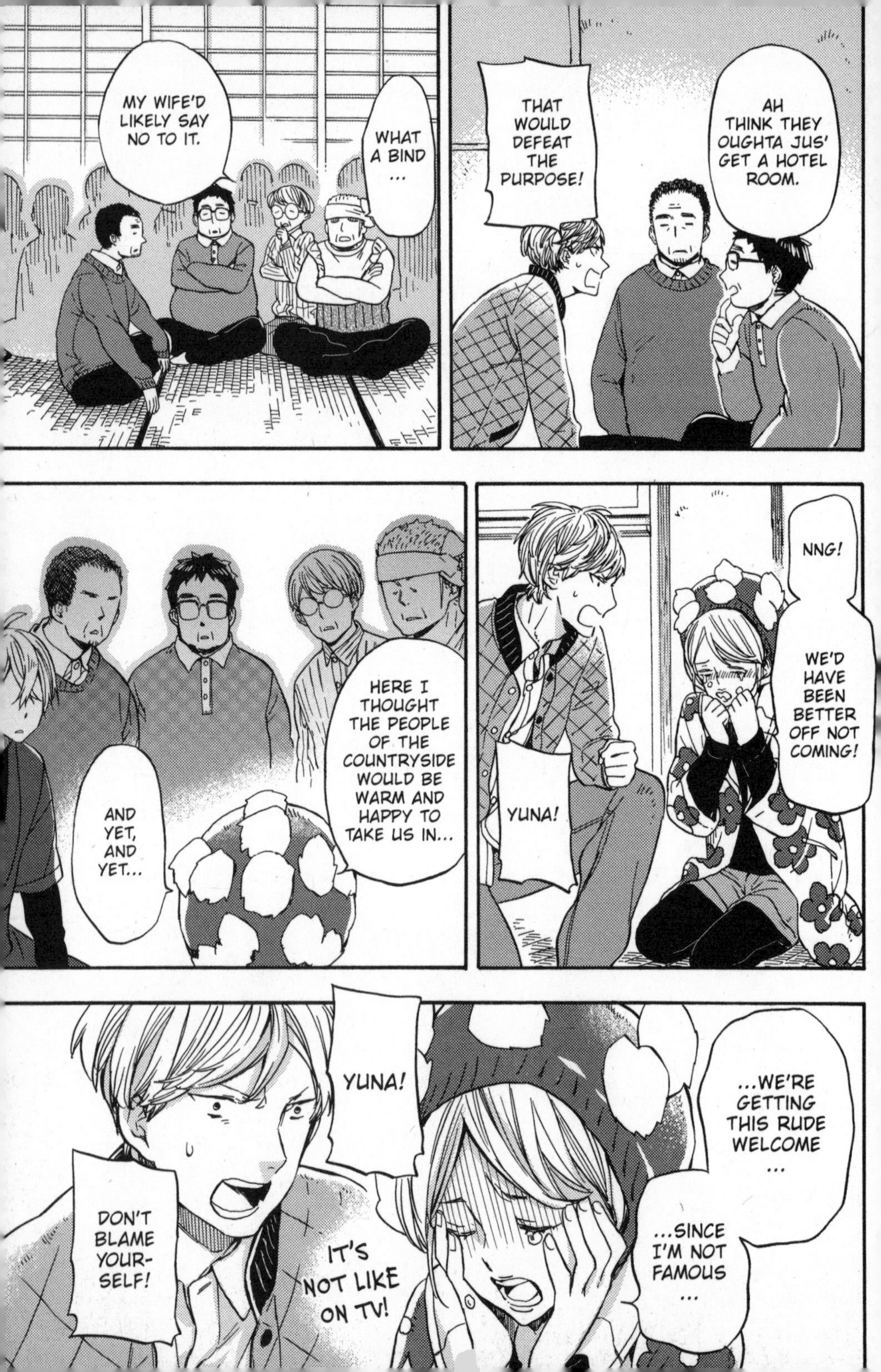
AH THINK THEY OUGHTA JUS' GET A HOTEL ROOM.
THAT WOULD DEFEAT THE PURPOSE!
WHAT A BIND ...
MY WIFE'D LIKELY SAY NO TO IT.
NNG!
WE'D HAVE BEEN BETTER OFF NOT COMING!
YUNA!
HERE I THOUGHT THE PEOPLE OF THE COUNTRYSIDE WOULD BE WARM AND HAPPY TO TAKE US IN...
AND YET, AND YET...
...WE'RE GETTING THIS RUDE WELCOME ...
...SINCE I'M NOT FAMOUS ...
YUNA!
IT'S NOT LIKE ON TV!
DON'T BLAME YOUR-SELF!

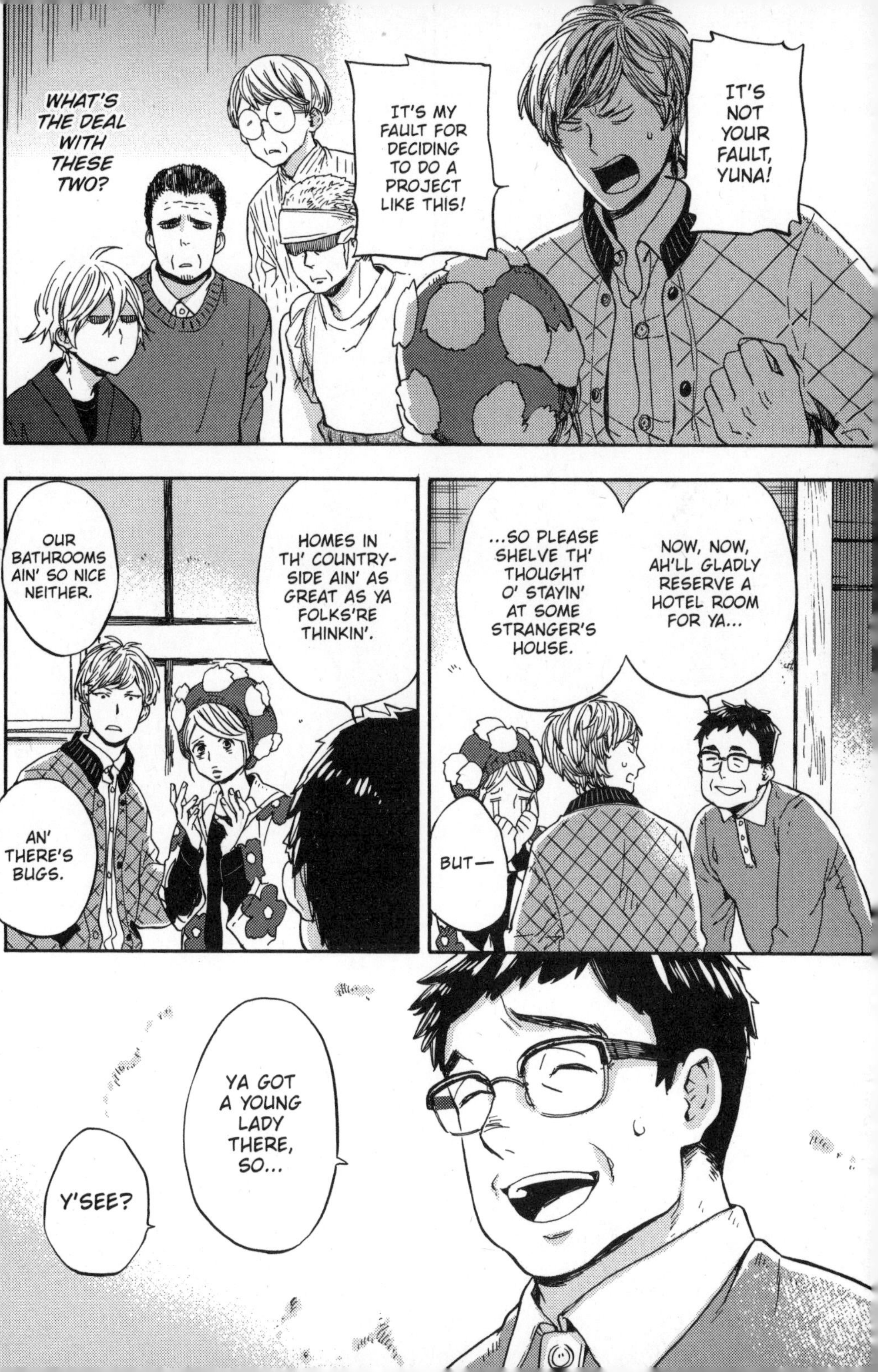
IT'S NOT YOUR FAULT, YUNA!
IT'S MY FAULT FOR DECIDING TO DO A PROJECT LIKE THIS!
WHAT'S THE DEAL WITH THESE TWO?
NOW, NOW, AH'LL GLADLY RESERVE A HOTEL ROOM FOR YA...
...SO PLEASE SHELVE TH' THOUGHT O' STAYIN' AT SOME STRANGER'S HOUSE.
BUT—
HOMES IN TH' COUNTRY-SIDE AIN' AS GREAT AS YA FOLKS'RE THINKIN'.
OUR BATHROOMS AIN' SO NICE NEITHER.
AN' THERE'S BUGS.
YA GOT A YOUNG LADY THERE, SO...
Y'SEE?

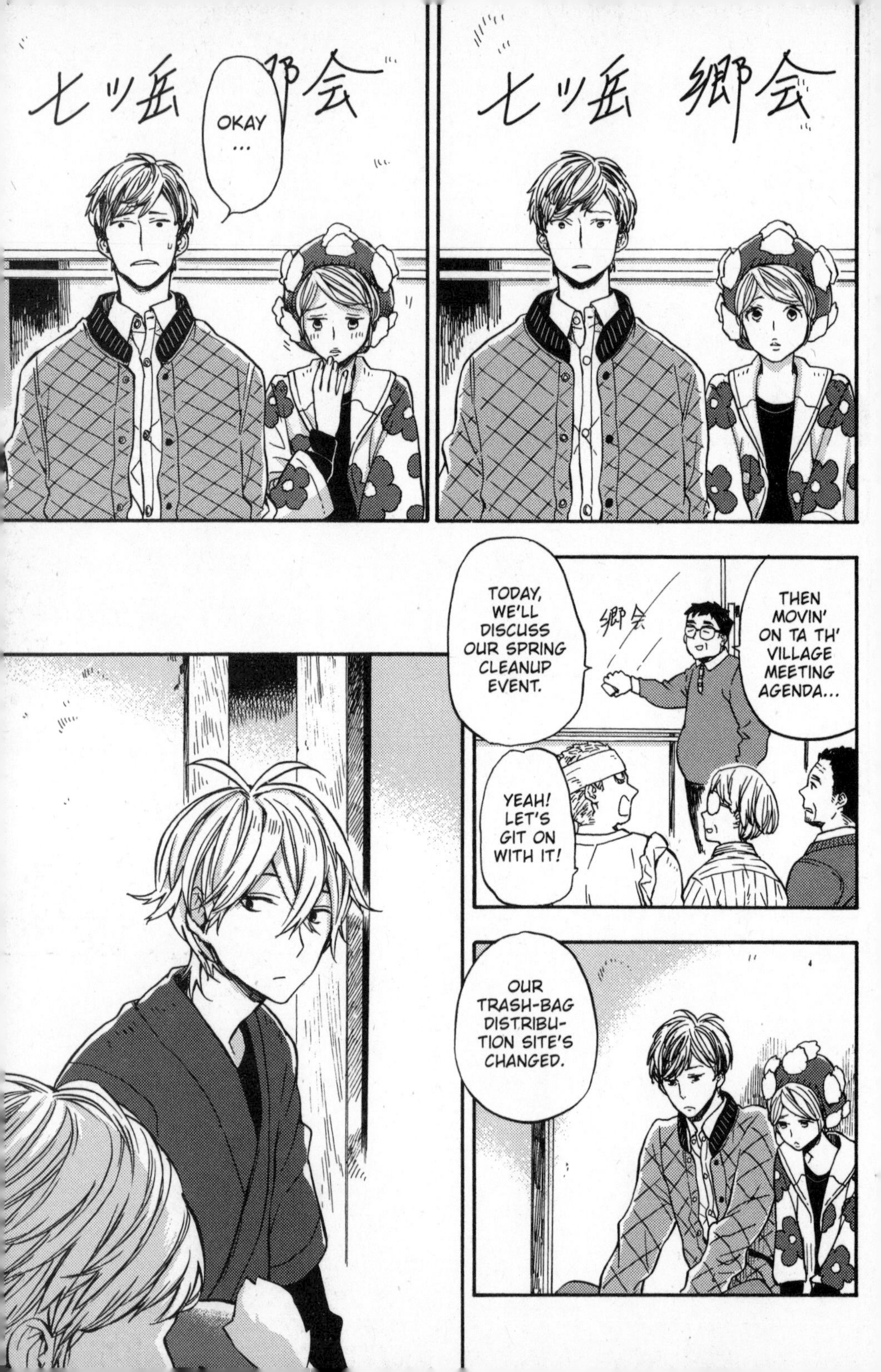
七ッ岳 郷会
七ッ岳
OKAY ...
THEN MOVIN' ON TA TH' VILLAGE MEETING AGENDA...
郷会
TODAY, WE'LL DISCUSS OUR SPRING CLEANUP EVENT.
YEAH! LET'S GIT ON WITH IT!
OUR TRASH-BAG DISTRIBU-TION SITE'S CHANGED.

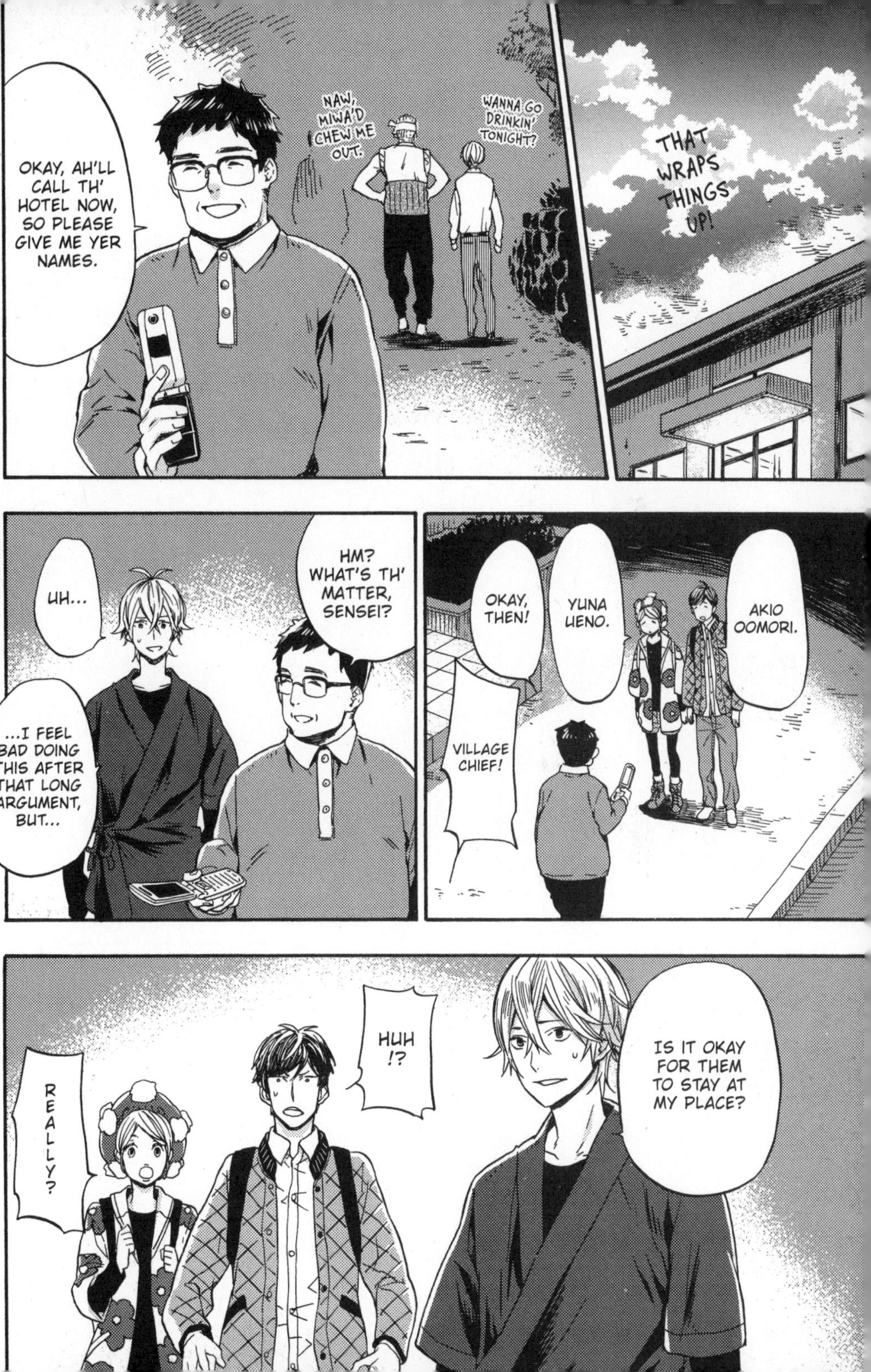
THAT WRAPS THINGS UP!
WANNA GO DRINKIN' TONIGHT?
NAW, MIWA'D CHEW ME OUT.
OKAY, AH'LL CALL TH' HOTEL NOW, SO PLEASE GIVE ME YER NAMES.
AKIO OOMORI.
YUNA UENO.
OKAY, THEN!
VILLAGE CHIEF!
HM? WHAT'S TH' MATTER, SENSEI?
UH...
...I FEEL BAD DOING THIS AFTER THAT LONG ARGUMENT, BUT...
IS IT OKAY FOR THEM TO STAY AT MY PLACE?
HUH!?
REALLY?

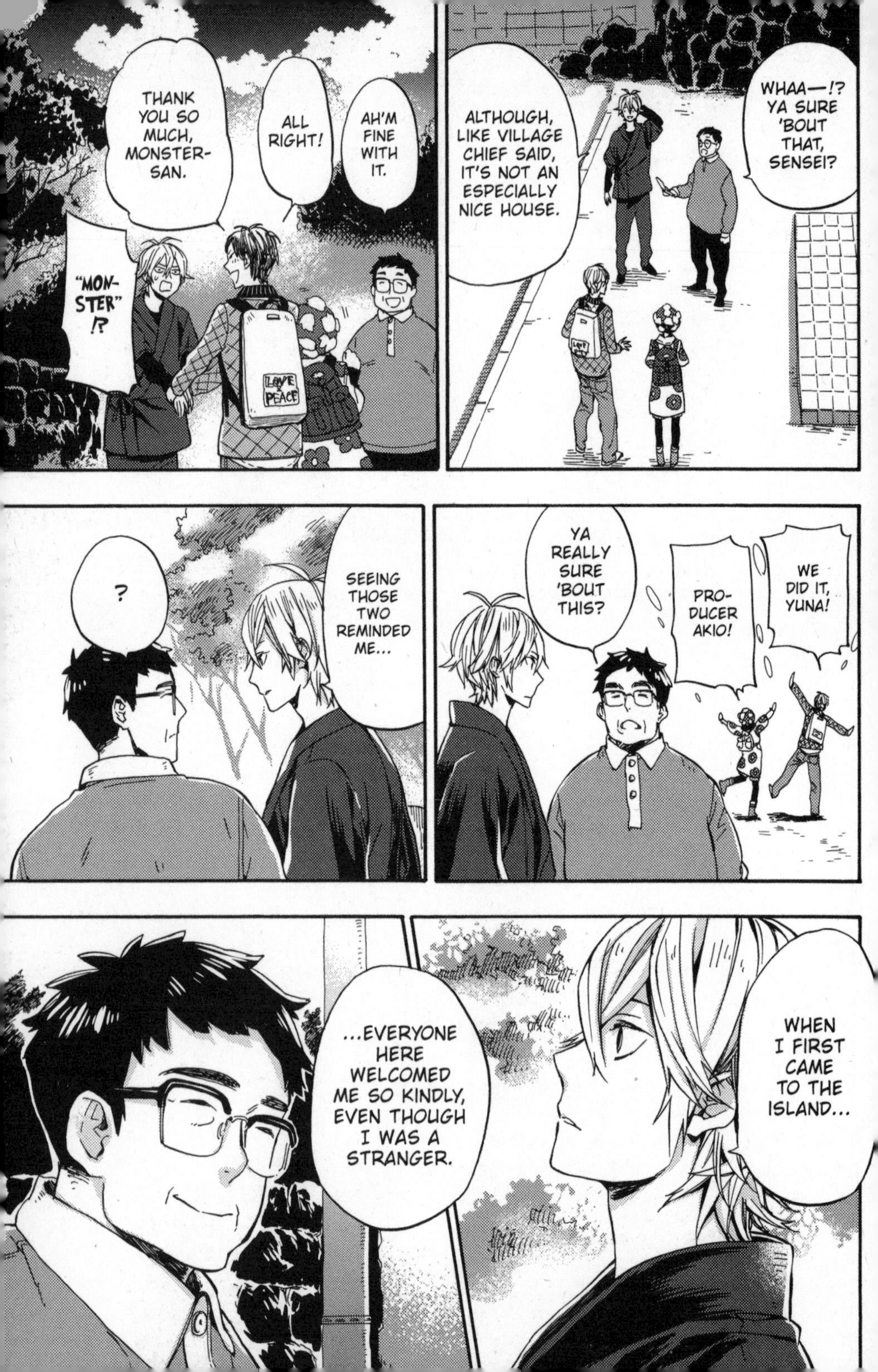
WHAA—!? YA SURE 'BOUT THAT, SENSEI?
ALTHOUGH, LIKE VILLAGE CHIEF SAID, IT'S NOT AN ESPECIALLY NICE HOUSE.
AH'M FINE WITH IT.
ALL RIGHT!
THANK YOU SO MUCH, MONSTER-SAN.
"MONSTER" !?
WE DID IT, YUNA!
PRODUCER AKIO!
YA REALLY SURE 'BOUT THIS?
SEEING THOSE TWO REMINDED ME...
?
WHEN I FIRST CAME TO THE ISLAND...
...EVERYONE HERE WELCOMED ME SO KINDLY, EVEN THOUGH I WAS A STRANGER.

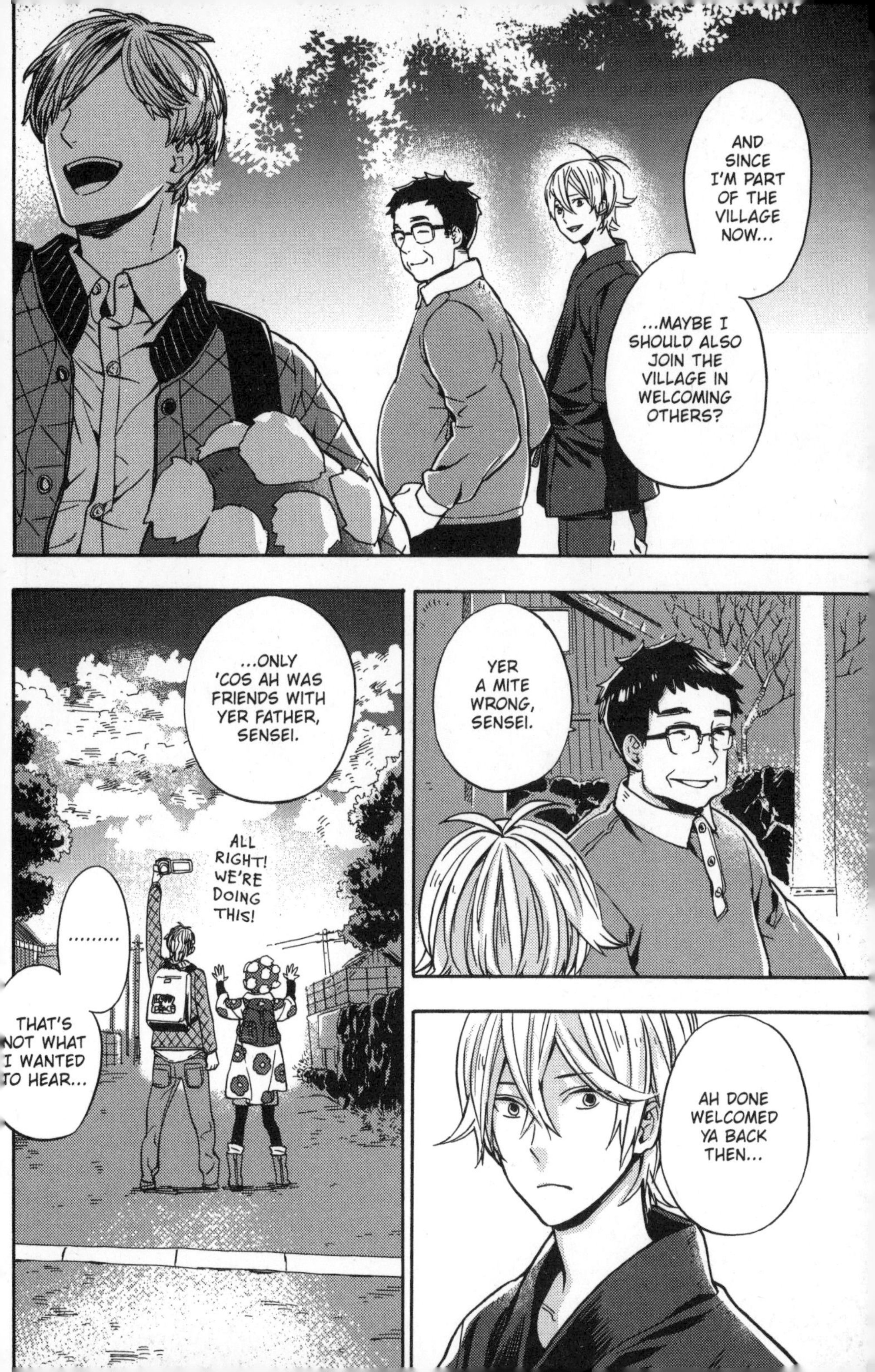
AND SINCE I'M PART OF THE VILLAGE NOW...
...MAYBE I SHOULD ALSO JOIN THE VILLAGE IN WELCOMING OTHERS?
YER A MITE WRONG, SENSEI.
AH DONE WELCOMED YA BACK THEN...
...ONLY 'COS AH WAS FRIENDS WITH YER FATHER, SENSEI.
ALL RIGHT! WE'RE DOING THIS!
....
THAT'S NOT WHAT I WANTED TO HEAR...

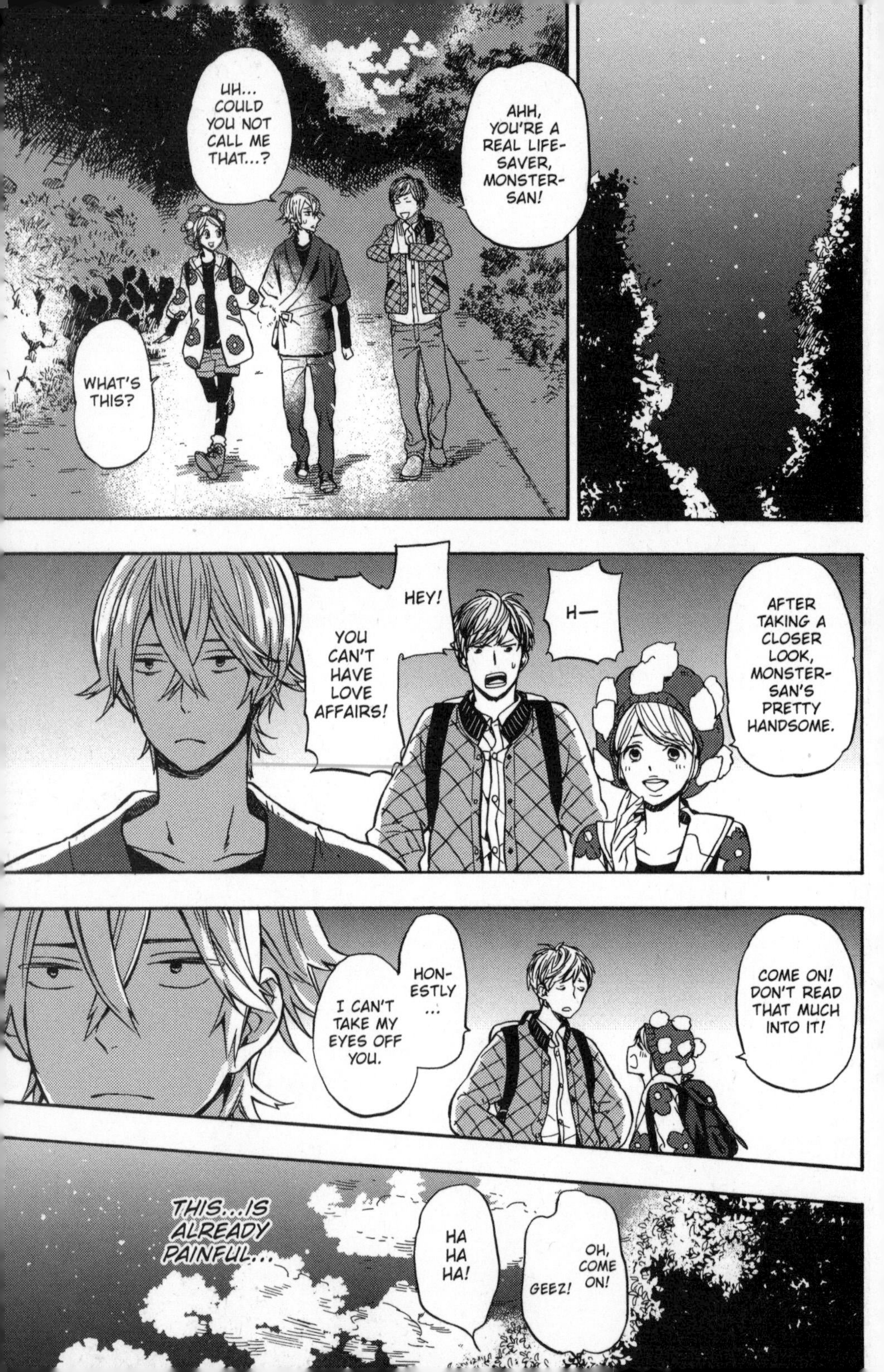
AHH, YOU'RE A REAL LIFE-SAVER, MONSTER-SAN!
UH... COULD YOU NOT CALL ME THAT...?
WHAT'S THIS?
AFTER TAKING A CLOSER LOOK, MONSTER-SAN'S PRETTY HANDSOME.
H—
HEY!
YOU CAN'T HAVE LOVE AFFAIRS!
COME ON! DON'T READ THAT MUCH INTO IT!
HON-ESTLY ...
I CAN'T TAKE MY EYES OFF YOU.
OH, COME ON!
GEEZ!
HA HA HA!
THIS...IS ALREADY PAINFUL...

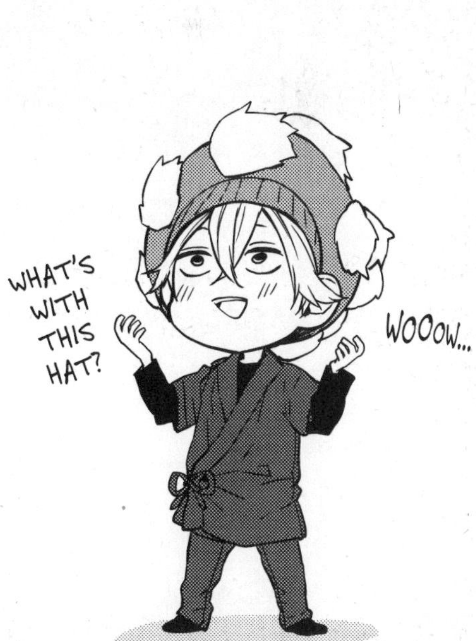
WOOOW...
WHAT'S WITH THIS HAT?

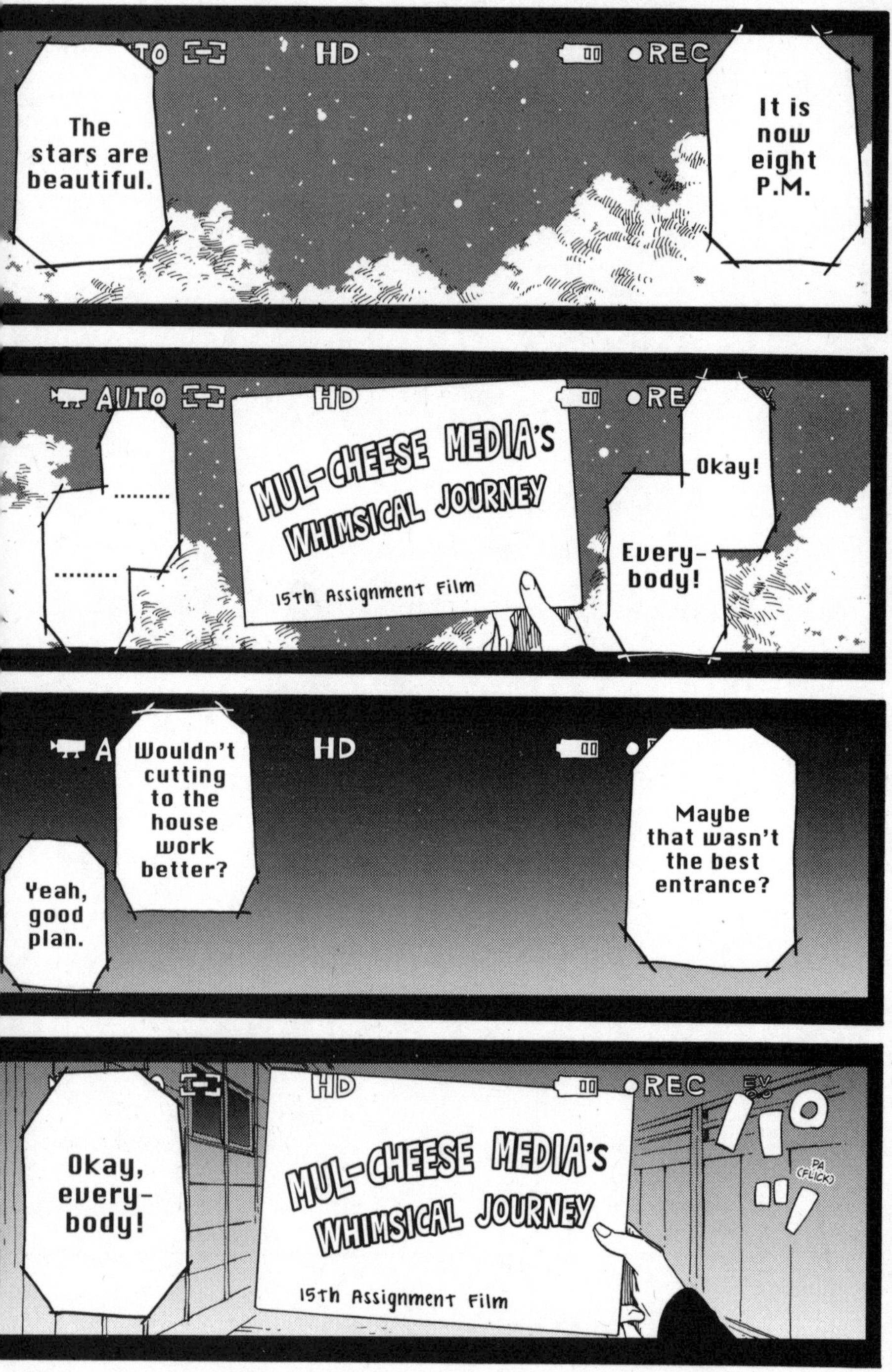
REC
HD
AUTO
It is now eight P.M.
The stars are beautiful.
REC
HD
AUTO
Okay!
Every-body!
MUL-CHEESE MEDIA's WHIMSICAL JOURNEY
15th Assignment Film
....
....
HD
Maybe that wasn't the best entrance?
Wouldn't cutting to the house work better?
Yeah, good plan.
PA (FLICK)
REC
HD
MUL-CHEESE MEDIA's WHIMSICAL JOURNEY
15th Assignment Film
Okay, every-body!

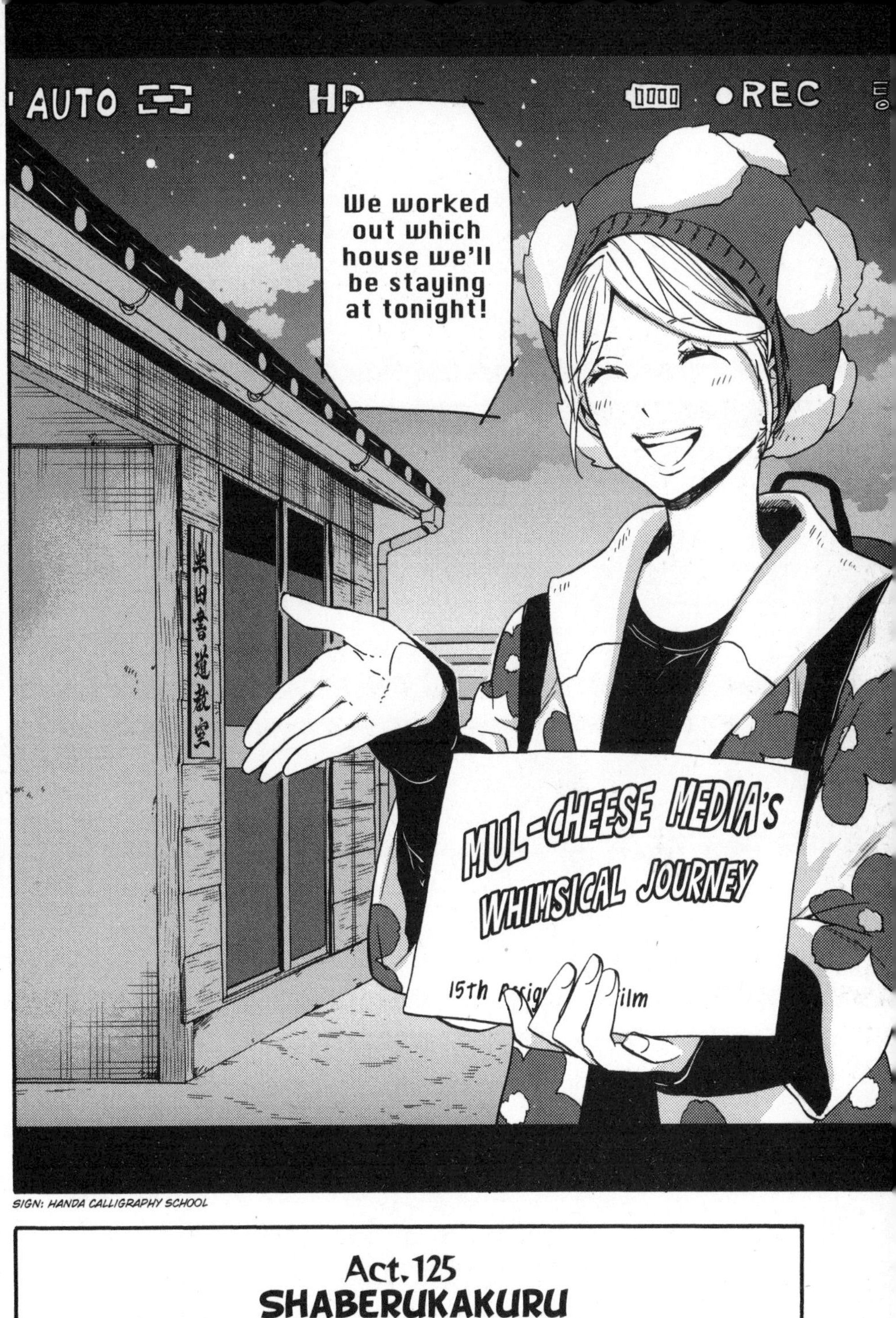
AUTO
HD
REC
We worked out which house we'll be staying at tonight!
半田書道教室
MUL-CHEESE MEDIA's
WHIMSICAL JOURNEY

SIGN: HANDA CALLIGRAPHY SCHOOL

Act. 125
SHABERUKAKURU
(Translation: Striking up Conversation)

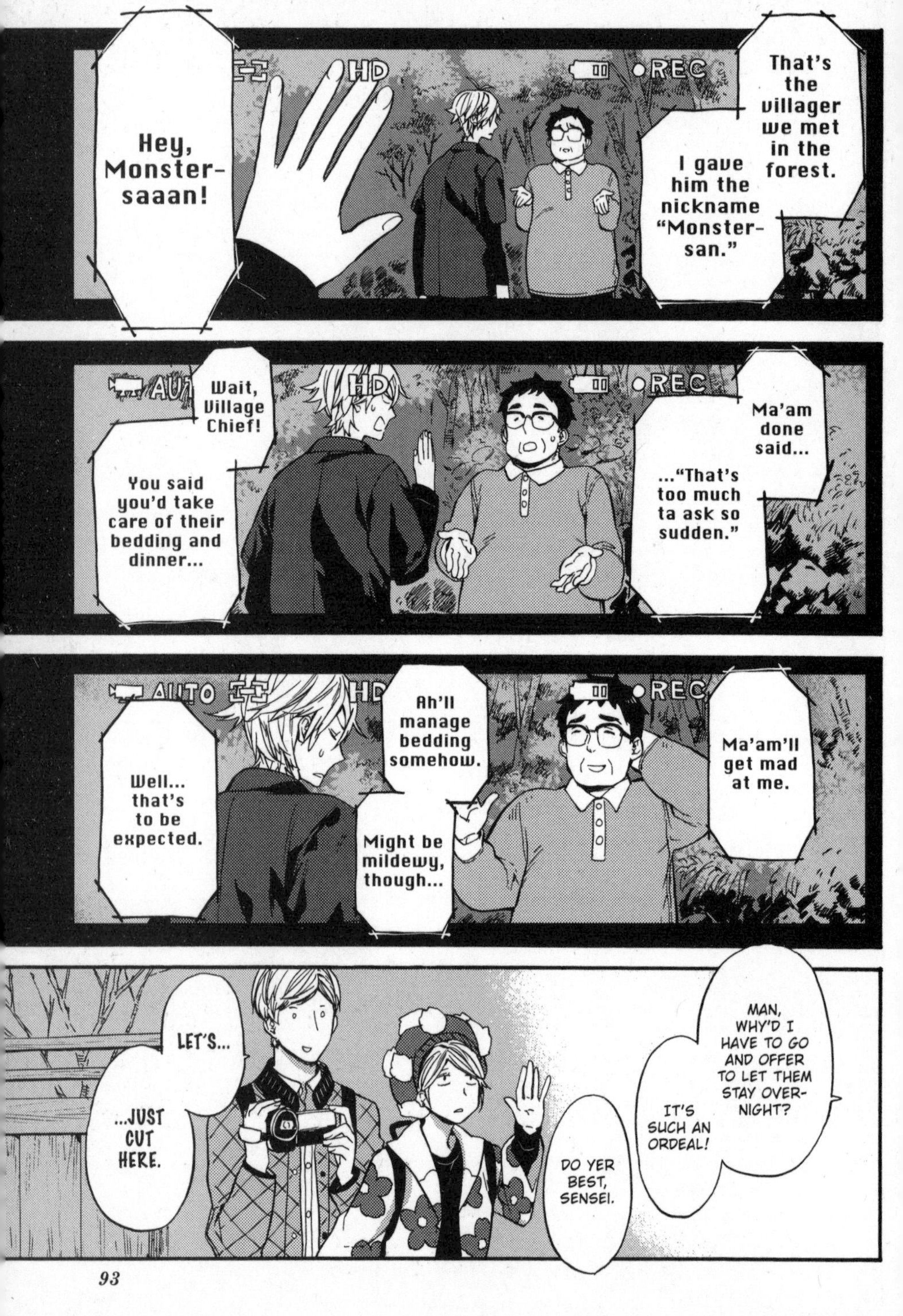
That's the villager we met in the forest.
I gave him the nickname "Monster-san."
Hey, Monster-saaan!
Ma'am done said...
..."That's too much ta ask so sudden."
Wait, Village Chief!
You said you'd take care of their bedding and dinner...
Ma'am'll get mad at me.
Ah'll manage bedding somehow.
Might be mildewy, though...
Well... that's to be expected.
MAN, WHY'D I HAVE TO GO AND OFFER TO LET THEM STAY OVER-NIGHT?
IT'S SUCH AN ORDEAL!
DO YER BEST, SENSEI.
LET'S...
...JUST CUT HERE.

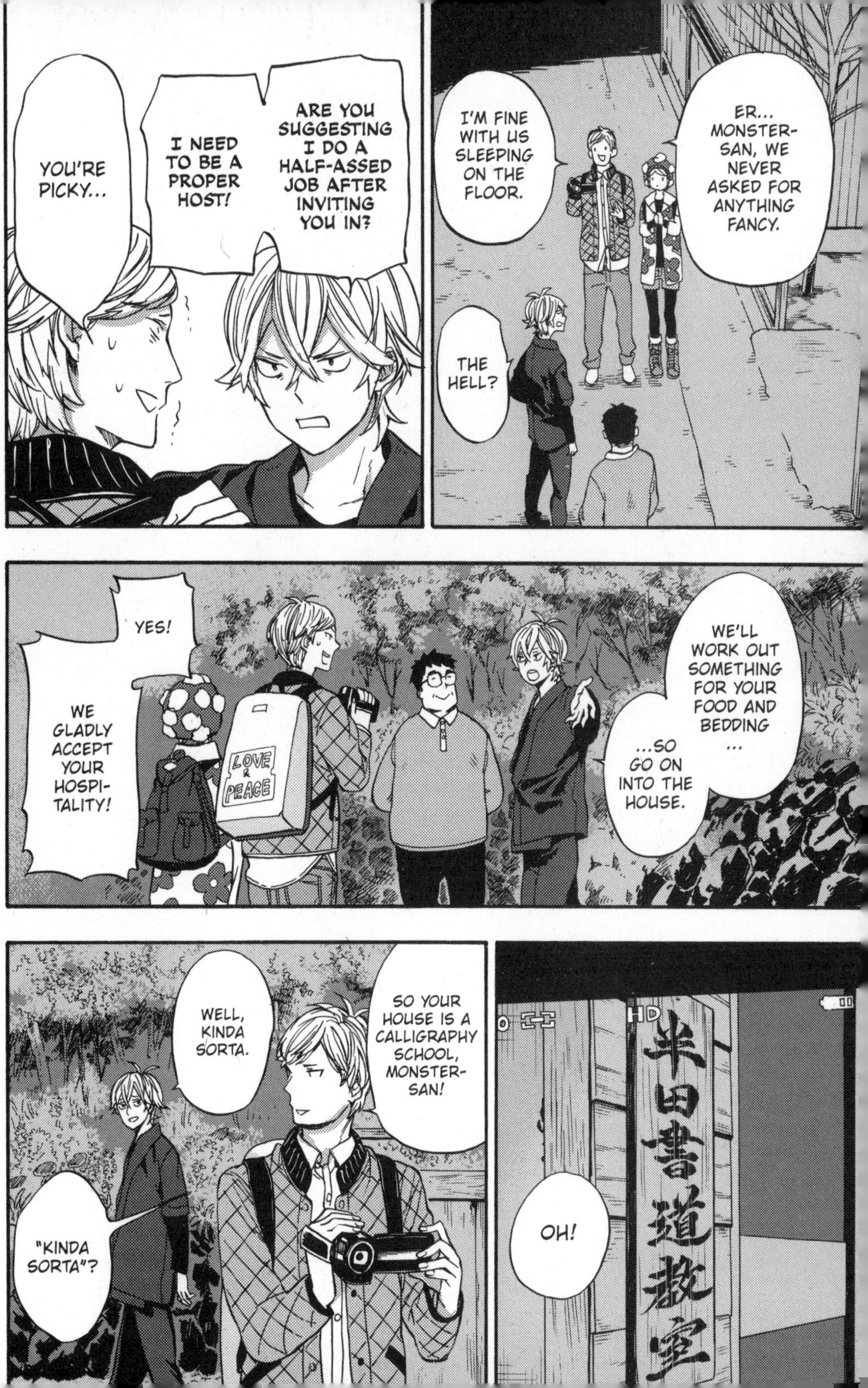
ER... MONSTER-SAN, WE NEVER ASKED FOR ANYTHING FANCY.
I'M FINE WITH US SLEEPING ON THE FLOOR.
THE HELL?
ARE YOU SUGGESTING I DO A HALF-ASSED JOB AFTER INVITING YOU IN?
I NEED TO BE A PROPER HOST!
YOU'RE PICKY...
WE'LL WORK OUT SOMETHING FOR YOUR FOOD AND BEDDING...
...SO GO ON INTO THE HOUSE.
YES!
WE GLADLY ACCEPT YOUR HOSPI-TALITY!
LOVE & PEACE
HD
半田書道教室
OH!
SO YOUR HOUSE IS A CALLIGRAPHY SCHOOL, MONSTER-SAN!
WELL, KINDA SORTA.
"KINDA SORTA"?

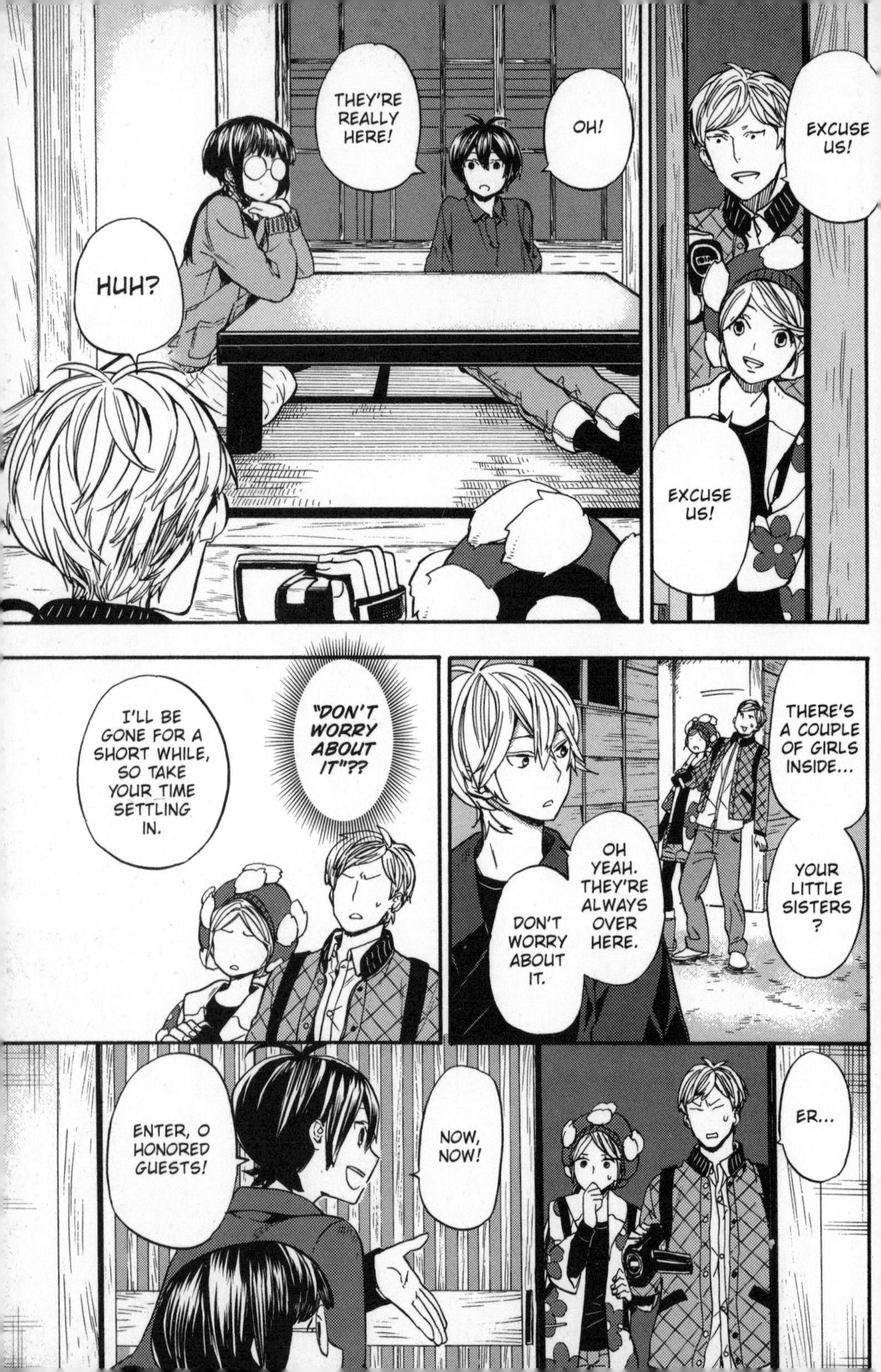
EXCUSE US!
EXCUSE US!
OH!
THEY'RE REALLY HERE!
HUH?
THERE'S A COUPLE OF GIRLS INSIDE...
YOUR LITTLE SISTERS?
OH YEAH. THEY'RE ALWAYS OVER HERE.
DON'T WORRY ABOUT IT.
"DON'T WORRY ABOUT IT"??
I'LL BE GONE FOR A SHORT WHILE, SO TAKE YOUR TIME SETTLING IN.
ER...
NOW, NOW!
ENTER, O HONORED GUESTS!

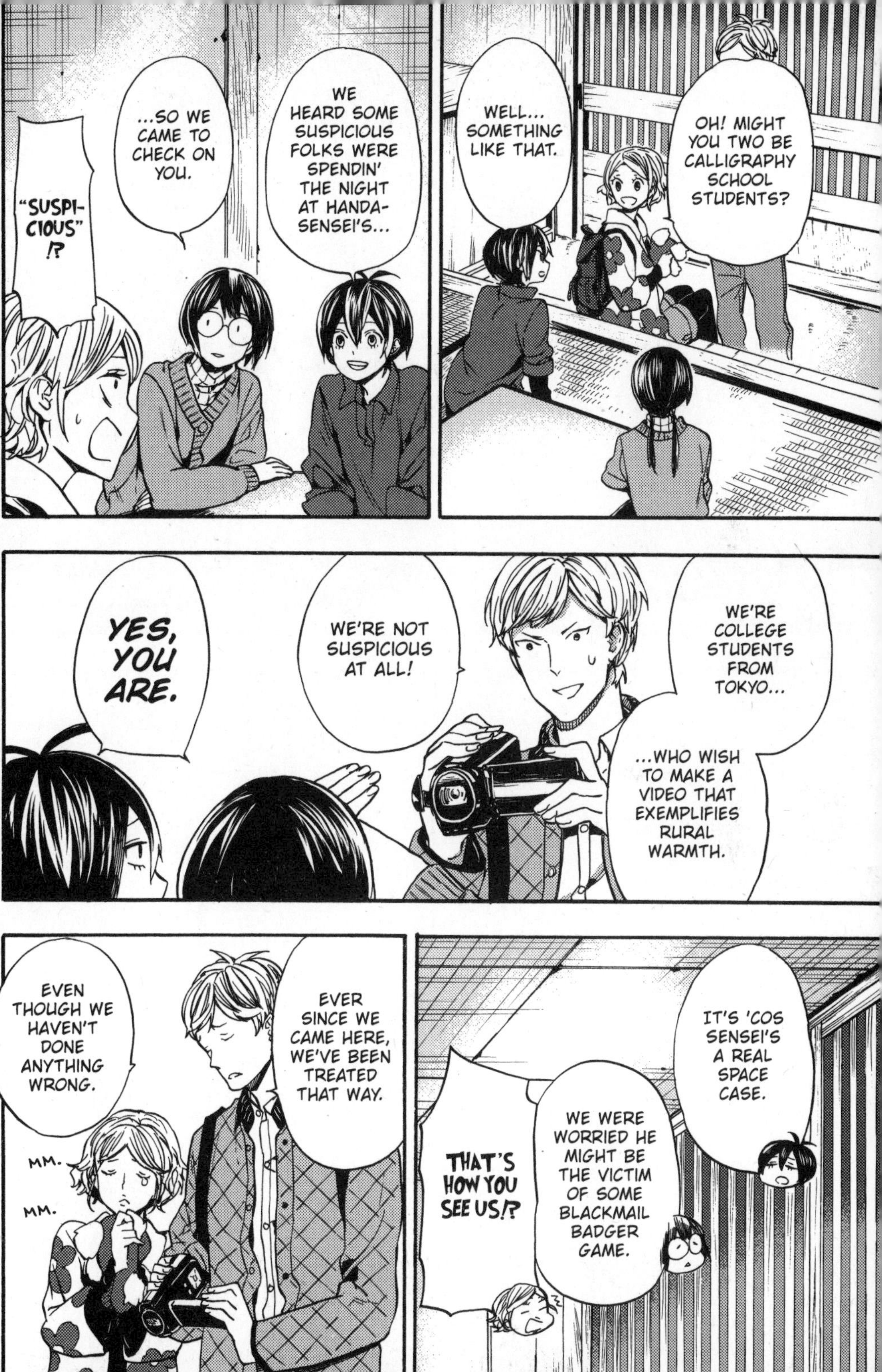
OH! MIGHT YOU TWO BE CALLIGRAPHY SCHOOL STUDENTS?
WELL... SOMETHING LIKE THAT.
WE HEARD SOME SUSPICIOUS FOLKS WERE SPENDIN' THE NIGHT AT HANDA-SENSEI'S...
...SO WE CAME TO CHECK ON YOU.
"SUSPICIOUS"!?
WE'RE COLLEGE STUDENTS FROM TOKYO...
...WHO WISH TO MAKE A VIDEO THAT EXEMPLIFIES RURAL WARMTH.
WE'RE NOT SUSPICIOUS AT ALL!
YES, YOU ARE.
IT'S 'COS SENSEI'S A REAL SPACE CASE.
WE WERE WORRIED HE MIGHT BE THE VICTIM OF SOME BLACKMAIL BADGER GAME.
THAT'S HOW YOU SEE US!?
EVER SINCE WE CAME HERE, WE'VE BEEN TREATED THAT WAY.
EVEN THOUGH WE HAVEN'T DONE ANYTHING WRONG.
MM.
MM.

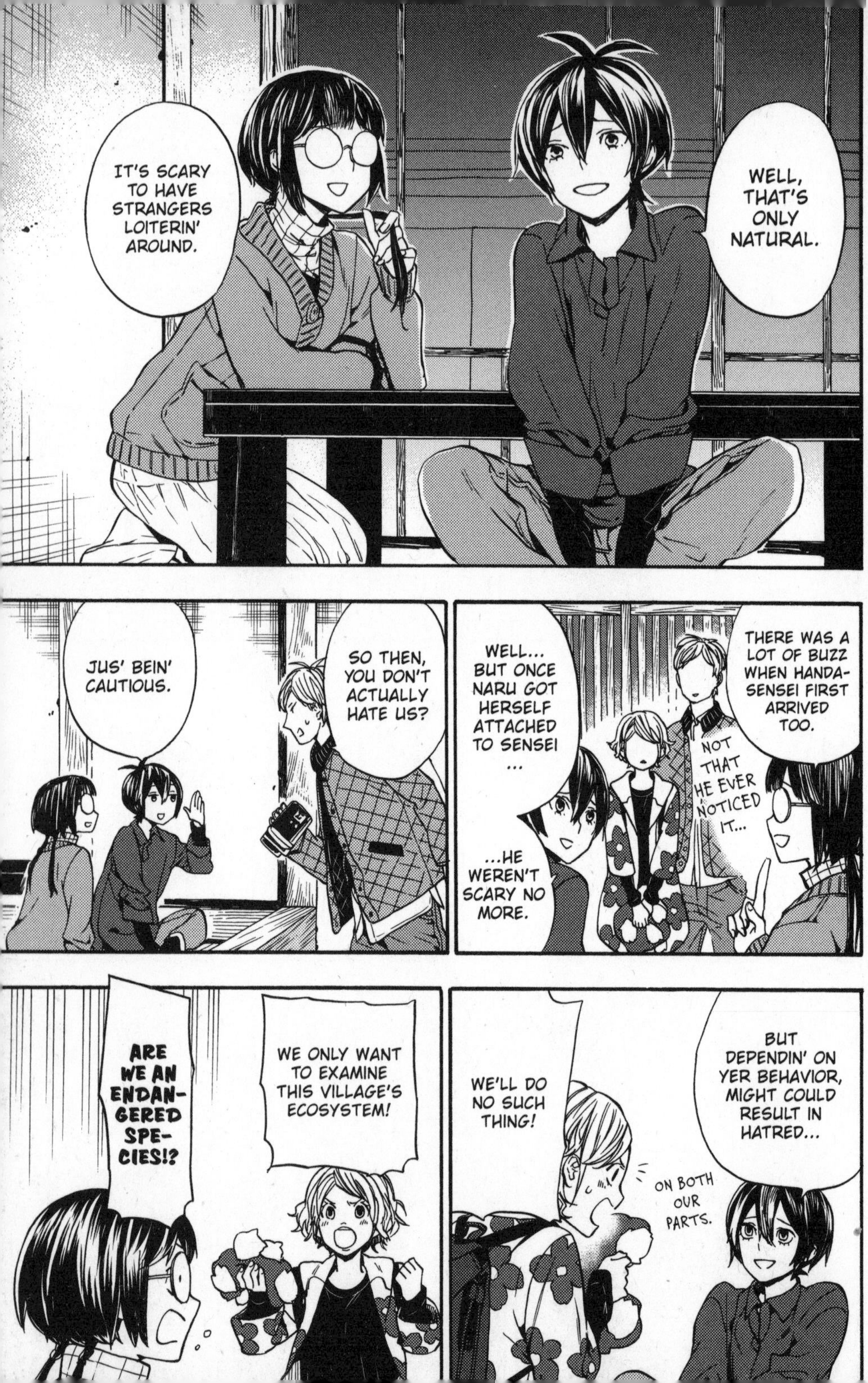
WELL, THAT'S ONLY NATURAL.
IT'S SCARY TO HAVE STRANGERS LOITERIN' AROUND.
THERE WAS A LOT OF BUZZ WHEN HANDA-SENSEI FIRST ARRIVED TOO.
NOT THAT HE EVER NOTICED IT...
WELL... BUT ONCE NARU GOT HERSELF ATTACHED TO SENSEI...
...HE WEREN'T SCARY NO MORE.
SO THEN, YOU DON'T ACTUALLY HATE US?
JUS' BEIN' CAUTIOUS.
BUT DEPENDIN' ON YER BEHAVIOR, MIGHT COULD RESULT IN HATRED...
ON BOTH OUR PARTS.
WE'LL DO NO SUCH THING!
WE ONLY WANT TO EXAMINE THIS VILLAGE'S ECOSYSTEM!
ARE WE AN ENDANGERED SPECIES!?

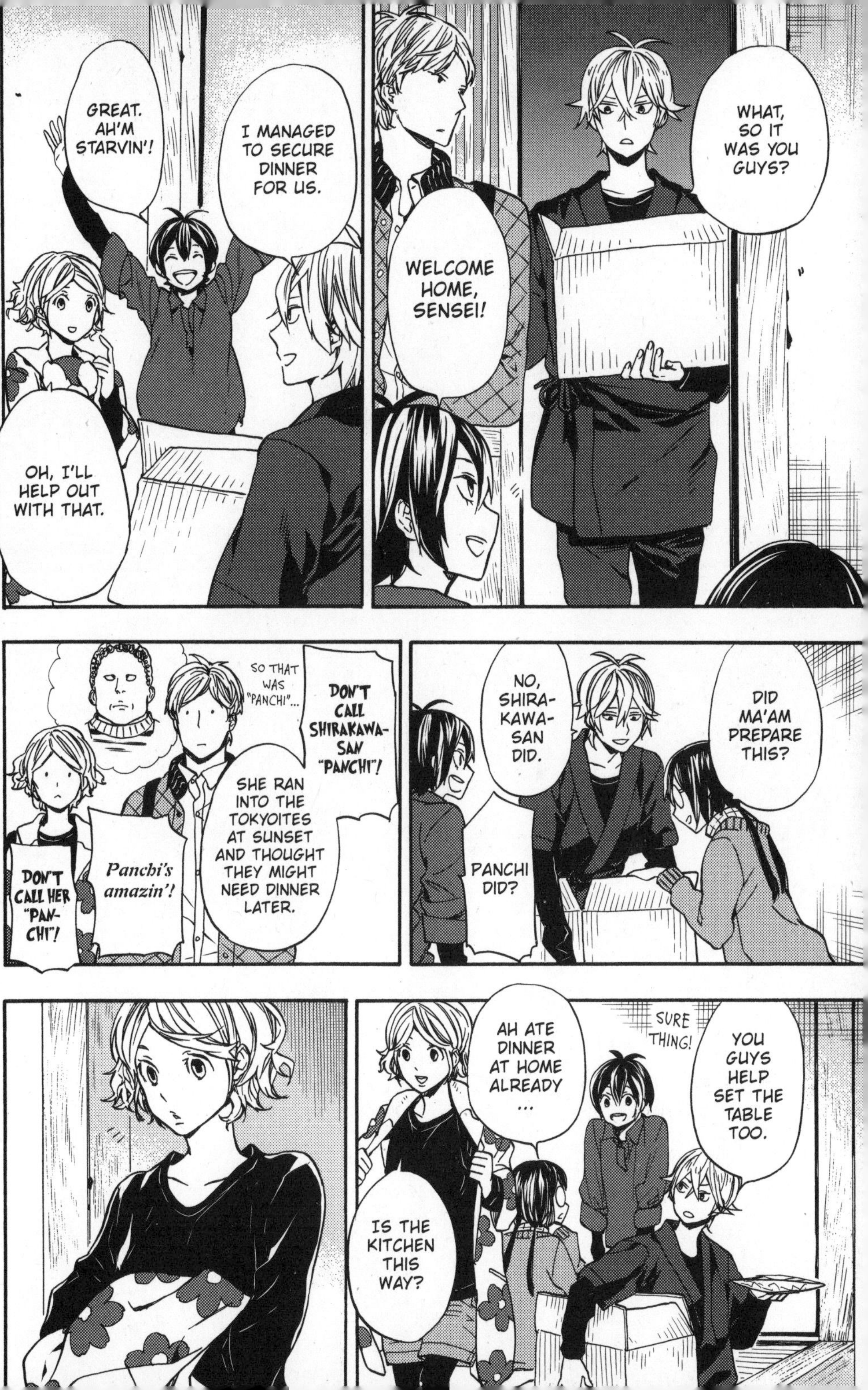
WHAT, SO IT WAS YOU GUYS?
WELCOME HOME, SENSEI!
I MANAGED TO SECURE DINNER FOR US.
GREAT. AH'M STARVIN'!
OH, I'LL HELP OUT WITH THAT.
DID MA'AM PREPARE THIS?
NO, SHIRAKAWA-SAN DID.
PANCHI DID?
DON'T CALL SHIRAKAWA-SAN "PANCHI"!
SO THAT WAS "PANCHI"...
SHE RAN INTO THE TOKYOITES AT SUNSET AND THOUGHT THEY MIGHT NEED DINNER LATER.
Panchi's amazin'!
DON'T CALL HER "PAN-CHI"!
YOU GUYS HELP SET THE TABLE TOO.
SURE THING!
AH ATE DINNER AT HOME ALREADY ...
IS THE KITCHEN THIS WAY?

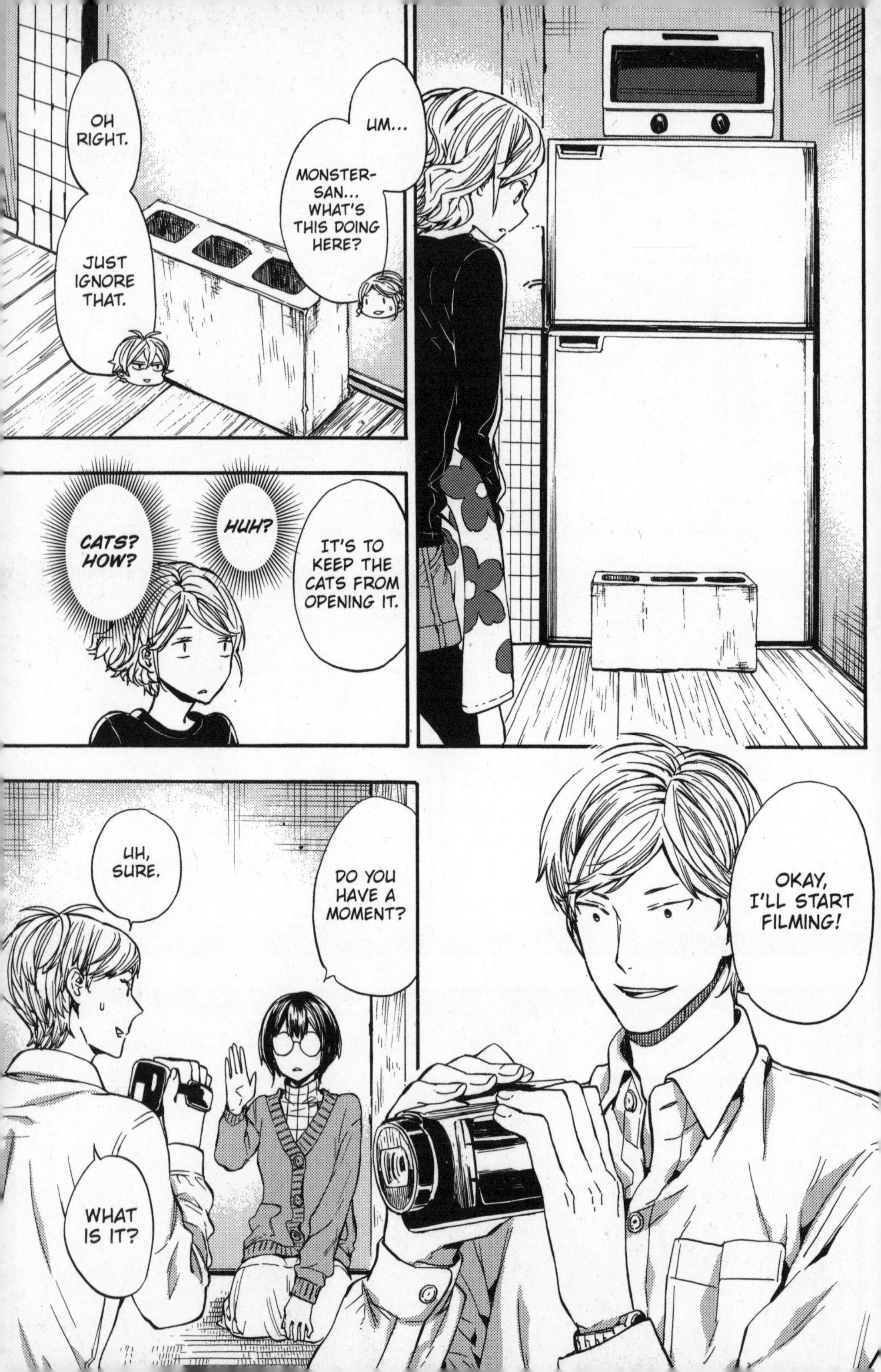
UM...
MONSTER-SAN... WHAT'S THIS DOING HERE?
OH RIGHT.
JUST IGNORE THAT.
IT'S TO KEEP THE CATS FROM OPENING IT.
HUH?
CATS? HOW?
OKAY, I'LL START FILMING!
DO YOU HAVE A MOMENT?
UH, SURE.
WHAT IS IT?

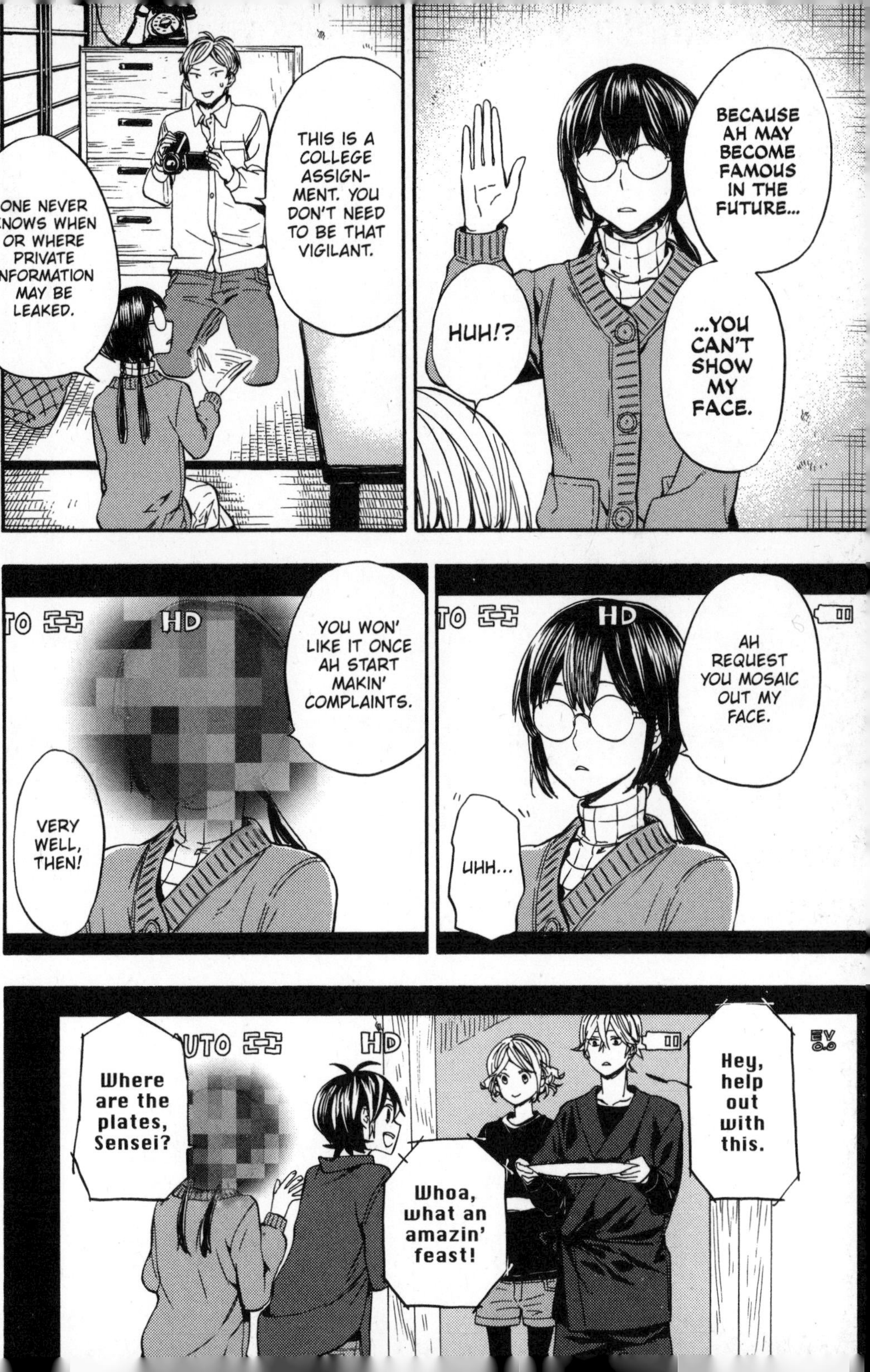
BECAUSE AH MAY BECOME FAMOUS IN THE FUTURE...
...YOU CAN'T SHOW MY FACE.
HUH!?
THIS IS A COLLEGE ASSIGN-MENT. YOU DON'T NEED TO BE THAT VIGILANT.
ONE NEVER KNOWS WHEN OR WHERE PRIVATE INFORMATION MAY BE LEAKED.
HD
AH REQUEST YOU MOSAIC OUT MY FACE.
UHH...
HD
YOU WON' LIKE IT ONCE AH START MAKIN' COMPLAINTS.
VERY WELL, THEN!
Hey, help out with this.
Whoa, what an amazin' feast!
HD
Where are the plates, Sensei?

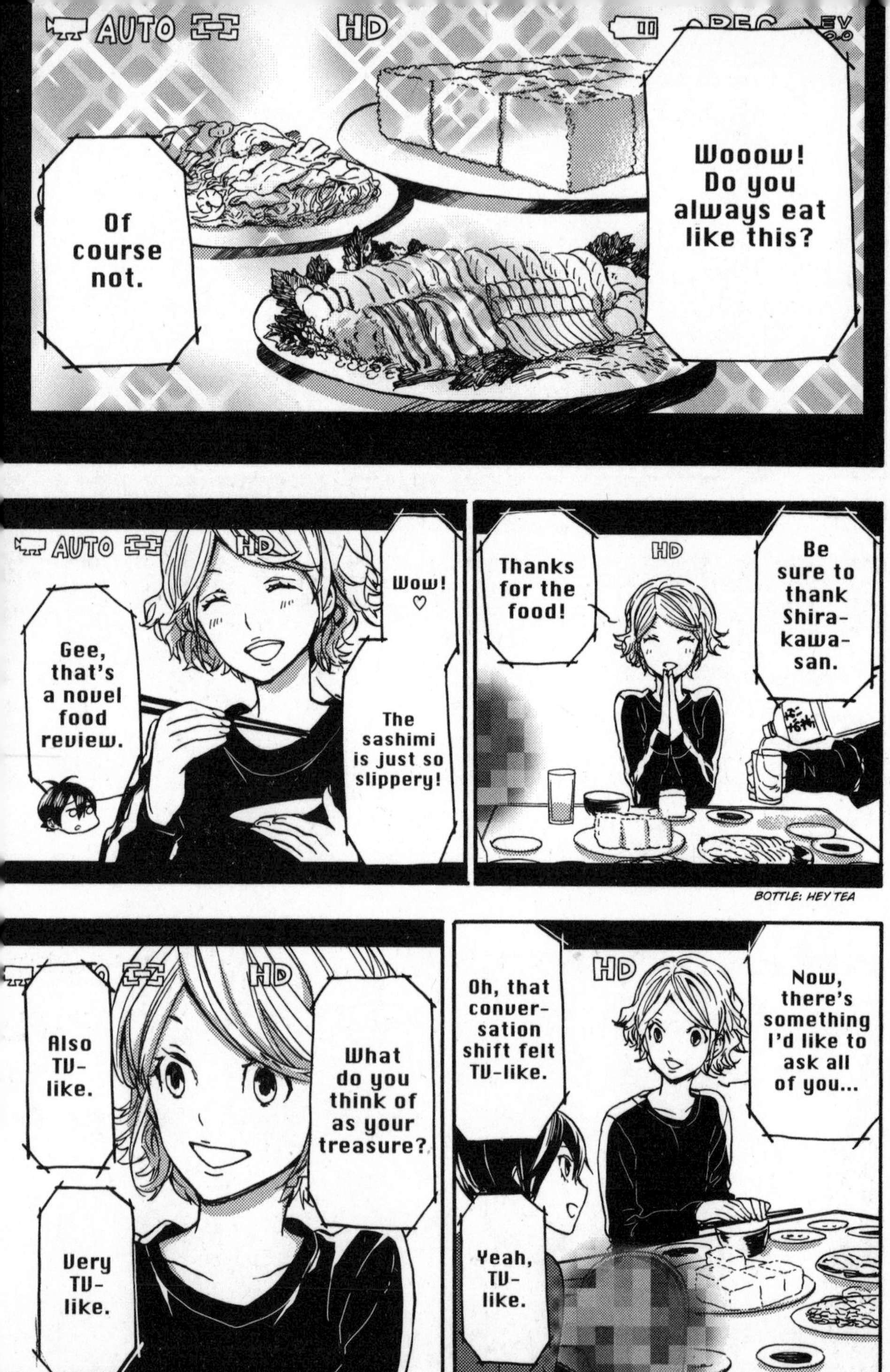
AUTO
HD
Wooow! Do you always eat like this?
Of course not.
HD
Be sure to thank Shira-kawa-san.
Thanks for the food!
AUTO
HD
Wow! ♡
The sashimi is just so slippery!
Gee, that's a novel food review.
BOTTLE: HEY TEA
HD
Now, there's something I'd like to ask all of you...
Oh, that conver-sation shift felt TV-like.
Yeah, TV-like.
HD
What do you think of as your treasure?
Also TV-like.
Very TV-like.

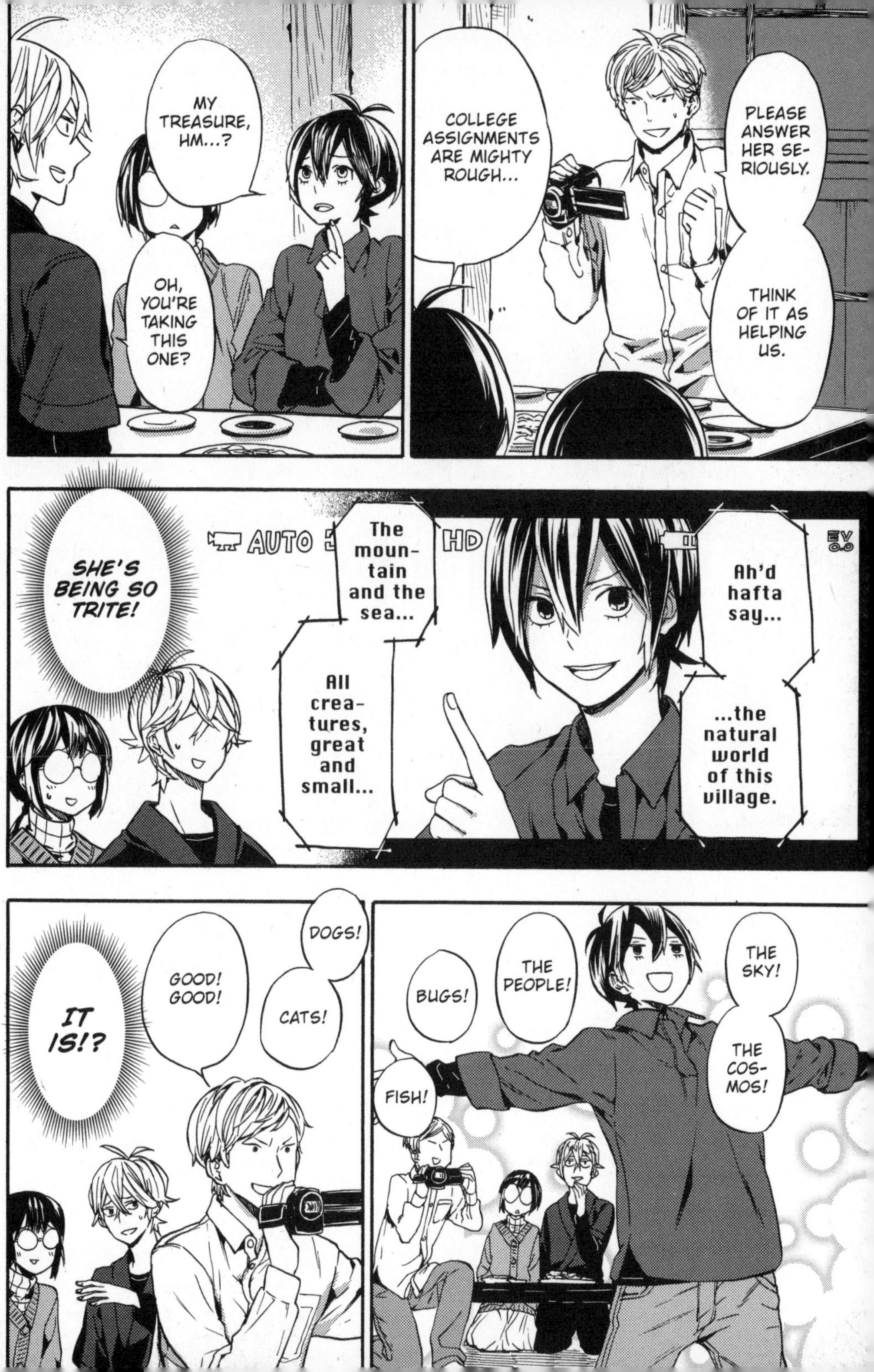
PLEASE ANSWER HER SERIOUSLY.
COLLEGE ASSIGNMENTS ARE MIGHTY ROUGH...
THINK OF IT AS HELPING US.
MY TREASURE, HM...?
OH, YOU'RE TAKING THIS ONE?
AUTO
HD
Ah'd hafta say...
...the natural world of this village.
The mountain and the sea...
All creatures, great and small...
SHE'S BEING SO TRITE!
THE SKY!
THE COSMOS!
THE PEOPLE!
BUGS!
FISH!
DOGS!
CATS!
GOOD! GOOD!
IT IS!?

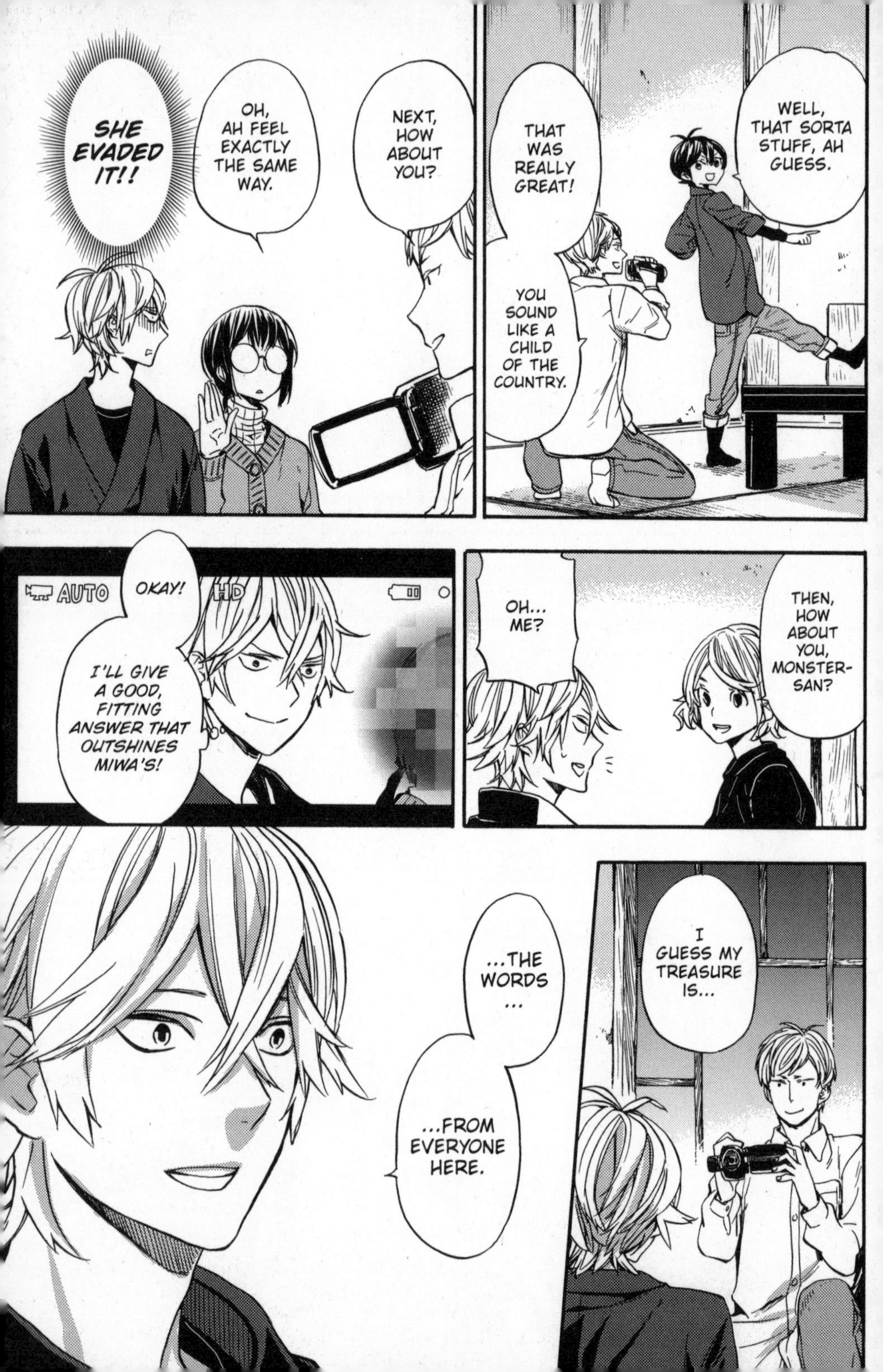
WELL, THAT SORTA STUFF, AH GUESS.
THAT WAS REALLY GREAT!
YOU SOUND LIKE A CHILD OF THE COUNTRY.
NEXT, HOW ABOUT YOU?
OH, AH FEEL EXACTLY THE SAME WAY.
SHE EVADED IT!!
THEN, HOW ABOUT YOU, MONSTER-SAN?
OH... ME?
AUTO
HD
OKAY!
I'LL GIVE A GOOD, FITTING ANSWER THAT OUTSHINES MIWA'S!
I GUESS MY TREASURE IS...
...THE WORDS ...
...FROM EVERYONE HERE.

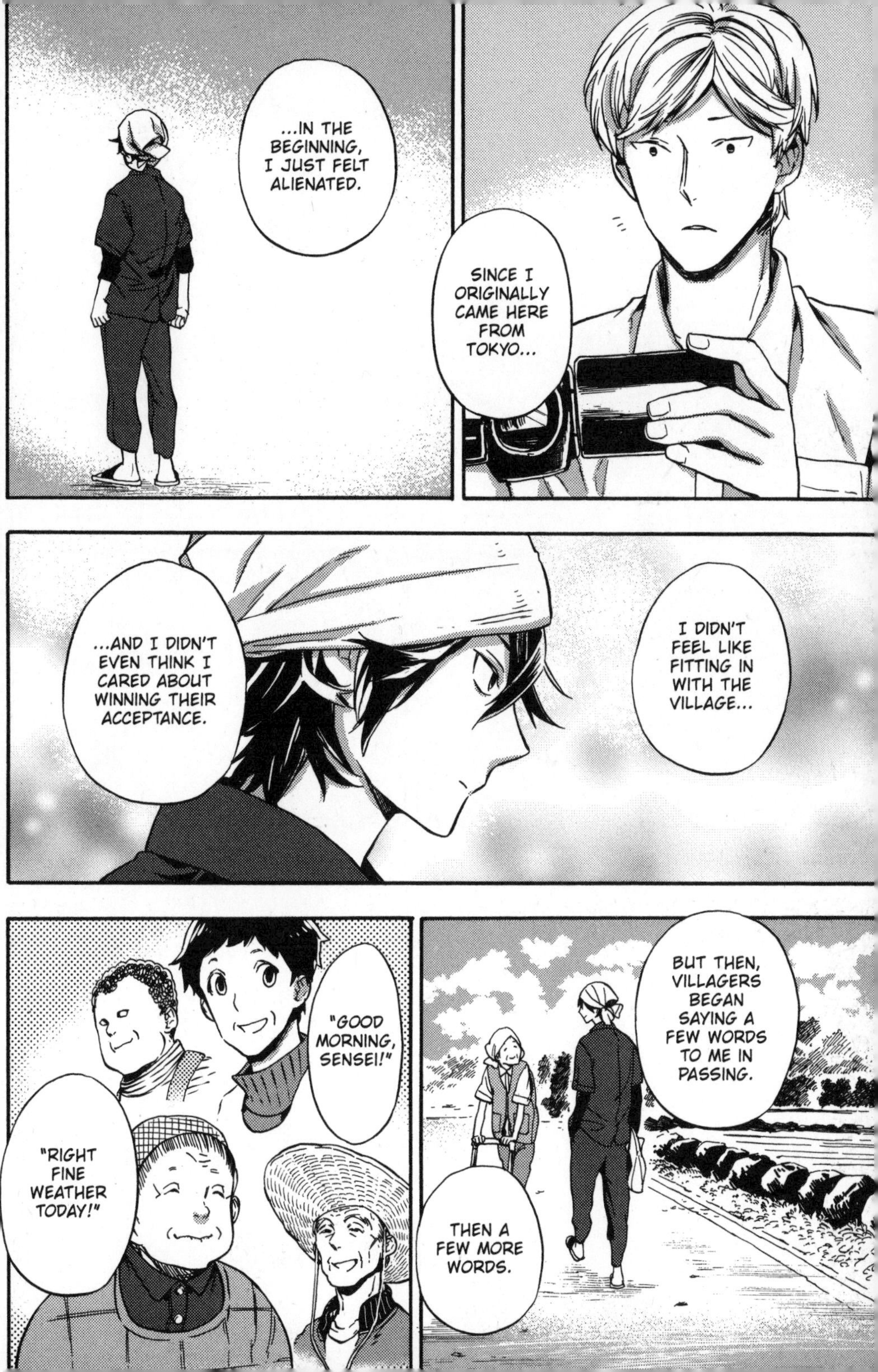
SINCE I ORIGINALLY CAME HERE FROM TOKYO...
...IN THE BEGINNING, I JUST FELT ALIENATED.
I DIDN'T FEEL LIKE FITTING IN WITH THE VILLAGE...
...AND I DIDN'T EVEN THINK I CARED ABOUT WINNING THEIR ACCEPTANCE.
BUT THEN, VILLAGERS BEGAN SAYING A FEW WORDS TO ME IN PASSING.
THEN A FEW MORE WORDS.
"GOOD MORNING, SENSEI!"
"RIGHT FINE WEATHER TODAY!"

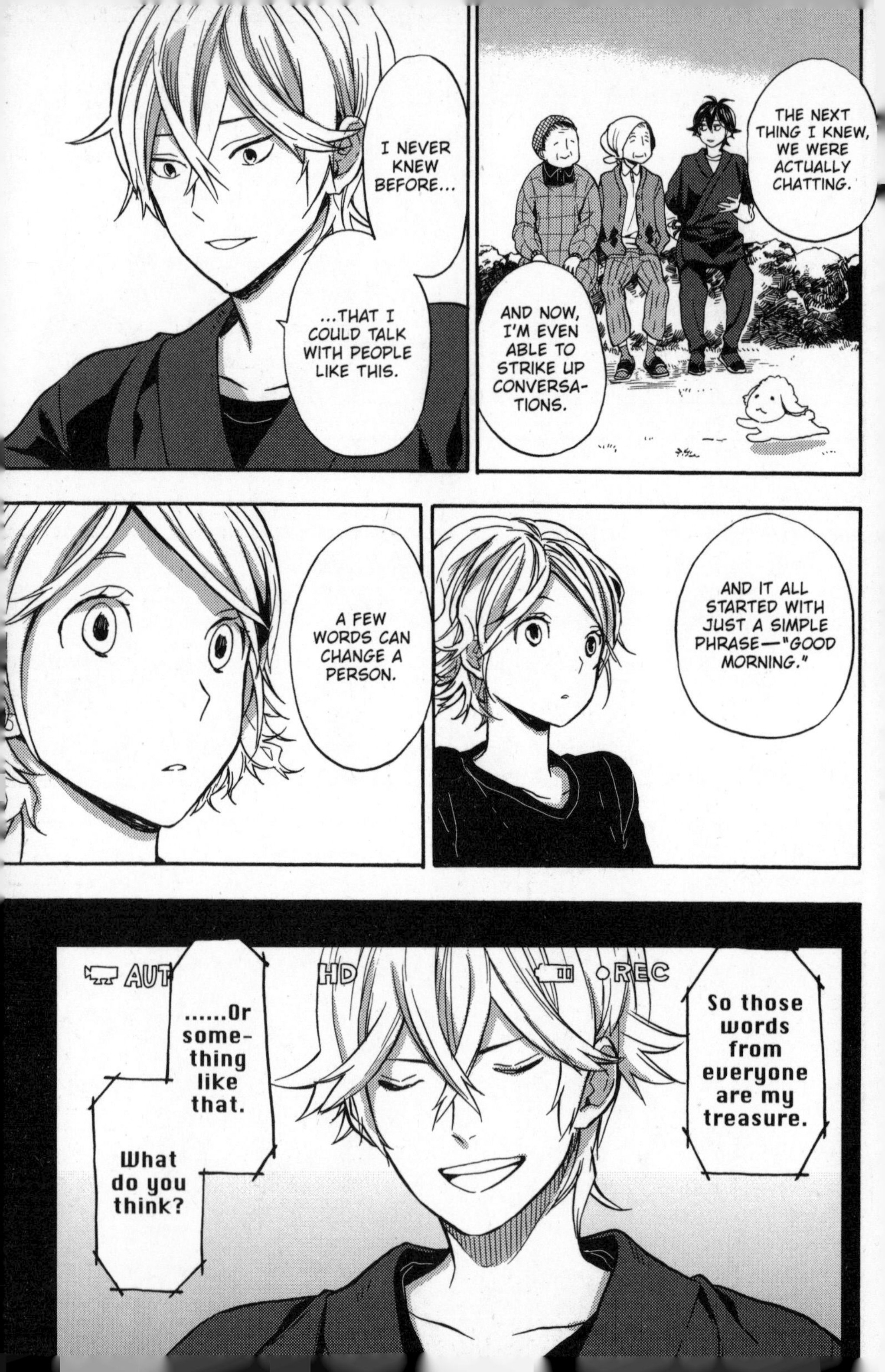
THE NEXT THING I KNEW, WE WERE ACTUALLY CHATTING.
AND NOW, I'M EVEN ABLE TO STRIKE UP CONVERSATIONS.
I NEVER KNEW BEFORE...
...THAT I COULD TALK WITH PEOPLE LIKE THIS.
AND IT ALL STARTED WITH JUST A SIMPLE PHRASE—"GOOD MORNING."
A FEW WORDS CAN CHANGE A PERSON.
AUT
HD
REC
So those words from everyone are my treasure.
......Or something like that.
What do you think?

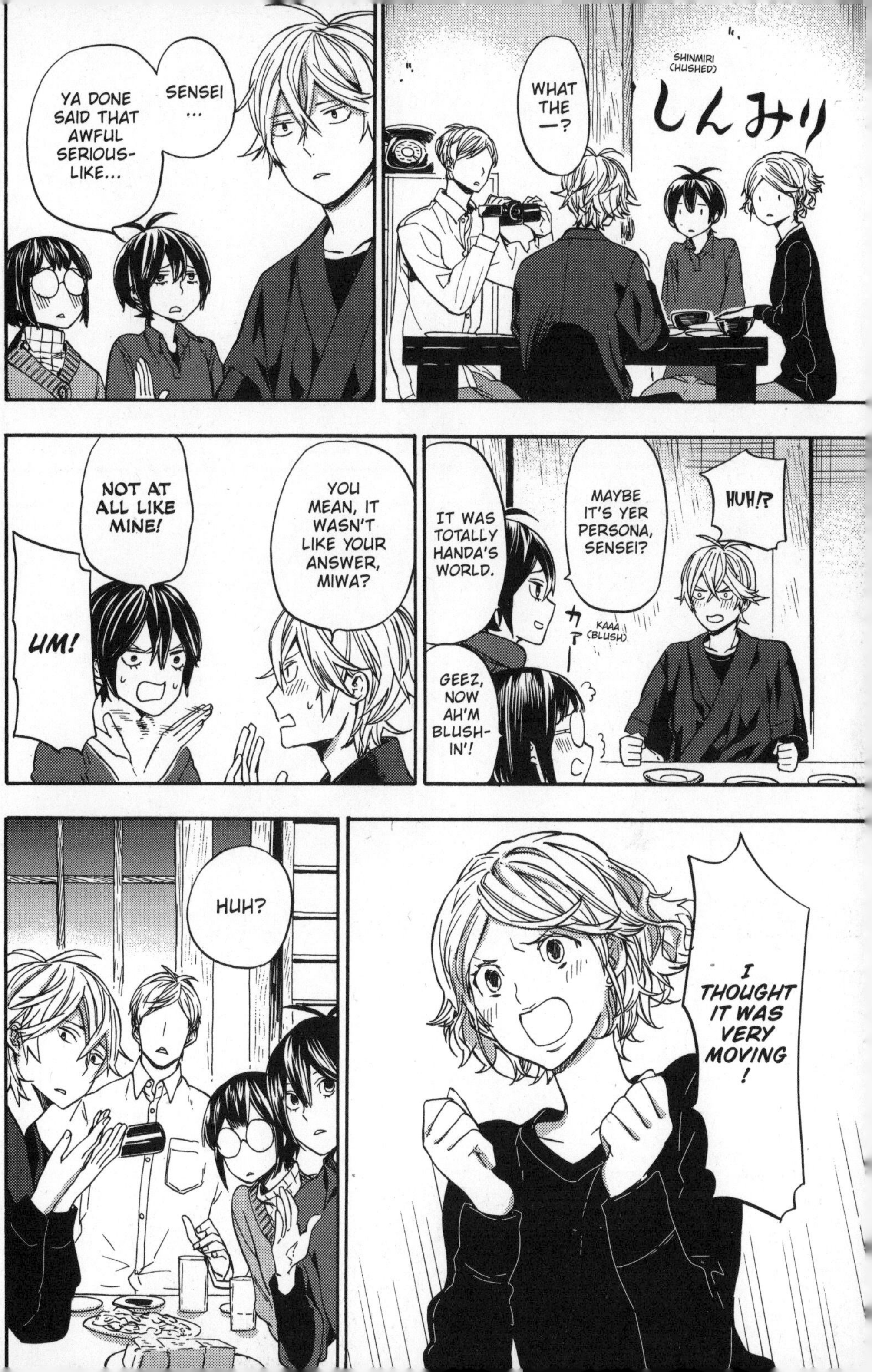

WHAT THE一?
しんみり
SHINMIRI (HUSHED)
SENSEI ...
YA DONE SAID THAT AWFUL SERIOUS-LIKE...
HUH!?
MAYBE IT'S YER PERSONA, SENSEI?
IT WAS TOTALLY HANDA'S WORLD.
カァー
KAAA (BLUSH)
GEEZ, NOW AH'M BLUSHIN'!
YOU MEAN, IT WASN'T LIKE YOUR ANSWER, MIWA?
NOT AT ALL LIKE MINE!
UM!
I THOUGHT IT WAS VERY MOVING!
HUH?

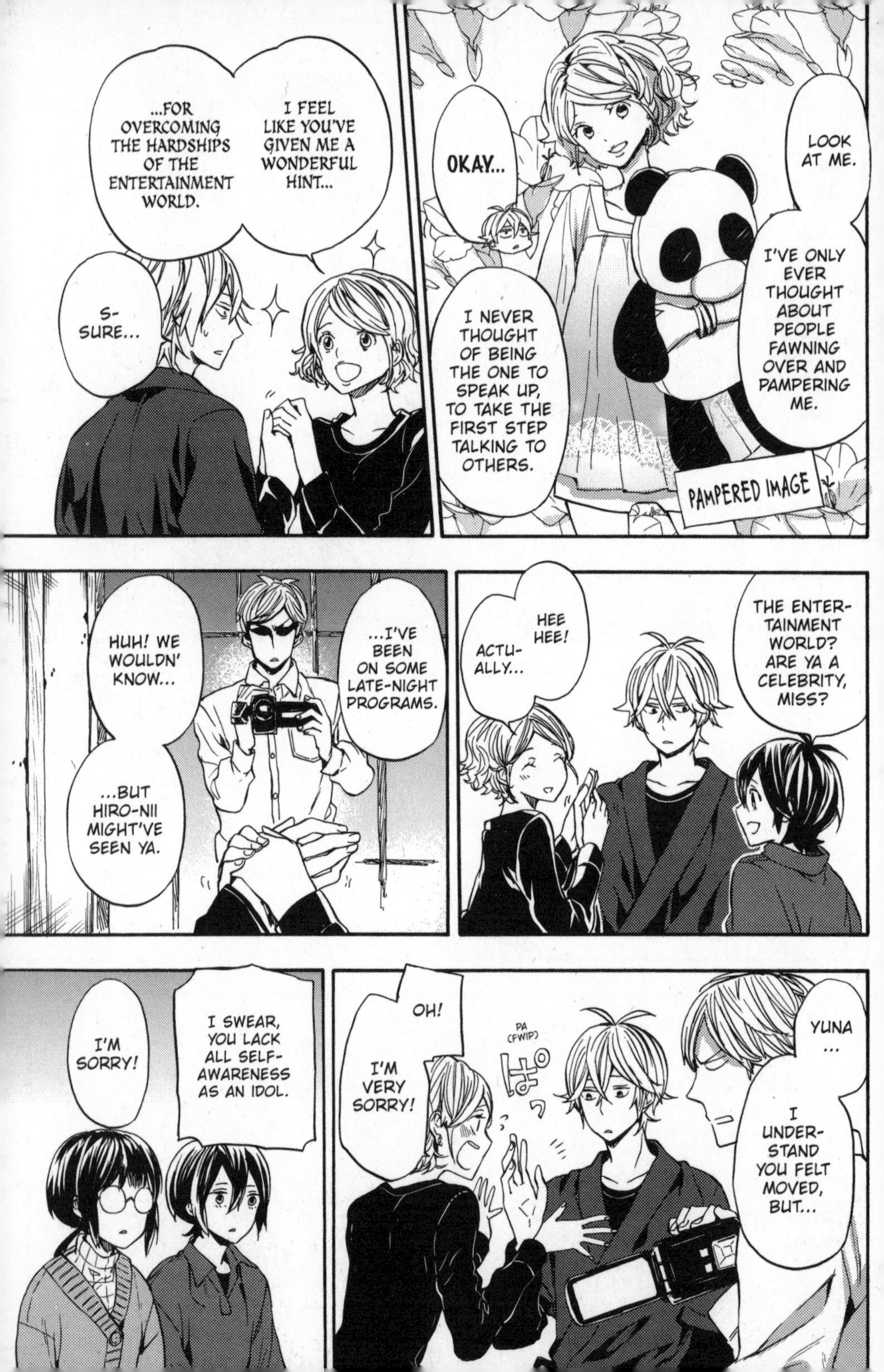
LOOK AT ME.
I'VE ONLY EVER THOUGHT ABOUT PEOPLE FAWNING OVER AND PAMPERING ME.
OKAY...
I NEVER THOUGHT OF BEING THE ONE TO SPEAK UP, TO TAKE THE FIRST STEP TALKING TO OTHERS.
PAMPERED IMAGE
I FEEL LIKE YOU'VE GIVEN ME A WONDERFUL HINT...
...FOR OVERCOMING THE HARDSHIPS OF THE ENTERTAINMENT WORLD.
S-SURE...
THE ENTER-TAINMENT WORLD? ARE YA A CELEBRITY, MISS?
HEE HEE!
ACTU-ALLY...
...I'VE BEEN ON SOME LATE-NIGHT PROGRAMS.
HUH! WE WOULDN' KNOW...
...BUT HIRO-NII MIGHT'VE SEEN YA.
YUNA...
I UNDER-STAND YOU FELT MOVED, BUT...
PA (FWIP)
ぱっ
OH!
I'M VERY SORRY!
I SWEAR, YOU LACK ALL SELF-AWARENESS AS AN IDOL.
I'M SORRY!

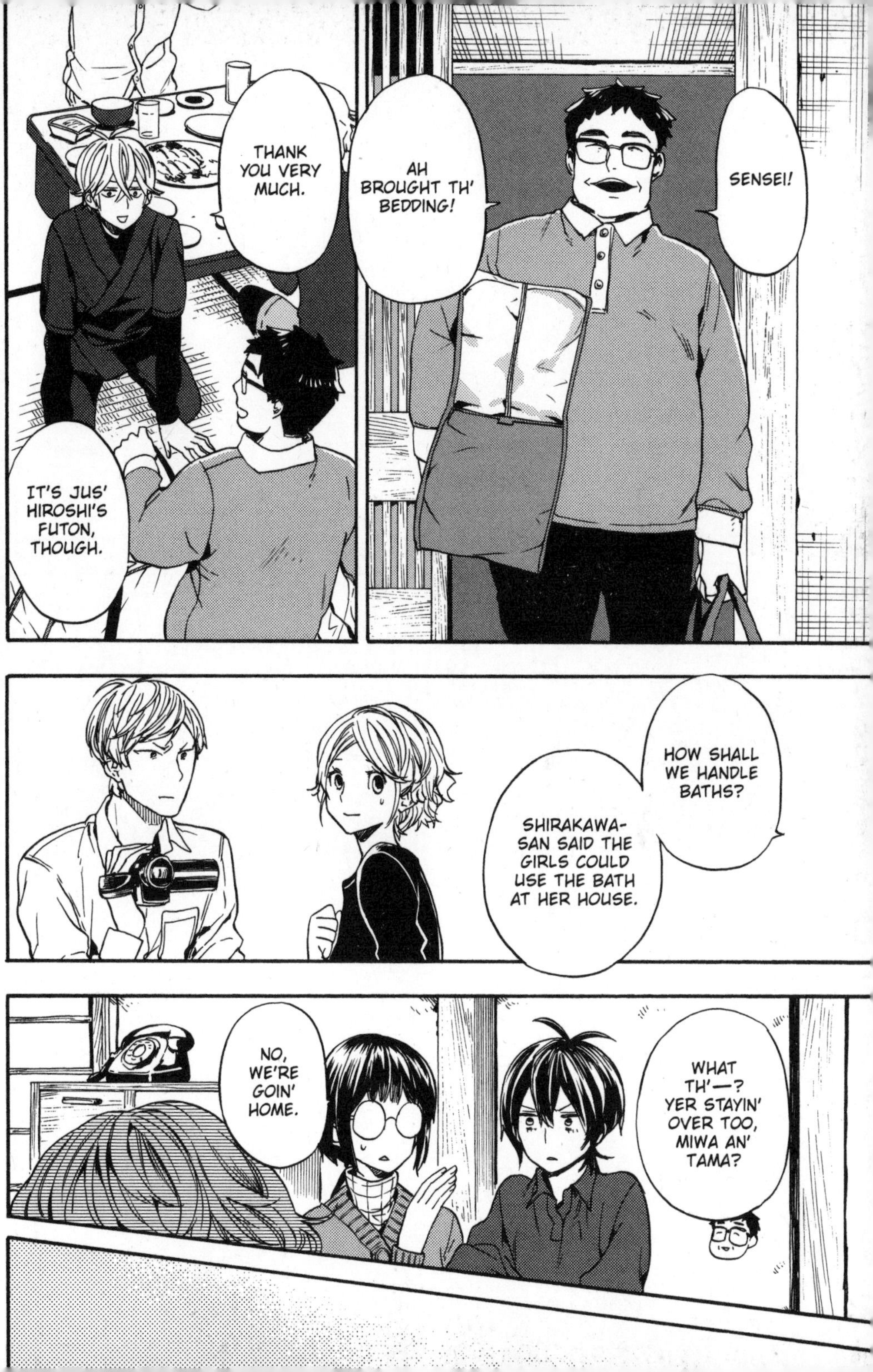
SENSEI!
AH BROUGHT TH' BEDDING!
THANK YOU VERY MUCH.
IT'S JUS' HIROSHI'S FUTON, THOUGH.
HOW SHALL WE HANDLE BATHS?
SHIRAKAWA-SAN SAID THE GIRLS COULD USE THE BATH AT HER HOUSE.
WHAT TH'—? YER STAYIN' OVER TOO, MIWA AN' TAMA?
NO, WE'RE GOIN' HOME.

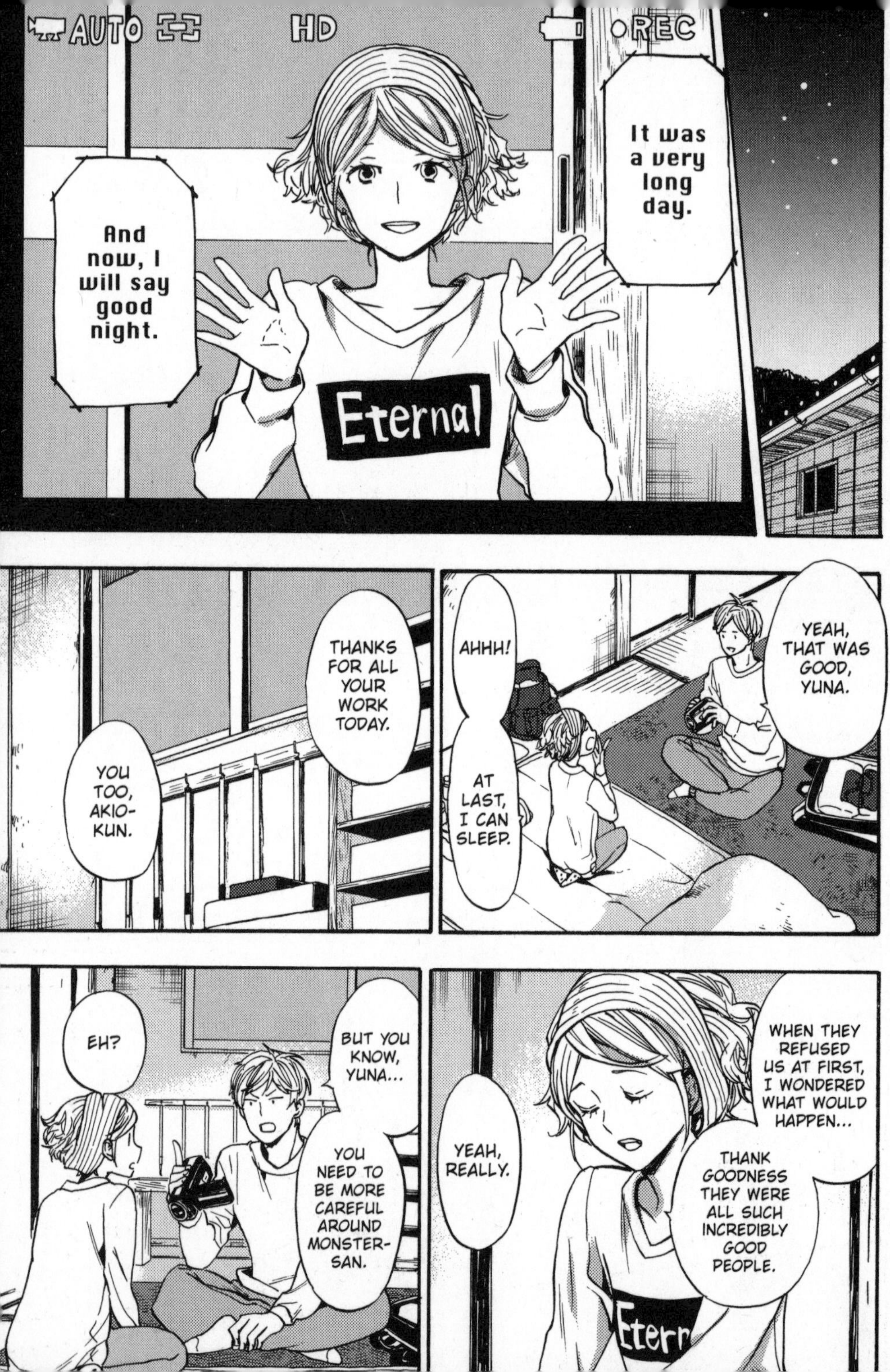
AUTO
HD
REC
It was a very long day.
And now, I will say good night.
Eternal
YEAH, THAT WAS GOOD, YUNA.
AHHH!
AT LAST, I CAN SLEEP.
THANKS FOR ALL YOUR WORK TODAY.
YOU TOO, AKIO-KUN.
WHEN THEY REFUSED US AT FIRST, I WONDERED WHAT WOULD HAPPEN...
THANK GOODNESS THEY WERE ALL SUCH INCREDIBLY GOOD PEOPLE.
YEAH, REALLY.
BUT YOU KNOW, YUNA...
YOU NEED TO BE MORE CAREFUL AROUND MONSTER-SAN.
EH?

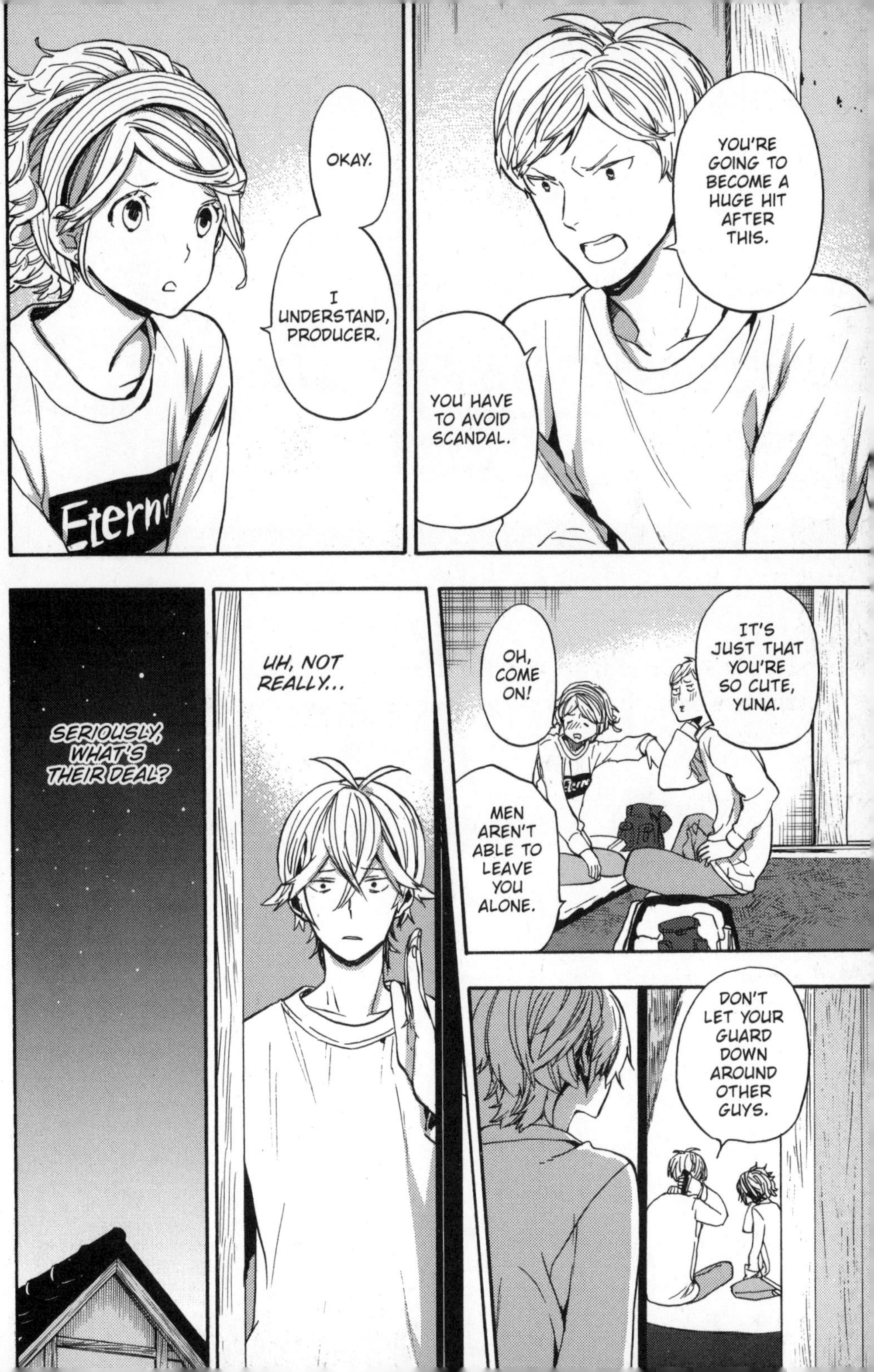

YOU'RE GOING TO BECOME A HUGE HIT AFTER THIS.
YOU HAVE TO AVOID SCANDAL.
OKAY.
I UNDERSTAND, PRODUCER.
Eterna
IT'S JUST THAT YOU'RE SO CUTE, YUNA.
OH, COME ON!
MEN AREN'T ABLE TO LEAVE YOU ALONE.
DON'T LET YOUR GUARD DOWN AROUND OTHER GUYS.
UH, NOT REALLY...
SERIOUSLY, WHAT'S THEIR DEAL?

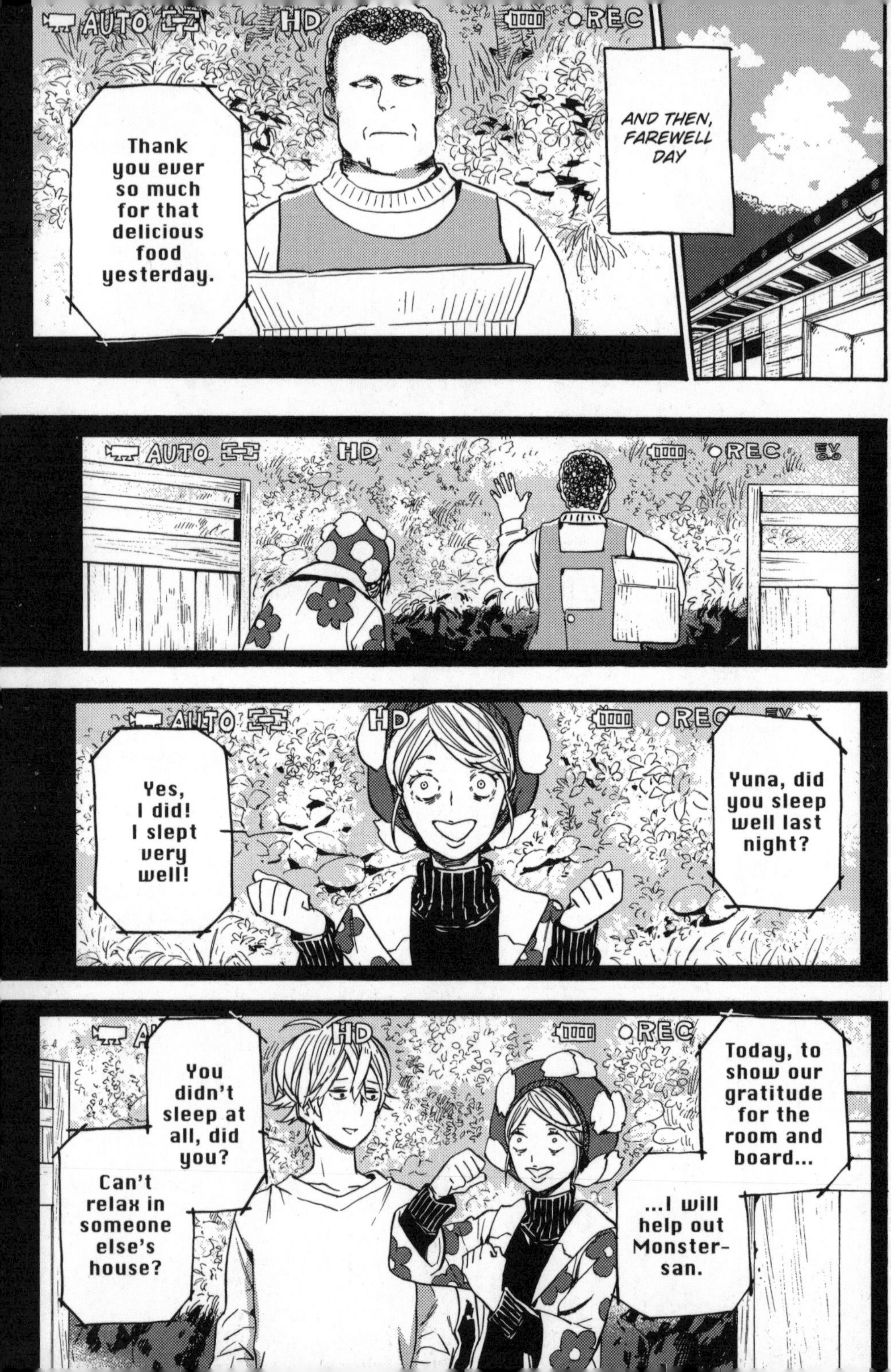
AND THEN, FAREWELL DAY
AUTO HD REC
Thank you ever so much for that delicious food yesterday.
AUTO HD REC
AUTO HD REC
Yuna, did you sleep well last night?
Yes, I did! I slept very well!
HD REC
Today, to show our gratitude for the room and board...
...I will help out Monster-san.
You didn't sleep at all, did you?
Can't relax in someone else's house?

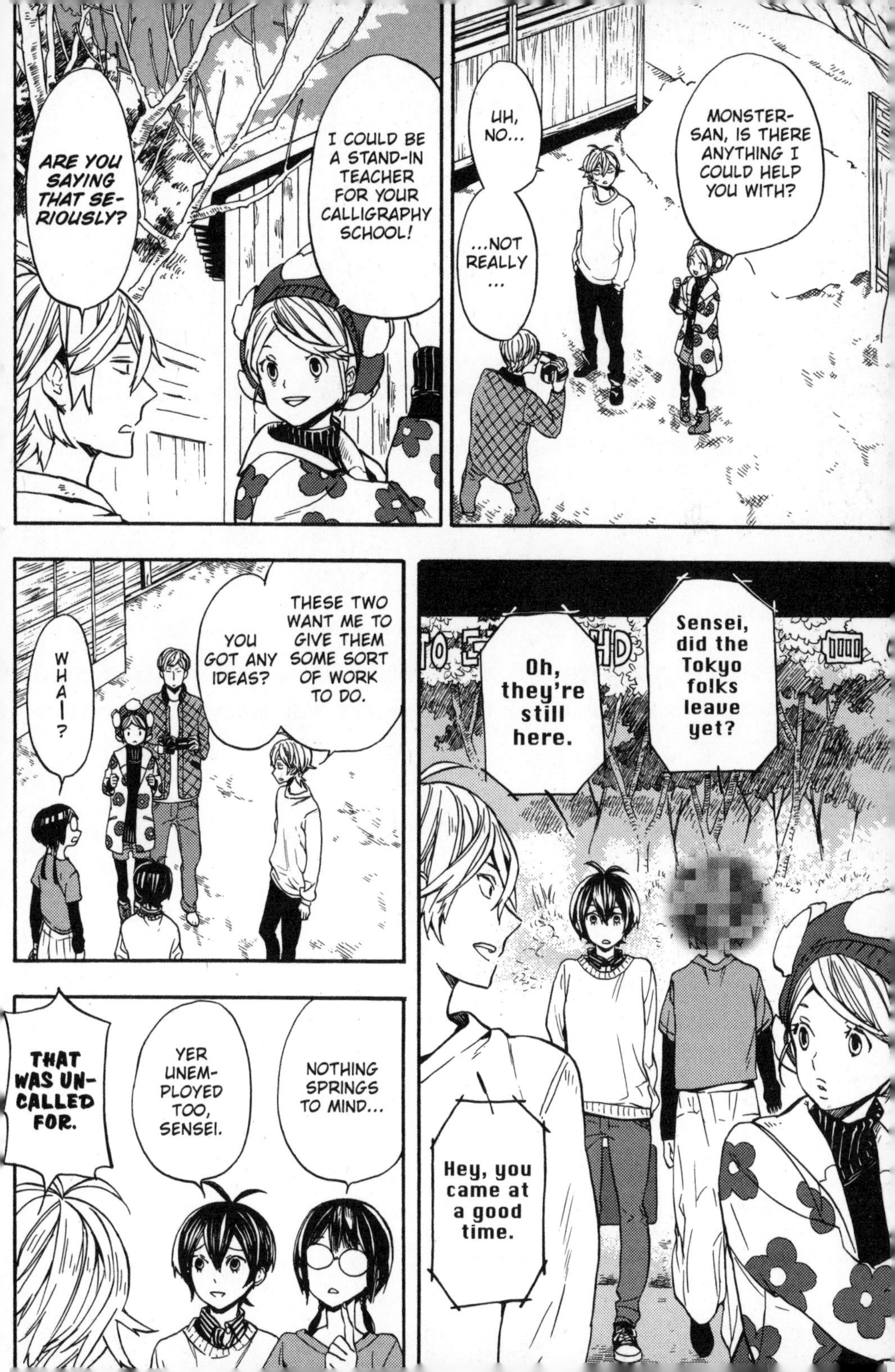

MONSTER-SAN, IS THERE ANYTHING I COULD HELP YOU WITH?
UH, NO...
...NOT REALLY...
I COULD BE A STAND-IN TEACHER FOR YOUR CALLIGRAPHY SCHOOL!
ARE YOU SAYING THAT SERIOUSLY?
Sensei, did the Tokyo folks leave yet?
Oh, they're still here.
Hey, you came at a good time.
THESE TWO WANT ME TO GIVE THEM SOME SORT OF WORK TO DO.
YOU GOT ANY IDEAS?
WHA—?
NOTHING SPRINGS TO MIND...
YER UNEMPLOYED TOO, SENSEI.
THAT WAS UNCALLED FOR.

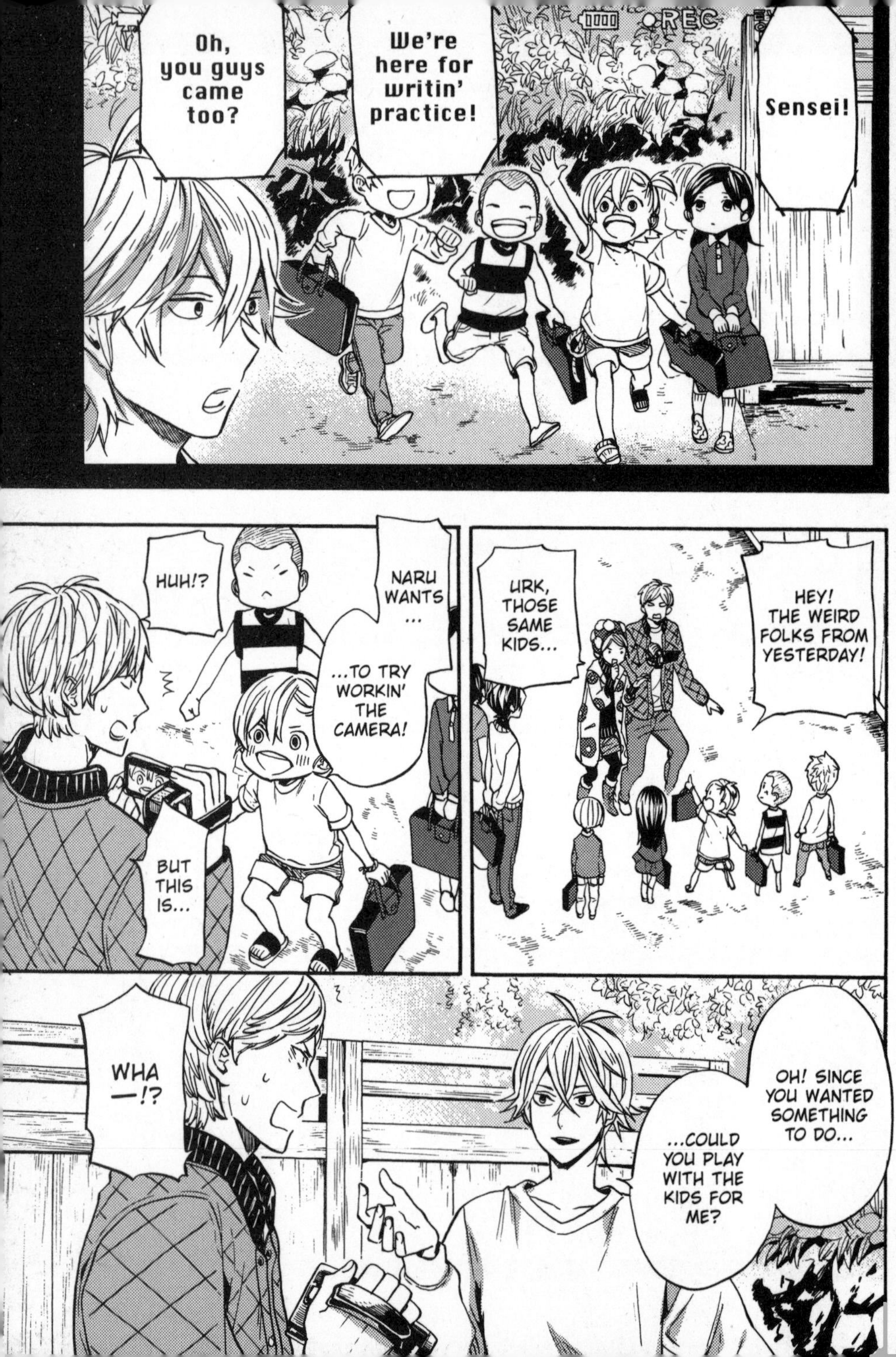
Sensei!
REC
We're here for writin' practice!
Oh, you guys came too?
HEY! THE WEIRD FOLKS FROM YESTERDAY!
URK, THOSE SAME KIDS...
NARU WANTS ...
...TO TRY WORKIN' THE CAMERA!
HUH!?
BUT THIS IS...
OH! SINCE YOU WANTED SOMETHING TO DO...
...COULD YOU PLAY WITH THE KIDS FOR ME?
WHA—!?

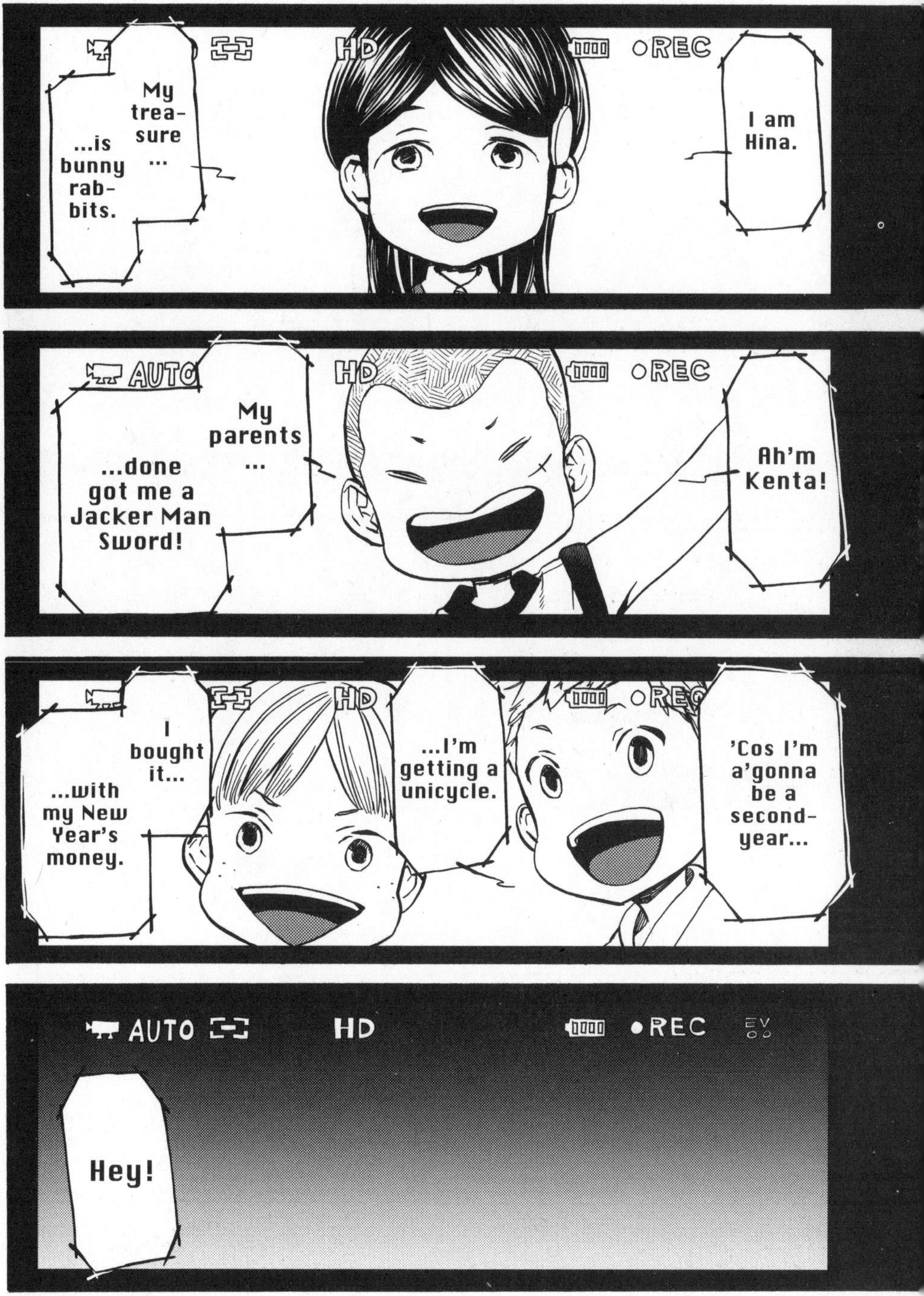
I am Hina.
My treasure...
...is bunny rabbits.
Ah'm Kenta!
My parents...
...done got me a Jacker Man Sword!
'Cos I'm a'gonna be a second-year...
...I'm getting a unicycle.
I bought it...
...with my New Year's money.
Hey!

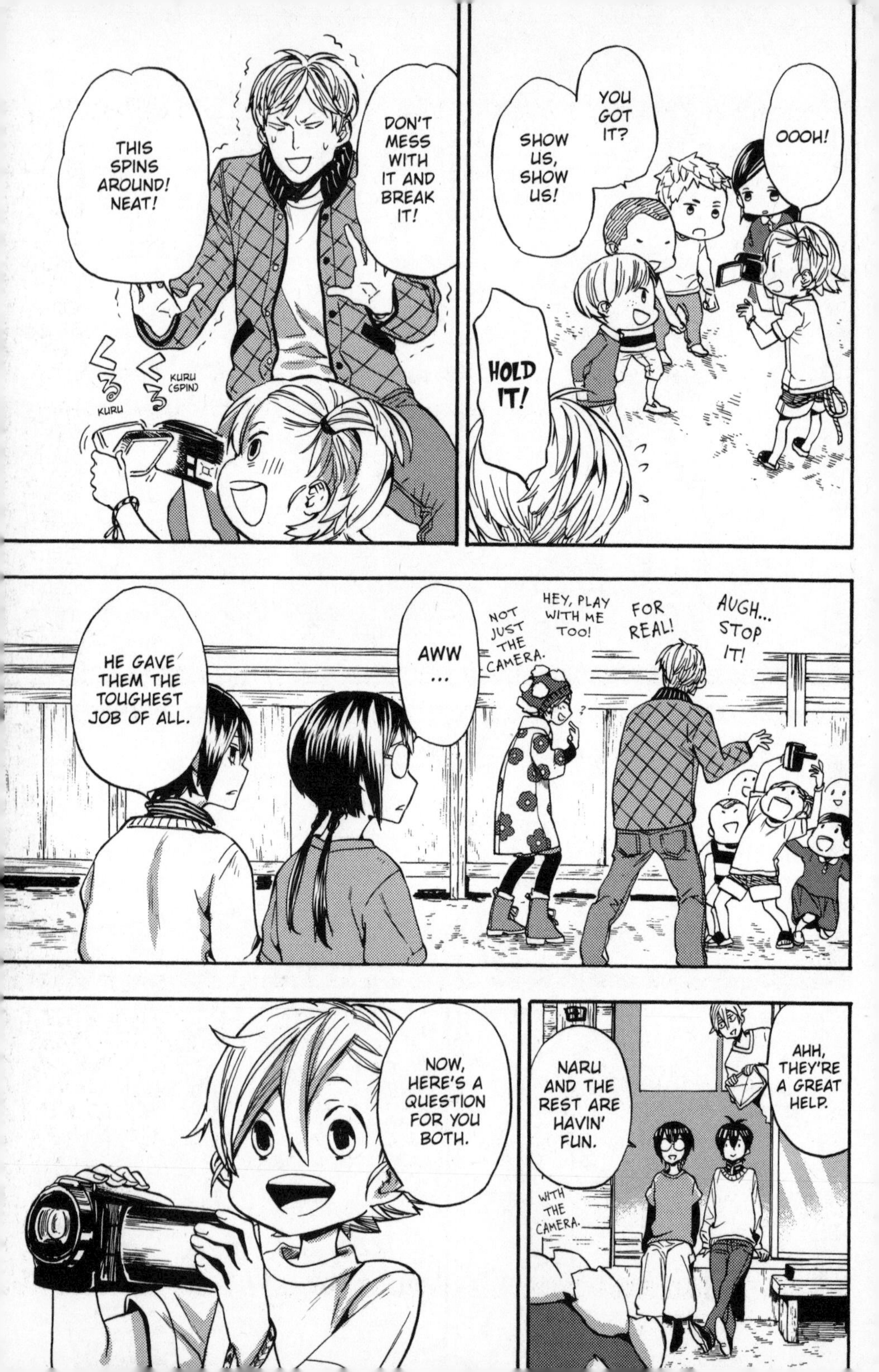
OOOH!
YOU GOT IT?
SHOW US, SHOW US!
HOLD IT!
DON'T MESS WITH IT AND BREAK IT!
THIS SPINS AROUND! NEAT!
KURU (SPIN)
KURU
AUGH... STOP IT!
FOR REAL!
HEY, PLAY WITH ME TOO!
NOT JUST THE CAMERA.
AWW ...
HE GAVE THEM THE TOUGHEST JOB OF ALL.
AHH, THEY'RE A GREAT HELP.
NARU AND THE REST ARE HAVIN' FUN.
WITH THE CAMERA.
NOW, HERE'S A QUESTION FOR YOU BOTH.

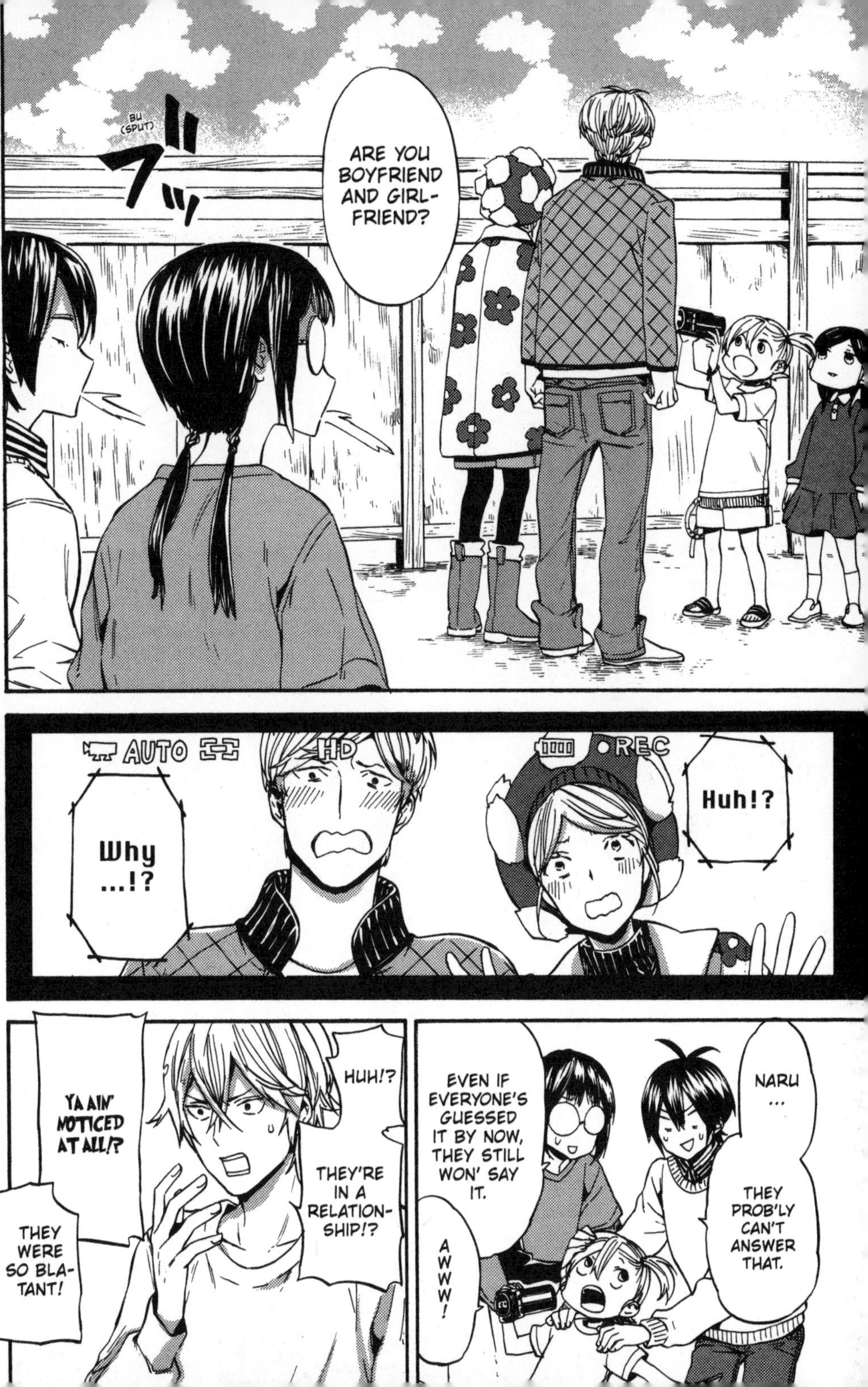
ARE YOU BOYFRIEND AND GIRL-FRIEND?
BU (SPUT)
Huh!?
Why ...!?
NARU ...
THEY PROB'LY CAN'T ANSWER THAT.
EVEN IF EVERYONE'S GUESSED IT BY NOW, THEY STILL WON' SAY IT.
AWWW!
HUH!?
THEY'RE IN A RELATIONSHIP!?
YA AIN' NOTICED AT ALL!?
THEY WERE SO BLA-TANT!

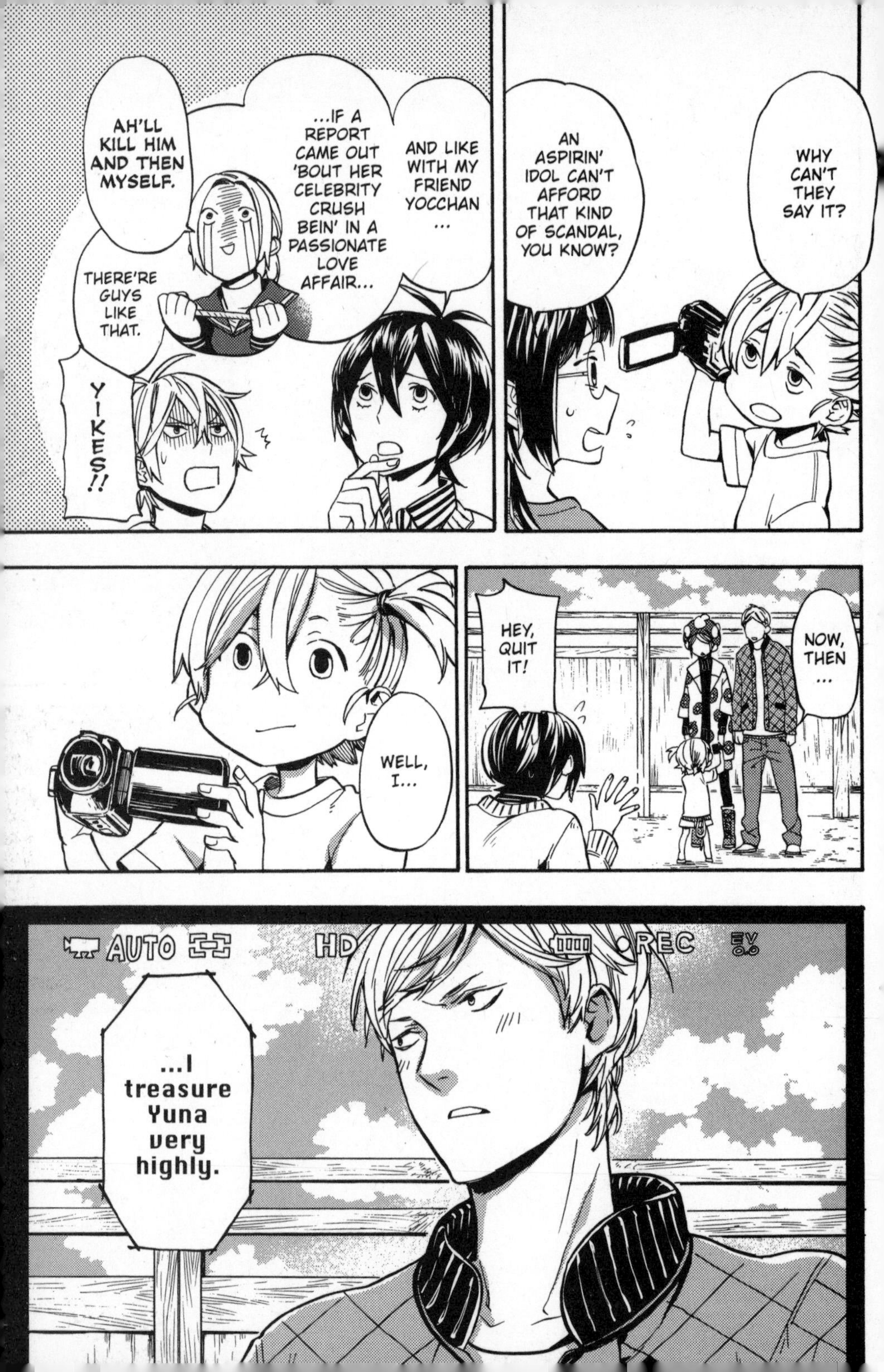
WHY CAN'T THEY SAY IT?
AN ASPIRIN' IDOL CAN'T AFFORD THAT KIND OF SCANDAL, YOU KNOW?
AND LIKE WITH MY FRIEND YOCCHAN ...
...IF A REPORT CAME OUT 'BOUT HER CELEBRITY CRUSH BEIN' IN A PASSIONATE LOVE AFFAIR...
AH'LL KILL HIM AND THEN MYSELF.
THERE'RE GUYS LIKE THAT.
YIKES!!
NOW, THEN ...
HEY, QUIT IT!
WELL, I...
AUTO
HD
REC
...I treasure Yuna very highly.

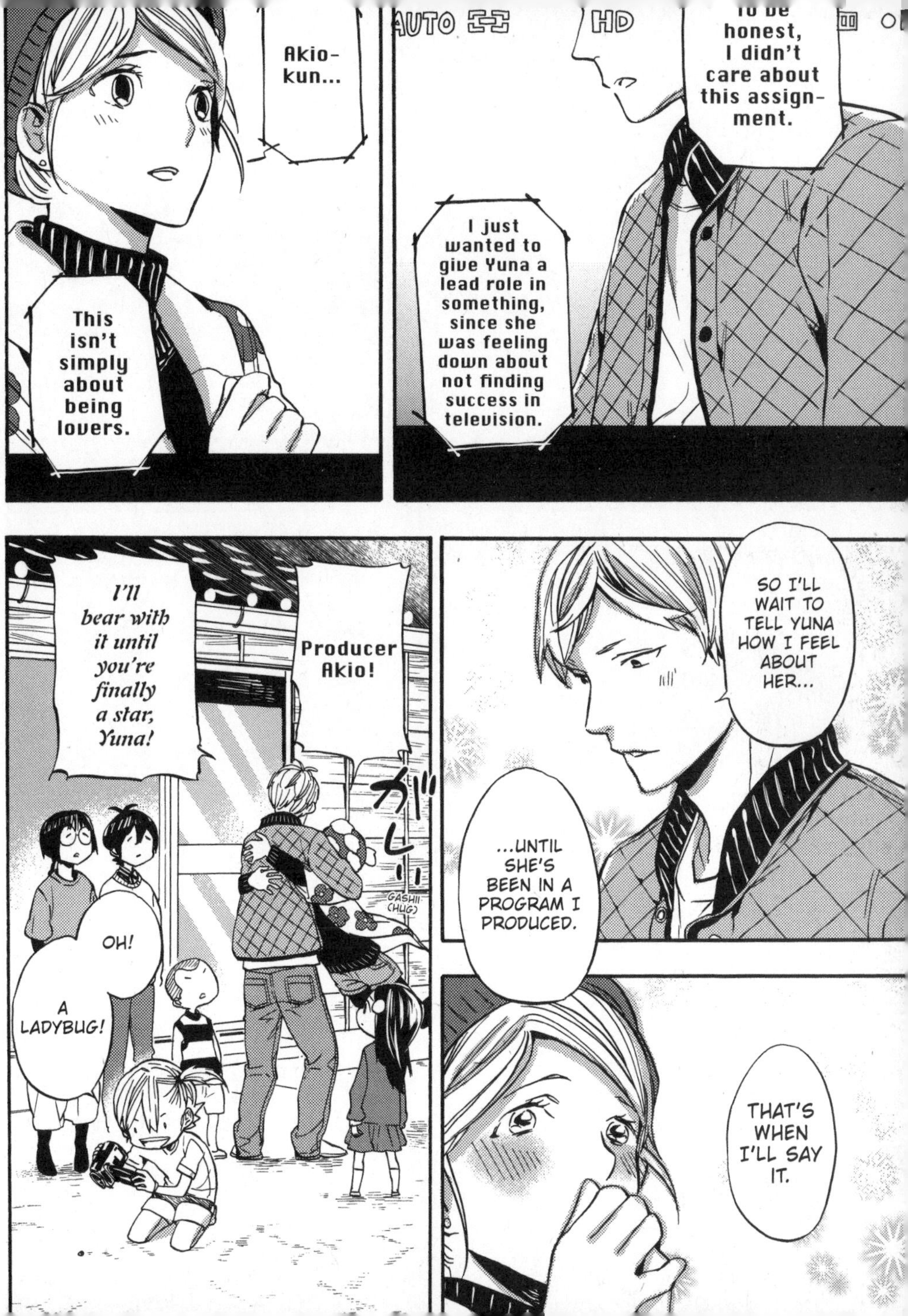
AUTO
HD
honest, I didn't care about this assignment.
I just wanted to give Yuna a lead role in something, since she was feeling down about not finding success in television.
Akio-kun...
This isn't simply about being lovers.
SO I'LL WAIT TO TELL YUNA HOW I FEEL ABOUT HER...
...UNTIL SHE'S BEEN IN A PROGRAM I PRODUCED.
THAT'S WHEN I'LL SAY IT.
I'll bear with it until you're finally a star, Yuna!
Producer Akio!
GASHI! (HUG)
OH!
A LADYBUG!

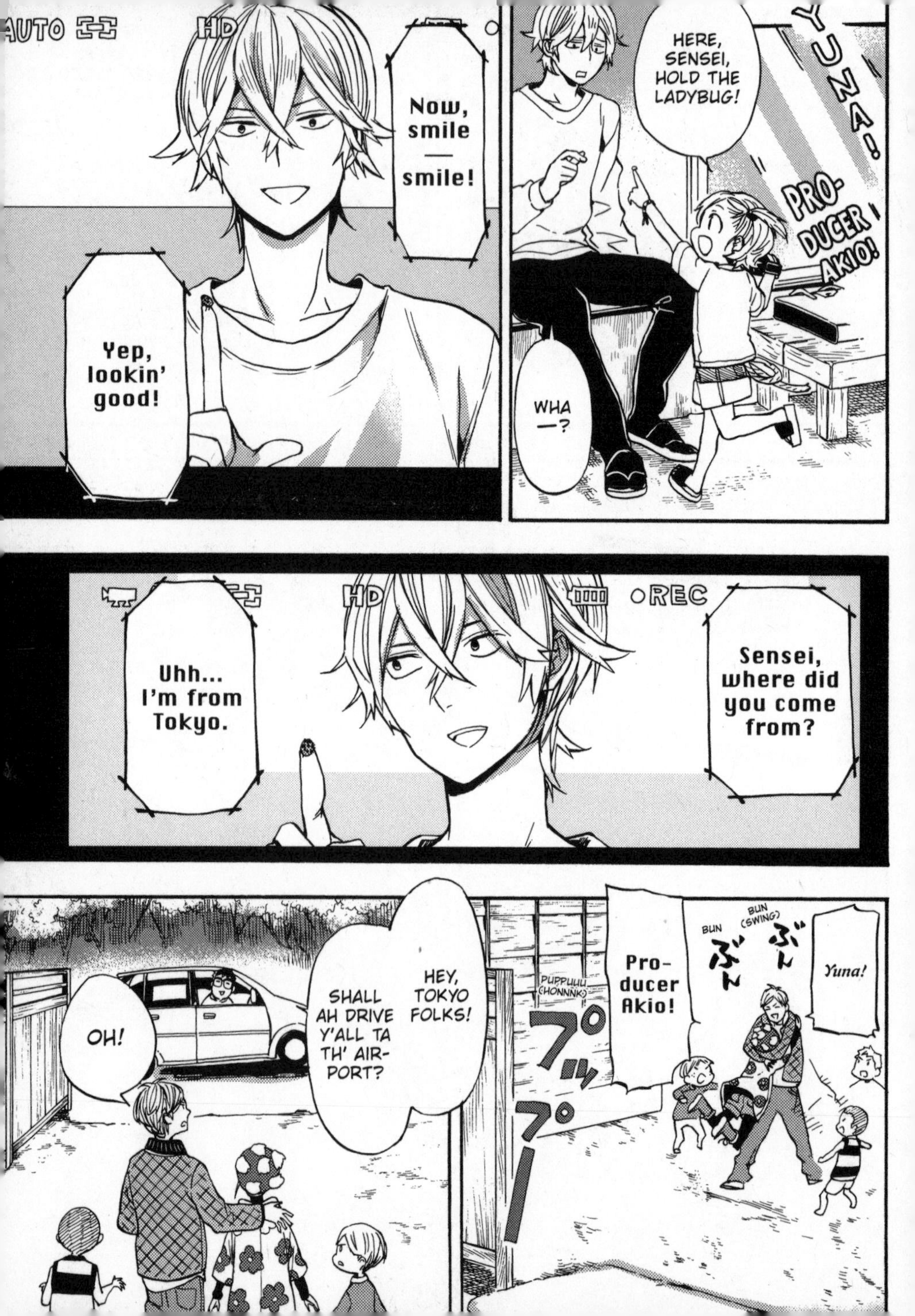
YUNA!
PRO-DUCER AKIO!
HERE, SENSEI, HOLD THE LADYBUG!
WHA—?
AUTO
HD
Now, smile—smile!
Yep, lookin' good!
HD
REC
Sensei, where did you come from?
Uhh... I'm from Tokyo.
Yuna!
BUN (SWING) ぶん
BUN ぶん
Pro-ducer Akio!
PUPPUUU (HONNNK)
プップー!
HEY, TOKYO FOLKS!
SHALL AH DRIVE Y'ALL TA TH' AIR-PORT?
OH!

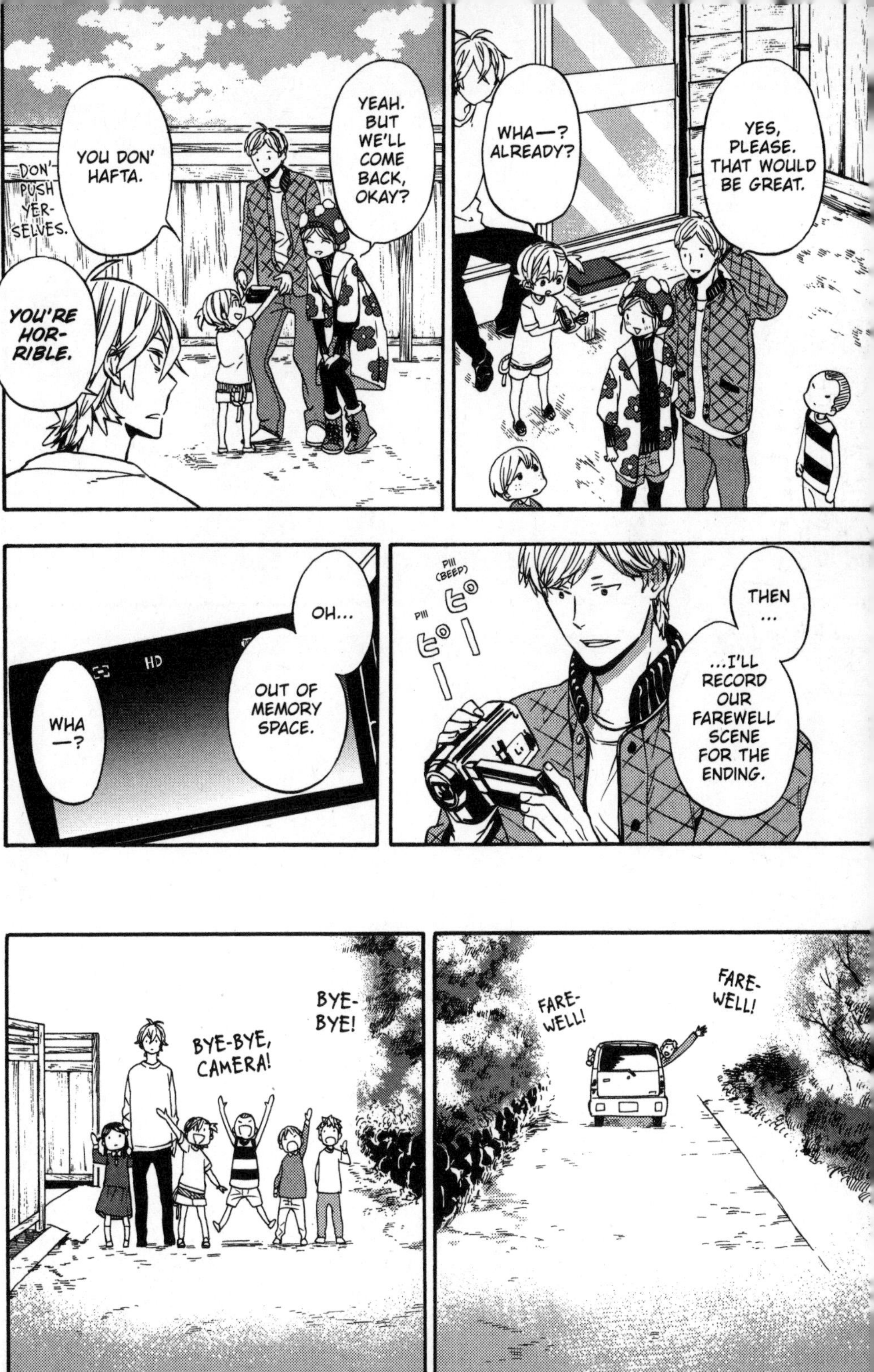
YES, PLEASE. THAT WOULD BE GREAT.
WHA—? ALREADY?
YEAH. BUT WE'LL COME BACK, OKAY?
YOU DON' HAFTA.
DON' PUSH YER-SELVES.
YOU'RE HOR-RIBLE.
PIII (BEEP)
ピー
PIII
ピー
THEN...
...I'LL RECORD OUR FAREWELL SCENE FOR THE ENDING.
OH...
OUT OF MEMORY SPACE.
HD
WHA—?
FARE-WELL!
FARE-WELL!
BYE-BYE!
BYE-BYE, CAMERA!

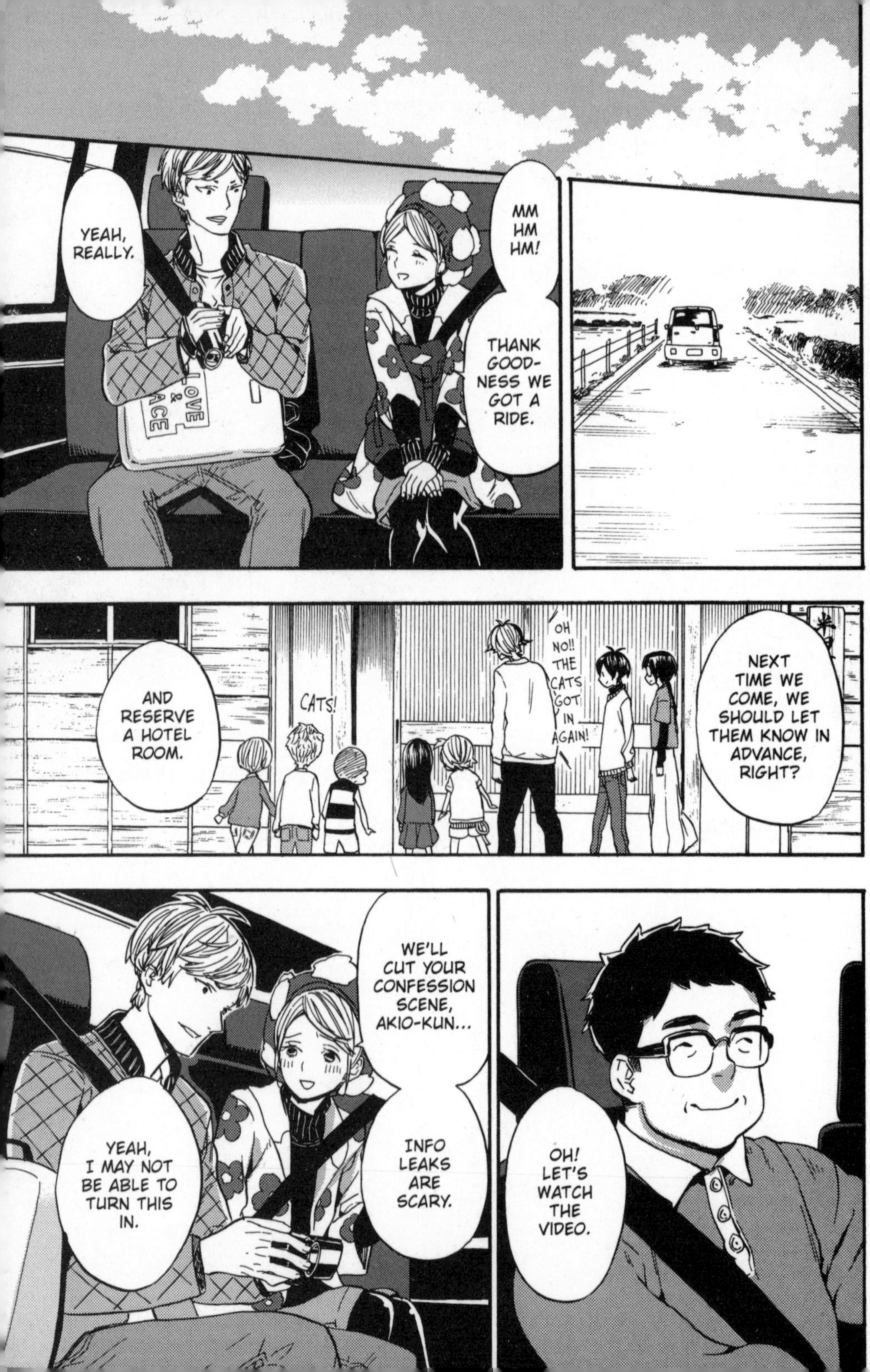
MM HM HM!
THANK GOODNESS WE GOT A RIDE.
YEAH, REALLY.
NEXT TIME WE COME, WE SHOULD LET THEM KNOW IN ADVANCE, RIGHT?
OH NO!! THE CATS GOT IN AGAIN!
CATS!
AND RESERVE A HOTEL ROOM.
OH! LET'S WATCH THE VIDEO.
WE'LL CUT YOUR CONFESSION SCENE, AKIO-KUN...
INFO LEAKS ARE SCARY.
YEAH, I MAY NOT BE ABLE TO TURN THIS IN.

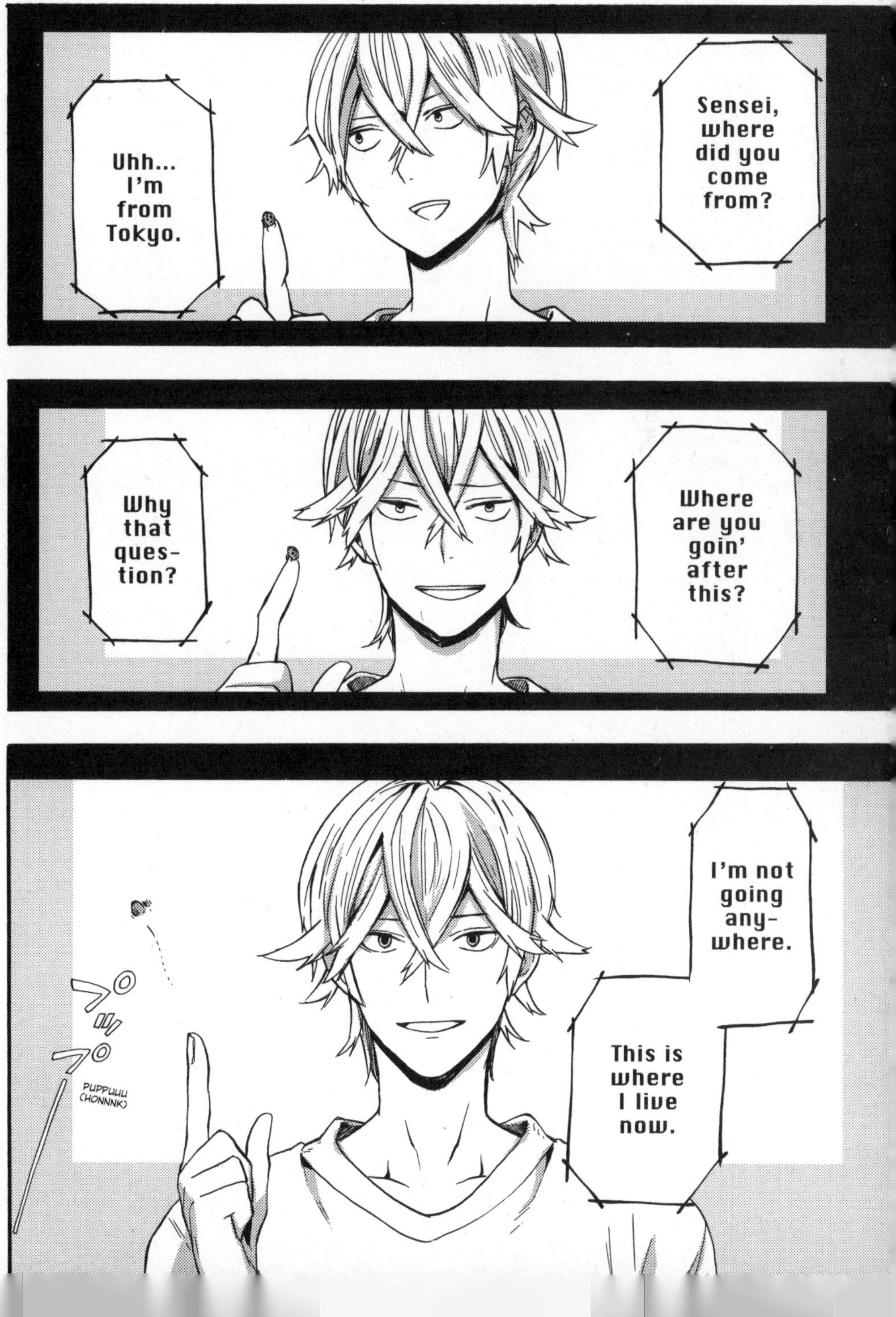

Sensei, where did you come from?
Uhh... I'm from Tokyo.
Where are you goin' after this?
Why that ques-tion?
I'm not going any-where.
This is where I live now.
PUPPUUU (HONNNK)

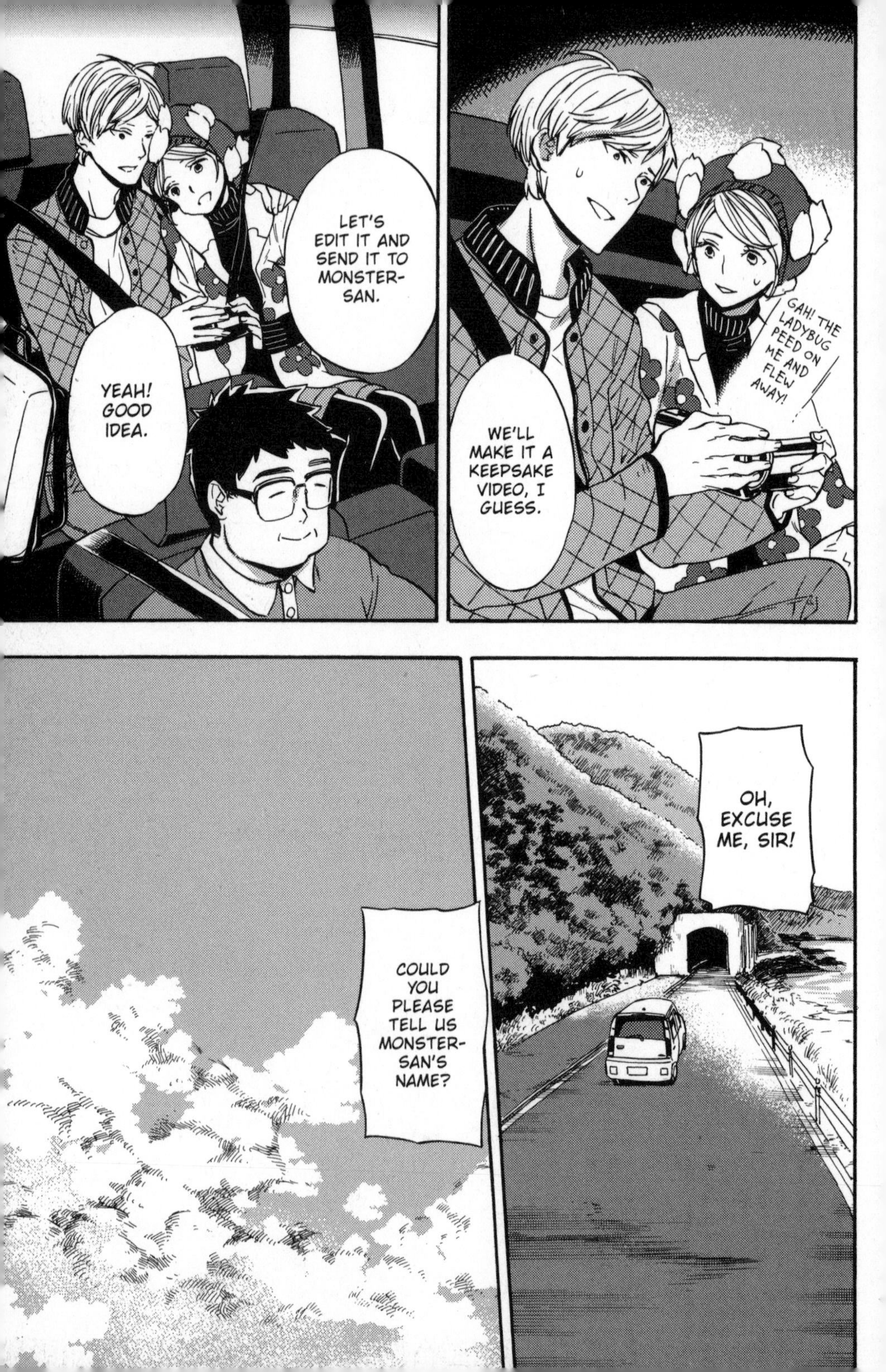
GAH! THE LADYBUG PEED ON ME AND FLEW AWAY!
WE'LL MAKE IT A KEEPSAKE VIDEO, I GUESS.
LET'S EDIT IT AND SEND IT TO MONSTER-SAN.
YEAH! GOOD IDEA.
OH, EXCUSE ME, SIR!
COULD YOU PLEASE TELL US MONSTER-SAN'S NAME?

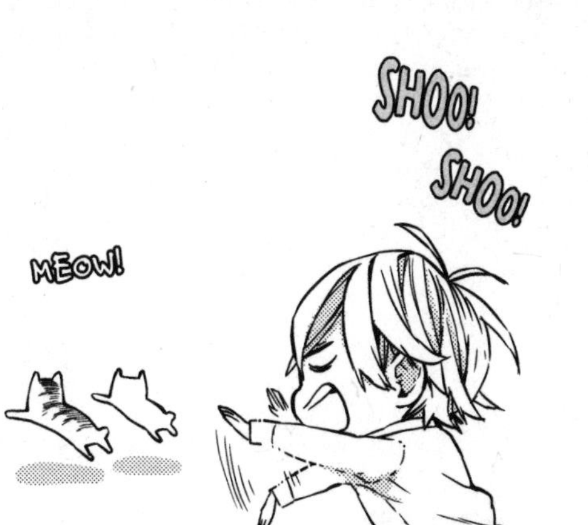
SHOO!
SHOO!
MEOW!

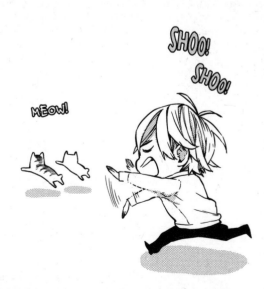

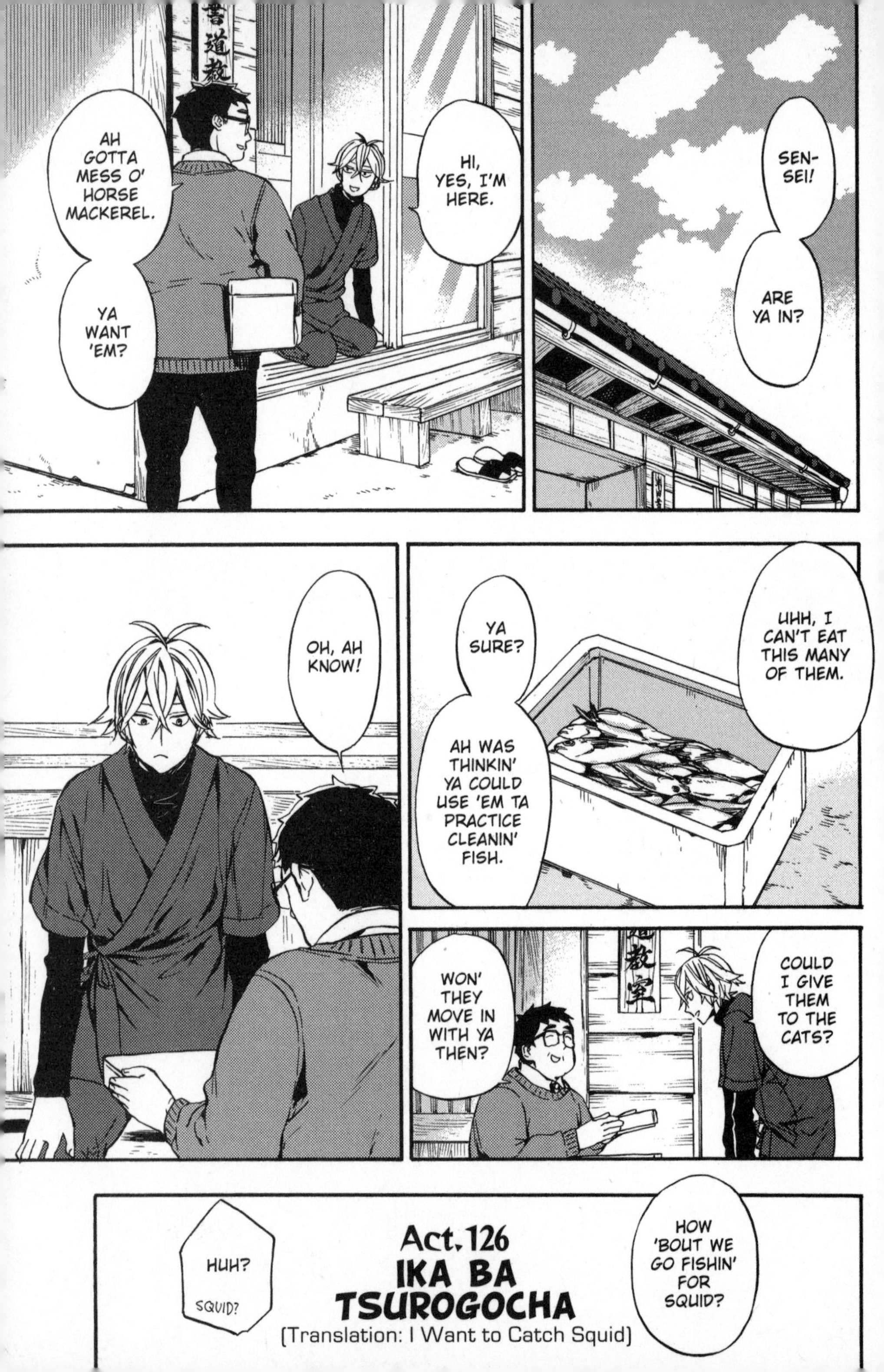
SEN-SEI!
ARE YA IN?
HI, YES, I'M HERE.
AH GOTTA MESS O' HORSE MACKEREL.
YA WANT 'EM?
UHH, I CAN'T EAT THIS MANY OF THEM.
YA SURE?
AH WAS THINKIN' YA COULD USE 'EM TA PRACTICE CLEANIN' FISH.
COULD I GIVE THEM TO THE CATS?
WON' THEY MOVE IN WITH YA THEN?
OH, AH KNOW!
HOW 'BOUT WE GO FISHIN' FOR SQUID?
Act. 126
IKA BA TSUROGOCHA
(Translation: I Want to Catch Squid)
HUH?
SQUID?

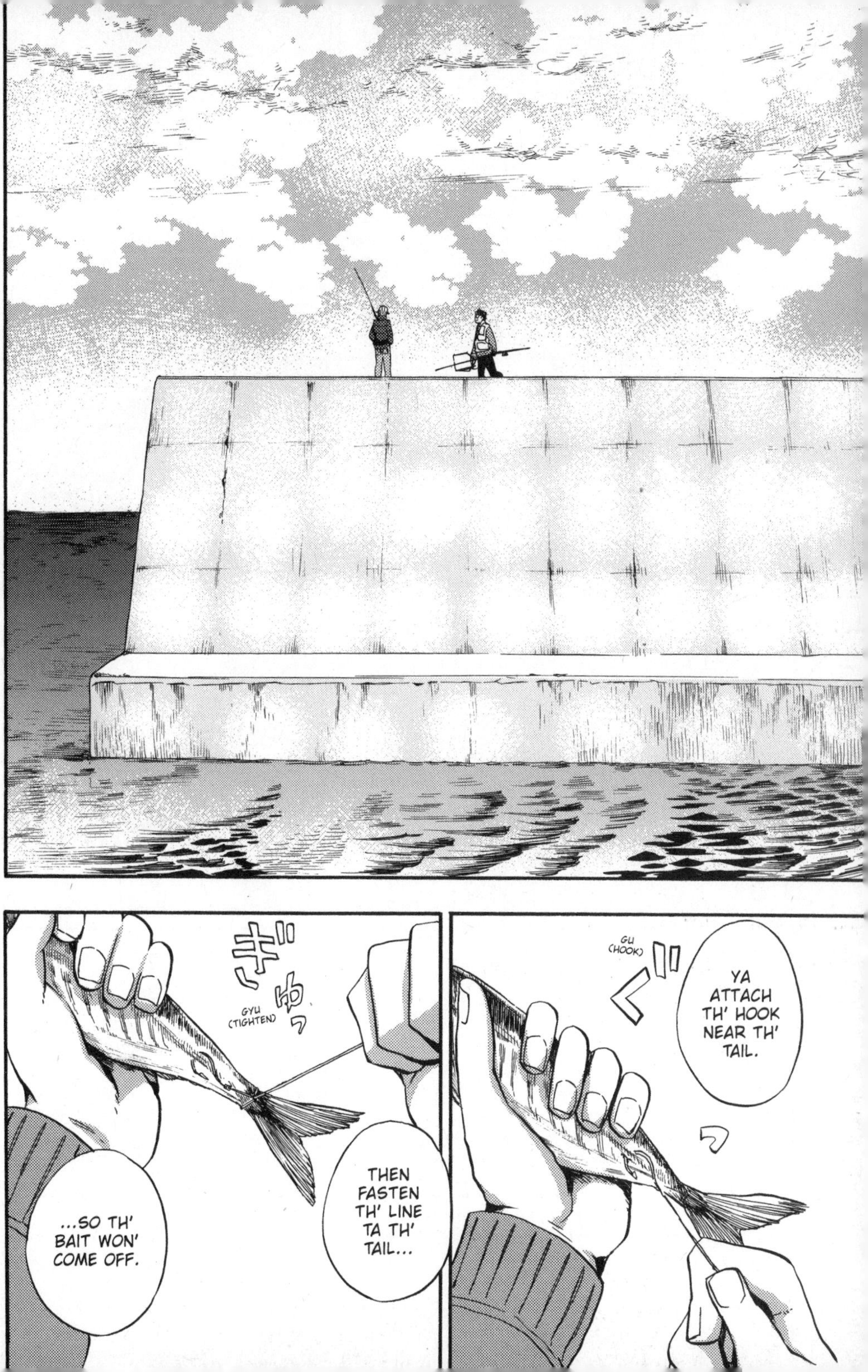
GU (HOOK)
YA ATTACH TH' HOOK NEAR TH' TAIL.
GYU (TIGHTEN)
THEN FASTEN TH' LINE TA TH' TAIL...
...SO TH' BAIT WON' COME OFF.

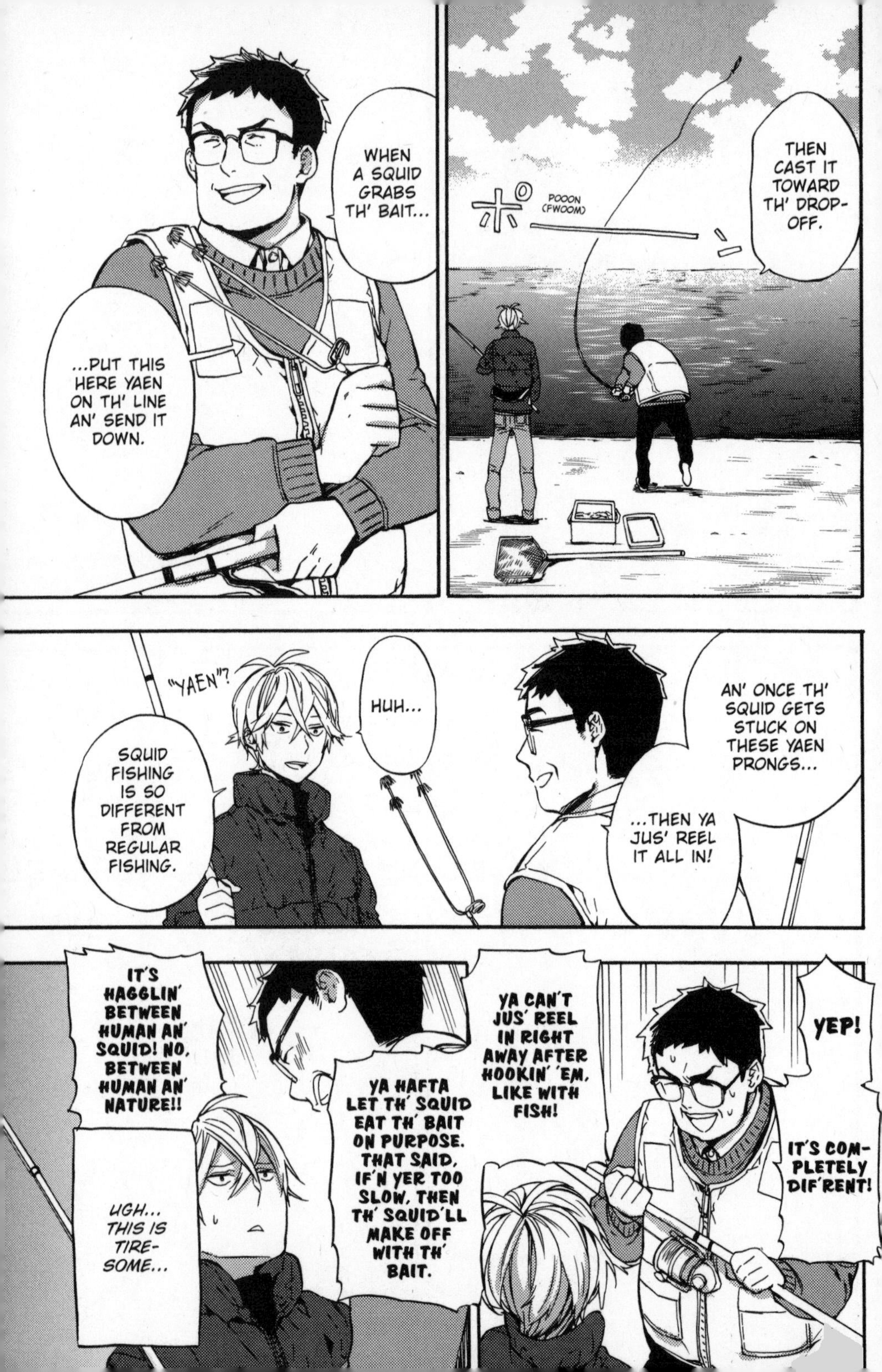
THEN CAST IT TOWARD TH' DROP-OFF.
POOON (FWOOM)
WHEN A SQUID GRABS TH' BAIT...
...PUT THIS HERE YAEN ON TH' LINE AN' SEND IT DOWN.
AN' ONCE TH' SQUID GETS STUCK ON THESE YAEN PRONGS...
...THEN YA JUS' REEL IT ALL IN!
HUH...
"YAEN"?
SQUID FISHING IS SO DIFFERENT FROM REGULAR FISHING.
YEP!
IT'S COMPLETELY DIF'RENT!
YA CAN'T JUS' REEL IN RIGHT AWAY AFTER HOOKIN' 'EM, LIKE WITH FISH!
YA HAFTA LET TH' SQUID EAT TH' BAIT ON PURPOSE. THAT SAID, IF'N YER TOO SLOW, THEN TH' SQUID'LL MAKE OFF WITH TH' BAIT.
IT'S HAGGLIN' BETWEEN HUMAN AN' SQUID! NO, BETWEEN HUMAN AN' NATURE!!
UGH... THIS IS TIRESOME...

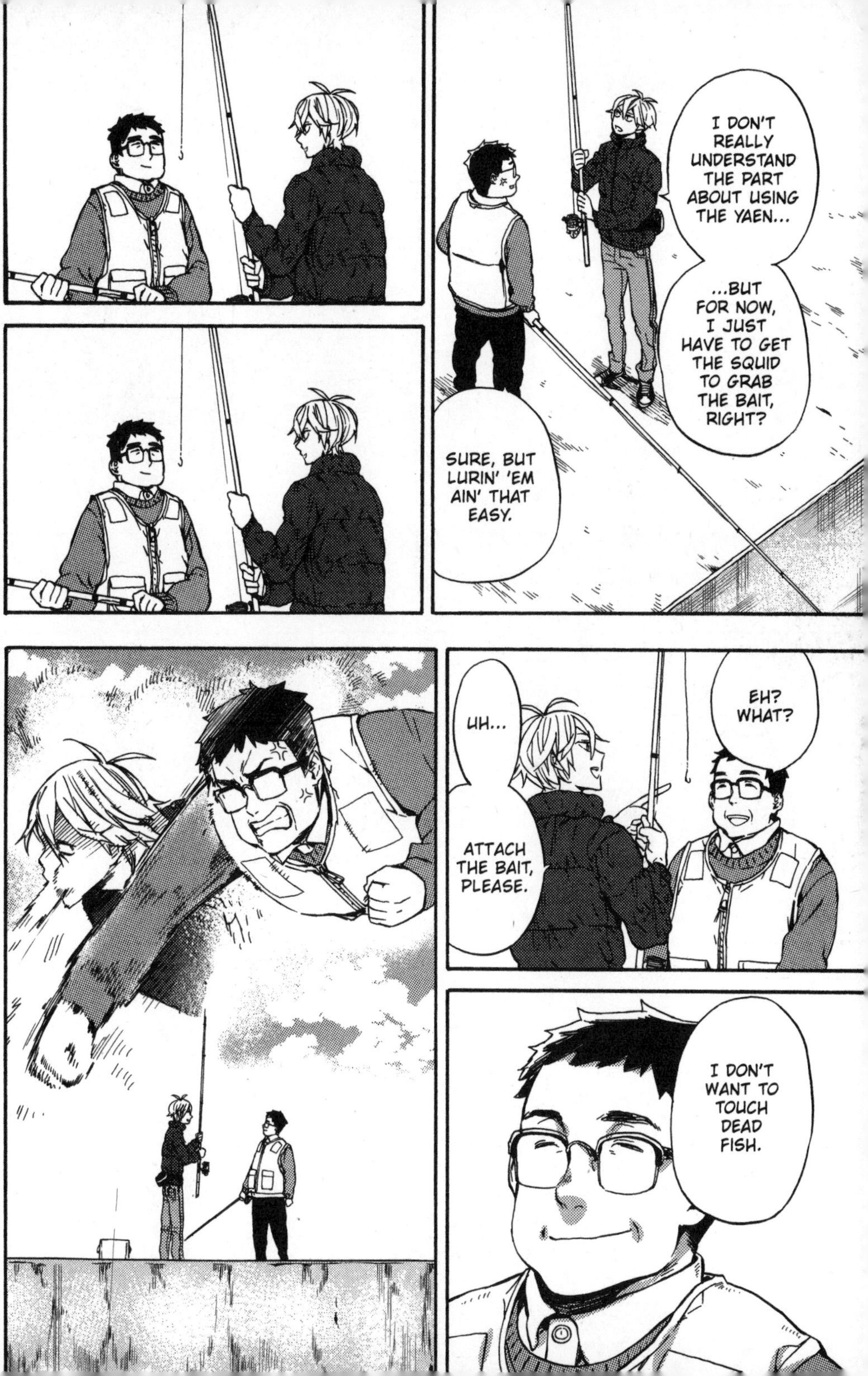
I DON'T REALLY UNDERSTAND THE PART ABOUT USING THE YAEN...
...BUT FOR NOW, I JUST HAVE TO GET THE SQUID TO GRAB THE BAIT, RIGHT?
SURE, BUT LURIN' 'EM AIN' THAT EASY.
EH? WHAT?
UH...
ATTACH THE BAIT, PLEASE.
I DON'T WANT TO TOUCH DEAD FISH.

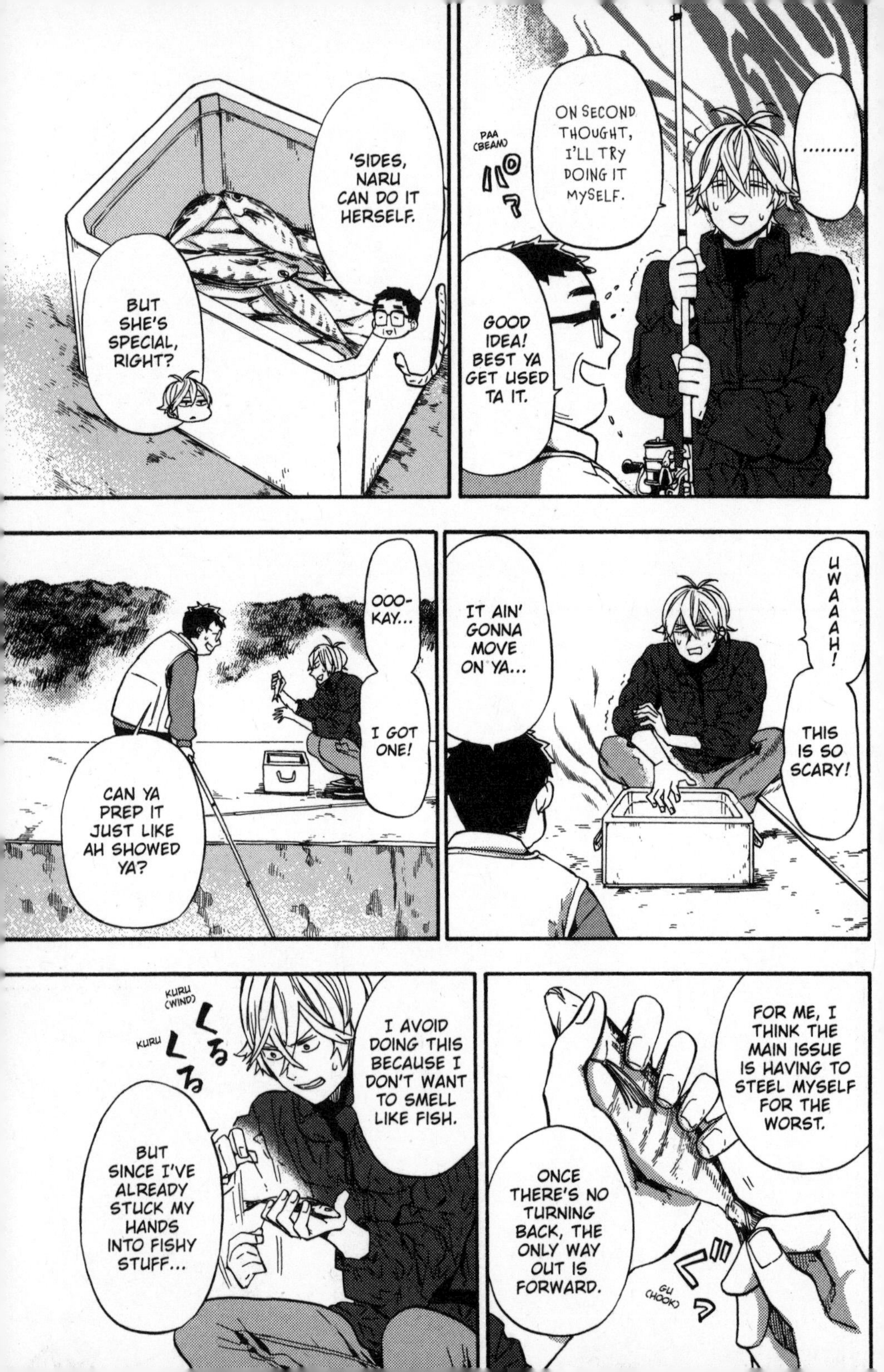
....
ON SECOND THOUGHT, I'LL TRY DOING IT MYSELF.
PAA (BEAM)
GOOD IDEA! BEST YA GET USED TA IT.
'SIDES, NARU CAN DO IT HERSELF.
BUT SHE'S SPECIAL, RIGHT?
UWAAAAH!
THIS IS SO SCARY!
IT AIN' GONNA MOVE ON YA...
OOO-KAY...
I GOT ONE!
CAN YA PREP IT JUST LIKE AH SHOWED YA?
FOR ME, I THINK THE MAIN ISSUE IS HAVING TO STEEL MYSELF FOR THE WORST.
ONCE THERE'S NO TURNING BACK, THE ONLY WAY OUT IS FORWARD.
GU (HOOK)
KURU (WIND)
KURU
I AVOID DOING THIS BECAUSE I DON'T WANT TO SMELL LIKE FISH.
BUT SINCE I'VE ALREADY STUCK MY HANDS INTO FISHY STUFF...

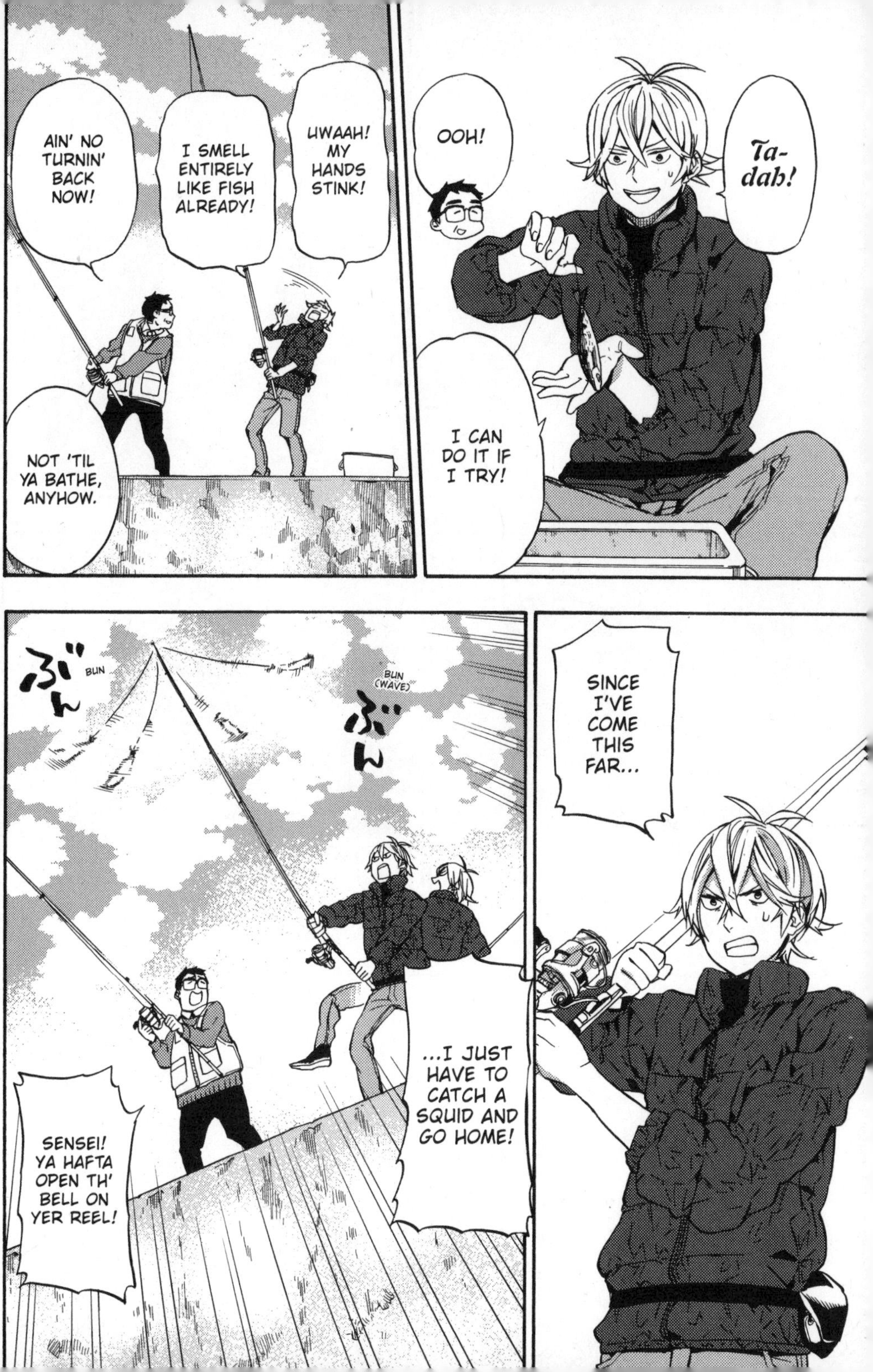
Ta-dah!
OOH!
I CAN DO IT IF I TRY!
UWAAH! MY HANDS STINK!
I SMELL ENTIRELY LIKE FISH ALREADY!
AIN' NO TURNIN' BACK NOW!
NOT 'TIL YA BATHE, ANYHOW.
SINCE I'VE COME THIS FAR...
...I JUST HAVE TO CATCH A SQUID AND GO HOME!
ぶん BUN (WAVE)
ぶん BUN
SENSEI! YA HAFTA OPEN TH' BELL ON YER REEL!

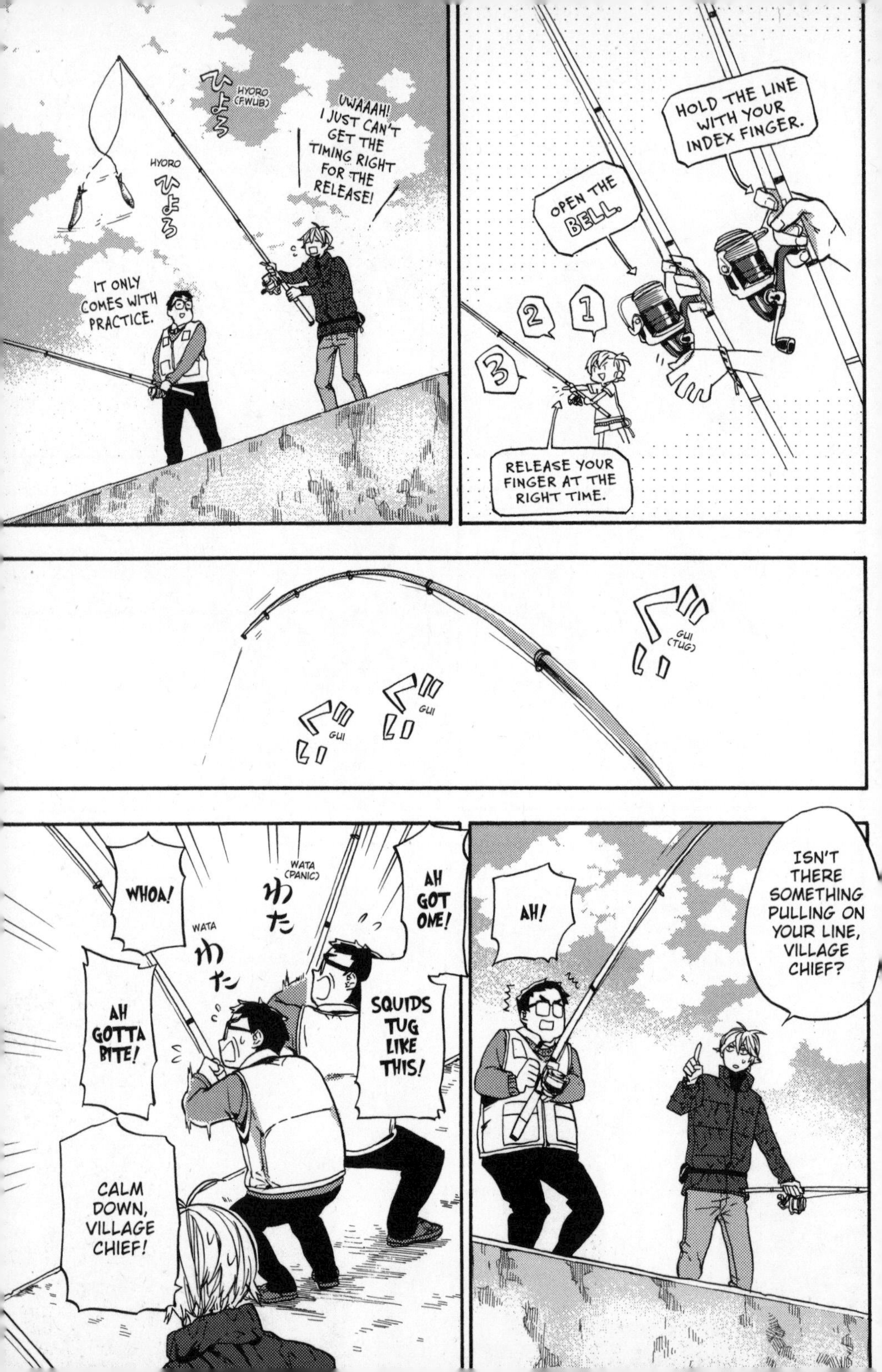
HOLD THE LINE WITH YOUR INDEX FINGER.
OPEN THE BELL.
1
2
3
RELEASE YOUR FINGER AT THE RIGHT TIME.
UWAAAH! I JUST CAN'T GET THE TIMING RIGHT FOR THE RELEASE!
ひょろ
HYORO (FWUB)
ひょろ
HYORO
IT ONLY COMES WITH PRACTICE.
GUI (TUG)
GUI
GUI
ISN'T THERE SOMETHING PULLING ON YOUR LINE, VILLAGE CHIEF?
AH!
AH GOT ONE!
わた
WATA (PANIC)
WHOA!
わた
WATA
SQUIDS TUG LIKE THIS!
AH GOTTA BITE!
CALM DOWN, VILLAGE CHIEF!

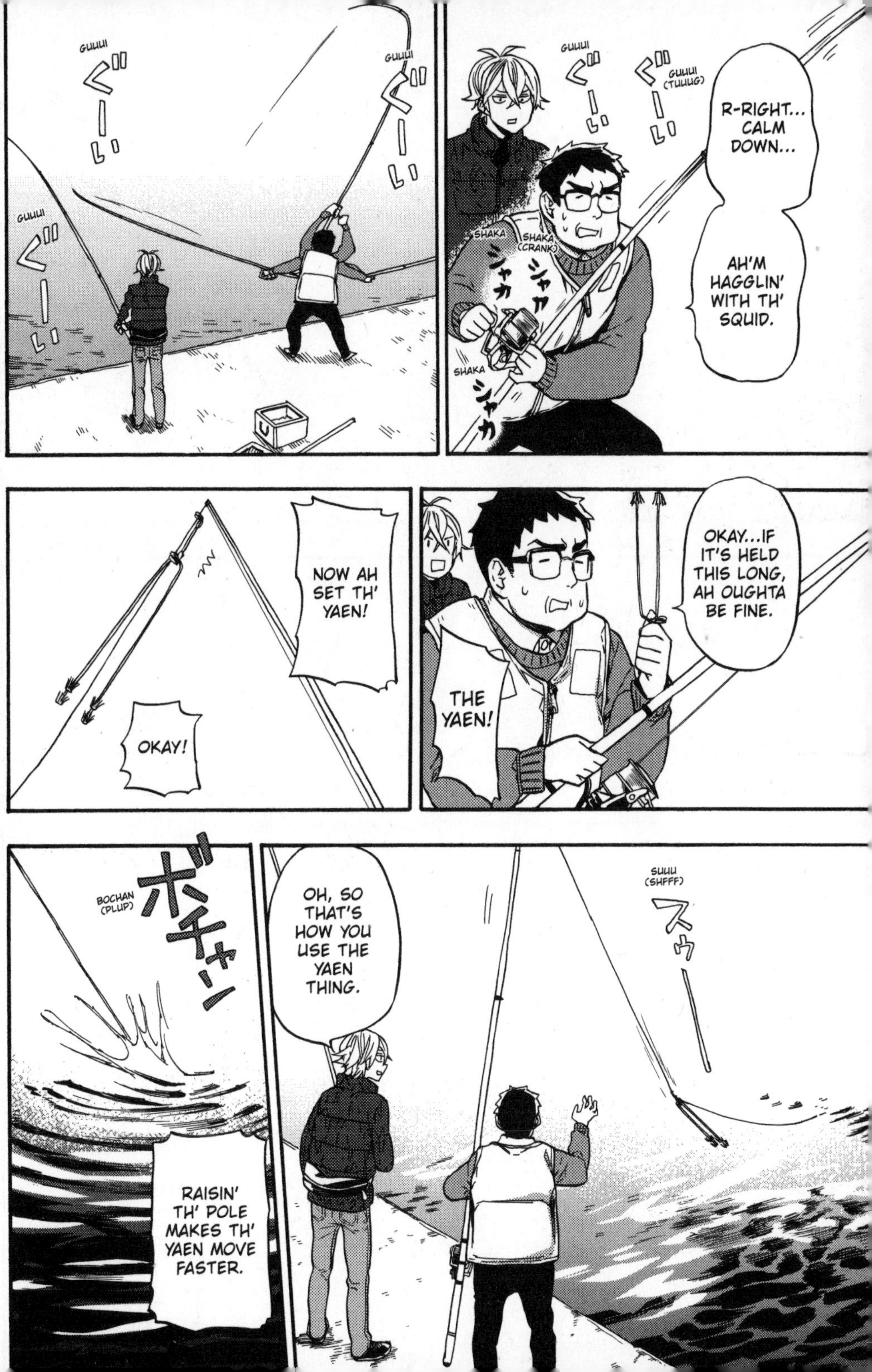
GUUUI
GUUUI (TUUUG)
R-RIGHT... CALM DOWN...
AH'M HAGGLIN' WITH TH' SQUID.
SHAKA
SHAKA (CRANK)
SHAKA
GUUUI
GUUUI
GUUUI
OKAY...IF IT'S HELD THIS LONG, AH OUGHTA BE FINE.
THE YAEN!
NOW AH SET TH' YAEN!
OKAY!
SUUU (SHFFF)
OH, SO THAT'S HOW YOU USE THE YAEN THING.
BOCHAN (PLUP)
RAISIN' TH' POLE MAKES TH' YAEN MOVE FASTER.

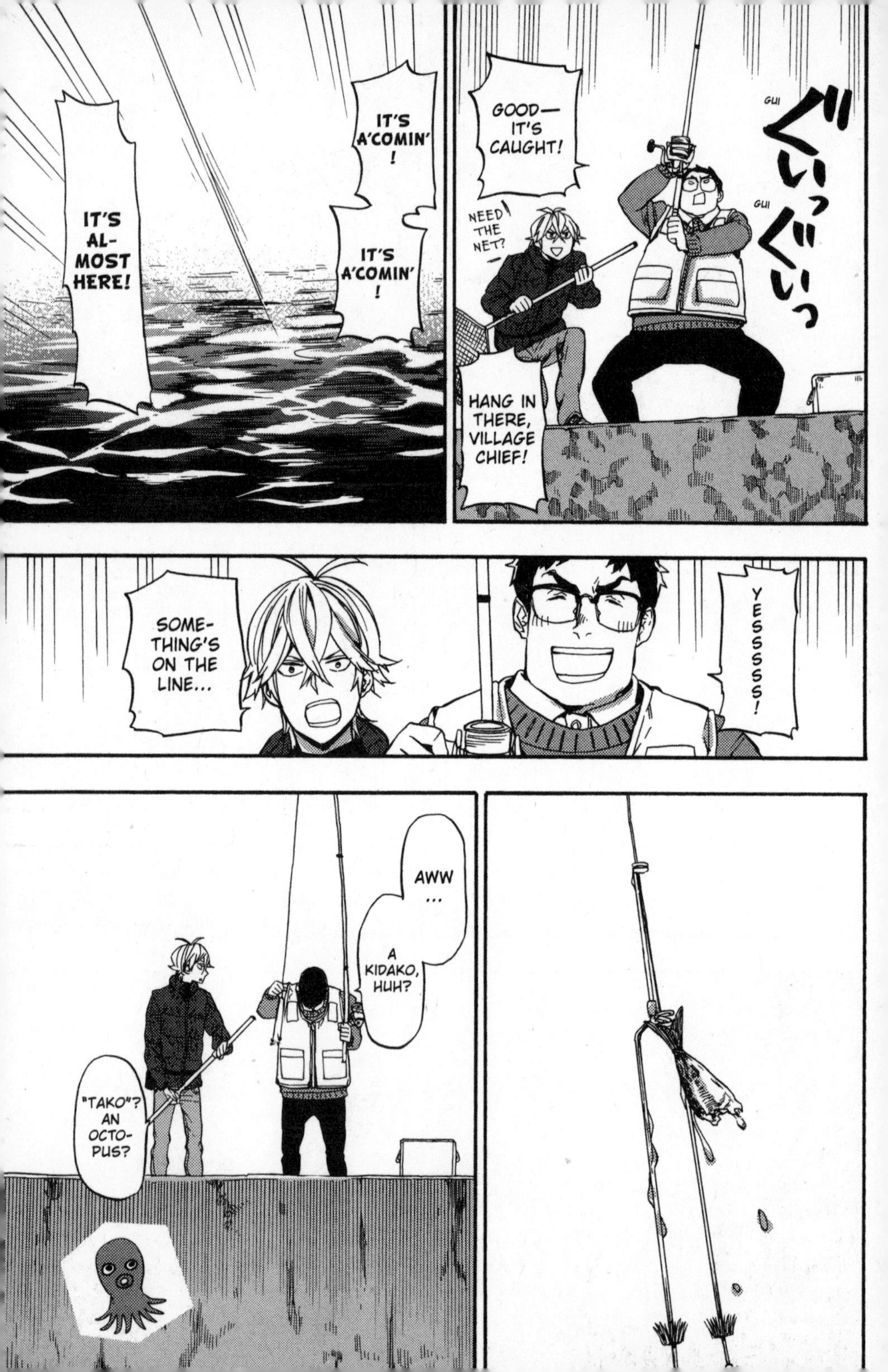
ぐいっ
GUI
ぐいっ
GUI
GOOD—IT'S CAUGHT!
NEED THE NET?
HANG IN THERE, VILLAGE CHIEF!
IT'S A'COMIN'!
IT'S A'COMIN'!
IT'S AL-MOST HERE!
YESSSSSS!
SOME-THING'S ON THE LINE...
AWW...
A KIDAKO, HUH?
"TAKO"? AN OCTO-PUS?

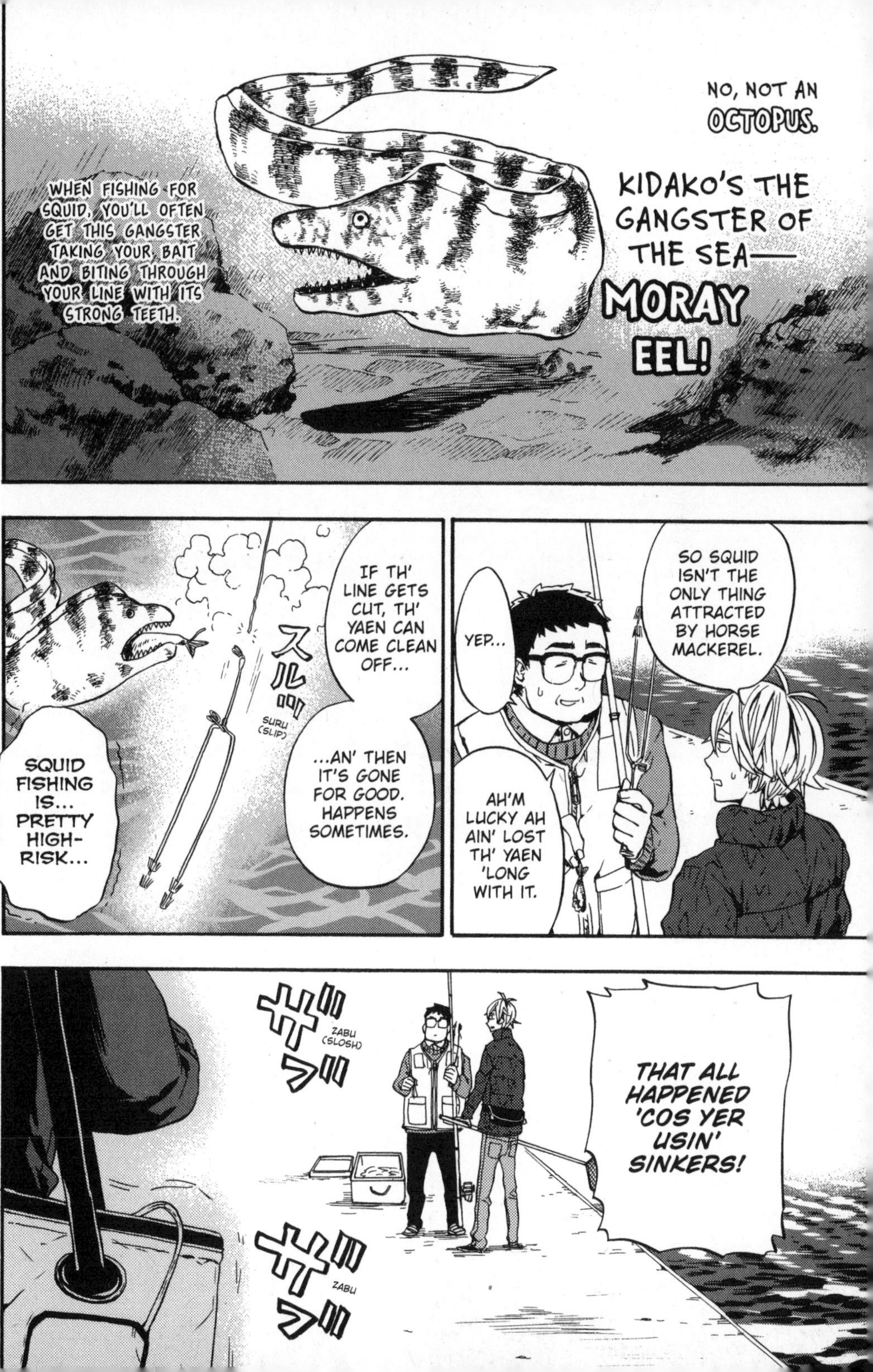
NO, NOT AN OCTOPUS.
KIDAKO'S THE GANGSTER OF THE SEA— MORAY EEL!
WHEN FISHING FOR SQUID, YOU'LL OFTEN GET THIS GANGSTER TAKING YOUR BAIT AND BITING THROUGH YOUR LINE WITH ITS STRONG TEETH.
SO SQUID ISN'T THE ONLY THING ATTRACTED BY HORSE MACKEREL.
YEP...
AH'M LUCKY AH AIN' LOST TH' YAEN 'LONG WITH IT.
IF TH' LINE GETS CUT, TH' YAEN CAN COME CLEAN OFF...
スルッ
SURU (SLIP)
...AN' THEN IT'S GONE FOR GOOD. HAPPENS SOMETIMES.
SQUID FISHING IS... PRETTY HIGH-RISK...
THAT ALL HAPPENED 'COS YER USIN' SINKERS!
ザブ
ZABU (SLOSH)
ザブ
ZABU

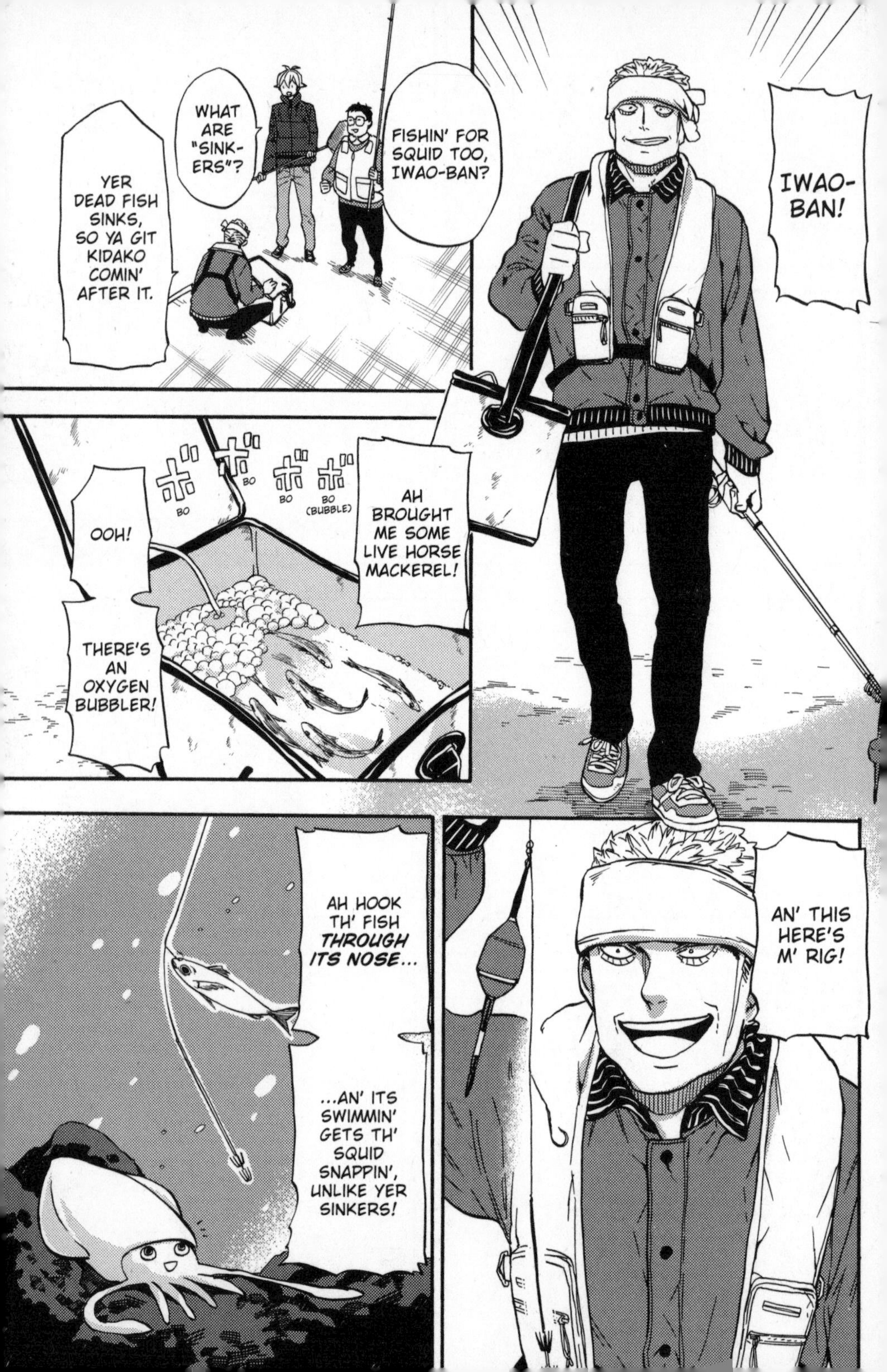
IWAO-BAN!
FISHIN' FOR SQUID TOO, IWAO-BAN?
WHAT ARE "SINKERS"?
YER DEAD FISH SINKS, SO YA GIT KIDAKO COMIN' AFTER IT.
AH BROUGHT ME SOME LIVE HORSE MACKEREL!
ボ BO (BUBBLE)
ボ BO
ボ BO
ボ BO
OOH!
THERE'S AN OXYGEN BUBBLER!
AN' THIS HERE'S M' RIG!
AH HOOK TH' FISH *THROUGH ITS NOSE*...
...AN' ITS SWIMMIN' GETS TH' SQUID SNAPPIN', UNLIKE YER SINKERS!

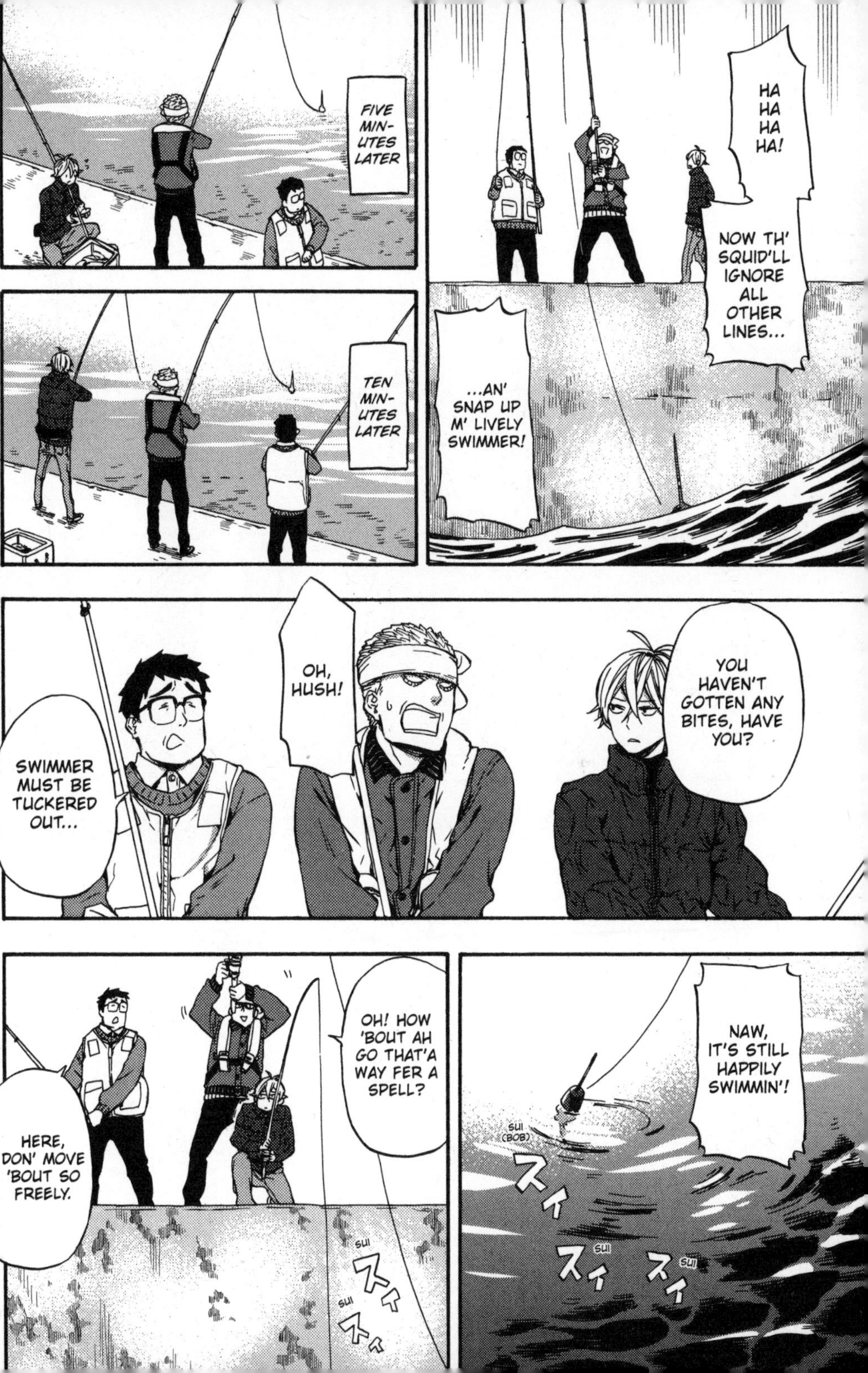
HA HA HA HA!
NOW TH' SQUID'LL IGNORE ALL OTHER LINES...
...AN' SNAP UP M' LIVELY SWIMMER!
FIVE MIN-UTES LATER
TEN MIN-UTES LATER
YOU HAVEN'T GOTTEN ANY BITES, HAVE YOU?
OH, HUSH!
SWIMMER MUST BE TUCKERED OUT...
NAW, IT'S STILL HAPPILY SWIMMIN'!
SUI (BOB)
スイ
SUI
スイ
SUI
スイ
OH! HOW 'BOUT AH GO THAT'A WAY FER A SPELL?
HERE, DON' MOVE 'BOUT SO FREELY.
SUI
スイ
SUI
スイ

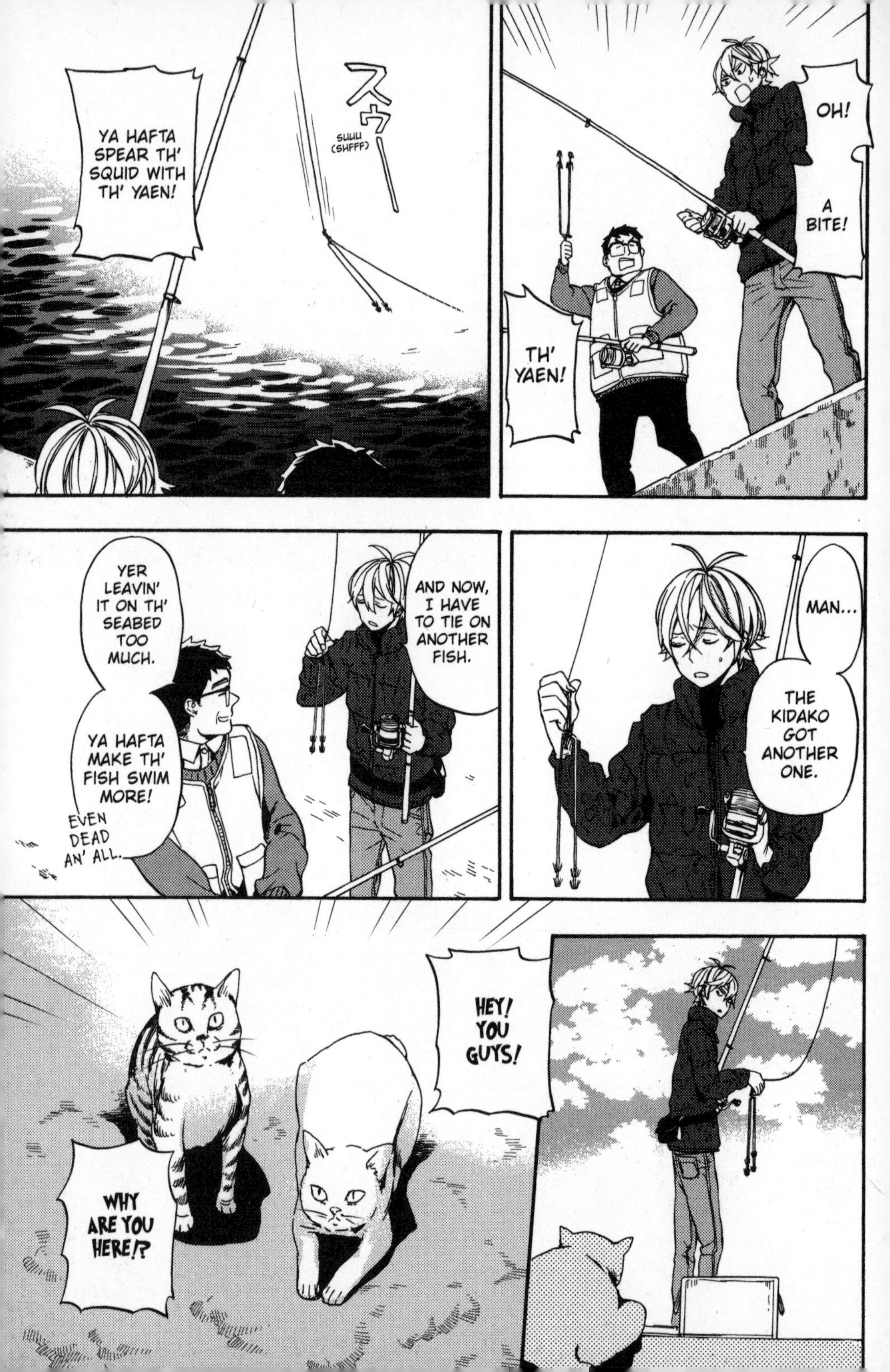
OH!
A BITE!
TH' YAEN!
スウ
SUUU (SHFFF)
YA HAFTA SPEAR TH' SQUID WITH TH' YAEN!
MAN...
THE KIDAKO GOT ANOTHER ONE.
AND NOW, I HAVE TO TIE ON ANOTHER FISH.
YER LEAVIN' IT ON TH' SEABED TOO MUCH.
YA HAFTA MAKE TH' FISH SWIM MORE!
EVEN DEAD AN' ALL.
HEY! YOU GUYS!
WHY ARE YOU HERE!?

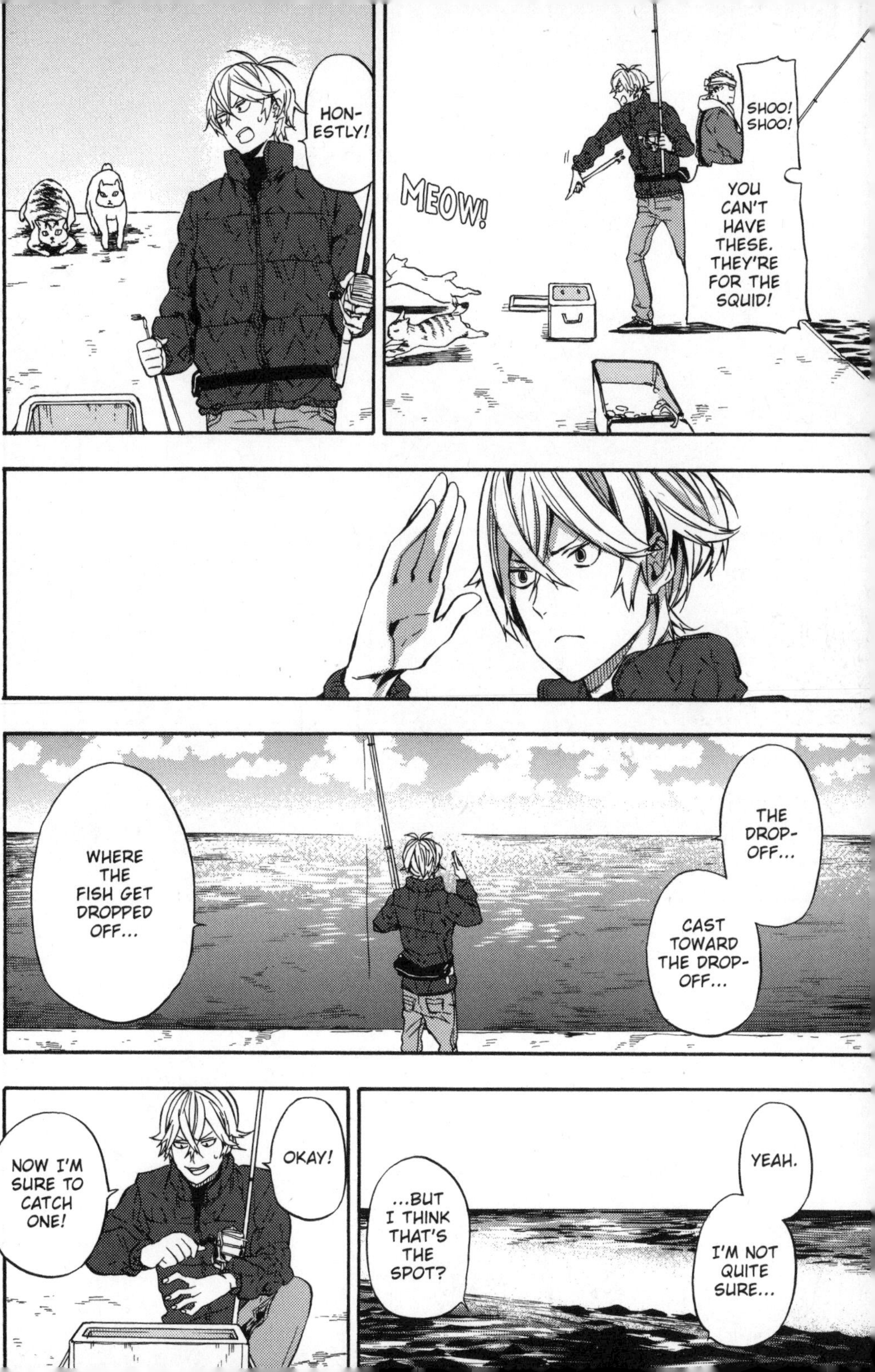
SHOO! SHOO!
YOU CAN'T HAVE THESE. THEY'RE FOR THE SQUID!
MEOW!
HON-ESTLY!
THE DROP-OFF...
CAST TOWARD THE DROP-OFF...
WHERE THE FISH GET DROPPED OFF...
YEAH.
I'M NOT QUITE SURE...
...BUT I THINK THAT'S THE SPOT?
OKAY!
NOW I'M SURE TO CATCH ONE!

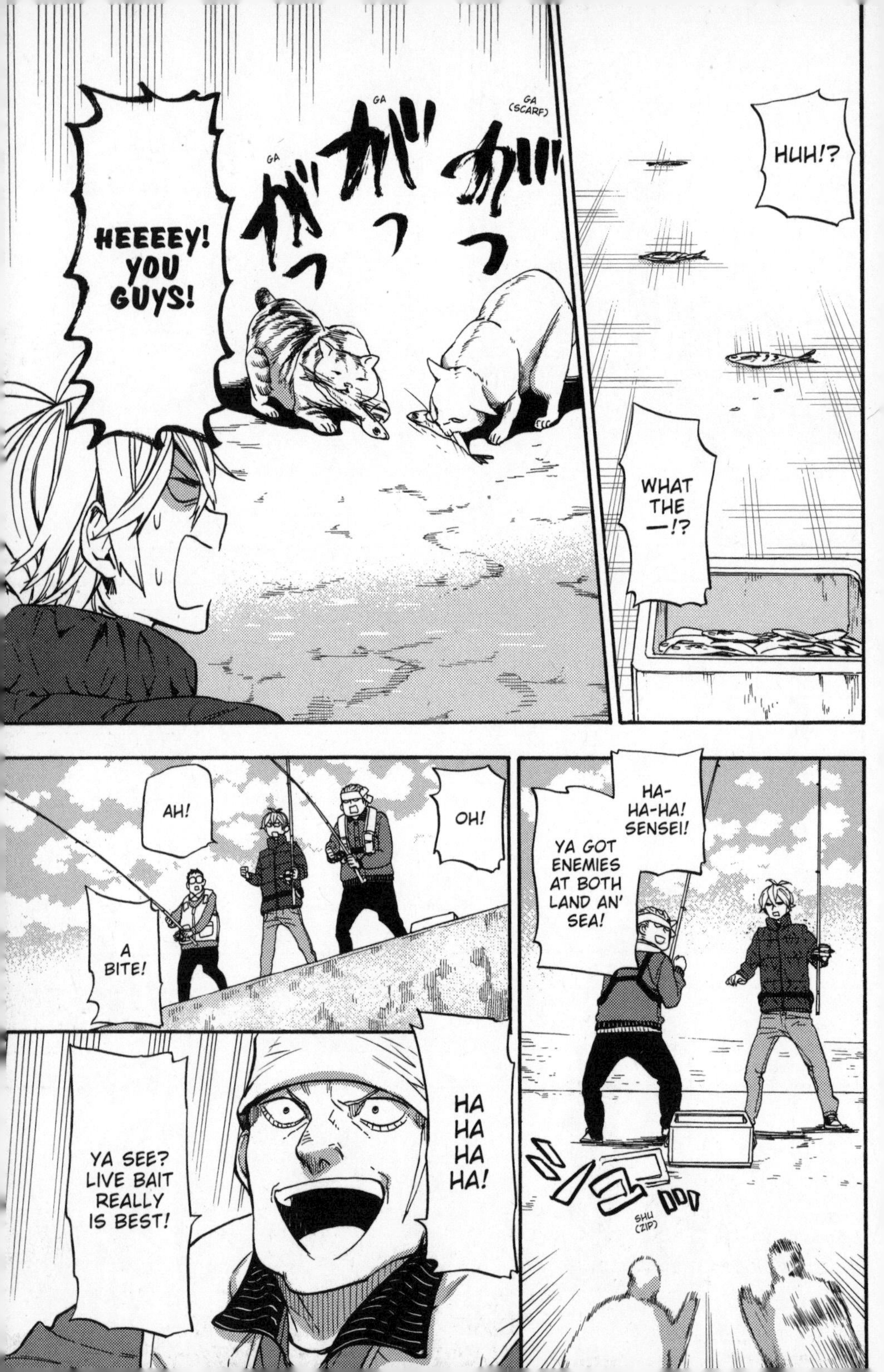
HUH!?
WHAT THE—!?
GA (SCARF)
GA
GA
HEEEEY! YOU GUYS!
HA-HA-HA! SENSEI!
YA GOT ENEMIES AT BOTH LAND AN' SEA!
SHU (ZIP)
OH!
AH!
A BITE!
HA HA HA HA!
YA SEE? LIVE BAIT REALLY IS BEST!

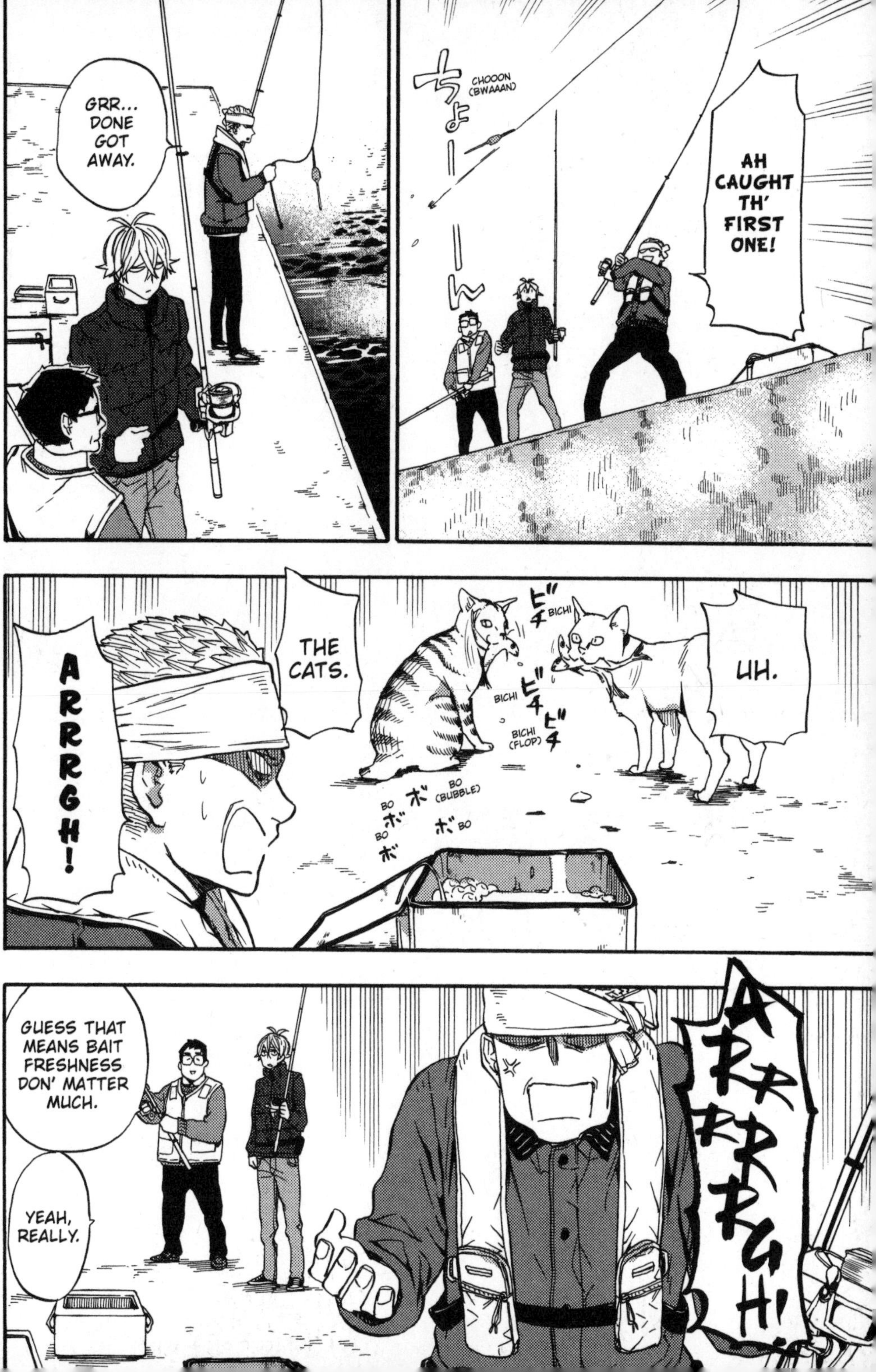
AH CAUGHT TH' FIRST ONE!
ちょーーん
CHOOON (BWAAAN)
GRR... DONE GOT AWAY.
UH.
ビチ BICHI
ビチ BICHI
ビチ BICHI (FLOP)
THE CATS.
ボ BO (BUBBLE)
ボ BO
ボ BO
ボ BO
ARRRGH!
ARRRRRRGH!
GUESS THAT MEANS BAIT FRESHNESS DON' MATTER MUCH.
YEAH, REALLY.

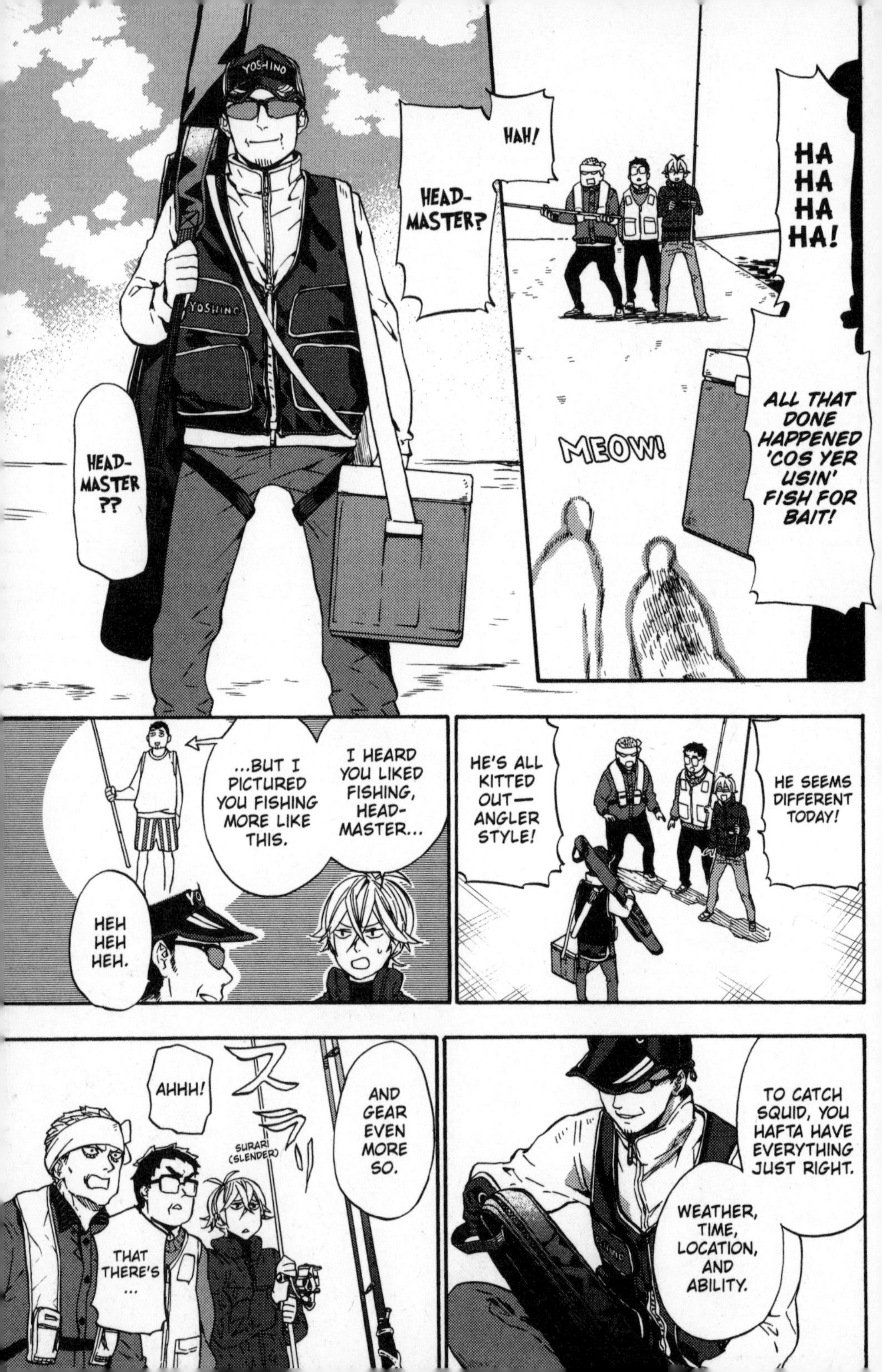
HA HA HA HA!
ALL THAT DONE HAPPENED 'COS YER USIN' FISH FOR BAIT!
MEOW!
HAH!
HEAD-MASTER?
YOSHINO
HEAD-MASTER??
HE SEEMS DIFFERENT TODAY!
HE'S ALL KITTED OUT—ANGLER STYLE!
I HEARD YOU LIKED FISHING, HEAD-MASTER...
...BUT I PICTURED YOU FISHING MORE LIKE THIS.
HEH HEH HEH.
TO CATCH SQUID, YOU HAFTA HAVE EVERYTHING JUST RIGHT.
WEATHER, TIME, LOCATION, AND ABILITY.
AND GEAR EVEN MORE SO.
AHHH!
SURARI (SLENDER)
THAT THERE'S ...

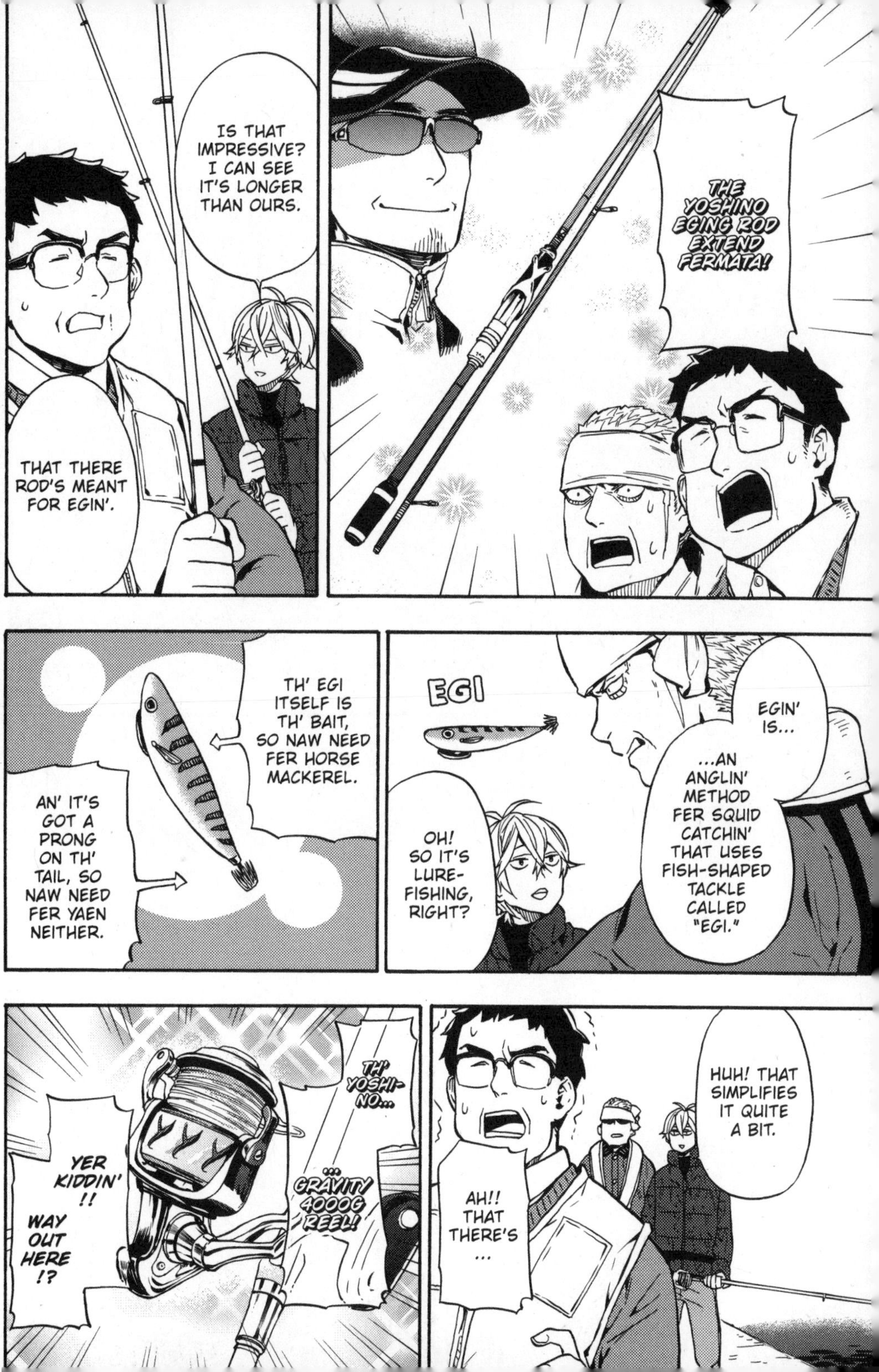
THE YOSHINO EGING ROD EXTEND FERMATA!
IS THAT IMPRESSIVE? I CAN SEE IT'S LONGER THAN OURS.
THAT THERE ROD'S MEANT FOR EGIN'.
EGIN' IS...
...AN ANGLIN' METHOD FER SQUID CATCHIN' THAT USES FISH-SHAPED TACKLE CALLED "EGI."
EGI
OH! SO IT'S LURE-FISHING, RIGHT?
TH' EGI ITSELF IS TH' BAIT, SO NAW NEED FER HORSE MACKEREL.
AN' IT'S GOT A PRONG ON TH' TAIL, SO NAW NEED FER YAEN NEITHER.
HUH! THAT SIMPLIFIES IT QUITE A BIT.
AH!! THAT THERE'S ...
TH' YOSHINO...
...GRAVITY 4000G REEL!
YER KIDDIN'!!
WAY OUT HERE!?

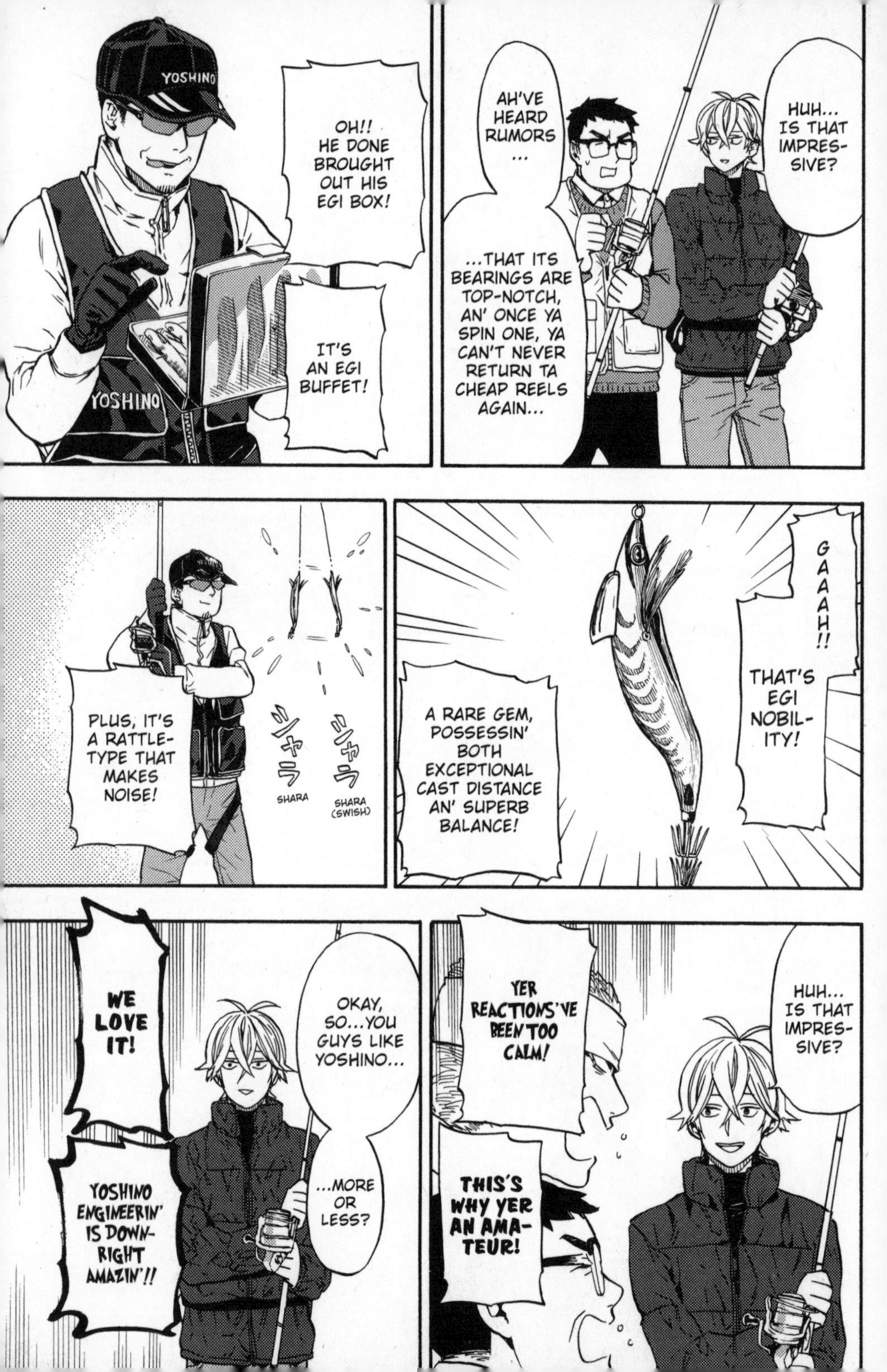
HUH... IS THAT IMPRES-SIVE?
AH'VE HEARD RUMORS ...
...THAT ITS BEARINGS ARE TOP-NOTCH, AN' ONCE YA SPIN ONE, YA CAN'T NEVER RETURN TA CHEAP REELS AGAIN...
YOSHINO
OH!! HE DONE BROUGHT OUT HIS EGI BOX!
IT'S AN EGI BUFFET!
YOSHINO
GAAAAH!!
THAT'S EGI NOBIL-ITY!
A RARE GEM, POSSESSIN' BOTH EXCEPTIONAL CAST DISTANCE AN' SUPERB BALANCE!
シャラ
SHARA (SWISH)
シャラ
SHARA
PLUS, IT'S A RATTLE-TYPE THAT MAKES NOISE!
HUH... IS THAT IMPRES-SIVE?
YER REACTIONS'VE BEEN TOO CALM!
THIS'S WHY YER AN AMA-TEUR!
OKAY, SO...YOU GUYS LIKE YOSHINO...
...MORE OR LESS?
WE LOVE IT!
YOSHINO ENGINEERIN' IS DOWN-RIGHT AMAZIN'!!

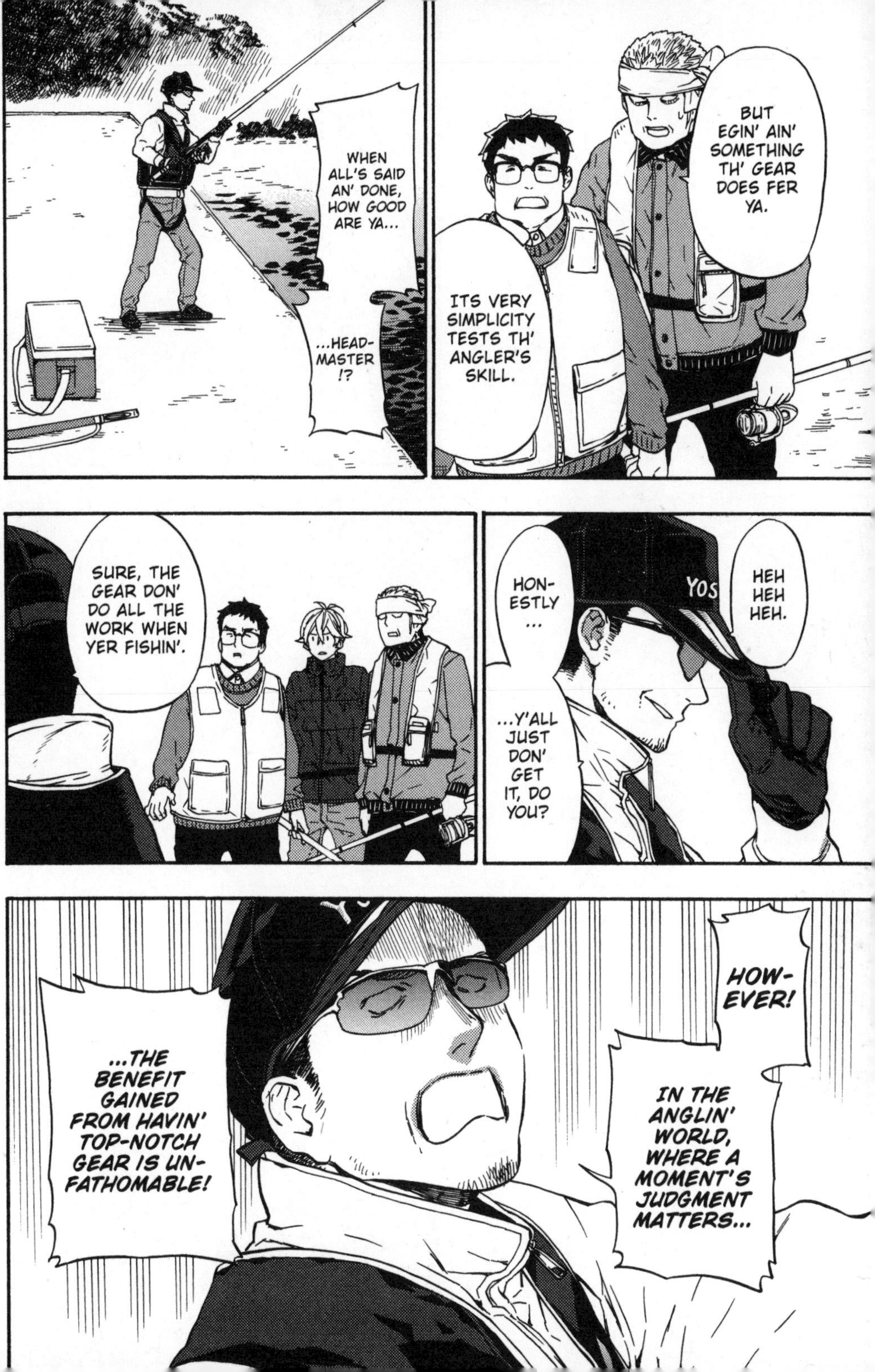
BUT EGIN' AIN' SOMETHING TH' GEAR DOES FER YA.
ITS VERY SIMPLICITY TESTS TH' ANGLER'S SKILL.
WHEN ALL'S SAID AN' DONE, HOW GOOD ARE YA...
...HEADMASTER!?
HEH HEH HEH.
YOS
HONESTLY...
...Y'ALL JUST DON' GET IT, DO YOU?
SURE, THE GEAR DON' DO ALL THE WORK WHEN YER FISHIN'.
HOWEVER!
IN THE ANGLIN' WORLD, WHERE A MOMENT'S JUDGMENT MATTERS...
...THE BENEFIT GAINED FROM HAVIN' TOP-NOTCH GEAR IS UNFATHOMABLE!

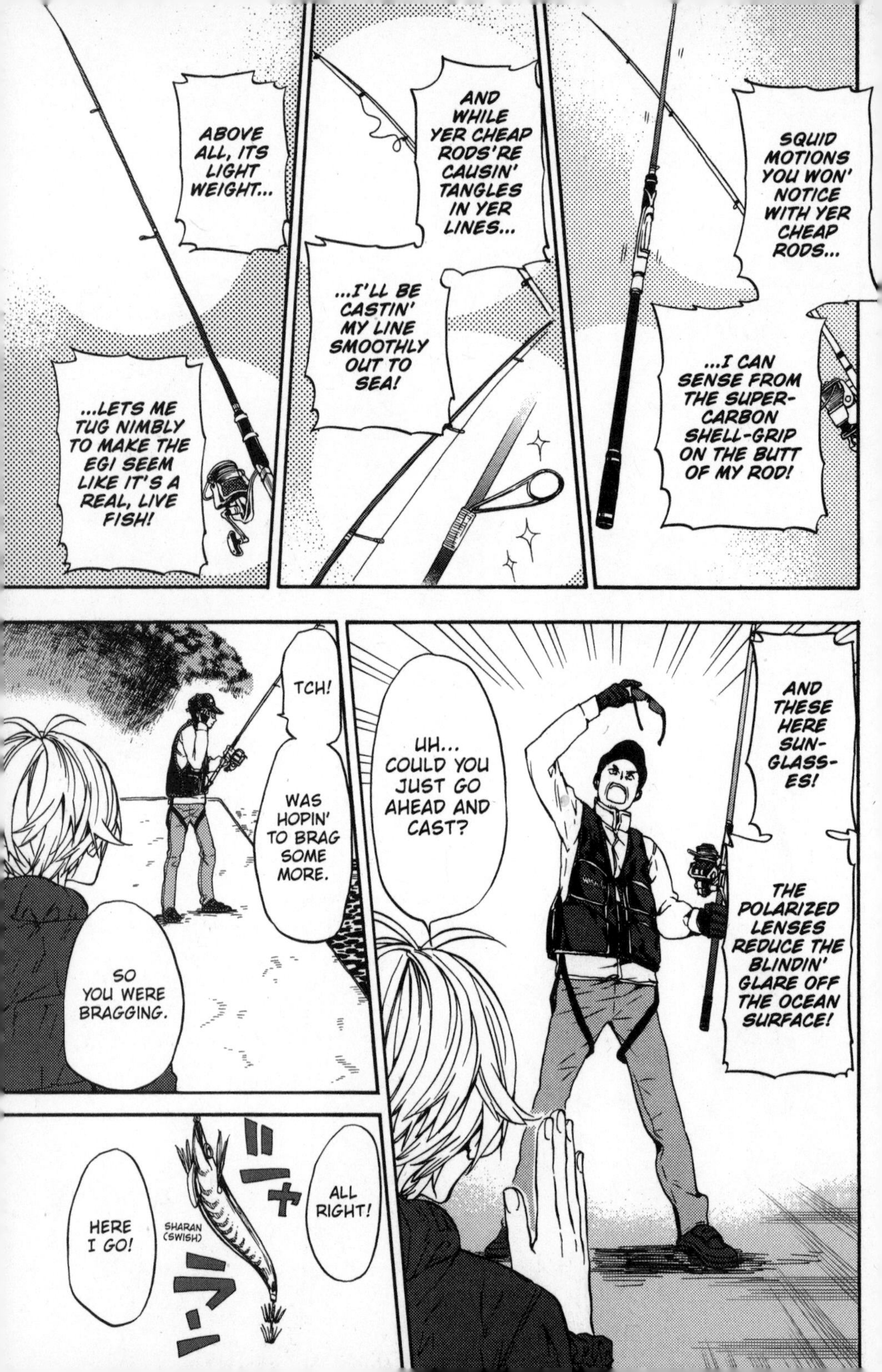
SQUID MOTIONS YOU WON' NOTICE WITH YER CHEAP RODS...
...I CAN SENSE FROM THE SUPER-CARBON SHELL-GRIP ON THE BUTT OF MY ROD!
AND WHILE YER CHEAP RODS'RE CAUSIN' TANGLES IN YER LINES...
...I'LL BE CASTIN' MY LINE SMOOTHLY OUT TO SEA!
ABOVE ALL, ITS LIGHT WEIGHT...
...LETS ME TUG NIMBLY TO MAKE THE EGI SEEM LIKE IT'S A REAL, LIVE FISH!
AND THESE HERE SUN-GLASS-ES!
THE POLARIZED LENSES REDUCE THE BLINDIN' GLARE OFF THE OCEAN SURFACE!
UH... COULD YOU JUST GO AHEAD AND CAST?
TCH!
WAS HOPIN' TO BRAG SOME MORE.
SO YOU WERE BRAGGING.
ALL RIGHT!
SHARAN (SWISH)
HERE I GO!

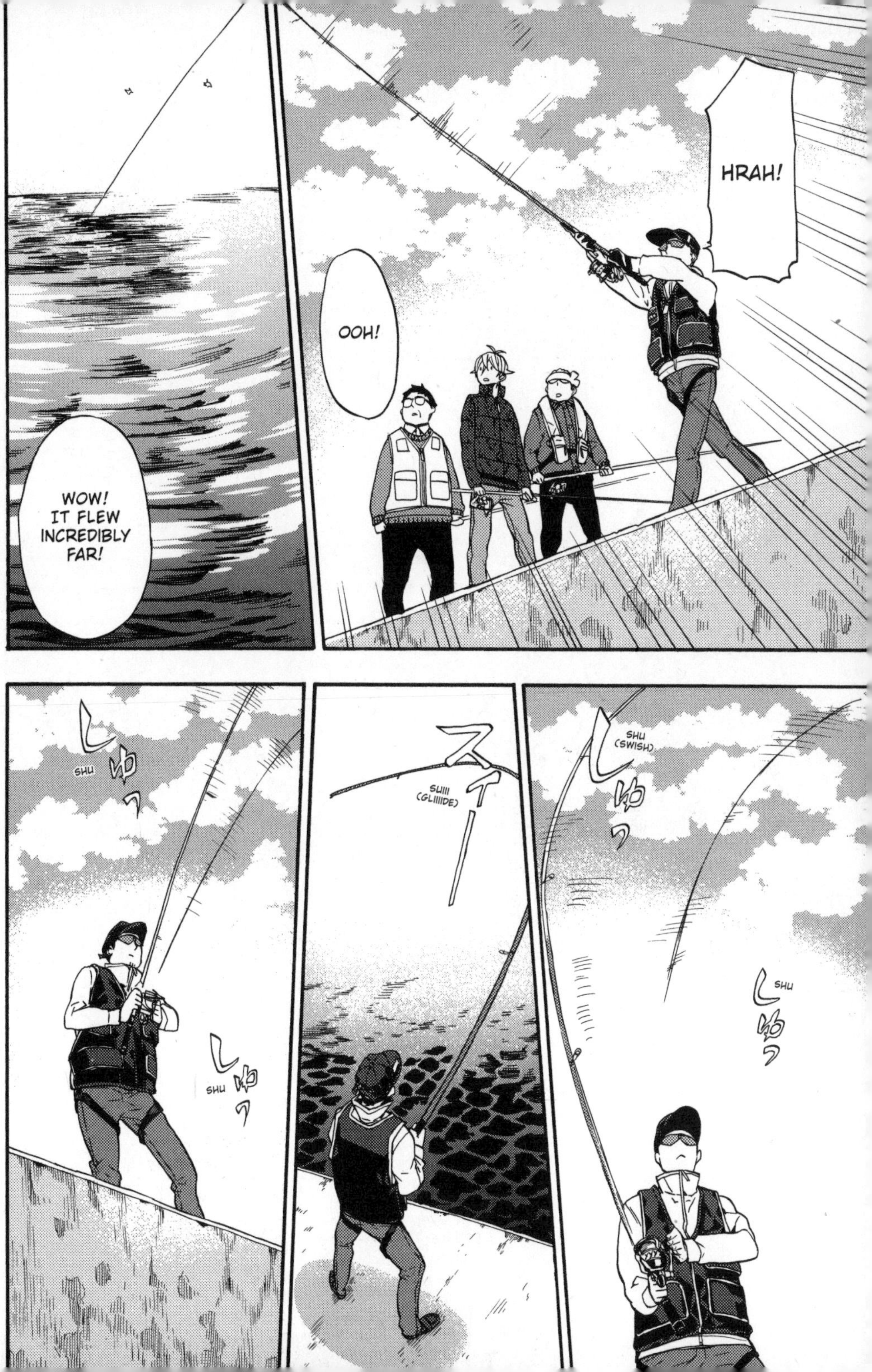
HRAH!
OOH!
WOW! IT FLEW INCREDIBLY FAR!
しゅっ
SHU (SWISH)
しゅっ
SHU
スイー
SUIII (GLIIIIDE)
しゅっ
SHU
しゅっ
SHU

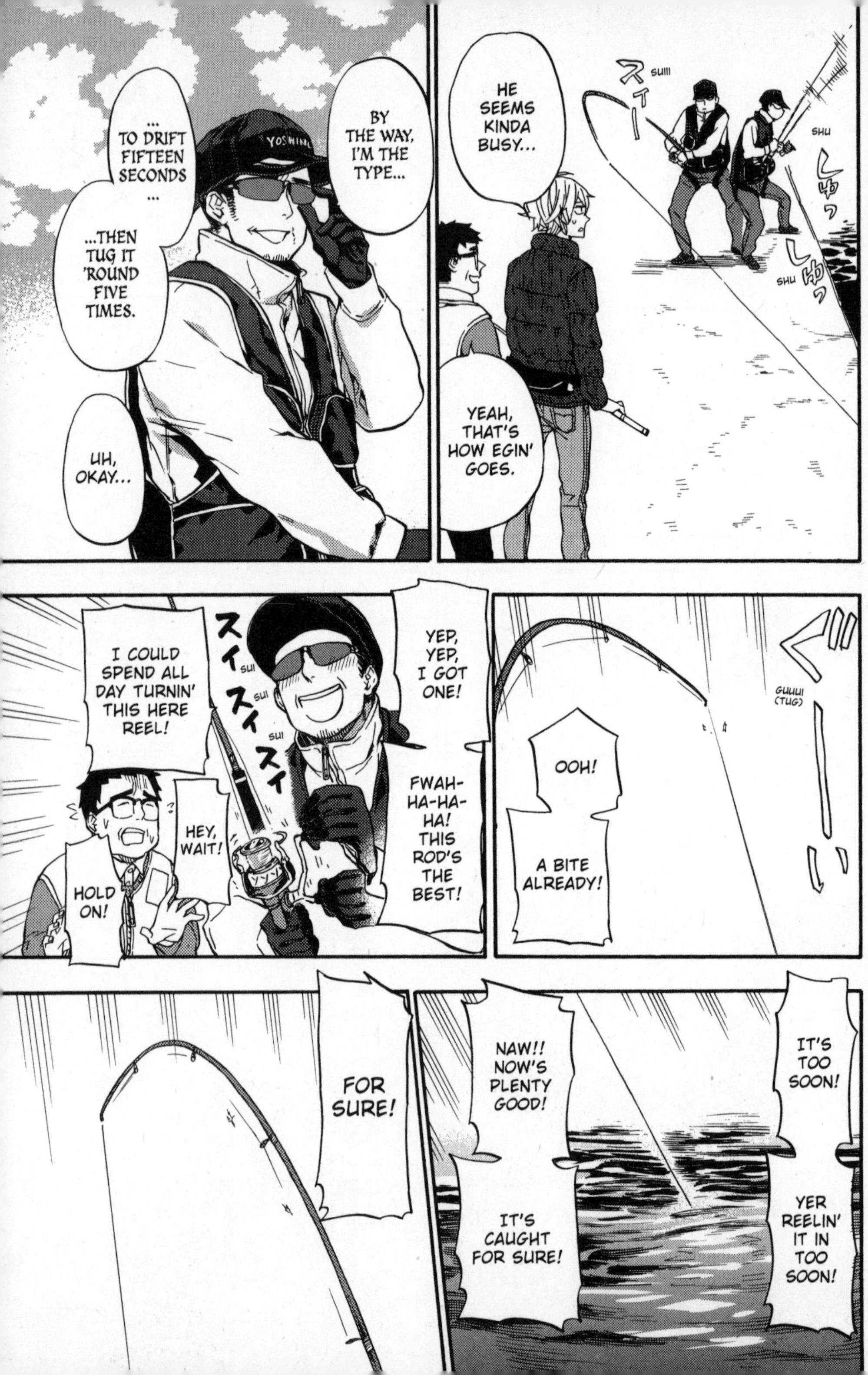
SUIII
HE SEEMS KINDA BUSY...
SHU
SHU
YEAH, THAT'S HOW EGIN' GOES.
BY THE WAY, I'M THE TYPE...
... TO DRIFT FIFTEEN SECONDS ...
...THEN TUG IT 'ROUND FIVE TIMES.
UH, OKAY...
GUUUI (TUG)
OOH!
A BITE ALREADY!
YEP, YEP, I GOT ONE!
FWAH-HA-HA-HA! THIS ROD'S THE BEST!
I COULD SPEND ALL DAY TURNIN' THIS HERE REEL!
SUI
SUI
SUI
HEY, WAIT!
HOLD ON!
IT'S TOO SOON!
NAW!! NOW'S PLENTY GOOD!
YER REELIN' IT IN TOO SOON!
IT'S CAUGHT FOR SURE!
FOR SURE!

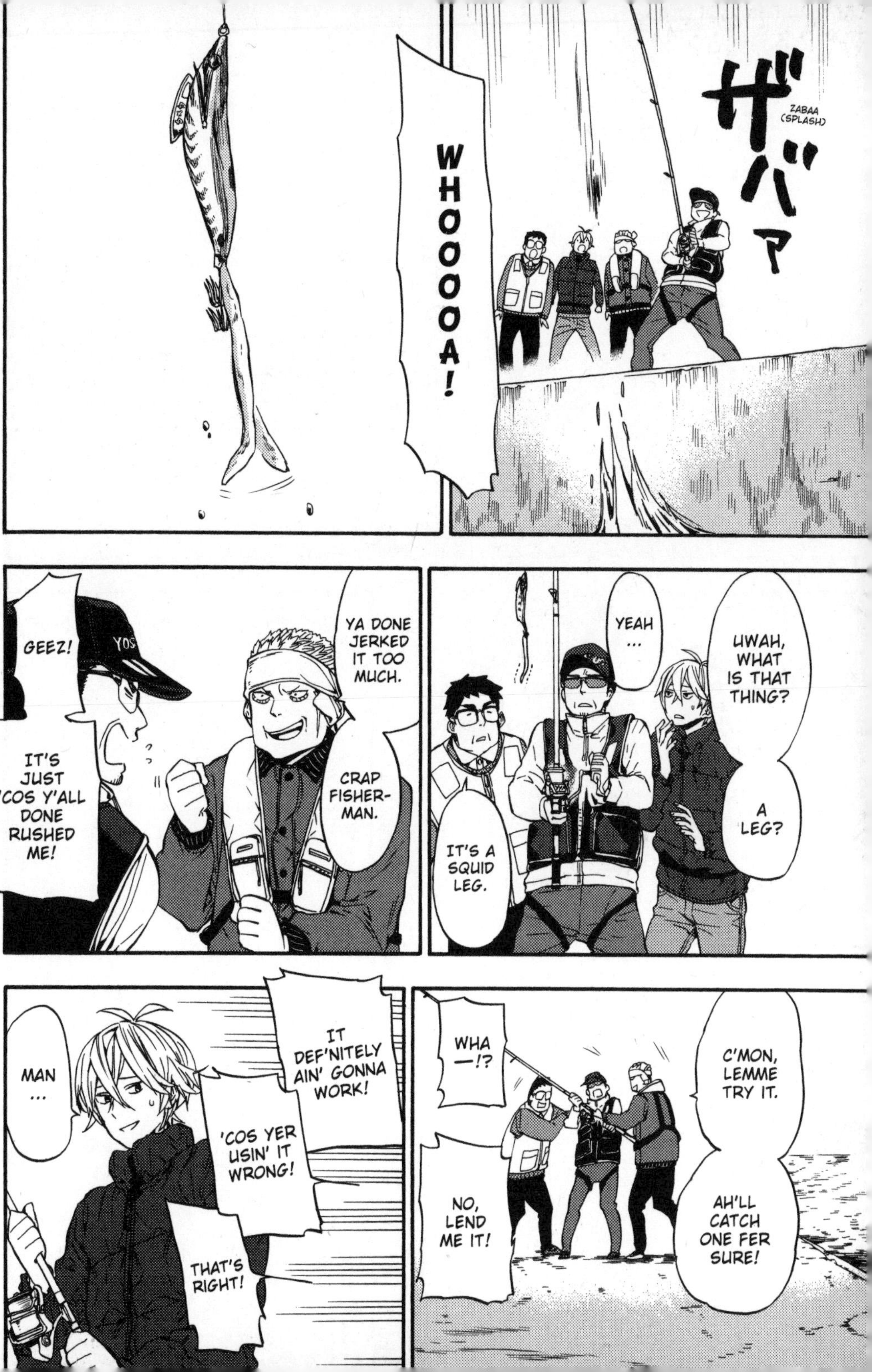
ザバァ
ZABAA (SPLASH)
WHOOOOA!
UWAH, WHAT IS THAT THING?
YEAH...
A LEG?
IT'S A SQUID LEG.
YA DONE JERKED IT TOO MUCH.
GEEZ!
CRAP FISHER-MAN.
IT'S JUST 'COS Y'ALL DONE RUSHED ME!
C'MON, LEMME TRY IT.
WHA—!?
AH'LL CATCH ONE FER SURE!
NO, LEND ME IT!
IT DEF'NITELY AIN' GONNA WORK!
MAN...
'COS YER USIN' IT WRONG!
THAT'S RIGHT!

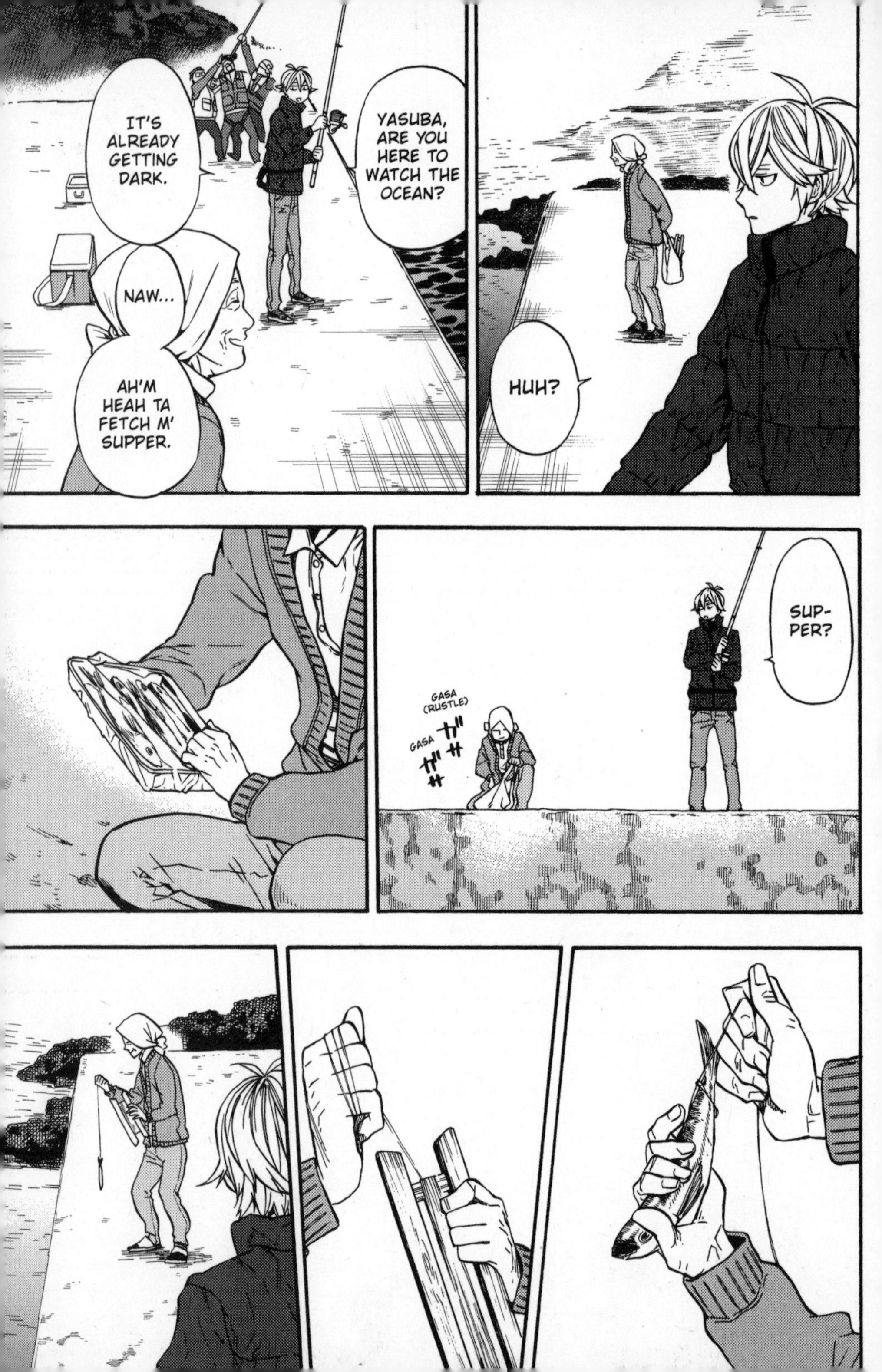
HUH?
YASUBA, ARE YOU HERE TO WATCH THE OCEAN?
IT'S ALREADY GETTING DARK.
NAW...
AH'M HEAH TA FETCH M' SUPPER.
SUP-PER?
GASA (RUSTLE)
GASA

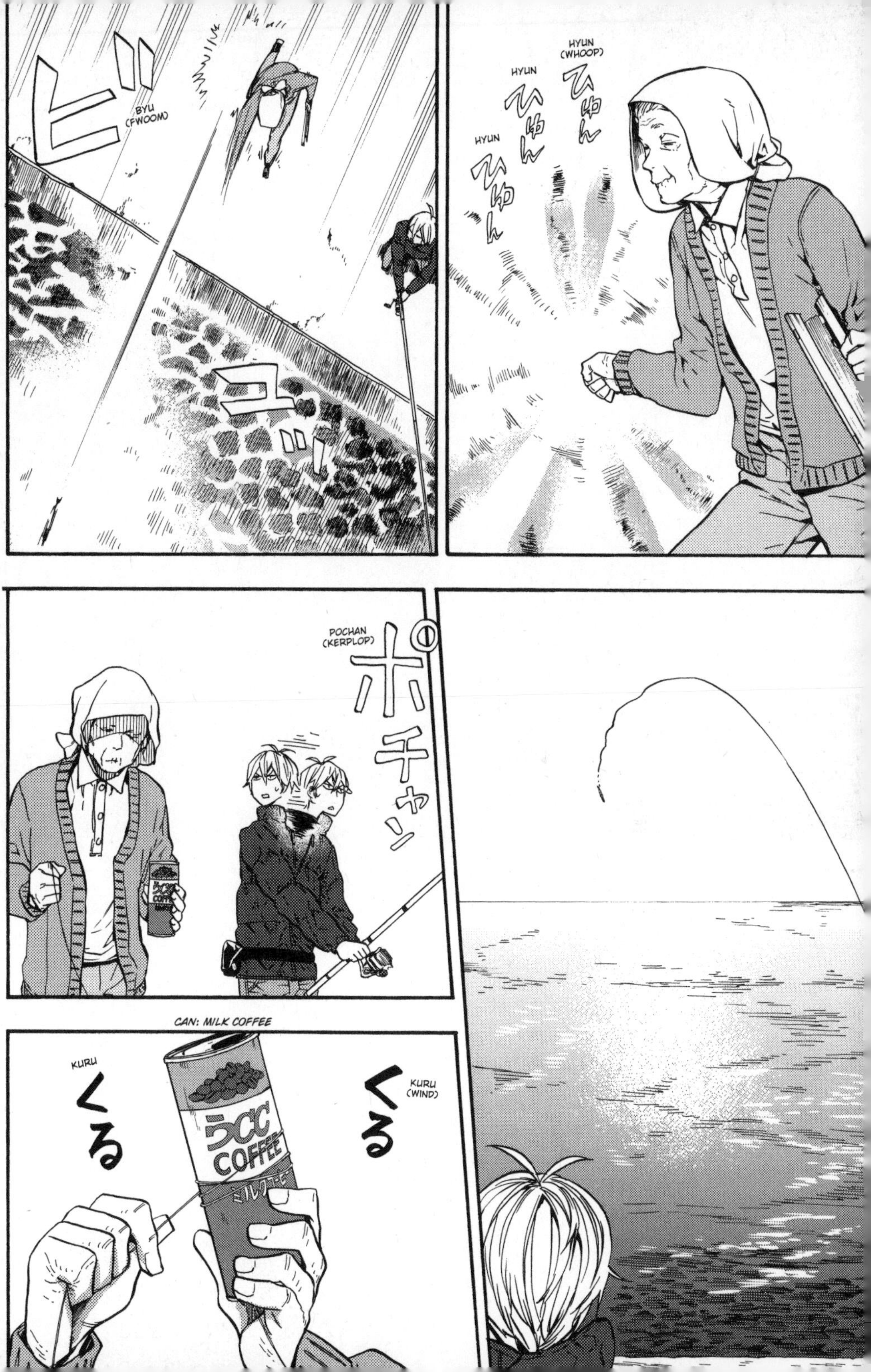
HYUN (WHOOP)
ひゅん
HYUN
ひゅん
HYUN
ひゅん
BYU (FWOOM)
ビュ
POCHAN (KERPLOP)
ポチャン
CAN: MILK COFFEE
KURU (WIND)
くる
KURU
くる
COFFEE

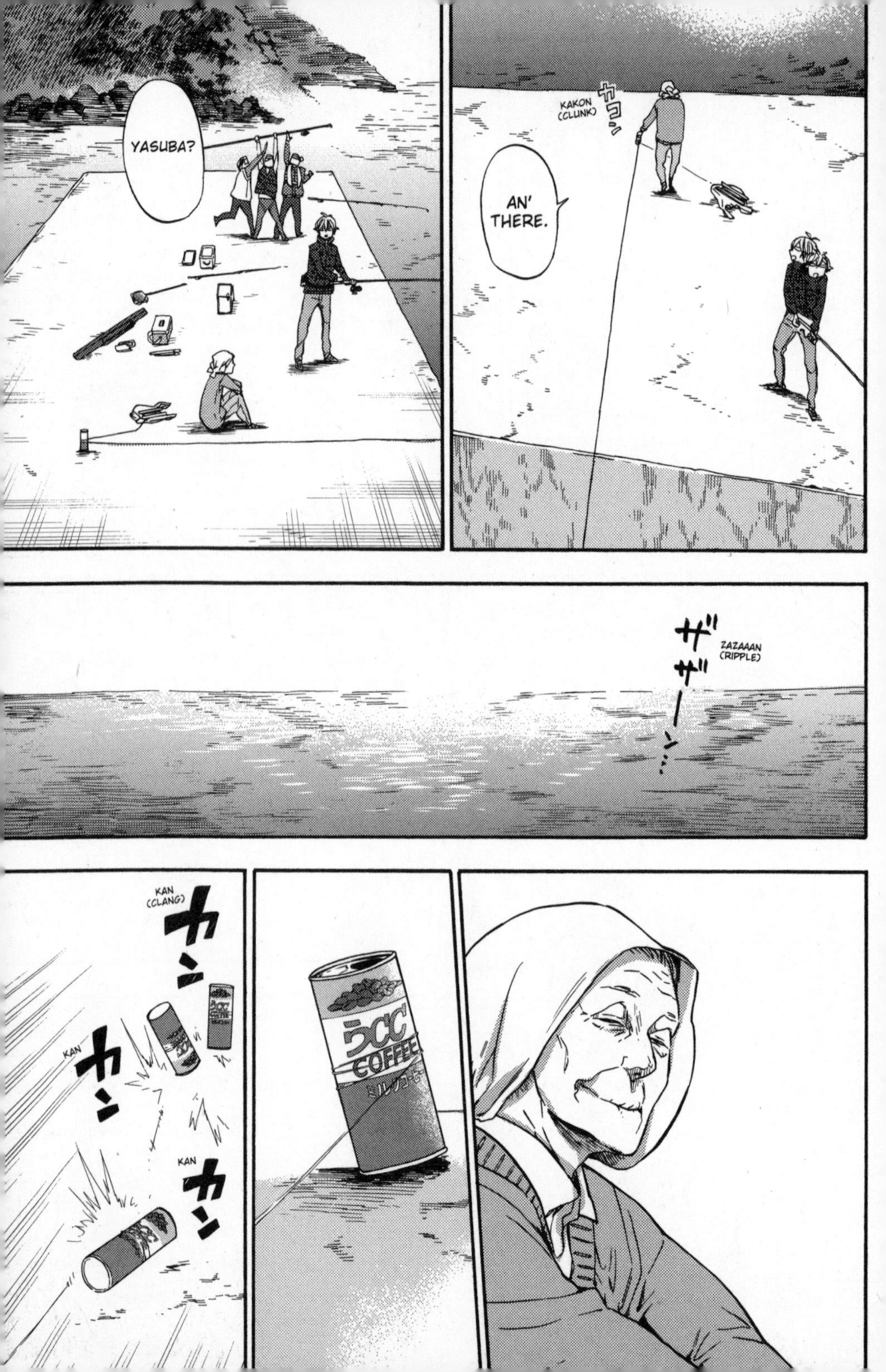

カコッ
KAKON (CLUNK)
AN' THERE.
YASUBA?
ザザーン…
ZAZAAAN (RIPPLE)
COFFEE
カン
KAN (CLANG)
カン
KAN
カン
KAN

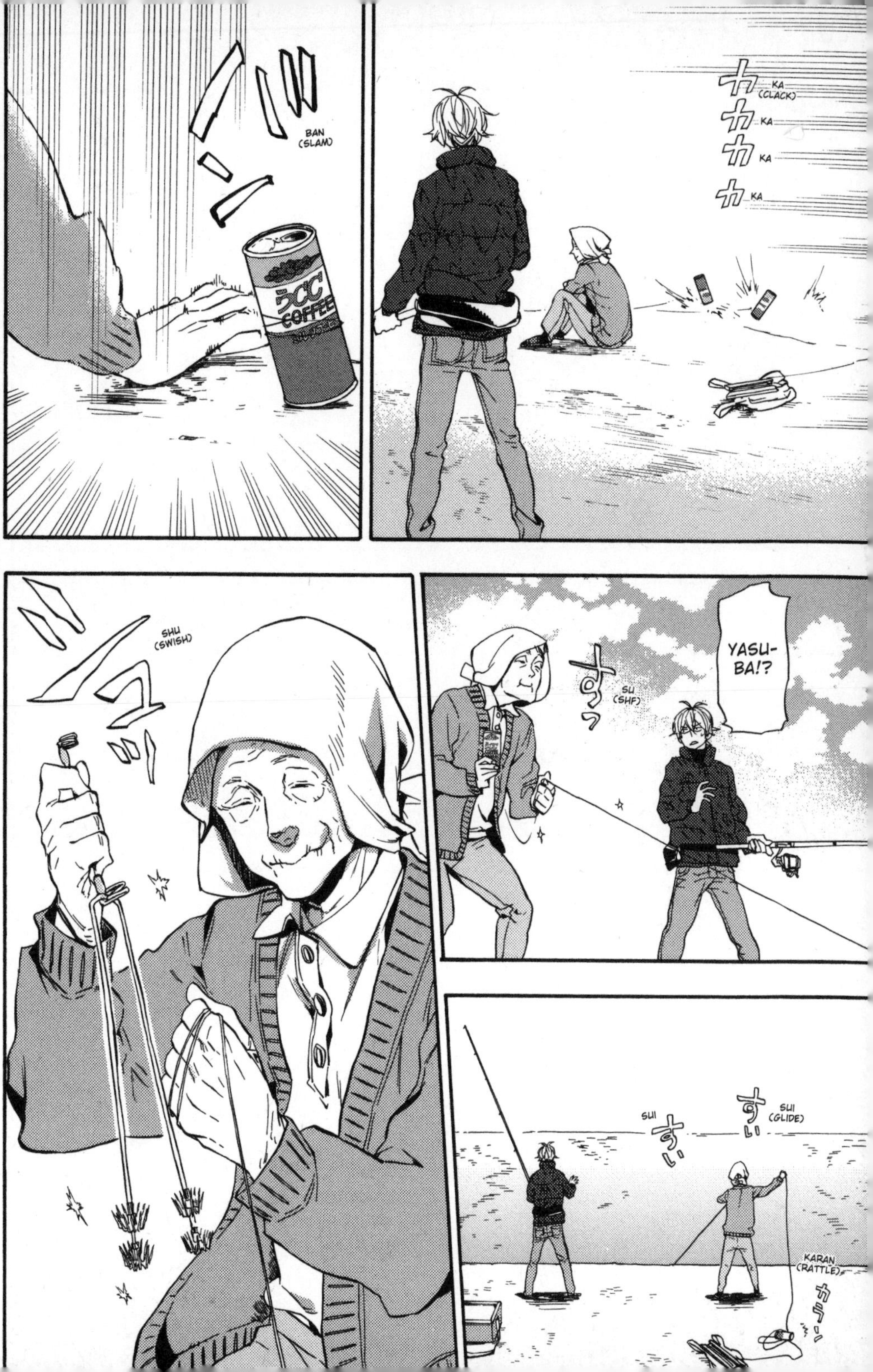
KA (CLACK)
KA
KA
KA
BAN (SLAM)
COFFEE
YASU-BA!?
SU (SHF)
SUI (GLIDE)
SUI
KARAN (RATTLE)
SHU (SWISH)

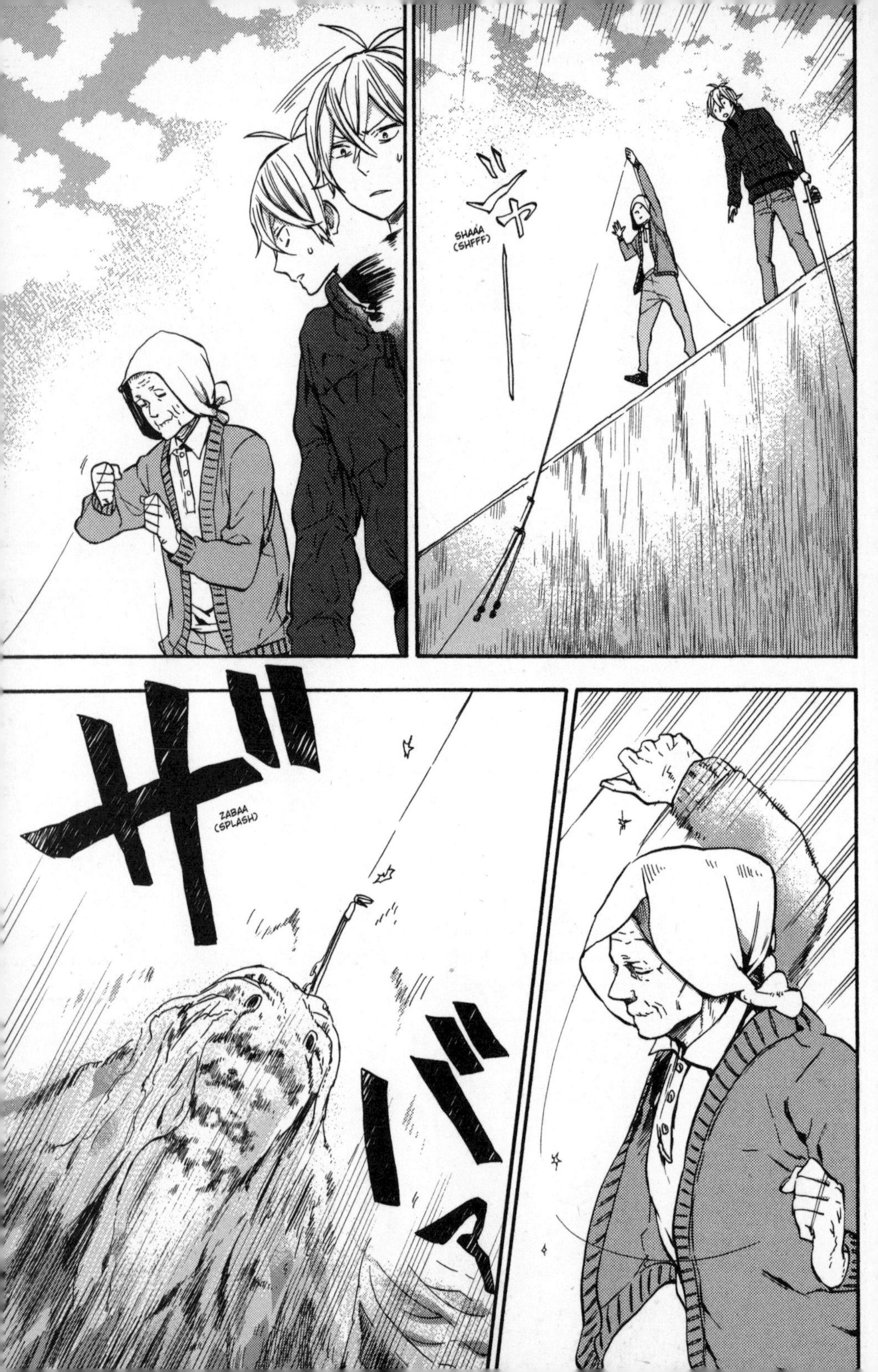
SHAAA (SHFFF)
ZABAA (SPLASH)

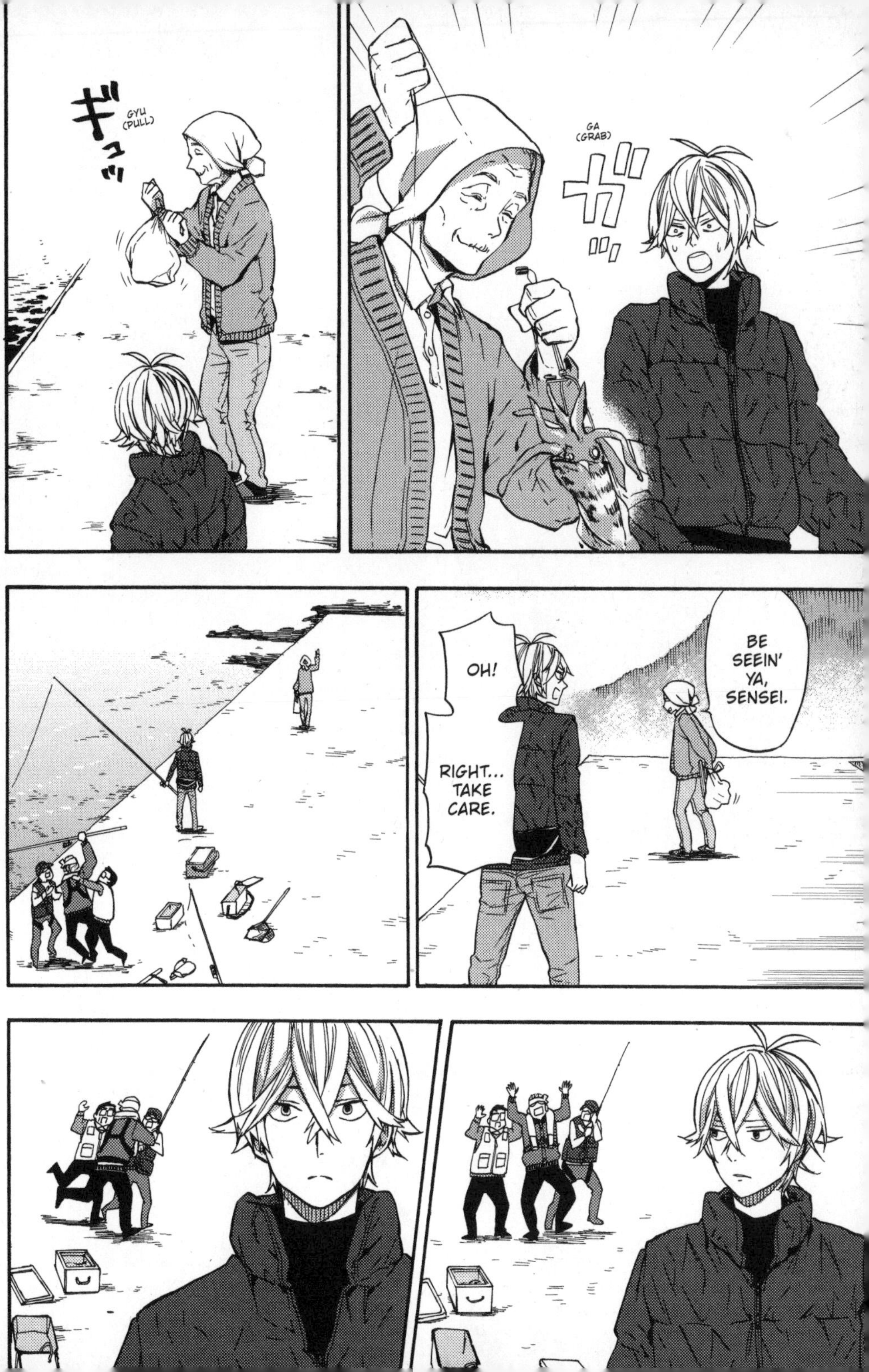
ガッ
GA (GRAB)
ギュッ
GYU (PULL)
BE SEEIN' YA, SENSEI.
OH!
RIGHT... TAKE CARE.

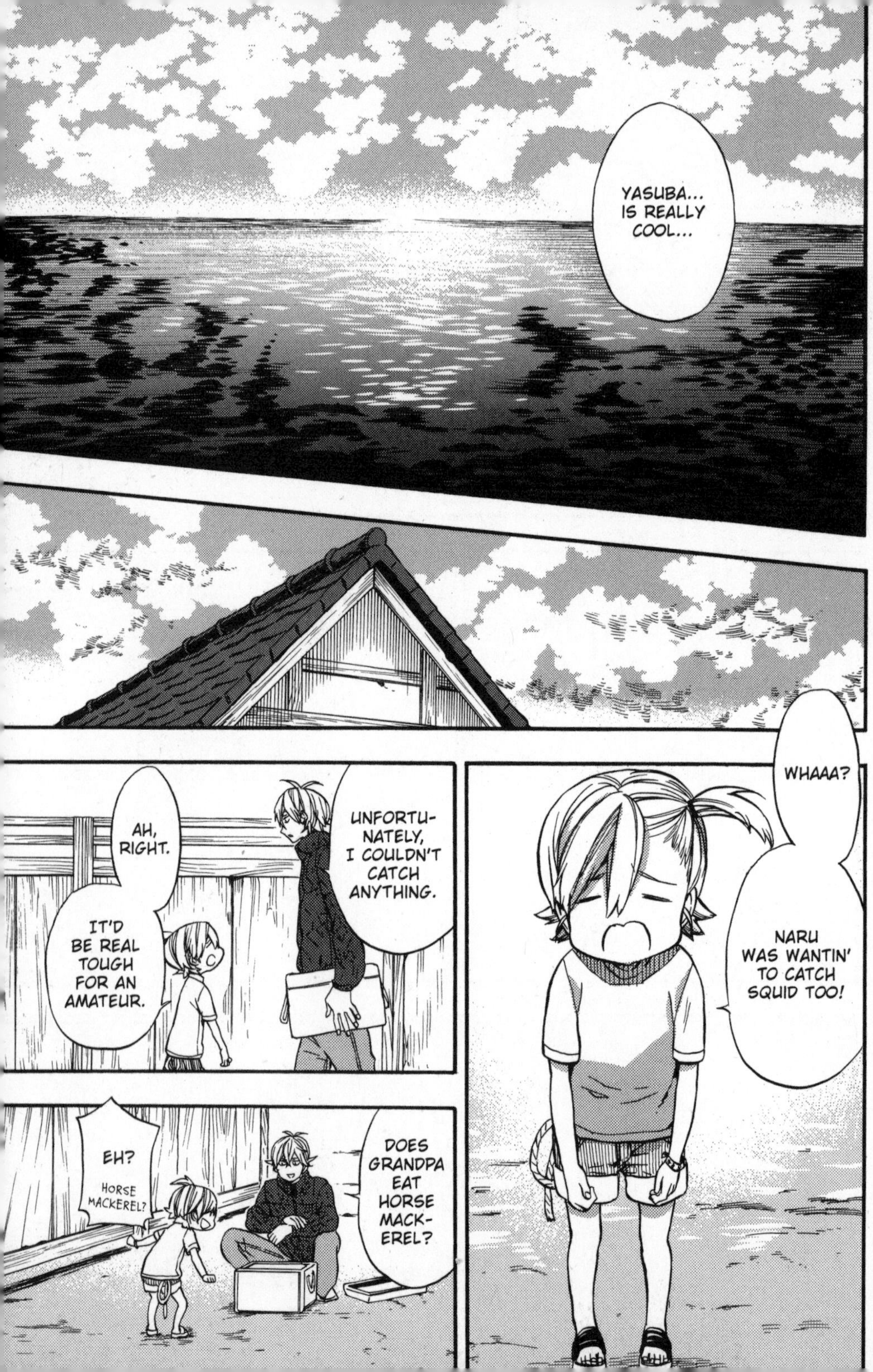
YASUBA... IS REALLY COOL...
WHAAA?
NARU WAS WANTIN' TO CATCH SQUID TOO!
UNFORTUNATELY, I COULDN'T CATCH ANYTHING.
AH, RIGHT.
IT'D BE REAL TOUGH FOR AN AMATEUR.
DOES GRANDPA EAT HORSE MACKEREL?
EH?
HORSE MACKEREL?

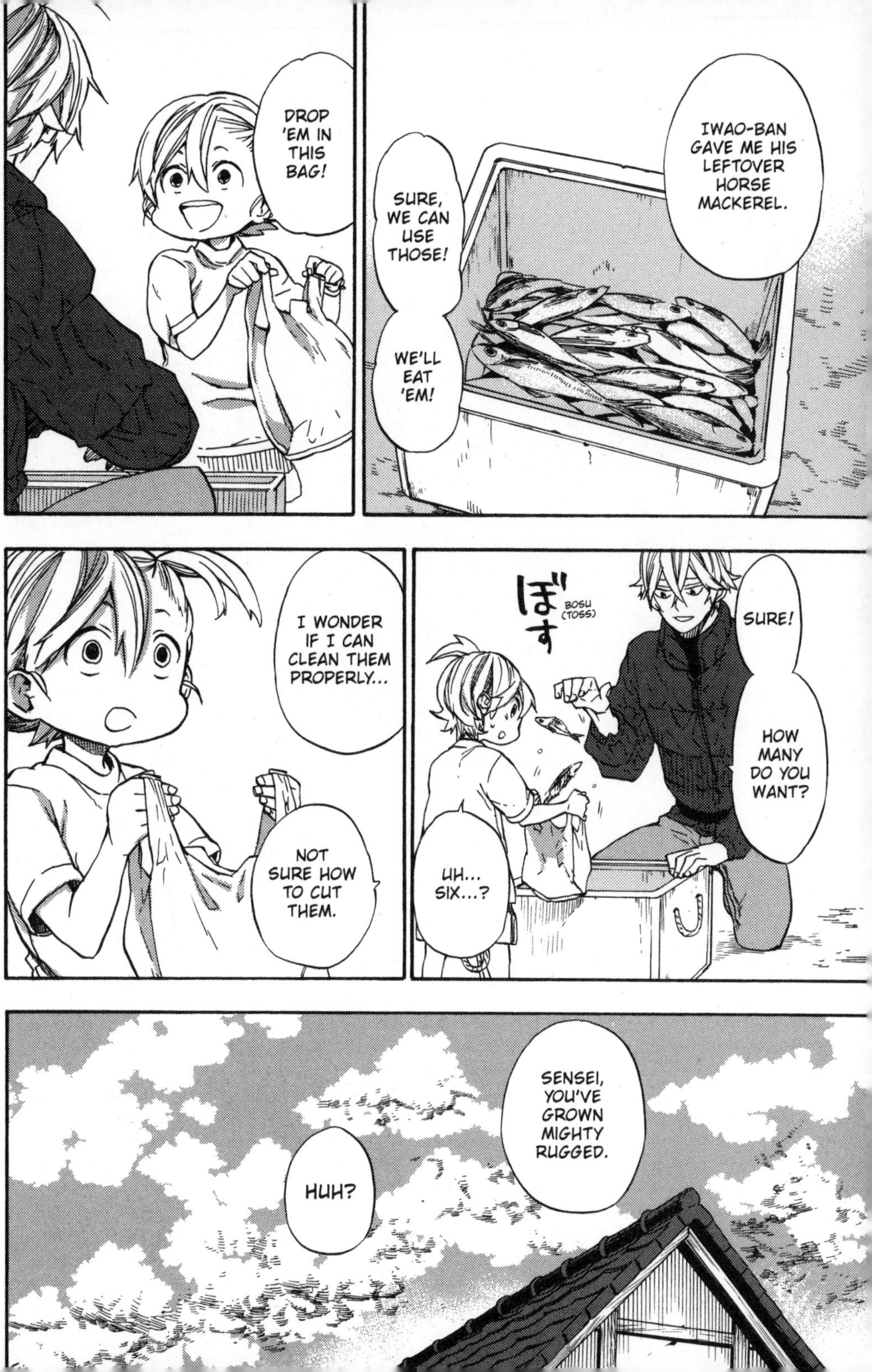
IWAO-BAN GAVE ME HIS LEFTOVER HORSE MACKEREL.
SURE, WE CAN USE THOSE!
WE'LL EAT 'EM!
DROP 'EM IN THIS BAG!
SURE!
ぼす BOSU (TOSS)
HOW MANY DO YOU WANT?
UH... SIX...?
I WONDER IF I CAN CLEAN THEM PROPERLY...
NOT SURE HOW TO CUT THEM.
SENSEI, YOU'VE GROWN MIGHTY RUGGED.
HUH?

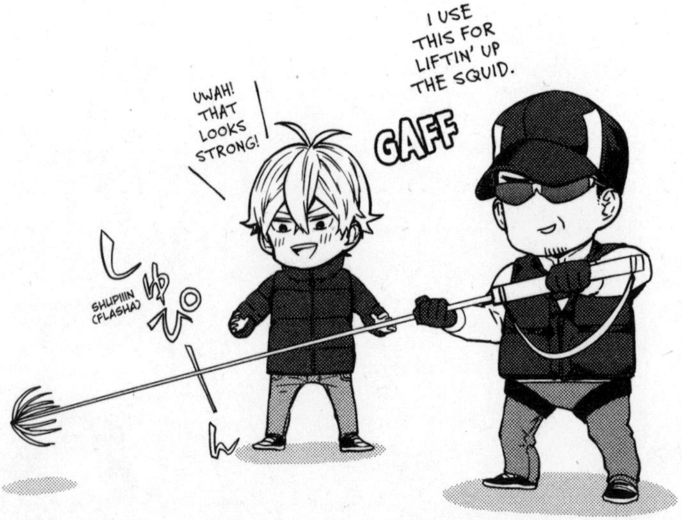
I USE THIS FOR LIFTIN' UP THE SQUID.
GAFF
UWAH! THAT LOOKS STRONG!
しゅぴーん
SHUPIIIN (FLASHA)

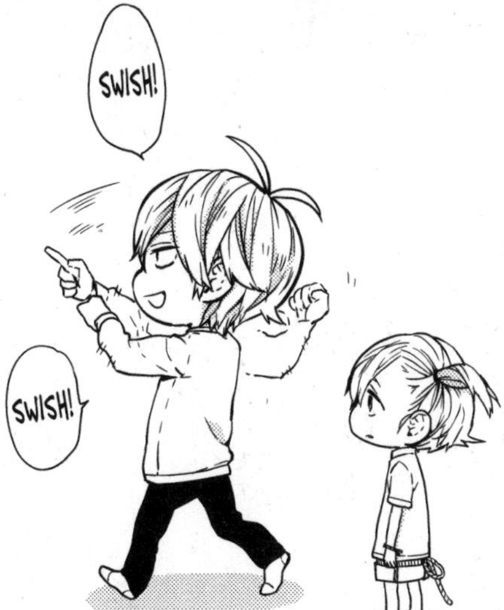
SWISH!
SWISH!

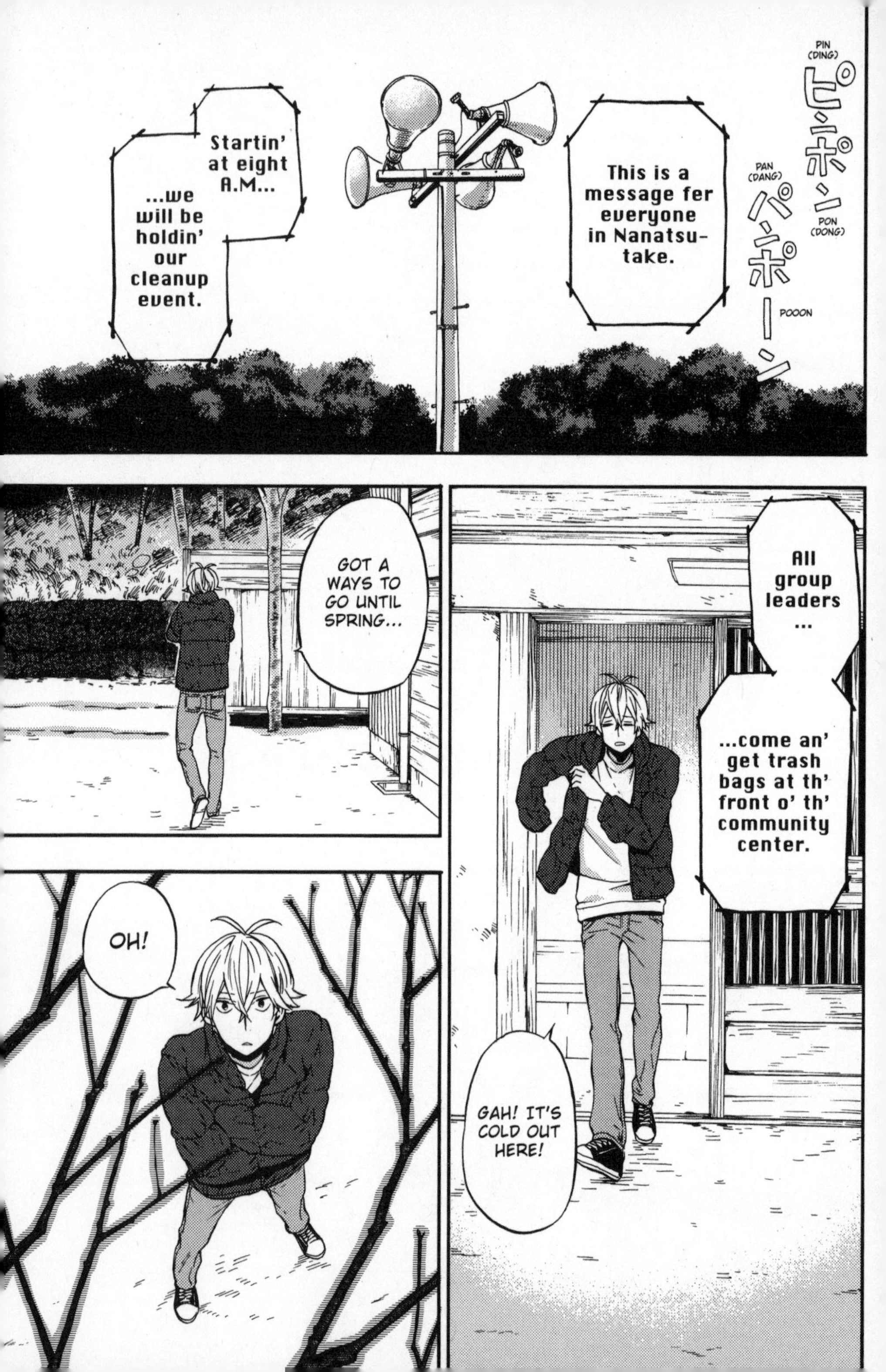
ピンポン
PIN (DING)
PON (DONG)
パンポーン
PAN (DANG)
POOON
This is a message fer everyone in Nanatsu-take.
Startin' at eight A.M...
...we will be holdin' our cleanup event.
All group leaders...
...come an' get trash bags at th' front o' th' community center.
GAH! IT'S COLD OUT HERE!
GOT A WAYS TO GO UNTIL SPRING...
OH!

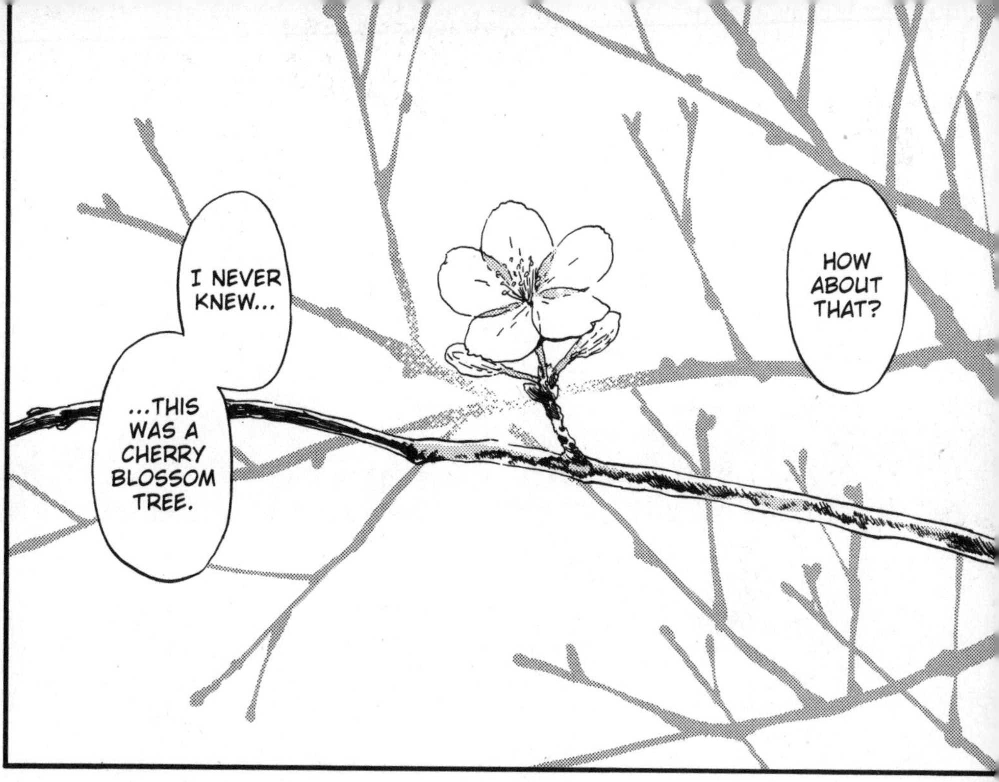
HOW ABOUT THAT?
I NEVER KNEW...
...THIS WAS A CHERRY BLOSSOM TREE.

Act.127

SAKURAN HANAN SEJORU

(Translation: Cherry Blossoms Are in Bloom)

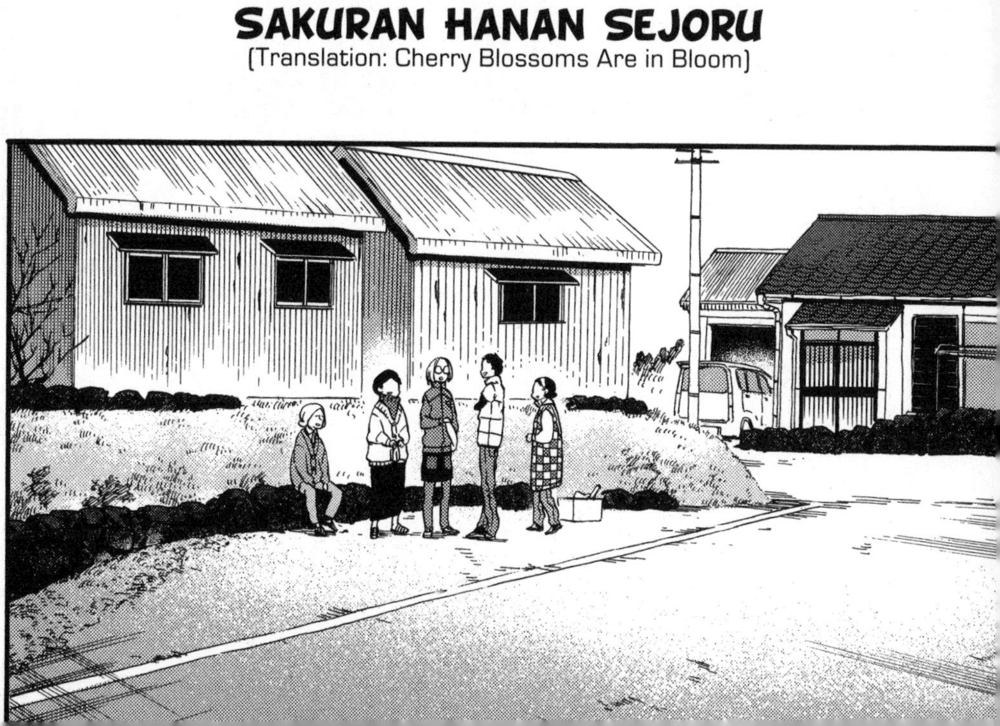

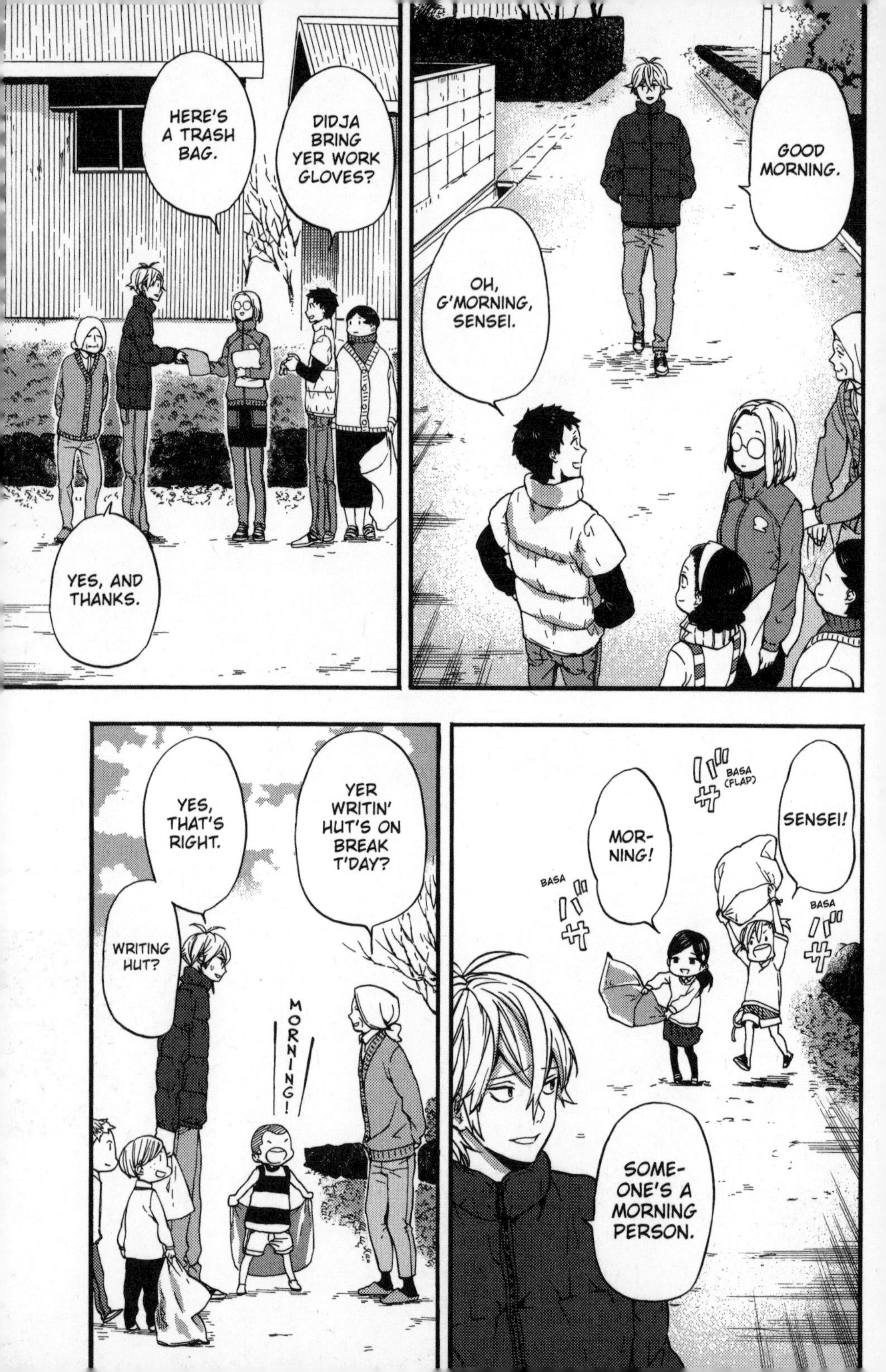
GOOD MORNING.
OH, G'MORNING, SENSEI.
DIDJA BRING YER WORK GLOVES?
HERE'S A TRASH BAG.
YES, AND THANKS.
SENSEI!
BASA (FLAP)
MOR-NING!
BASA
BASA
SOME-ONE'S A MORNING PERSON.
YER WRITIN' HUT'S ON BREAK T'DAY?
YES, THAT'S RIGHT.
MORNING!
WRITING HUT?

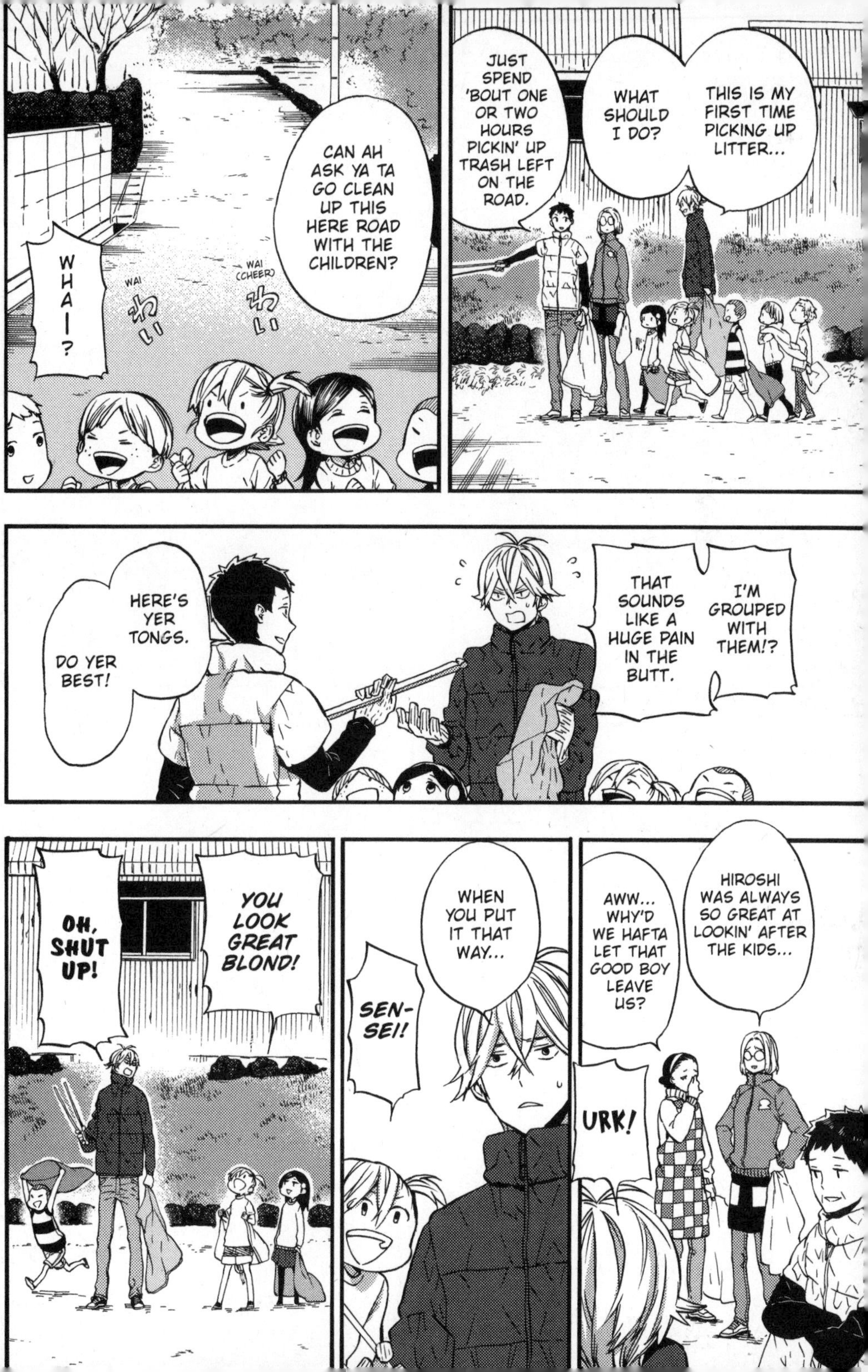
THIS IS MY FIRST TIME PICKING UP LITTER...
WHAT SHOULD I DO?
JUST SPEND 'BOUT ONE OR TWO HOURS PICKIN' UP TRASH LEFT ON THE ROAD.
CAN AH ASK YA TA GO CLEAN UP THIS HERE ROAD WITH THE CHILDREN?
WAI (CHEER)
わい
WAI
わい
WHAI?
I'M GROUPED WITH THEM!?
THAT SOUNDS LIKE A HUGE PAIN IN THE BUTT.
HERE'S YER TONGS.
DO YER BEST!
HIROSHI WAS ALWAYS SO GREAT AT LOOKIN' AFTER THE KIDS...
AWW... WHY'D WE HAFTA LET THAT GOOD BOY LEAVE US?
URK!
WHEN YOU PUT IT THAT WAY...
SEN-SEI!
YOU LOOK GREAT BLOND!
OH, SHUT UP!

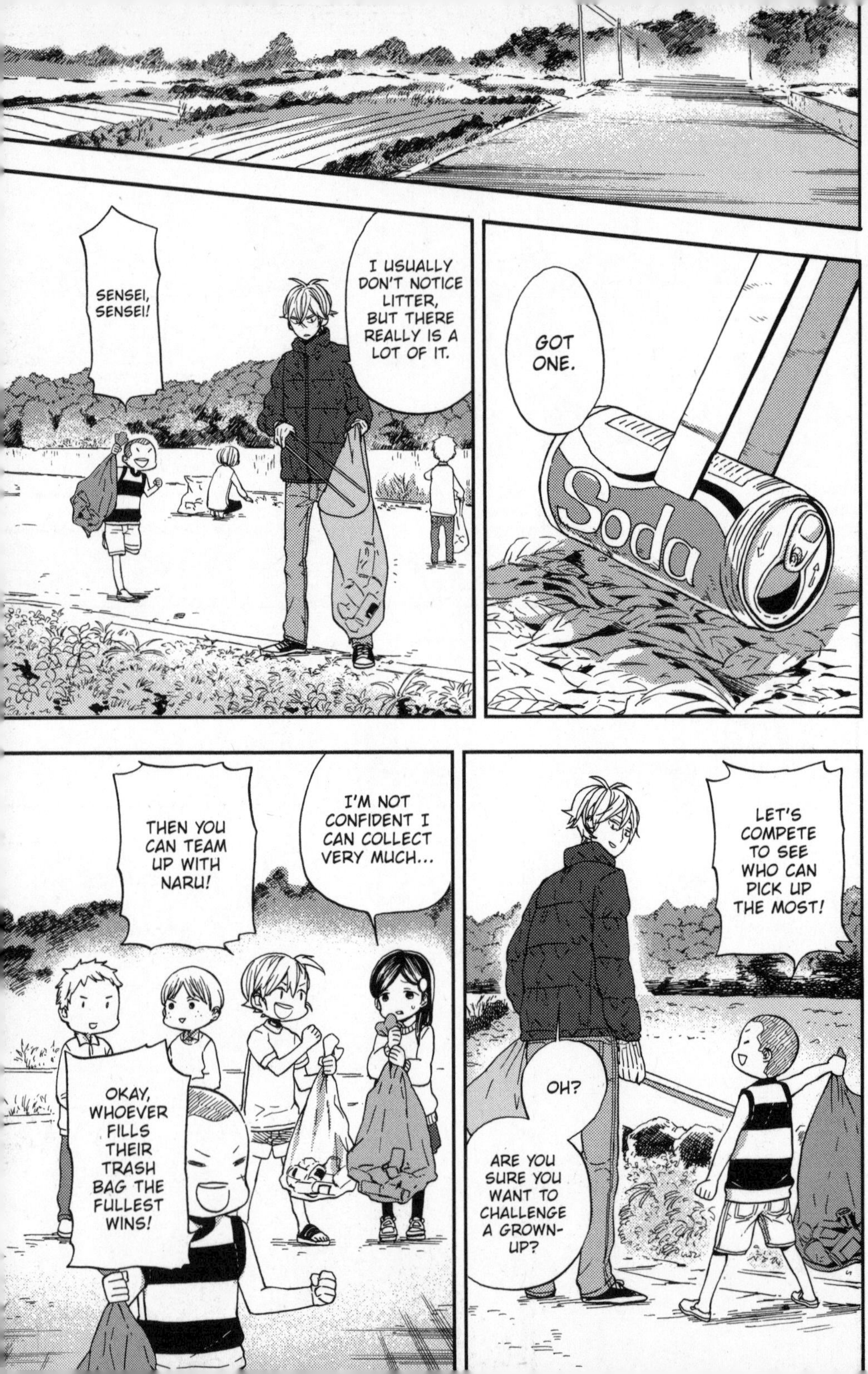
GOT ONE.
Soda
I USUALLY DON'T NOTICE LITTER, BUT THERE REALLY IS A LOT OF IT.
SENSEI, SENSEI!
LET'S COMPETE TO SEE WHO CAN PICK UP THE MOST!
OH?
ARE YOU SURE YOU WANT TO CHALLENGE A GROWN-UP?
I'M NOT CONFIDENT I CAN COLLECT VERY MUCH...
THEN YOU CAN TEAM UP WITH NARU!
OKAY, WHOEVER FILLS THEIR TRASH BAG THE FULLEST WINS!

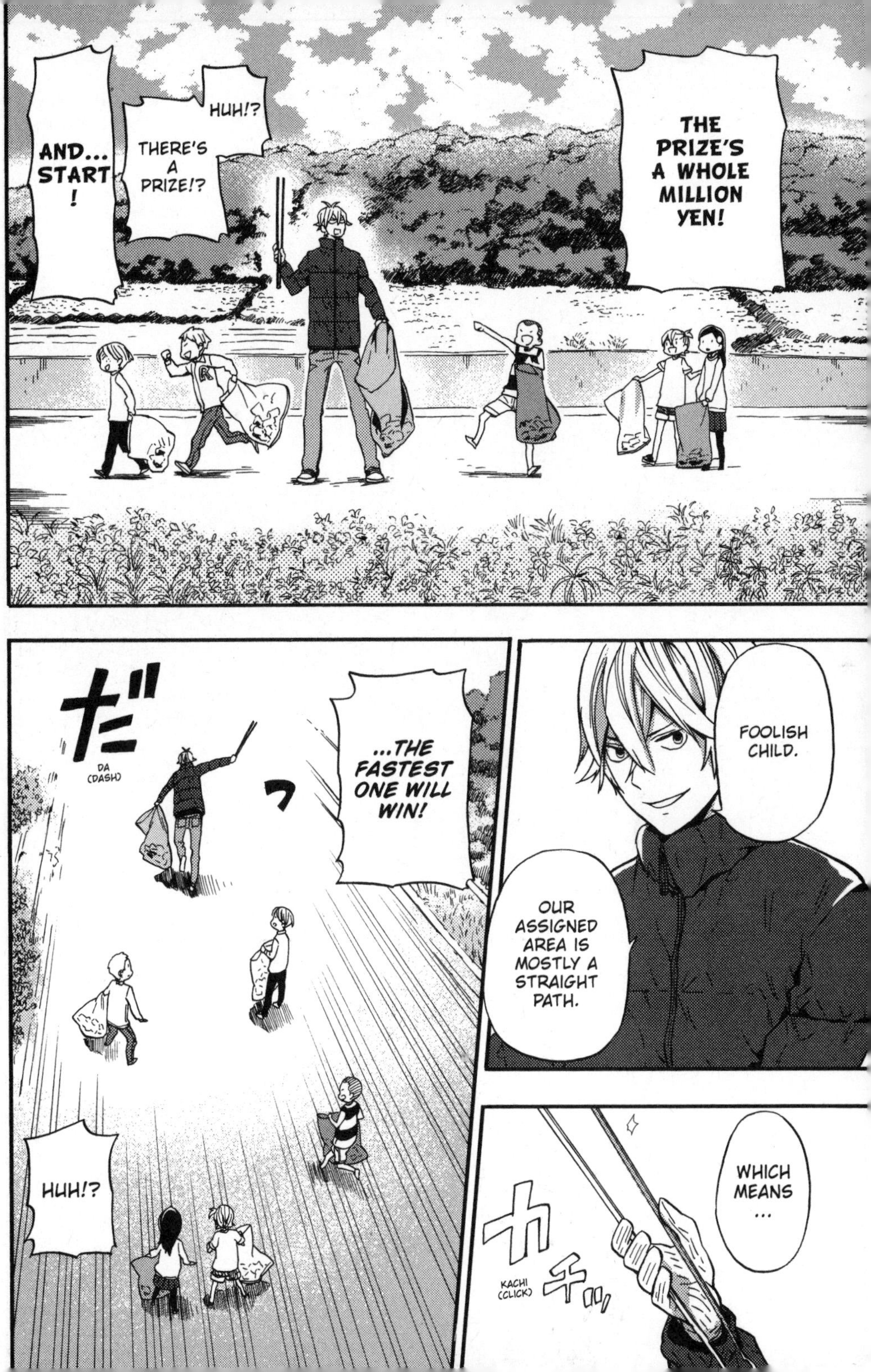

THE PRIZE'S A WHOLE MILLION YEN!
HUH!?
THERE'S A PRIZE!?
AND... START!
FOOLISH CHILD.
OUR ASSIGNED AREA IS MOSTLY A STRAIGHT PATH.
WHICH MEANS...
カチッ
KACHI (CLICK)
...THE FASTEST ONE WILL WIN!
だ
DA (DASH)
HUH!?

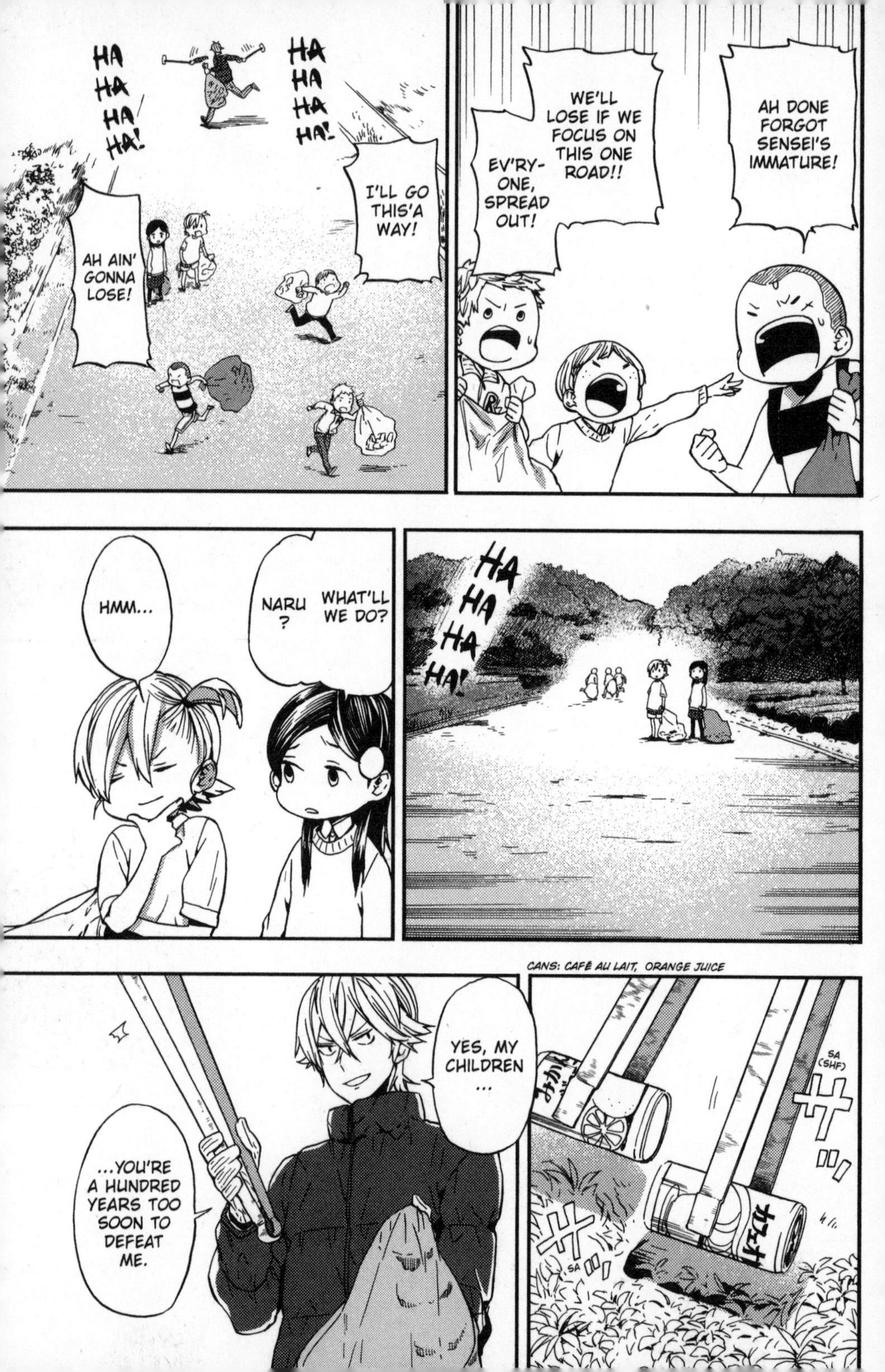
AH DONE FORGOT SENSEI'S IMMATURE!
WE'LL LOSE IF WE FOCUS ON THIS ONE ROAD!!
EV'RY-ONE, SPREAD OUT!
I'LL GO THIS'A WAY!
HA HA HA HA!
HA HA HA HA!
AH AIN' GONNA LOSE!
HA HA HA HA!
WHAT'LL WE DO?
NARU?
HMM...
CANS: CAFÉ AU LAIT, ORANGE JUICE
SA (SHF)
SA
YES, MY CHILDREN ...
...YOU'RE A HUNDRED YEARS TOO SOON TO DEFEAT ME.

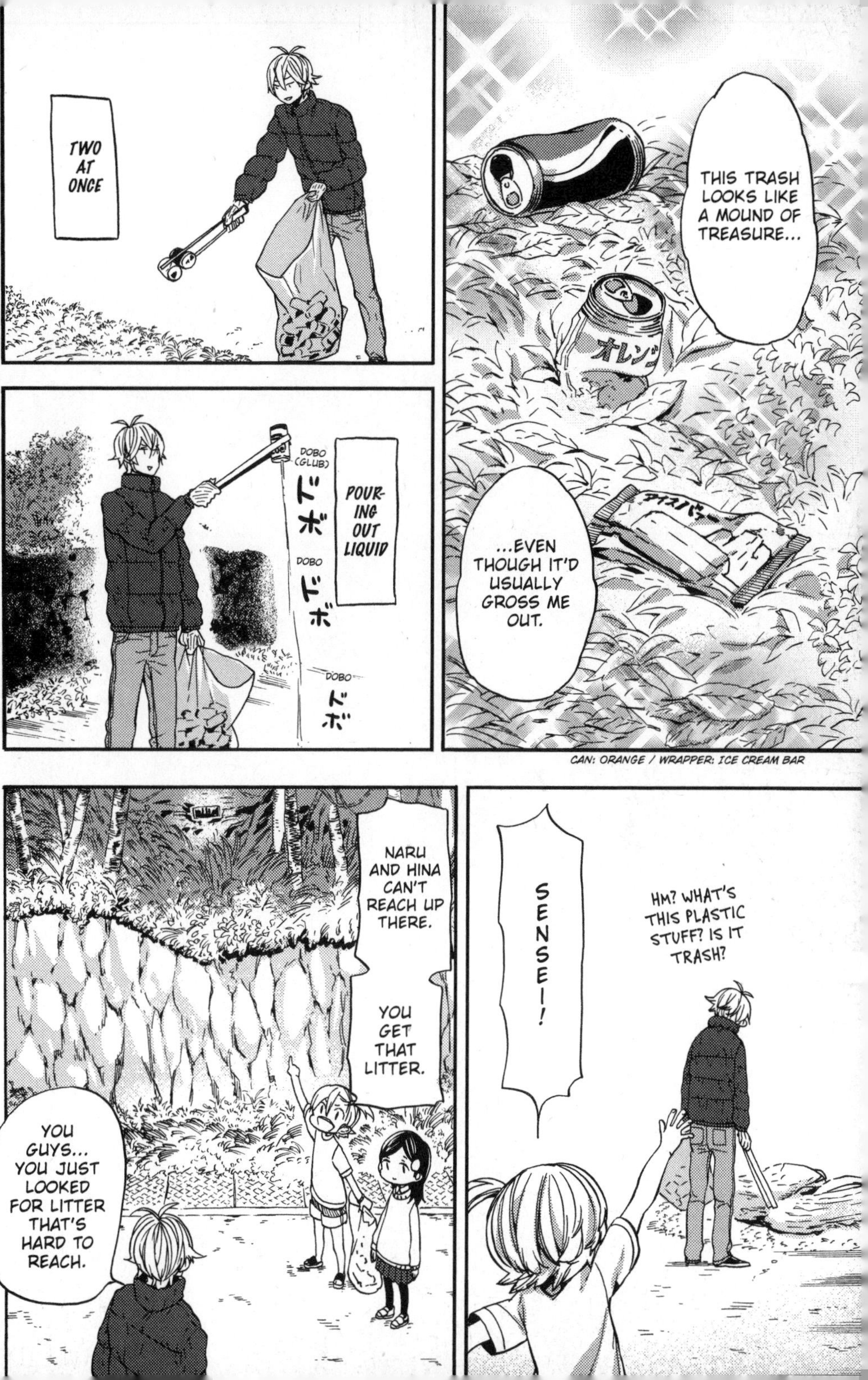
THIS TRASH LOOKS LIKE A MOUND OF TREASURE...
...EVEN THOUGH IT'D USUALLY GROSS ME OUT.
CAN: ORANGE / WRAPPER: ICE CREAM BAR
TWO AT ONCE
DOBO (GLUB) ドボ
POUR-ING OUT LIQUID
DOBO ドボ
DOBO ドボ
SENSEI!
HM? WHAT'S THIS PLASTIC STUFF? IS IT TRASH?
NARU AND HINA CAN'T REACH UP THERE.
YOU GET THAT LITTER.
YOU GUYS... YOU JUST LOOKED FOR LITTER THAT'S HARD TO REACH.

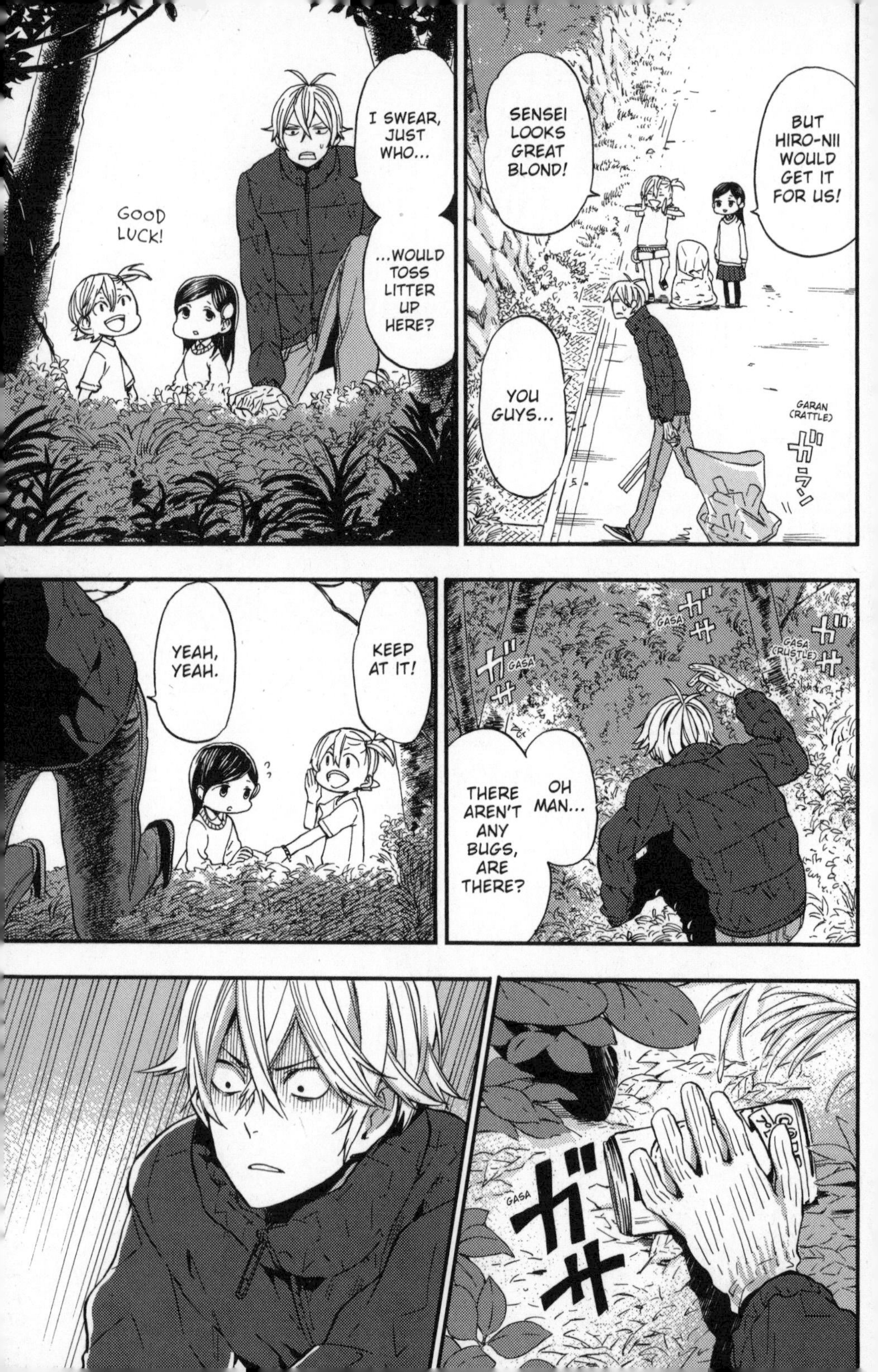
BUT HIRO-NII WOULD GET IT FOR US!
SENSEI LOOKS GREAT BLOND!
YOU GUYS...
GARAN (RATTLE)
I SWEAR, JUST WHO...
...WOULD TOSS LITTER UP HERE?
GOOD LUCK!
GASA (RUSTLE)
GASA
GASA
OH MAN...
THERE AREN'T ANY BUGS, ARE THERE?
KEEP AT IT!
YEAH, YEAH.
GASA

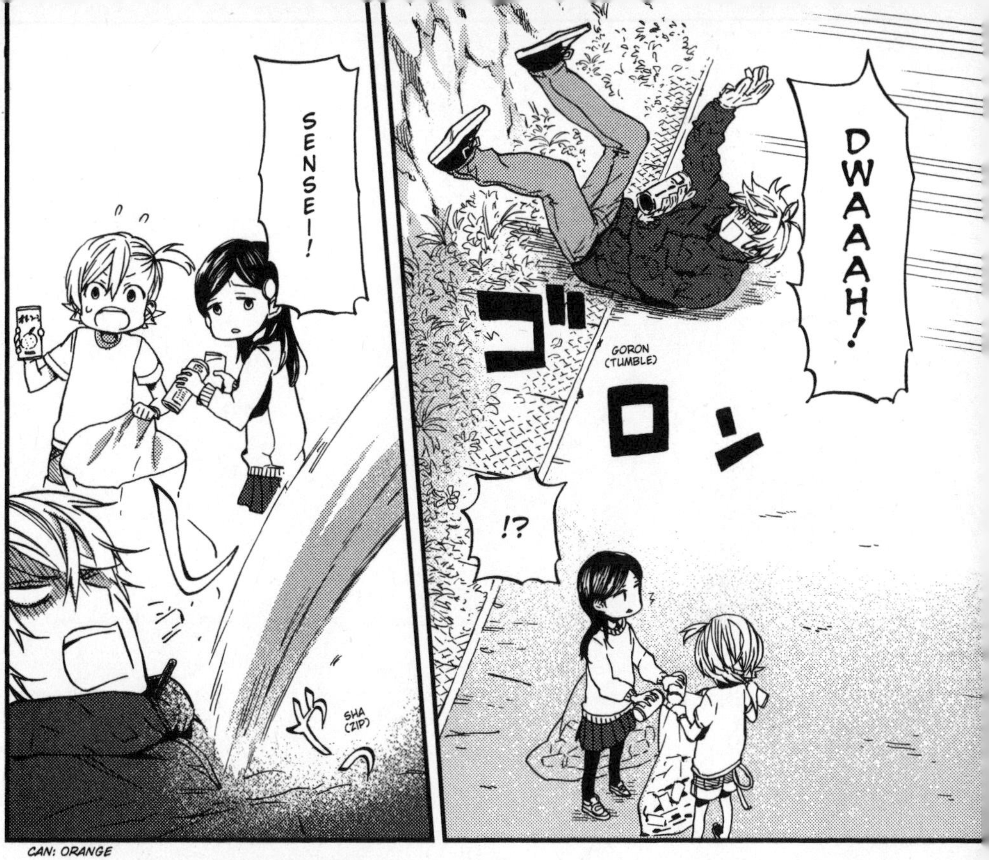
DWAAAH!
GORON (TUMBLE)
ゴロン
!?
SENSEI!
SHA (ZIP)
シャ

CAN: ORANGE

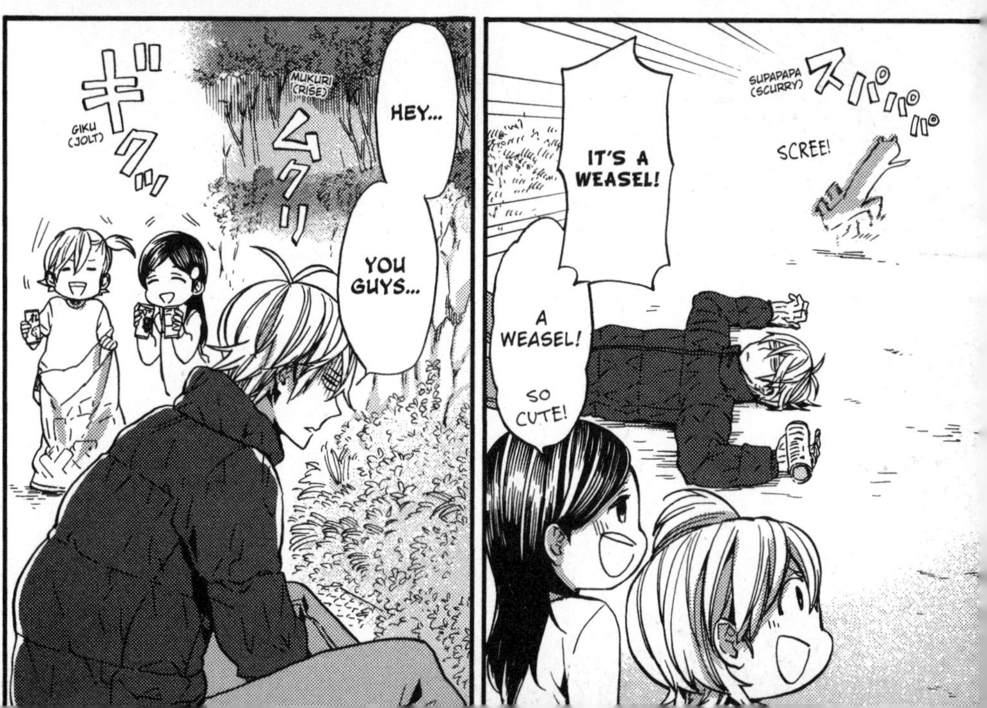
SUPAPAPA (SCURRY)
スパパパ
SCREE!
IT'S A WEASEL!
A WEASEL!
SO CUTE!
HEY...
YOU GUYS...
MUKURI (RISE)
ムクリ
GIKU (JOLT)
ギクッ

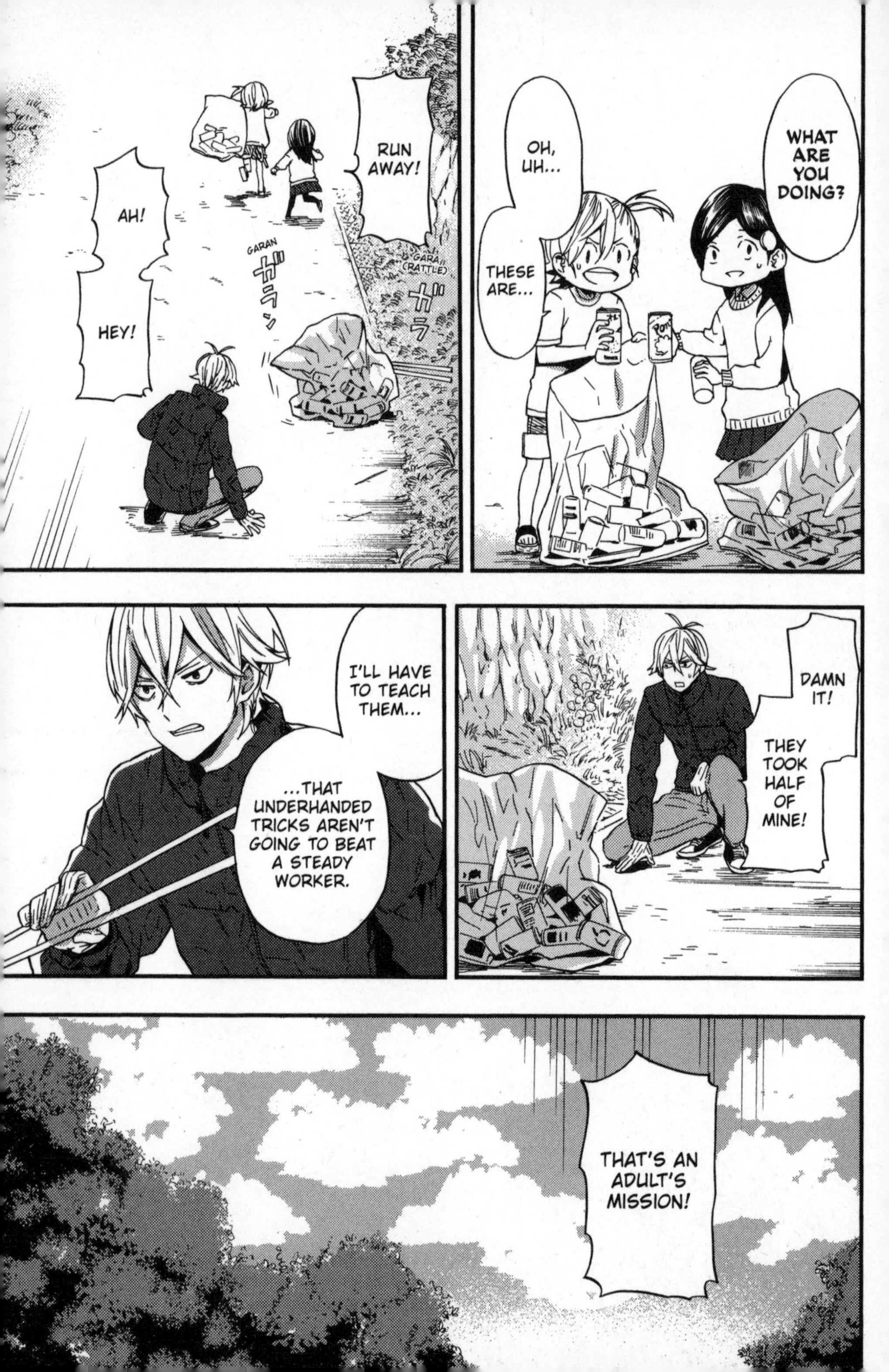
WHAT ARE YOU DOING?
OH, UH...
THESE ARE...
RUN AWAY!
GARA (RATTLE)
GARAN
AH!
HEY!
DAMN IT!
THEY TOOK HALF OF MINE!
I'LL HAVE TO TEACH THEM...
...THAT UNDERHANDED TRICKS AREN'T GOING TO BEAT A STEADY WORKER.
THAT'S AN ADULT'S MISSION!

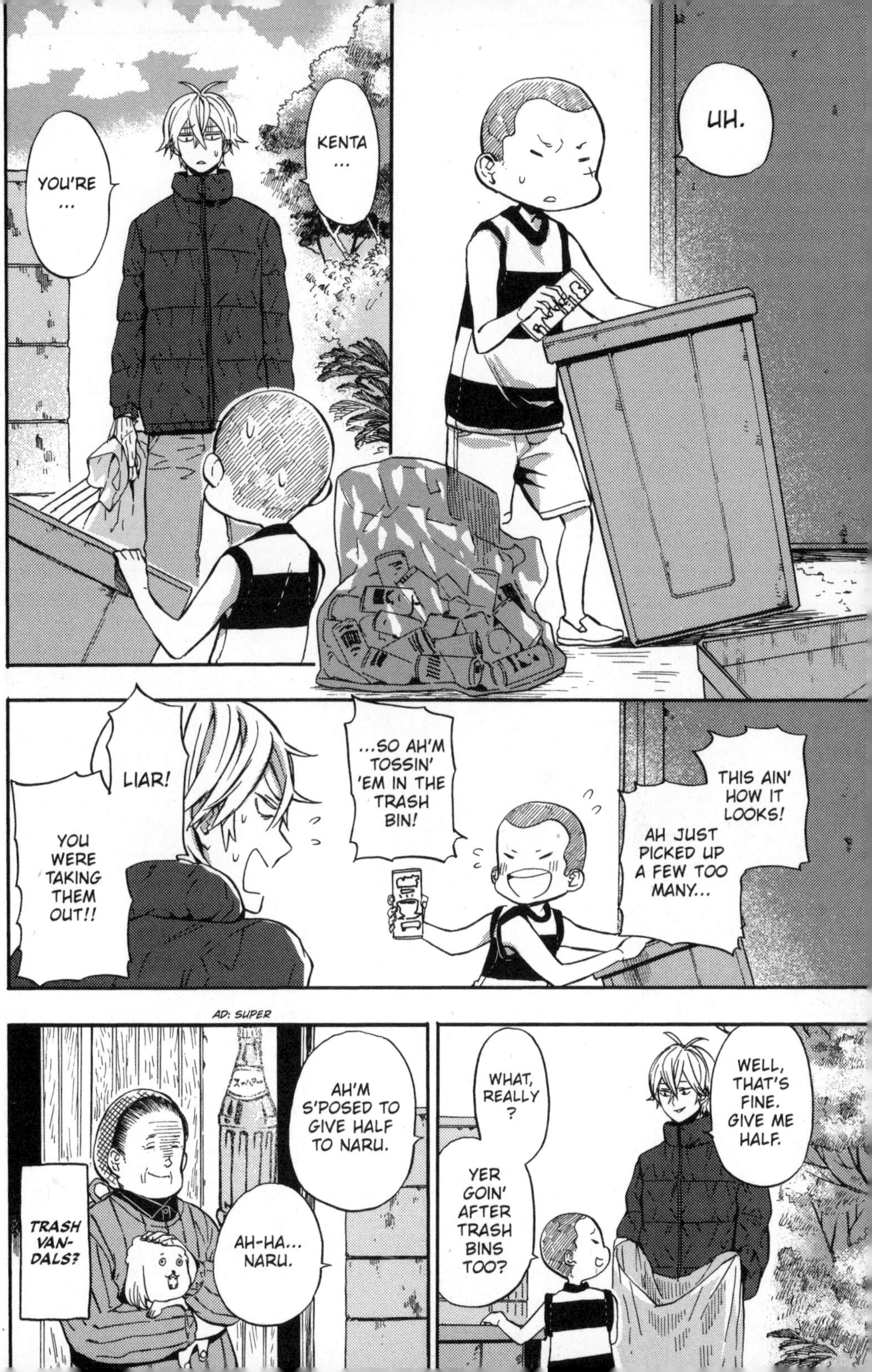
UH.
KENTA...
YOU'RE...
THIS AIN' HOW IT LOOKS!
AH JUST PICKED UP A FEW TOO MANY...
...SO AH'M TOSSIN' 'EM IN THE TRASH BIN!
LIAR!
YOU WERE TAKING THEM OUT!!
WELL, THAT'S FINE. GIVE ME HALF.
WHAT, REALLY?
YER GOIN' AFTER TRASH BINS TOO?
AD: SUPER
AH'M S'POSED TO GIVE HALF TO NARU.
AH-HA... NARU.
TRASH VANDALS?

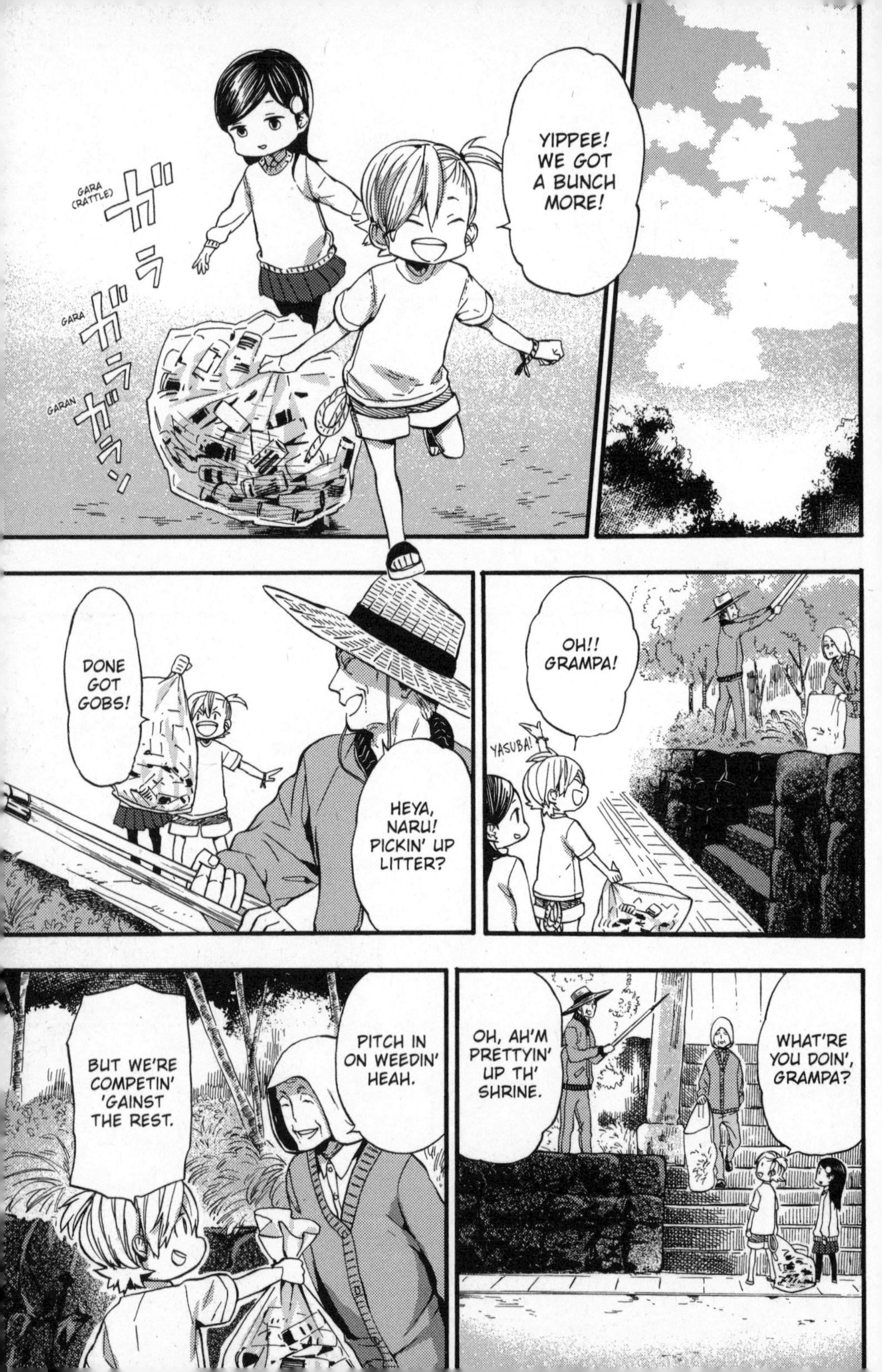
YIPPEE! WE GOT A BUNCH MORE!
GARA (RATTLE)
GARA
GARAN
OH!! GRAMPA!
YASUBA!
HEYA, NARU! PICKIN' UP LITTER?
DONE GOT GOBS!
WHAT'RE YOU DOIN', GRAMPA?
OH, AH'M PRETTYIN' UP TH' SHRINE.
PITCH IN ON WEEDIN' HEAH.
BUT WE'RE COMPETIN' 'GAINST THE REST.

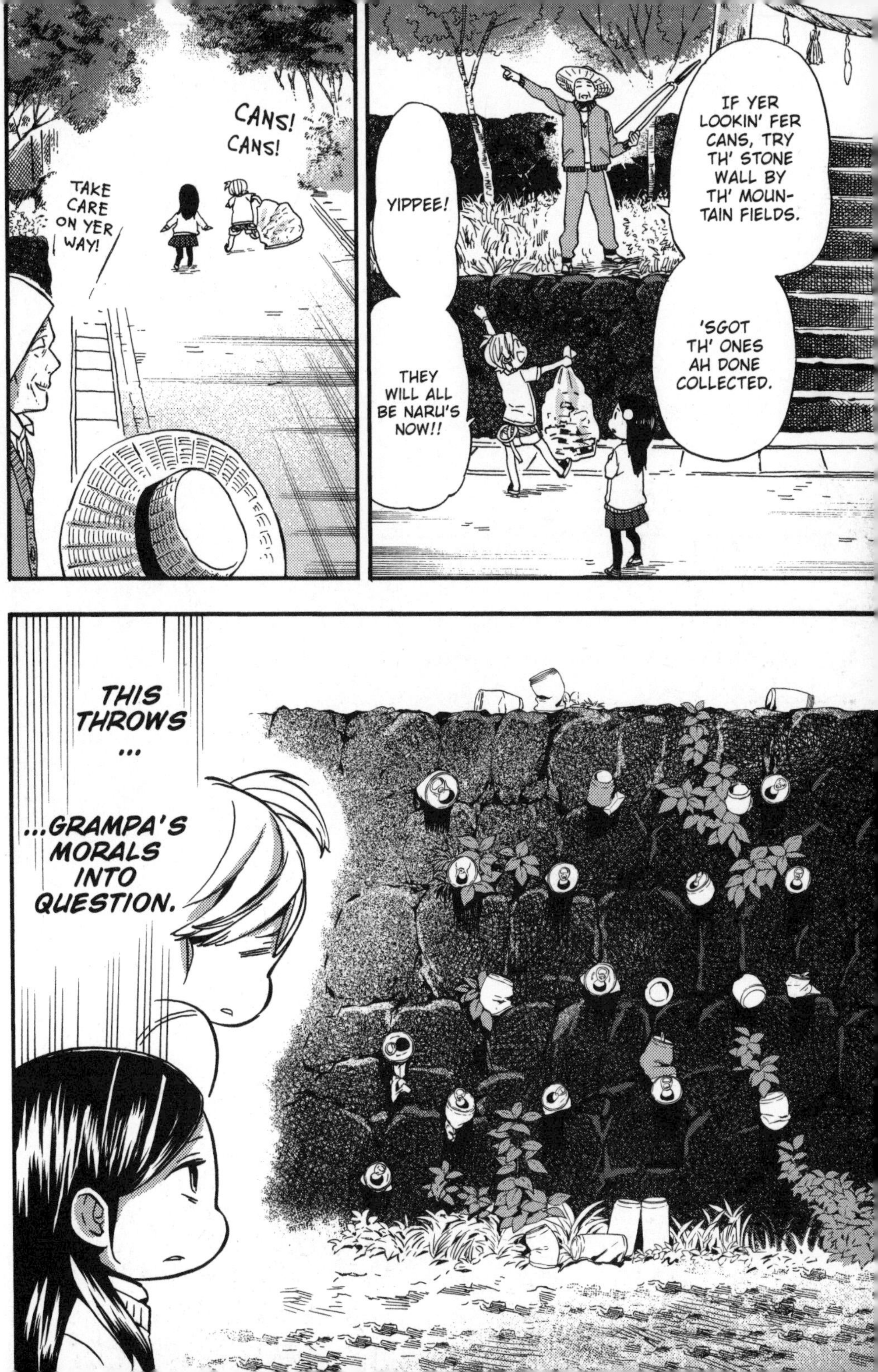
IF YER LOOKIN' FER CANS, TRY TH' STONE WALL BY TH' MOUN-TAIN FIELDS.
'SGOT TH' ONES AH DONE COLLECTED.
YIPPEE!
THEY WILL ALL BE NARU'S NOW!!
CANS! CANS!
TAKE CARE ON YER WAY!
THIS THROWS ...
...GRAMPA'S MORALS INTO QUESTION.

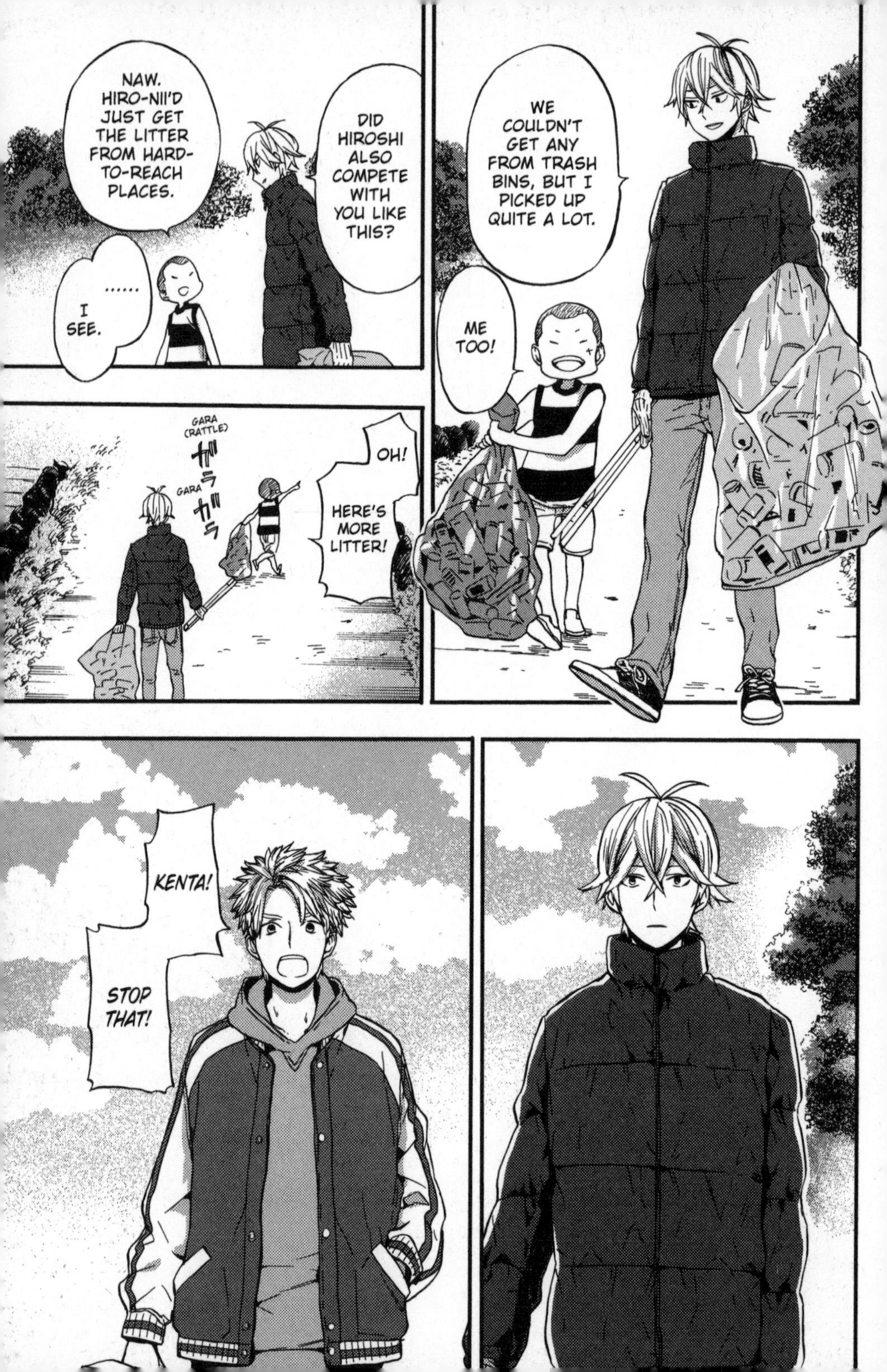
WE COULDN'T GET ANY FROM TRASH BINS, BUT I PICKED UP QUITE A LOT.
ME TOO!
DID HIROSHI ALSO COMPETE WITH YOU LIKE THIS?
NAW. HIRO-NII'D JUST GET THE LITTER FROM HARD-TO-REACH PLACES.
......
I SEE.
OH!
HERE'S MORE LITTER!
GARA (RATTLE)
ガラ
GARA
ガラ
KENTA!
STOP THAT!

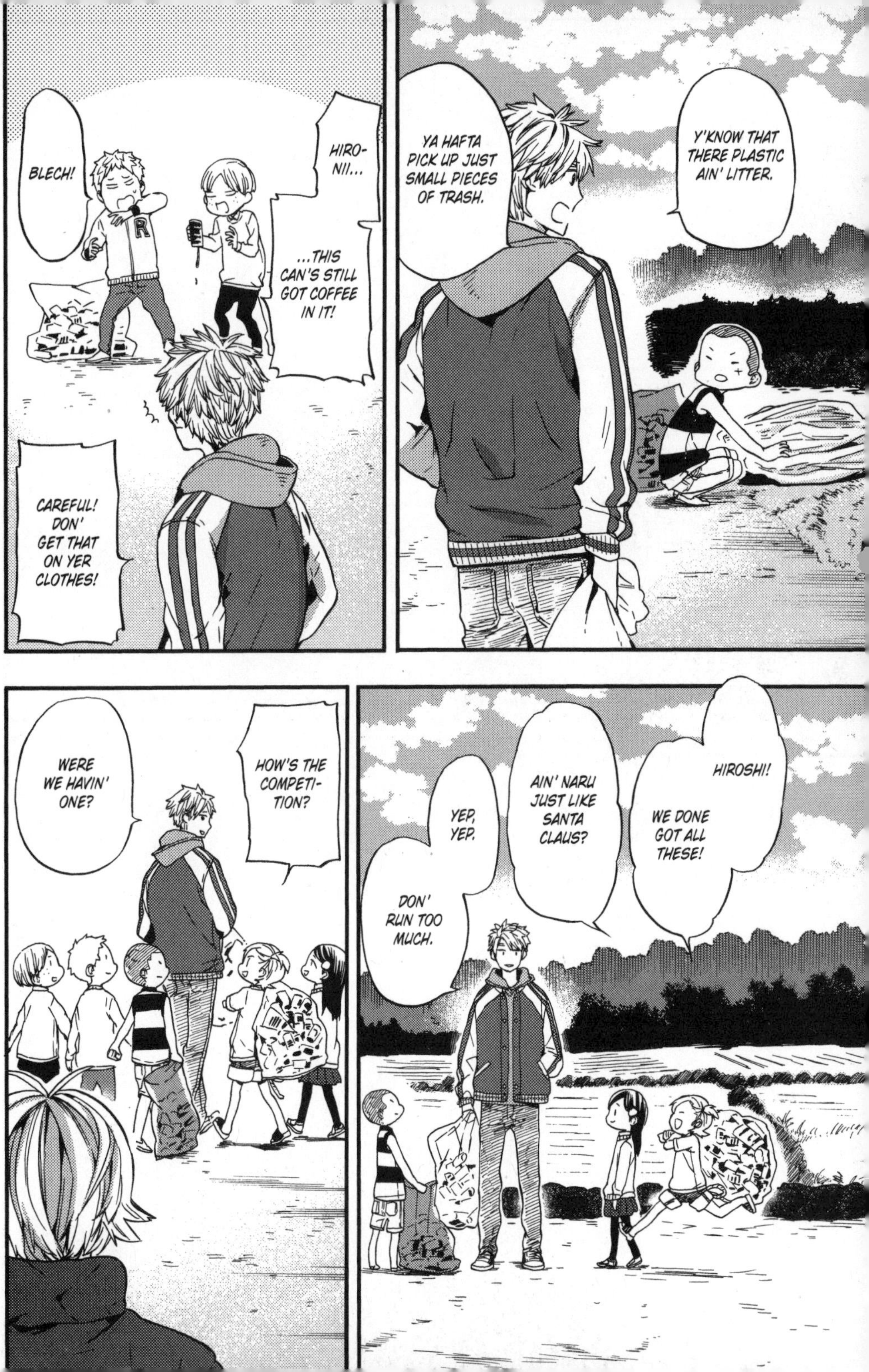
Y'KNOW THAT THERE PLASTIC AIN' LITTER.
YA HAFTA PICK UP JUST SMALL PIECES OF TRASH.
HIRO-NII...
...THIS CAN'S STILL GOT COFFEE IN IT!
BLECH!
CAREFUL! DON' GET THAT ON YER CLOTHES!
HIROSHI!
WE DONE GOT ALL THESE!
AIN' NARU JUST LIKE SANTA CLAUS?
YEP, YEP.
DON' RUN TOO MUCH.
HOW'S THE COMPETITION?
WERE WE HAVIN' ONE?

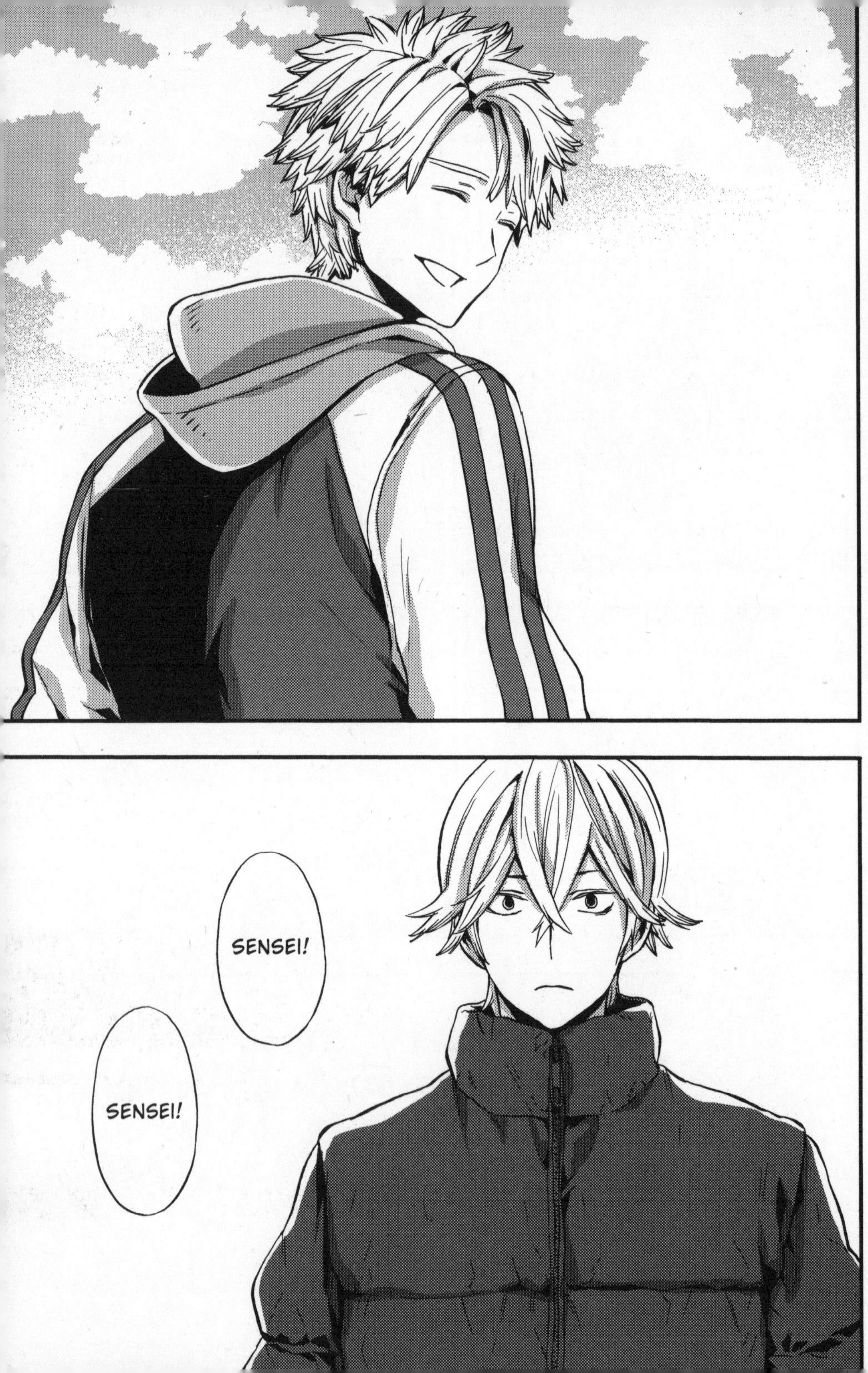
SENSEI!
SENSEI!

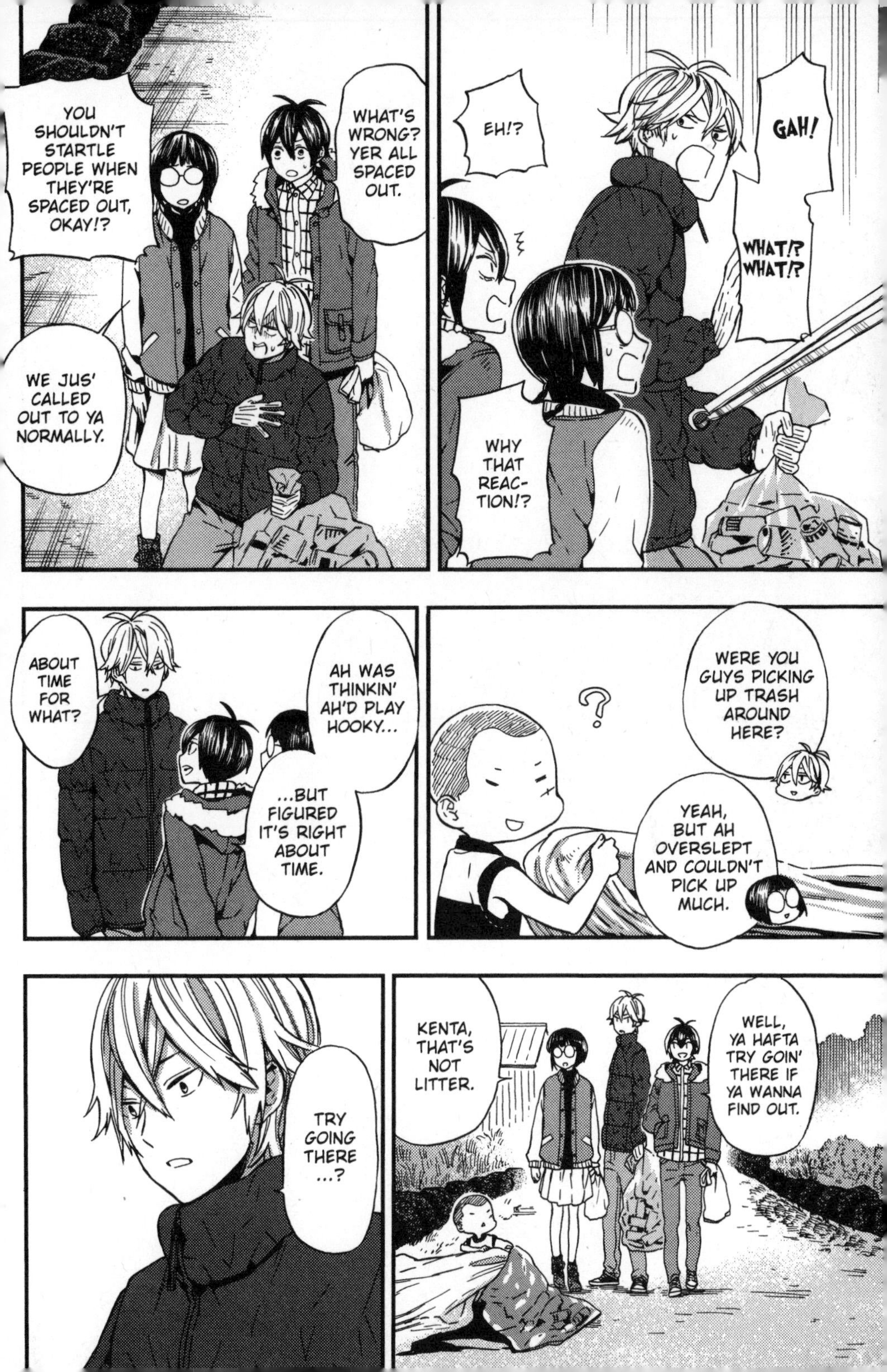
GAH!
EH!?
WHAT!? WHAT!?
WHY THAT REAC-TION!?
WHAT'S WRONG? YER ALL SPACED OUT.
YOU SHOULDN'T STARTLE PEOPLE WHEN THEY'RE SPACED OUT, OKAY!?
WE JUS' CALLED OUT TO YA NORMALLY.
WERE YOU GUYS PICKING UP TRASH AROUND HERE?
?
YEAH, BUT AH OVERSLEPT AND COULDN'T PICK UP MUCH.
AH WAS THINKIN' AH'D PLAY HOOKY...
...BUT FIGURED IT'S RIGHT ABOUT TIME.
ABOUT TIME FOR WHAT?
WELL, YA HAFTA TRY GOIN' THERE IF YA WANNA FIND OUT.
KENTA, THAT'S NOT LITTER.
TRY GOING THERE ...?

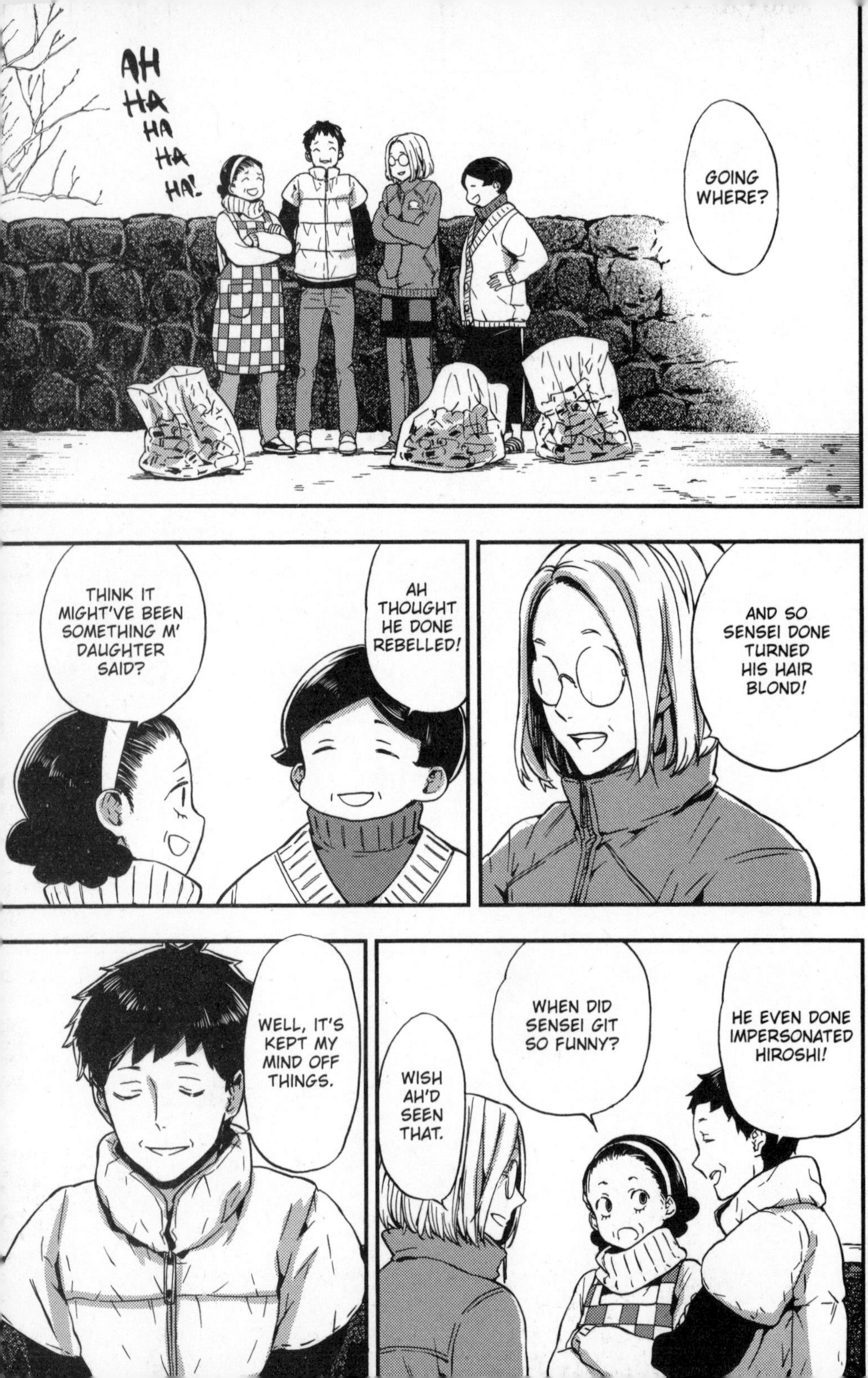
GOING WHERE?
AH HA HA HA HA!
AND SO SENSEI DONE TURNED HIS HAIR BLOND!
AH THOUGHT HE DONE REBELLED!
THINK IT MIGHT'VE BEEN SOMETHING M' DAUGHTER SAID?
HE EVEN DONE IMPERSONATED HIROSHI!
WHEN DID SENSEI GIT SO FUNNY?
WISH AH'D SEEN THAT.
WELL, IT'S KEPT MY MIND OFF THINGS.

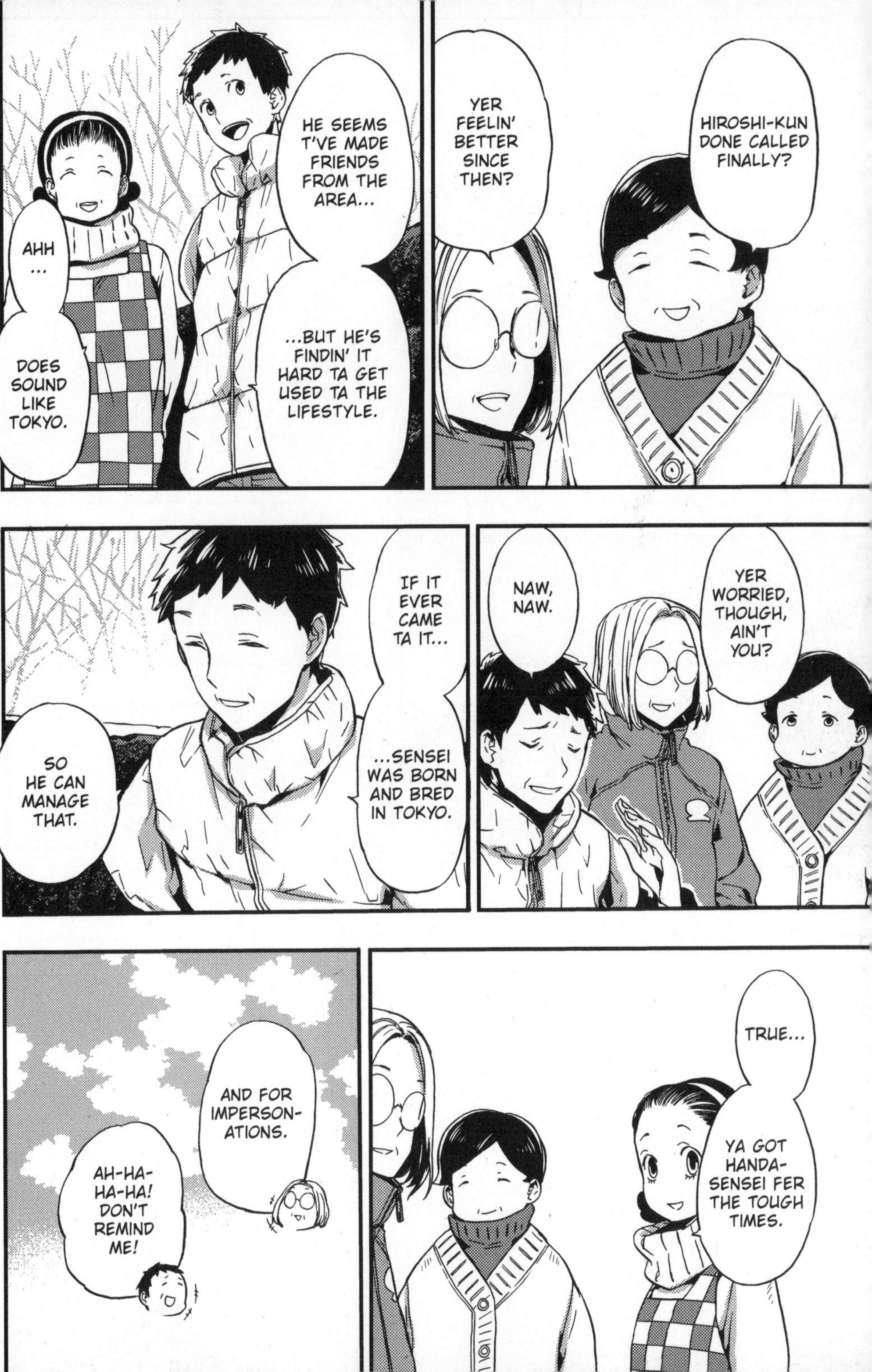
HIROSHI-KUN DONE CALLED FINALLY?
YER FEELIN' BETTER SINCE THEN?
HE SEEMS T'VE MADE FRIENDS FROM THE AREA...
...BUT HE'S FINDIN' IT HARD TA GET USED TA THE LIFESTYLE.
AHH ...
DOES SOUND LIKE TOKYO.
YER WORRIED, THOUGH, AIN'T YOU?
NAW, NAW.
IF IT EVER CAME TA IT...
...SENSEI WAS BORN AND BRED IN TOKYO.
SO HE CAN MANAGE THAT.
TRUE...
YA GOT HANDA-SENSEI FER THE TOUGH TIMES.
AND FOR IMPERSON-ATIONS.
AH-HA-HA-HA! DON'T REMIND ME!

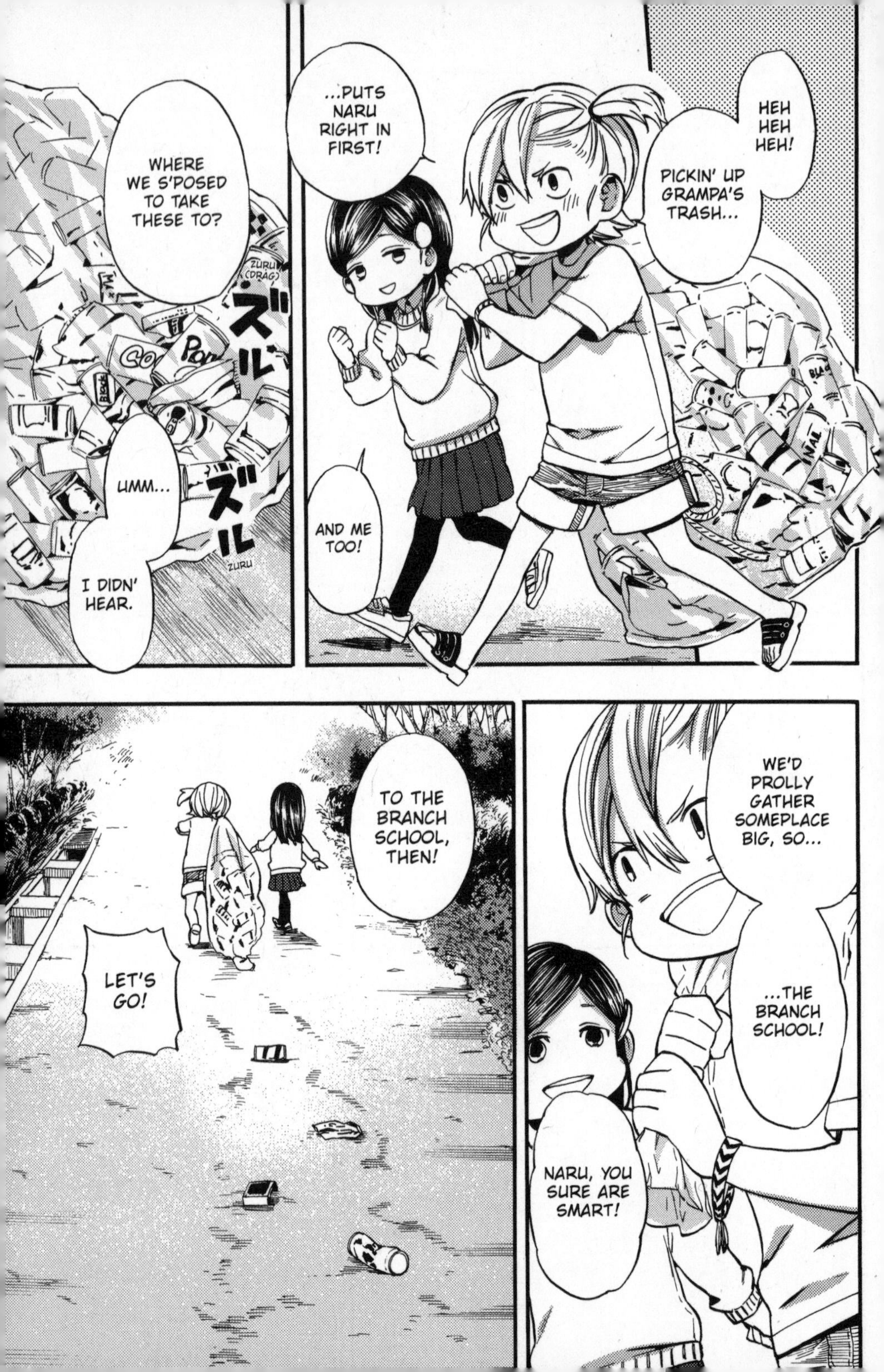
HEH HEH HEH!
PICKIN' UP GRAMPA'S TRASH...
...PUTS NARU RIGHT IN FIRST!
AND ME TOO!
WHERE WE S'POSED TO TAKE THESE TO?
ZURU (DRAG)
ズル
UMM...
ズル
ZURU
I DIDN' HEAR.
WE'D PROLLY GATHER SOMEPLACE BIG, SO...
...THE BRANCH SCHOOL!
NARU, YOU SURE ARE SMART!
TO THE BRANCH SCHOOL, THEN!
LET'S GO!

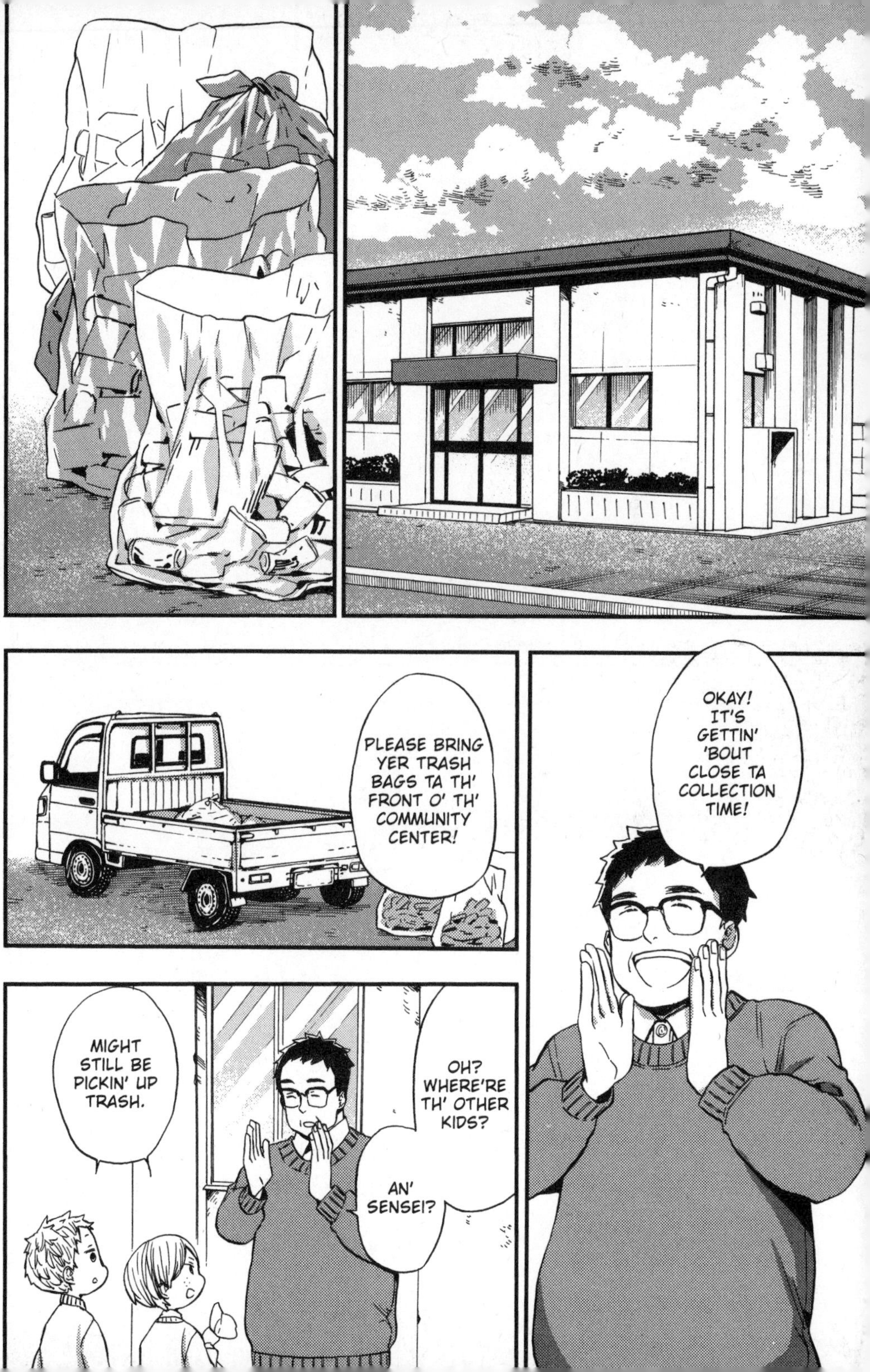
OKAY! IT'S GETTIN' 'BOUT CLOSE TA COLLECTION TIME!
PLEASE BRING YER TRASH BAGS TA TH' FRONT O' TH' COMMUNITY CENTER!
OH? WHERE'RE TH' OTHER KIDS?
AN' SENSEI?
MIGHT STILL BE PICKIN' UP TRASH.

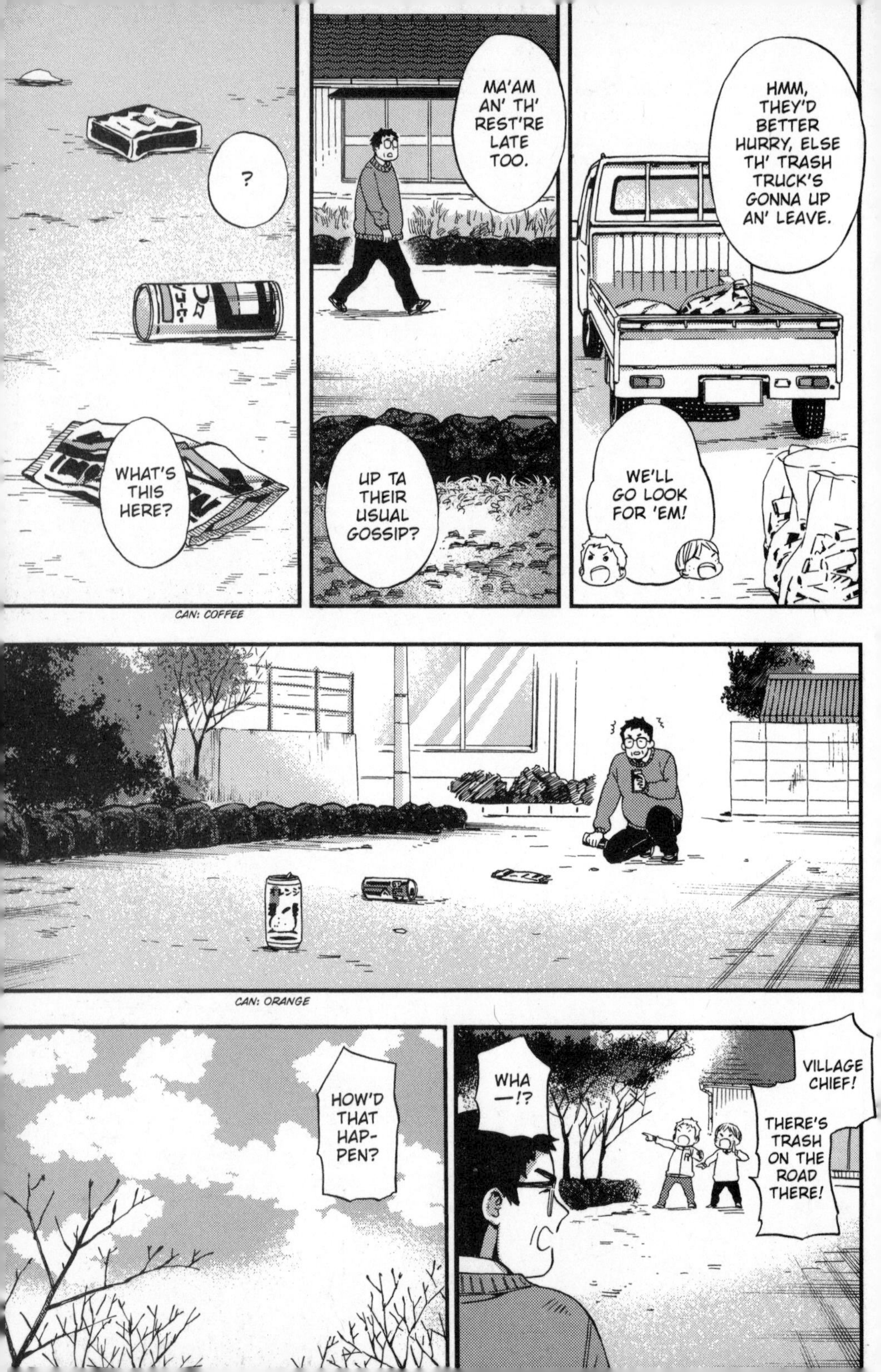
HMM, THEY'D BETTER HURRY, ELSE TH' TRASH TRUCK'S GONNA UP AN' LEAVE.
WE'LL GO LOOK FOR 'EM!
MA'AM AN' TH' REST'RE LATE TOO.
UP TA THEIR USUAL GOSSIP?
?
WHAT'S THIS HERE?
CAN: COFFEE
CAN: ORANGE
VILLAGE CHIEF!
THERE'S TRASH ON THE ROAD THERE!
WHA—!?
HOW'D THAT HAP-PEN?

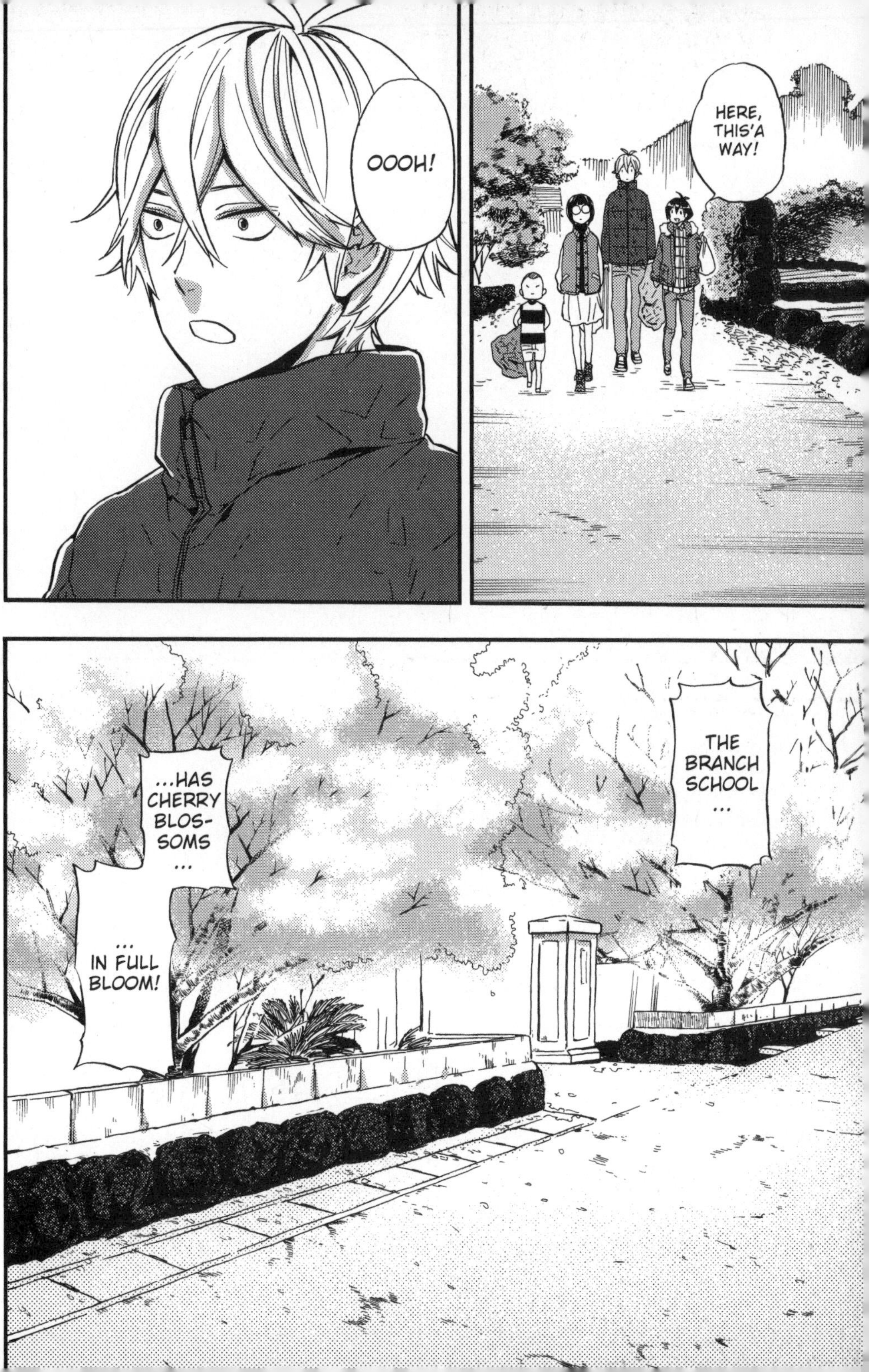
HERE, THIS'A WAY!
OOOH!
THE BRANCH SCHOOL ...
...HAS CHERRY BLOS-SOMS ...
... IN FULL BLOOM!

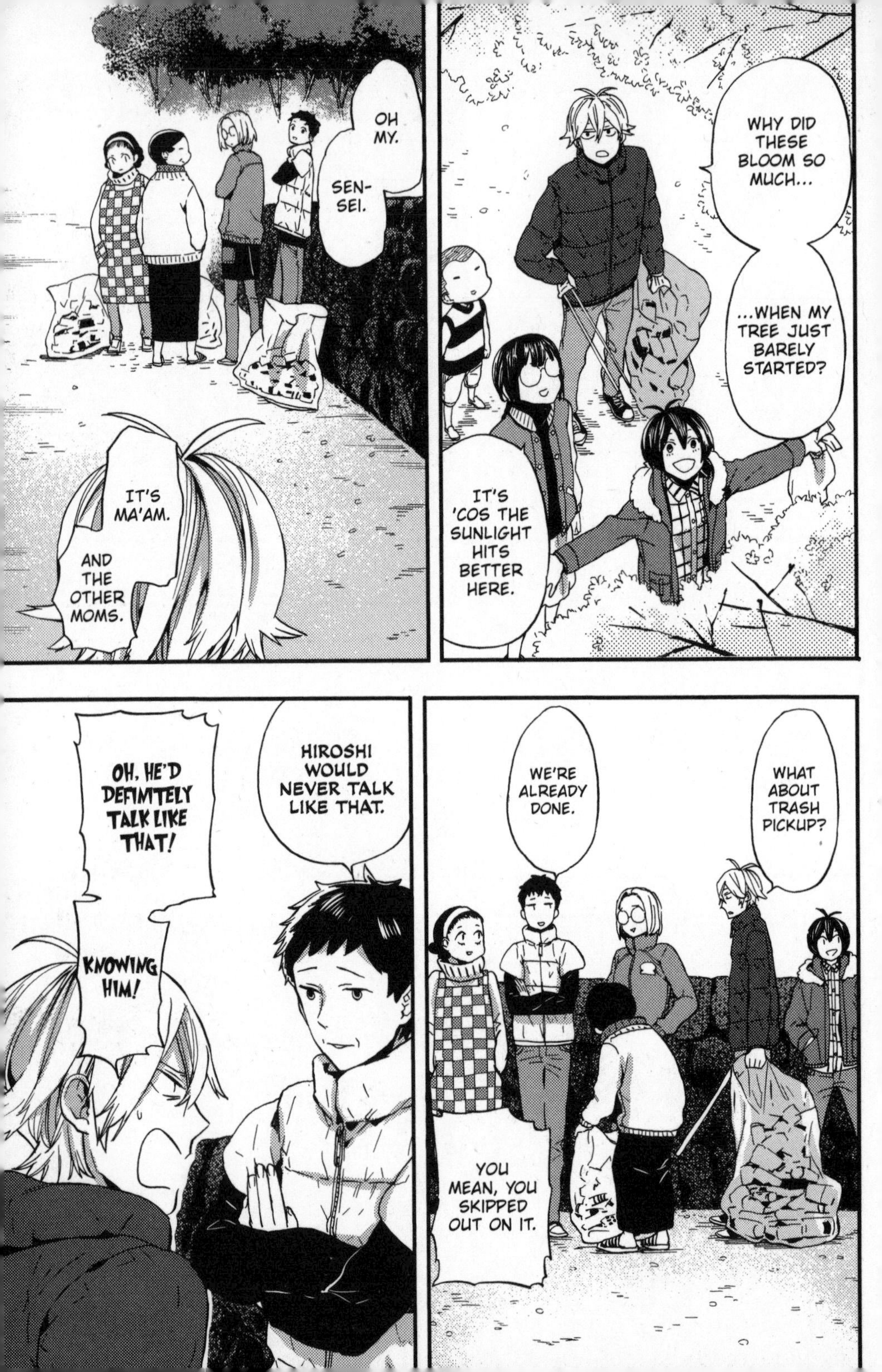
WHY DID THESE BLOOM SO MUCH...
...WHEN MY TREE JUST BARELY STARTED?
IT'S 'COS THE SUNLIGHT HITS BETTER HERE.
OH MY.
SEN-SEI.
IT'S MA'AM.
AND THE OTHER MOMS.
WHAT ABOUT TRASH PICKUP?
WE'RE ALREADY DONE.
YOU MEAN, YOU SKIPPED OUT ON IT.
HIROSHI WOULD NEVER TALK LIKE THAT.
OH, HE'D DEFIMTELY TALK LIKE THAT!
KNOWING HIM!

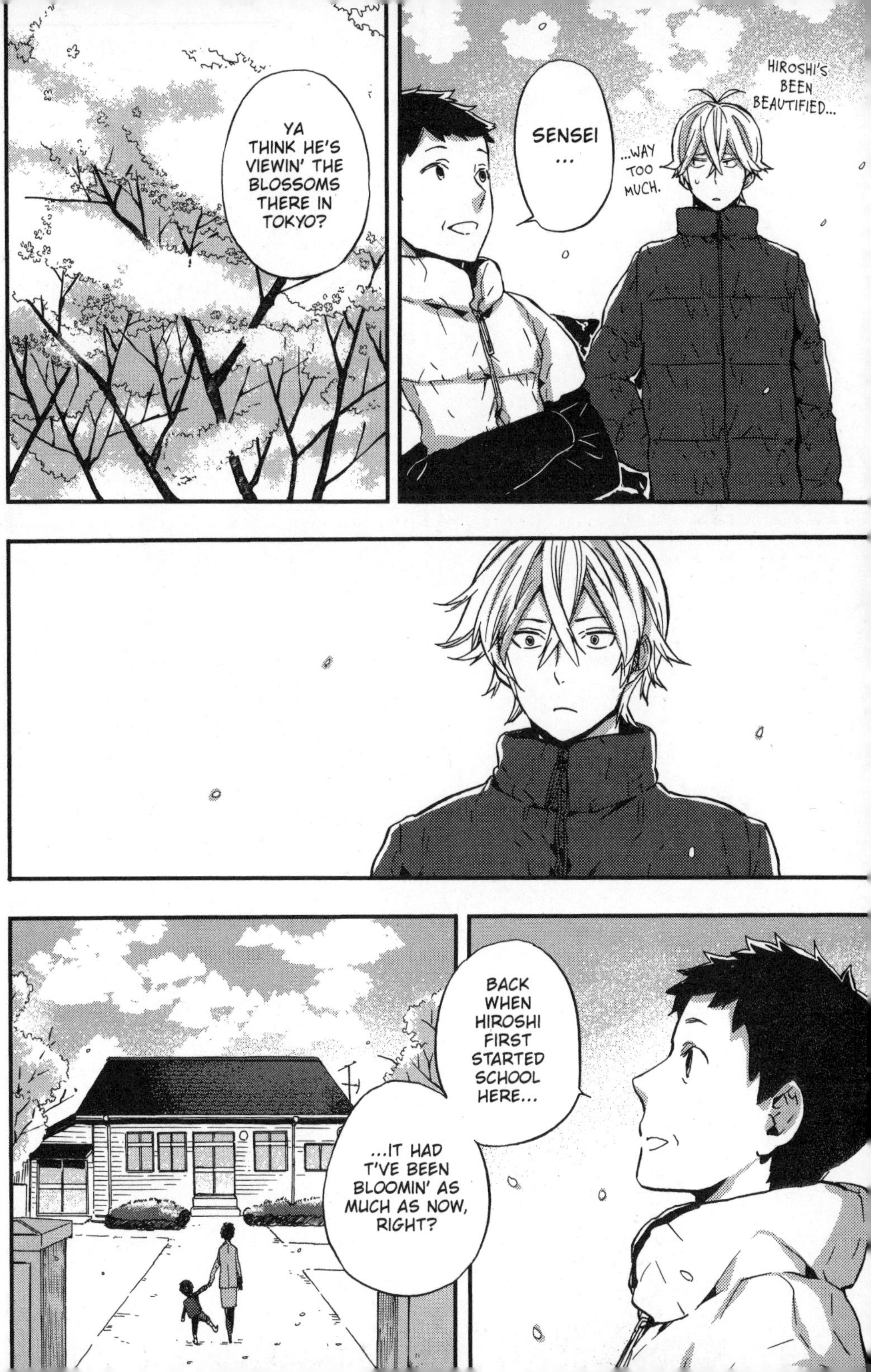
HIROSHI'S BEEN BEAUTIFIED...
...WAY TOO MUCH.
SENSEI ...
YA THINK HE'S VIEWIN' THE BLOSSOMS THERE IN TOKYO?
BACK WHEN HIROSHI FIRST STARTED SCHOOL HERE...
...IT HAD T'VE BEEN BLOOMIN' AS MUCH AS NOW, RIGHT?

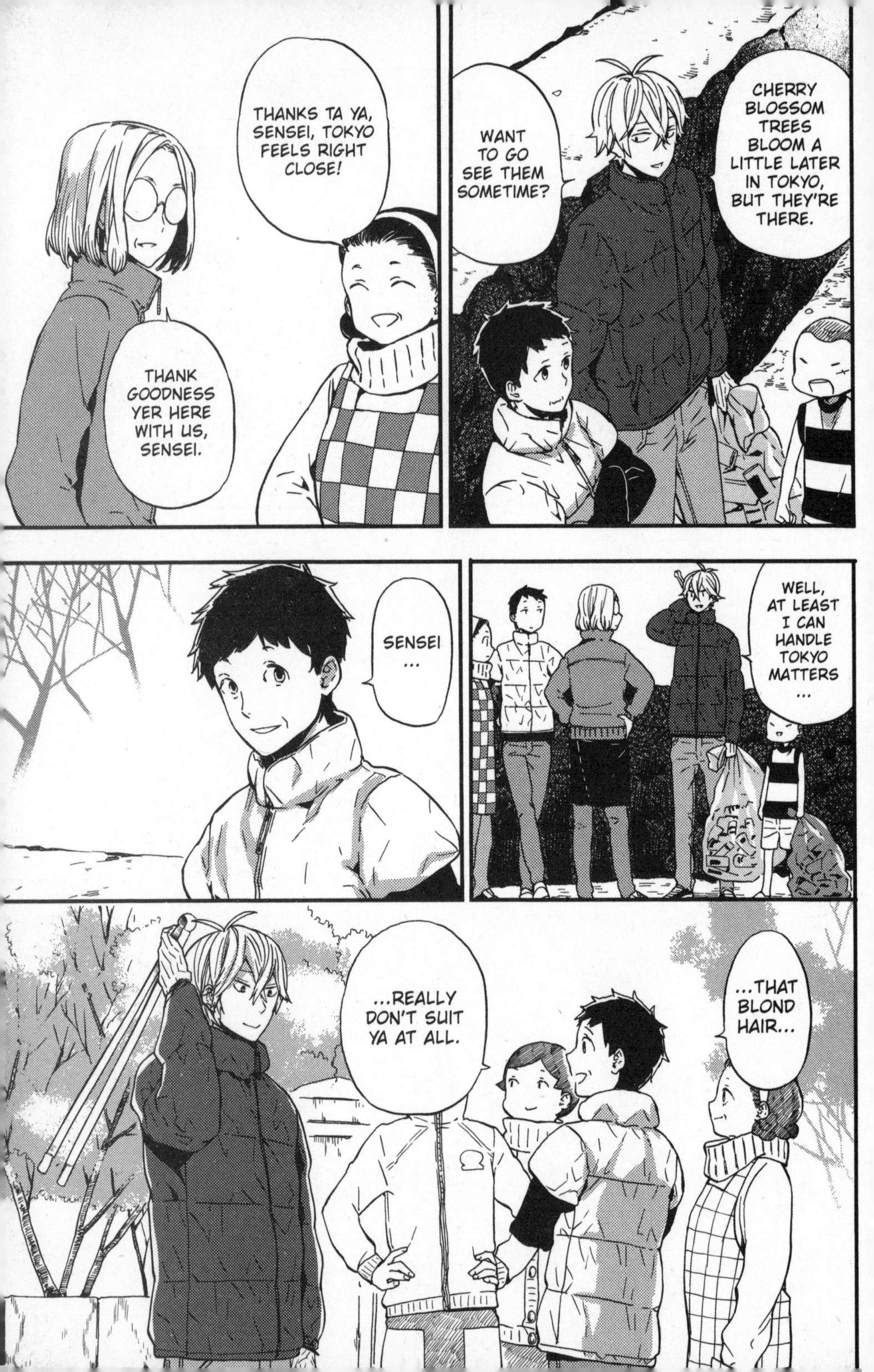
CHERRY BLOSSOM TREES BLOOM A LITTLE LATER IN TOKYO, BUT THEY'RE THERE.
WANT TO GO SEE THEM SOMETIME?
THANKS TA YA, SENSEI, TOKYO FEELS RIGHT CLOSE!
THANK GOODNESS YER HERE WITH US, SENSEI.
WELL, AT LEAST I CAN HANDLE TOKYO MATTERS ...
SENSEI ...
...THAT BLOND HAIR...
...REALLY DON'T SUIT YA AT ALL.

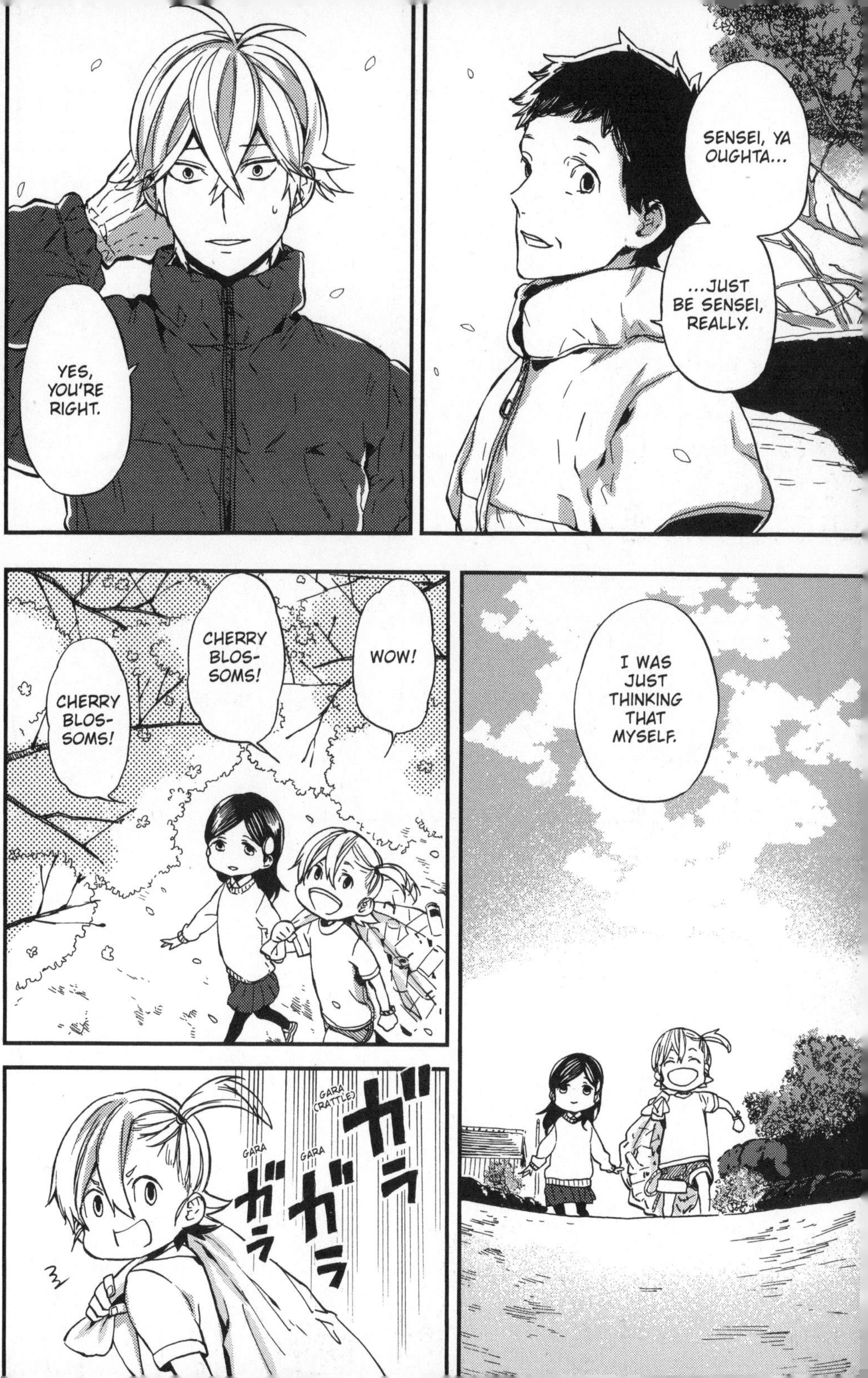
SENSEI, YA OUGHTA...
...JUST BE SENSEI, REALLY.
YES, YOU'RE RIGHT.
I WAS JUST THINKING THAT MYSELF.
WOW!
CHERRY BLOSSOMS!
CHERRY BLOSSOMS!
ガラ
GARA (RATTLE)
ガラ
GARA
ガラ
GARA

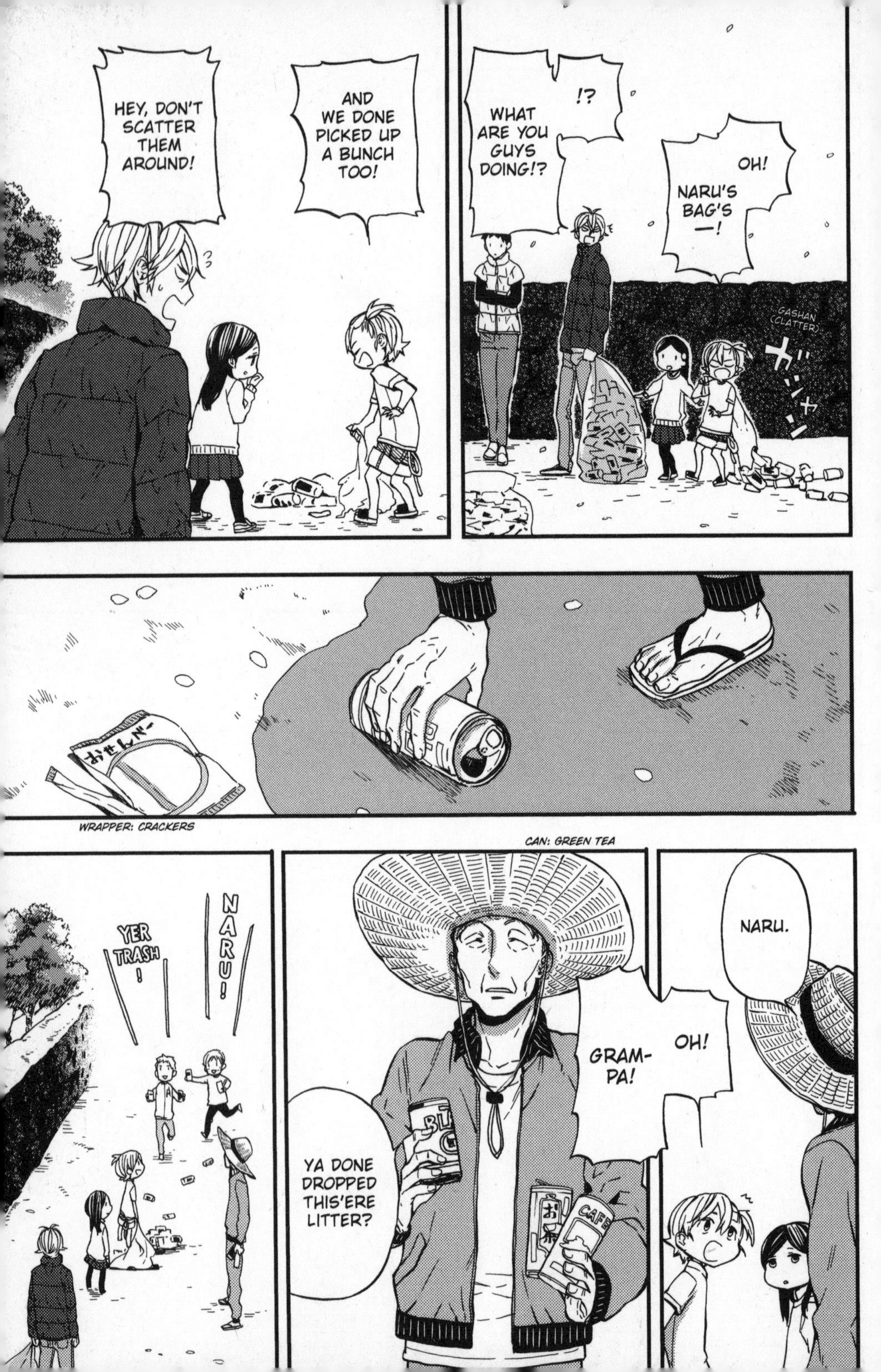
OH! NARU'S BAG'S—!
GASHAN (CLATTER)
!? WHAT ARE YOU GUYS DOING!?
AND WE DONE PICKED UP A BUNCH TOO!
HEY, DON'T SCATTER THEM AROUND!
おせんべい
WRAPPER: CRACKERS
CAN: GREEN TEA
NARU.
OH!
GRAMPA!
YA DONE DROPPED THIS'ERE LITTER?
NARU!
YER TRASH!

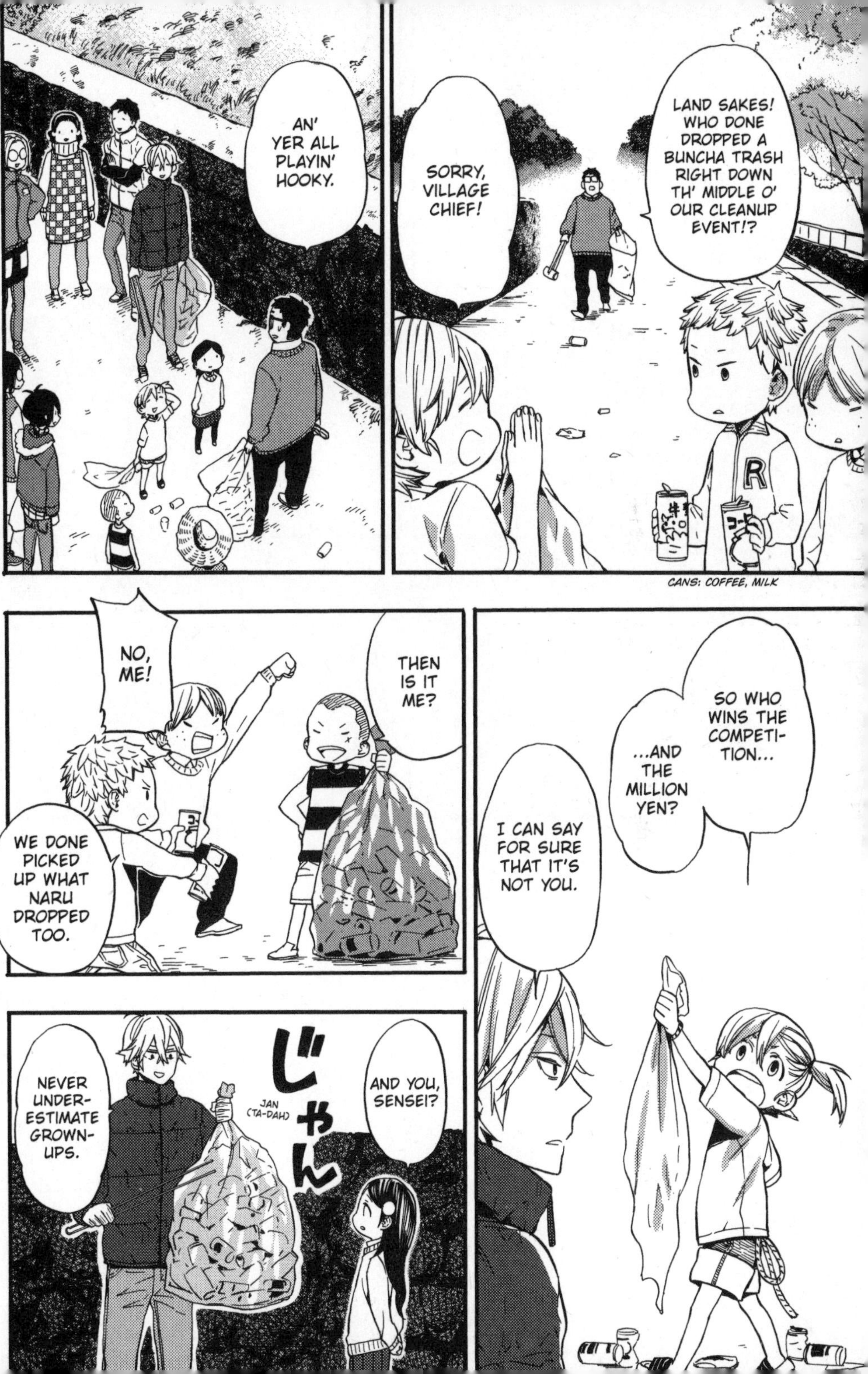
LAND SAKES! WHO DONE DROPPED A BUNCHA TRASH RIGHT DOWN TH' MIDDLE O' OUR CLEANUP EVENT!?
SORRY, VILLAGE CHIEF!
CANS: COFFEE, MILK
AN' YER ALL PLAYIN' HOOKY.
SO WHO WINS THE COMPETITION...
...AND THE MILLION YEN?
I CAN SAY FOR SURE THAT IT'S NOT YOU.
THEN IS IT ME?
NO, ME!
WE DONE PICKED UP WHAT NARU DROPPED TOO.
AND YOU, SENSEI?
じゃん
JAN (TA-DAH)
NEVER UNDERESTIMATE GROWN-UPS.

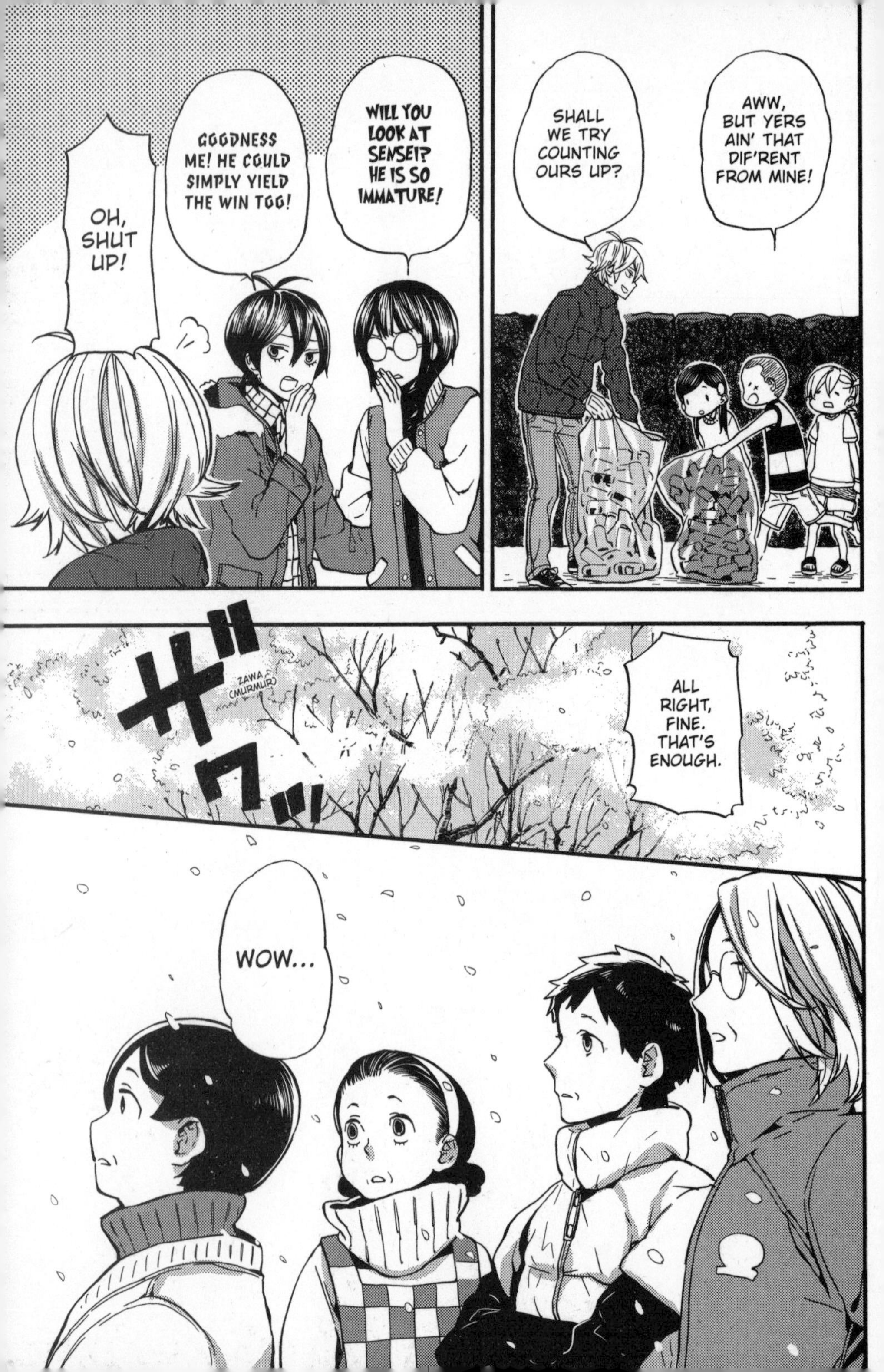
AWW, BUT YERS AIN' THAT DIF'RENT FROM MINE!
SHALL WE TRY COUNTING OURS UP?
WILL YOU LOOK AT SENSEI? HE IS SO IMMATURE!
GOODNESS ME! HE COULD SIMPLY YIELD THE WIN TOO!
OH, SHUT UP!
ALL RIGHT, FINE. THAT'S ENOUGH.
ZAWA (MURMUR)
WOW...

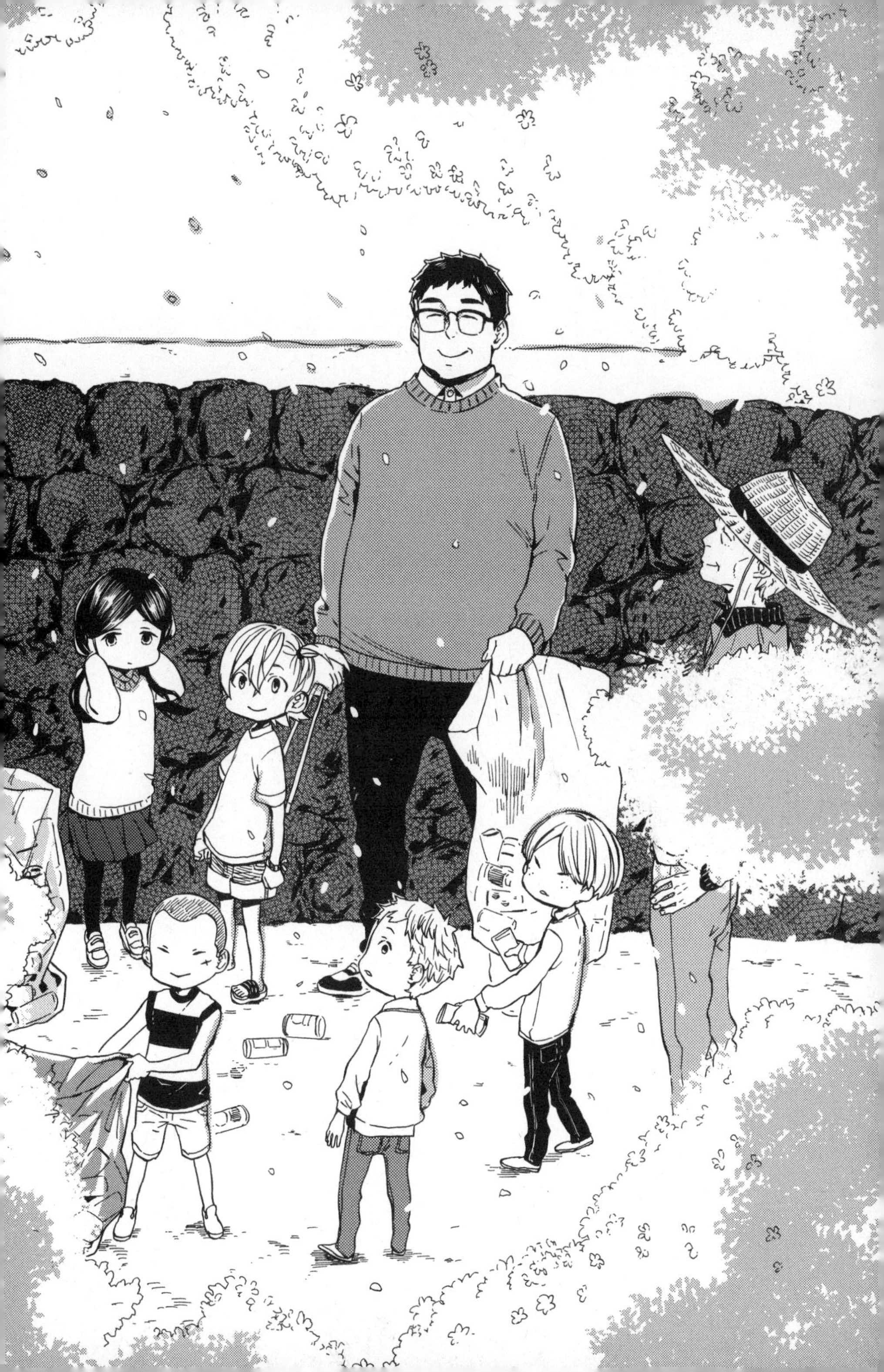

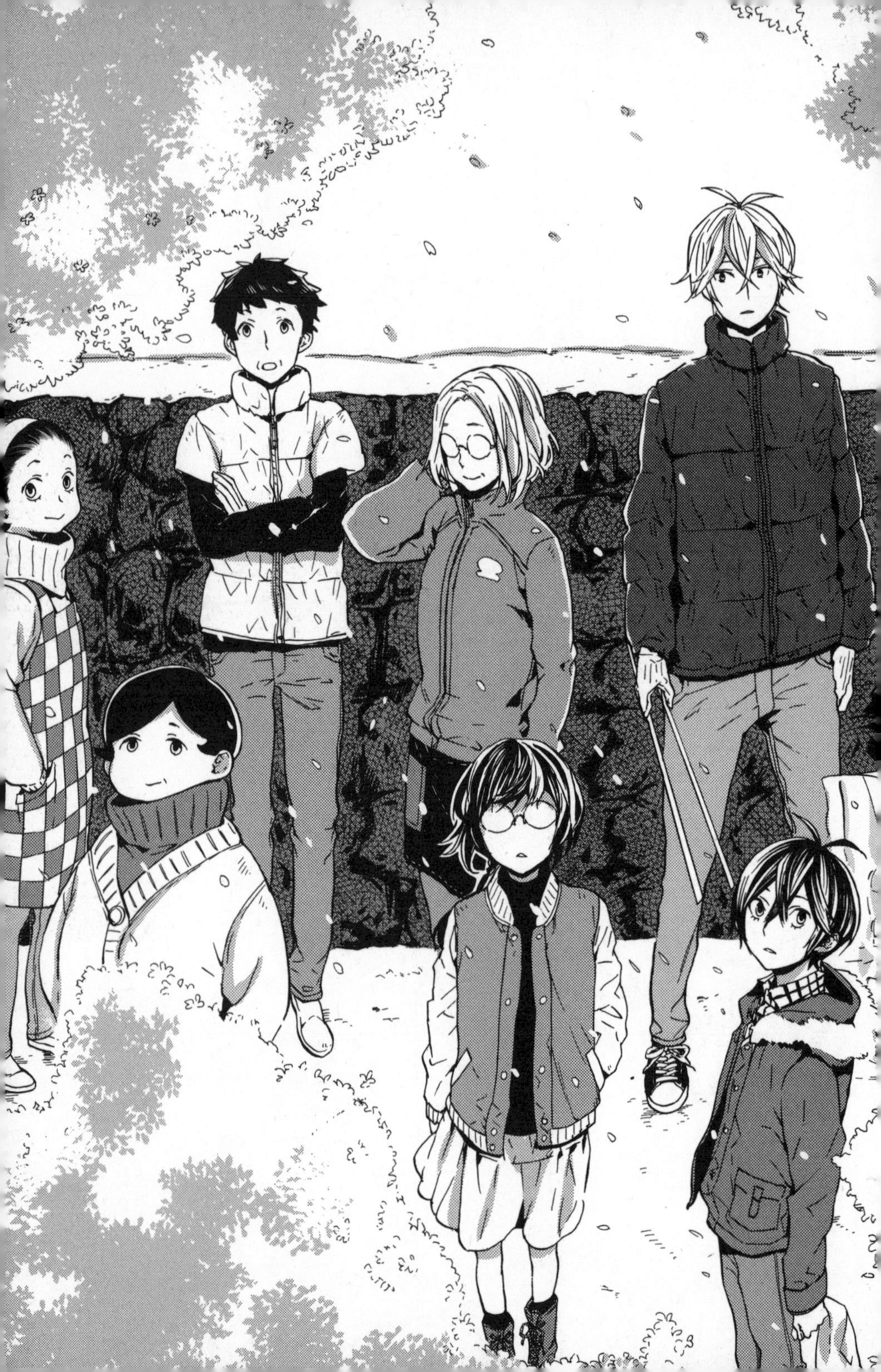

SPRING
REALLY
HAS
COME...

BOX: BLACK HAIR—BLACK

BASA
(FLAP)

GOSH!
(SCRUB)

GOSHI

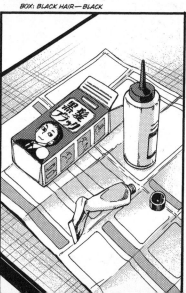

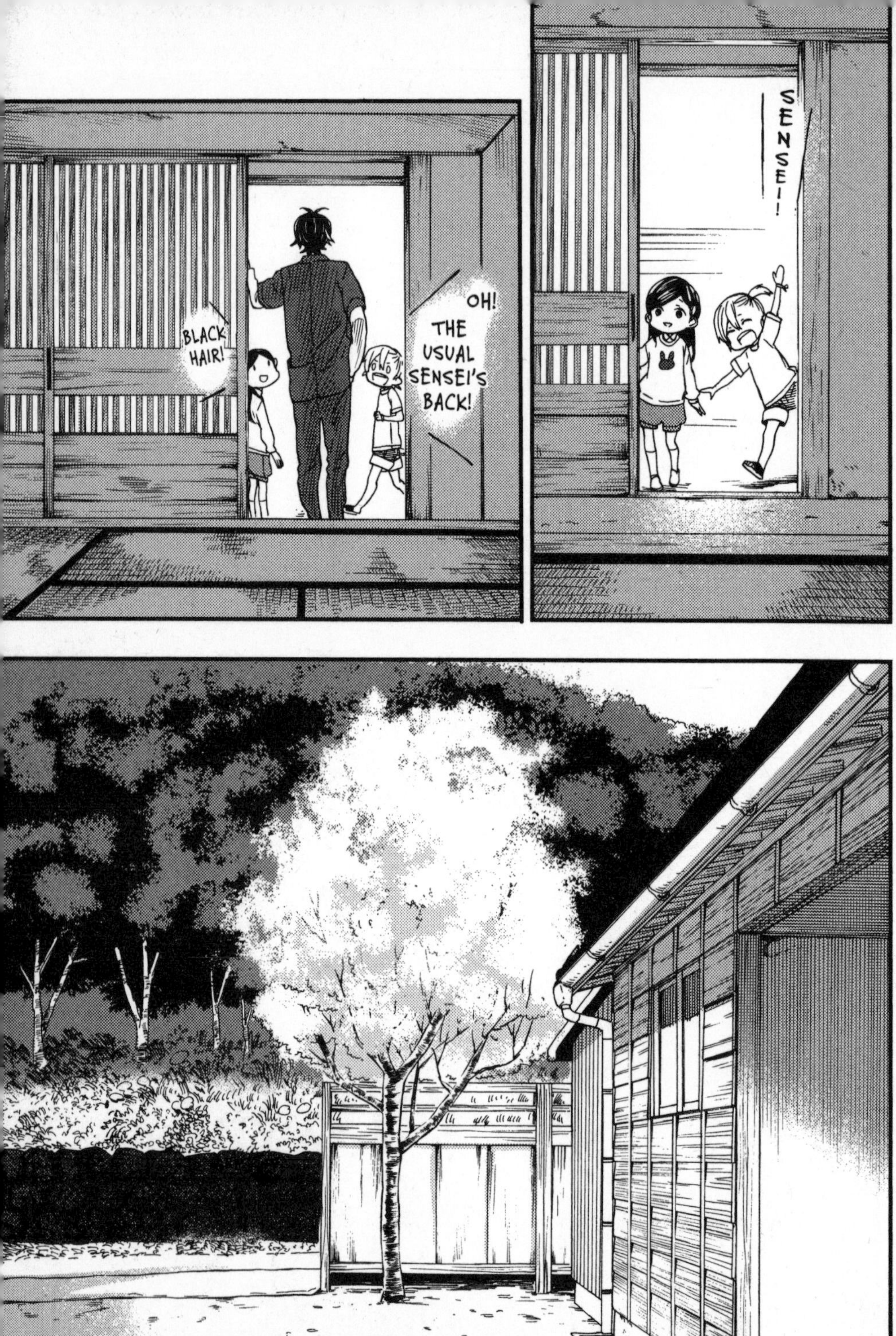
SENSEI!
OH! THE USUAL SENSEI'S BACK!
BLACK HAIR!
TO BE CONTINUED IN BARAKAMON 18

BONUS: DANPO THE 17TH

(Translation: Pond)

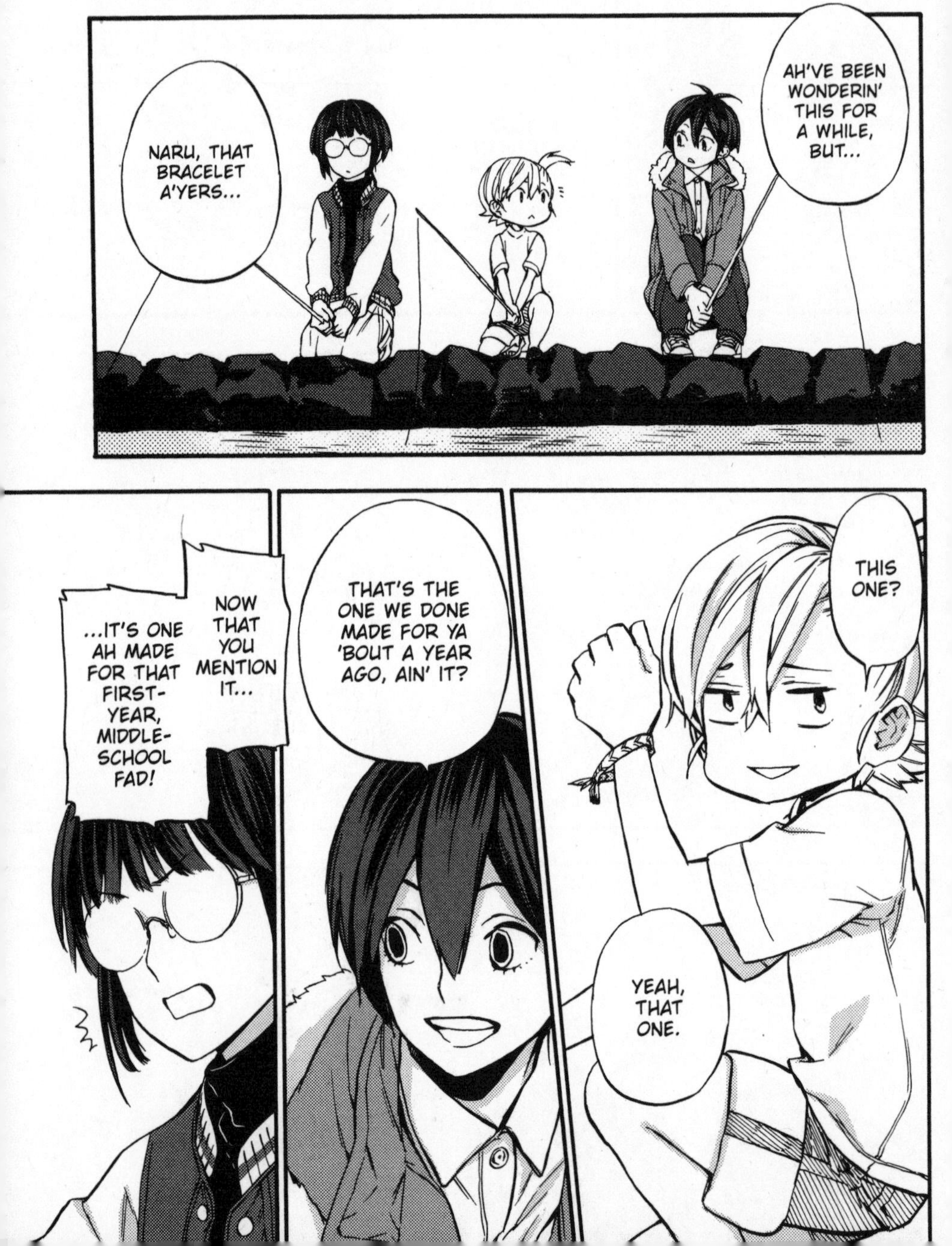
AH'VE BEEN WONDERIN' THIS FOR A WHILE, BUT...
NARU, THAT BRACELET A'YERS...
THIS ONE?
YEAH, THAT ONE.
THAT'S THE ONE WE DONE MADE FOR YA 'BOUT A YEAR AGO, AIN' IT?
NOW THAT YOU MENTION IT...
...IT'S ONE AH MADE FOR THAT FIRST-YEAR, MIDDLE-SCHOOL FAD!

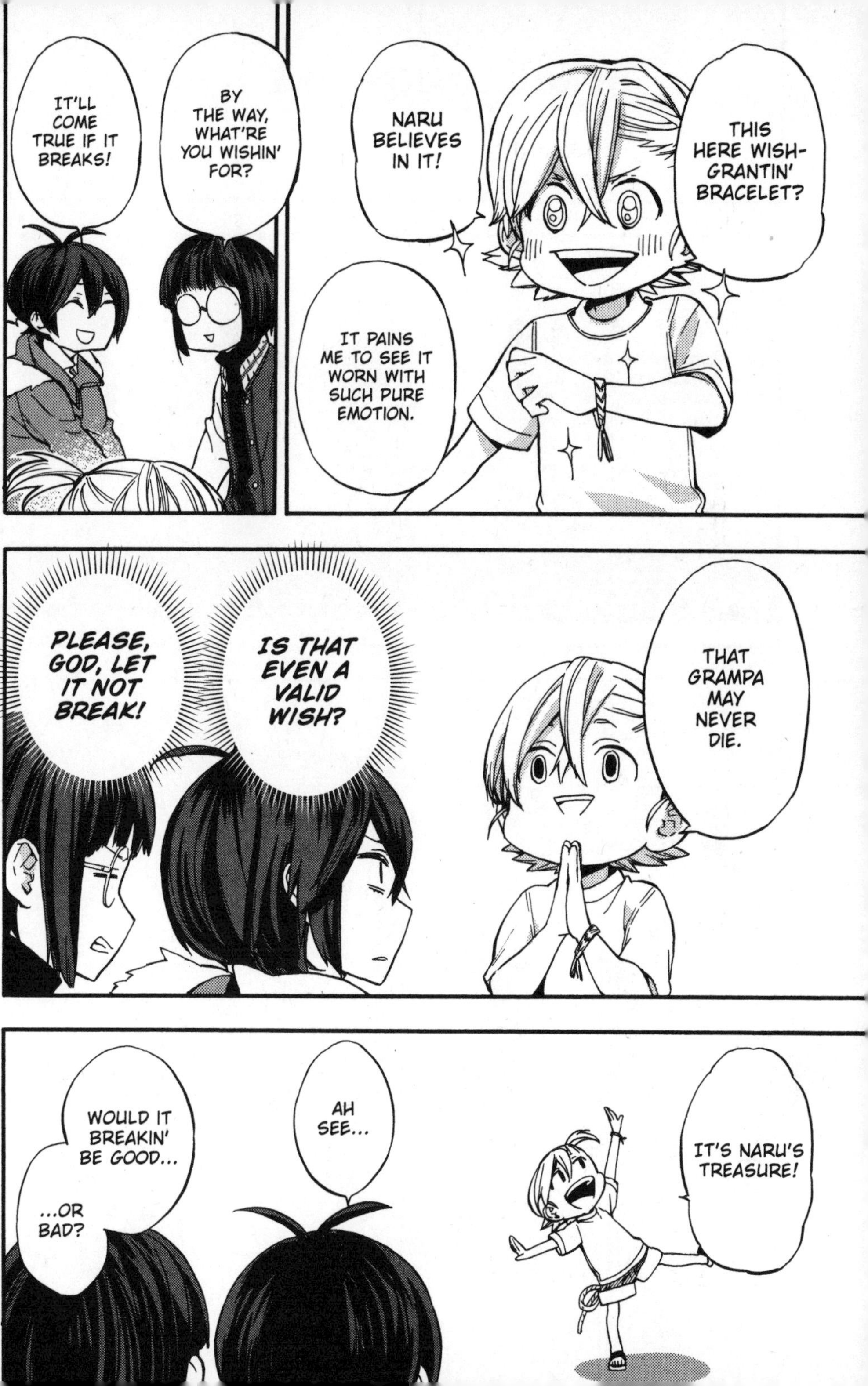
THIS HERE WISH-GRANTIN' BRACELET?
NARU BELIEVES IN IT!
IT PAINS ME TO SEE IT WORN WITH SUCH PURE EMOTION.
BY THE WAY, WHAT'RE YOU WISHIN' FOR?
IT'LL COME TRUE IF IT BREAKS!
THAT GRAMPA MAY NEVER DIE.
IS THAT EVEN A VALID WISH?
PLEASE, GOD, LET IT NOT BREAK!
IT'S NARU'S TREASURE!
AH SEE...
WOULD IT BREAKIN' BE GOOD...
...OR BAD?

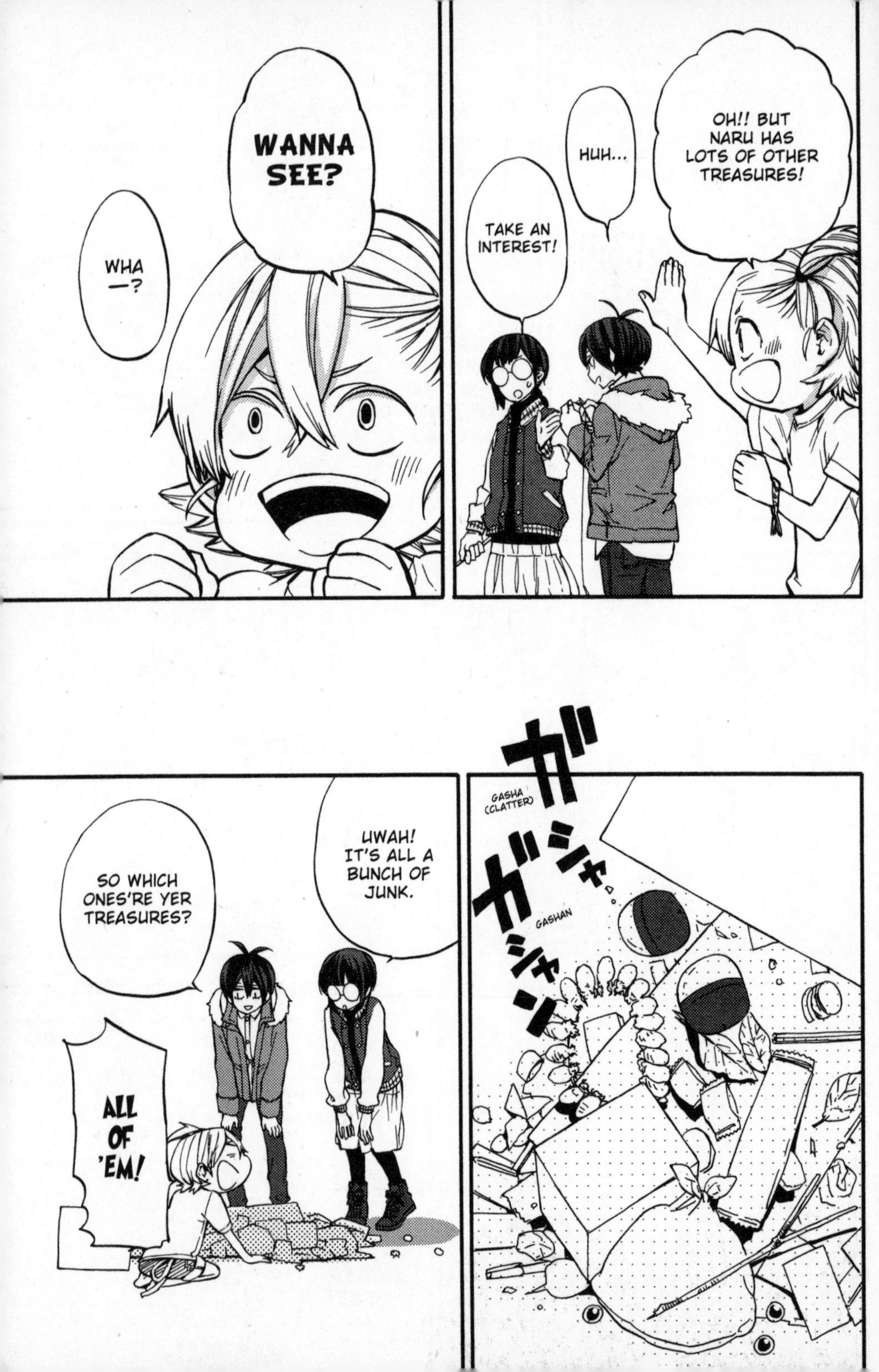
OH!! BUT NARU HAS LOTS OF OTHER TREASURES!
HUH...
TAKE AN INTEREST!
WANNA SEE?
WHA—?
ガシャ
GASHA (CLATTER)
ガシャン
GASHAN
UWAH! IT'S ALL A BUNCH OF JUNK.
SO WHICH ONES'RE YER TREASURES?
ALL OF 'EM!

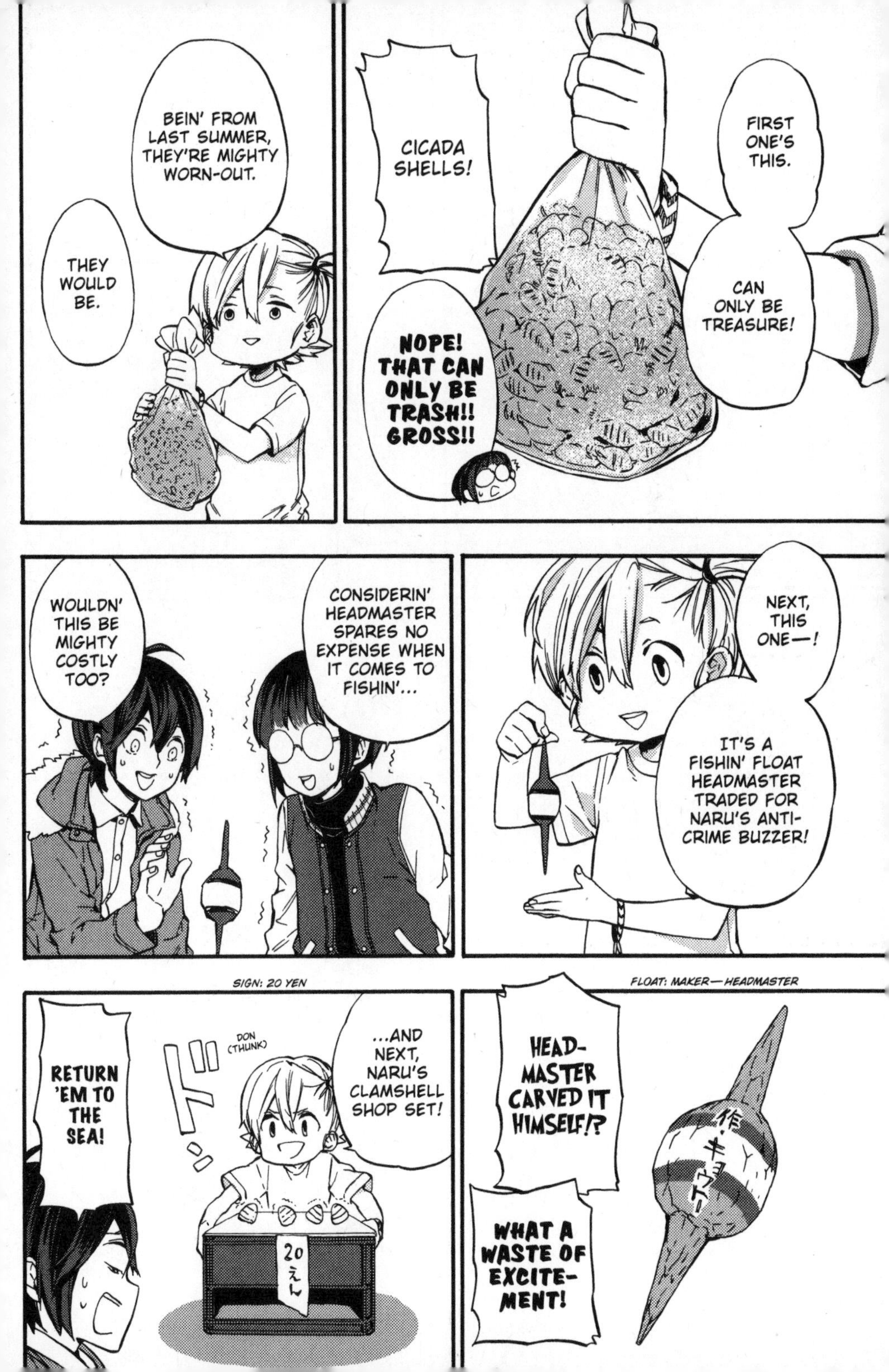
FIRST ONE'S THIS.
CAN ONLY BE TREASURE!
CICADA SHELLS!
NOPE! THAT CAN ONLY BE TRASH!! GROSS!!
BEIN' FROM LAST SUMMER, THEY'RE MIGHTY WORN-OUT.
THEY WOULD BE.
NEXT, THIS ONE—!
IT'S A FISHIN' FLOAT HEADMASTER TRADED FOR NARU'S ANTI-CRIME BUZZER!
CONSIDERIN' HEADMASTER SPARES NO EXPENSE WHEN IT COMES TO FISHIN'...
WOULDN' THIS BE MIGHTY COSTLY TOO?
FLOAT: MAKER—HEADMASTER
SIGN: 20 YEN
HEAD-MASTER CARVED IT HIMSELF!?
WHAT A WASTE OF EXCITEMENT!
...AND NEXT, NARU'S CLAMSHELL SHOP SET!
ドン
DON (THUNK)
20えん
RETURN 'EM TO THE SEA!

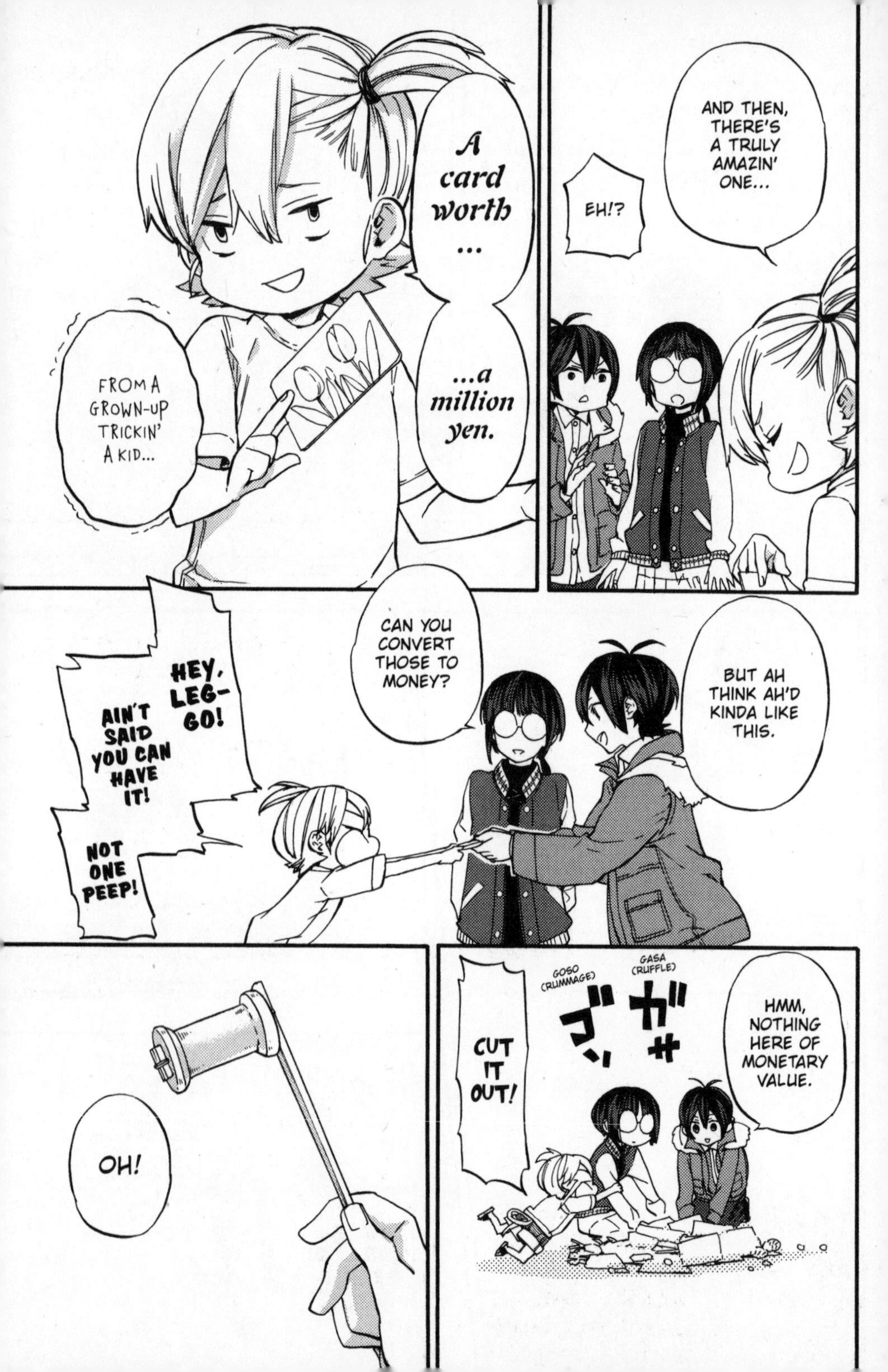
AND THEN, THERE'S A TRULY AMAZIN' ONE...
EH!?
A card worth...
...a million yen.
FROM A GROWN-UP TRICKIN' A KID...
BUT AH THINK AH'D KINDA LIKE THIS.
CAN YOU CONVERT THOSE TO MONEY?
HEY, LEG-GO!
AIN'T SAID YOU CAN HAVE IT!
NOT ONE PEEP!
ガサ
GASA (RUFFLE)
ゴソ
GOSO (RUMMAGE)
HMM, NOTHING HERE OF MONETARY VALUE.
CUT IT OUT!
OH!

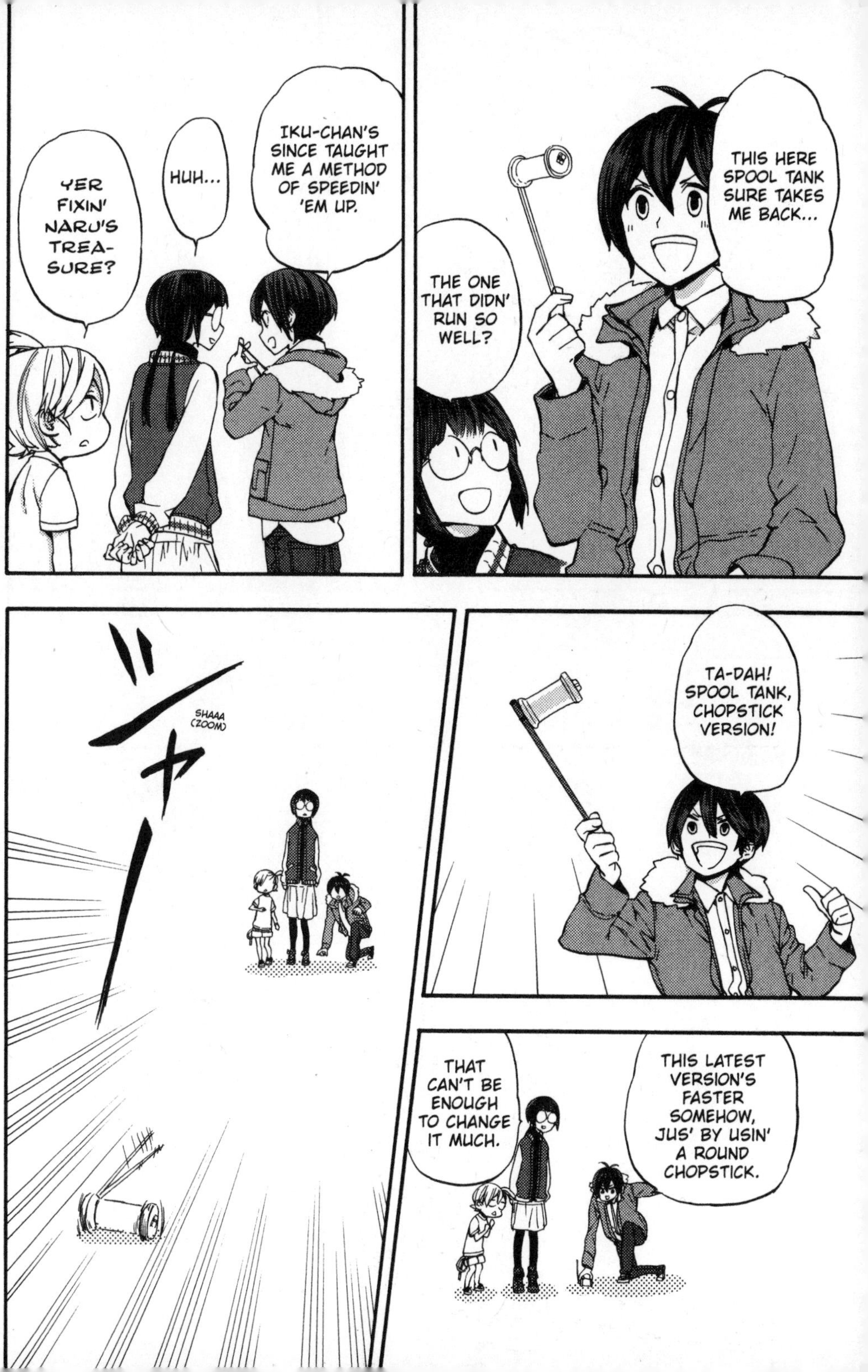
THIS HERE SPOOL TANK SURE TAKES ME BACK...
THE ONE THAT DIDN' RUN SO WELL?
IKU-CHAN'S SINCE TAUGHT ME A METHOD OF SPEEDIN' 'EM UP.
HUH...
YER FIXIN' NARU'S TREASURE?
TA-DAH! SPOOL TANK, CHOPSTICK VERSION!
THIS LATEST VERSION'S FASTER SOMEHOW, JUS' BY USIN' A ROUND CHOPSTICK.
THAT CAN'T BE ENOUGH TO CHANGE IT MUCH.
SHAAA (ZOOM)

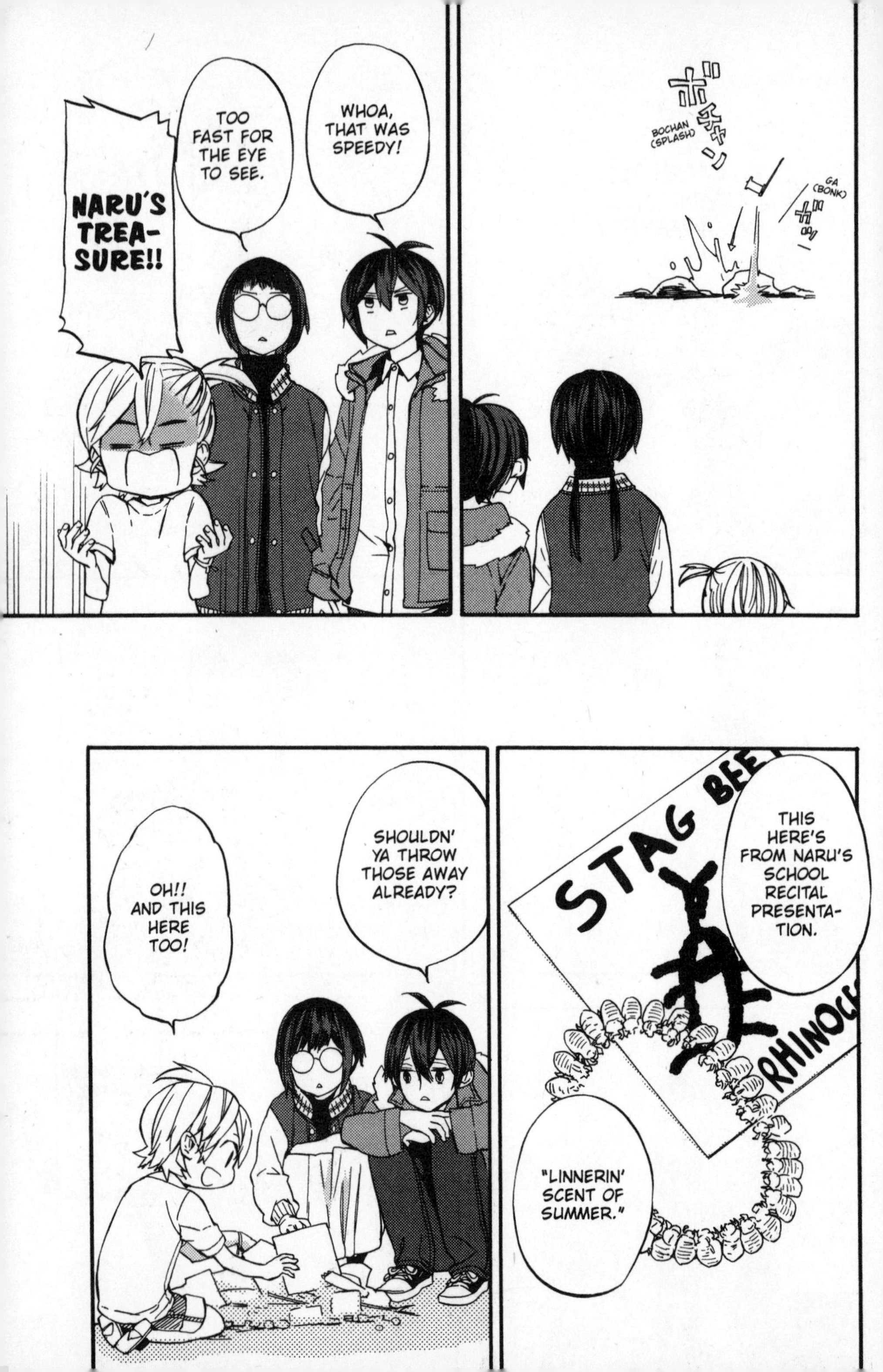
BOCHAN (SPLASH)
GA (BONK)
WHOA, THAT WAS SPEEDY!
TOO FAST FOR THE EYE TO SEE.
NARU'S TREA-SURE!!
THIS HERE'S FROM NARU'S SCHOOL RECITAL PRESENTA-TION.
STAG BEE
RHINOC
"LINNERIN' SCENT OF SUMMER."
SHOULDN' YA THROW THOSE AWAY ALREADY?
OH!! AND THIS HERE TOO!

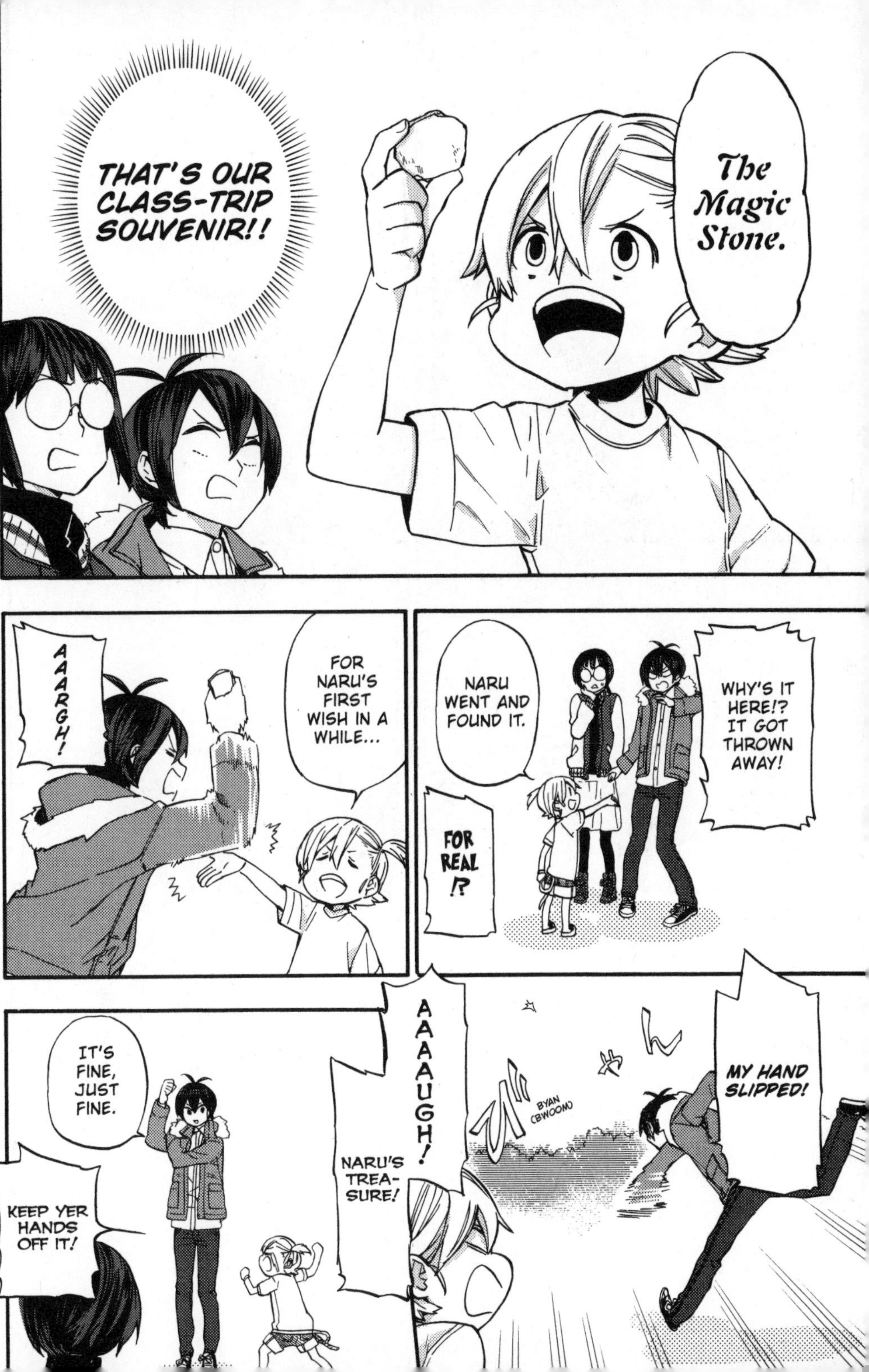
The Magic Stone.
THAT'S OUR CLASS-TRIP SOUVENIR!!
WHY'S IT HERE!? IT GOT THROWN AWAY!
NARU WENT AND FOUND IT.
FOR REAL !?
FOR NARU'S FIRST WISH IN A WHILE...
AAARGH!
MY HAND SLIPPED!
BYAN (BWOOM)
AAAAUGH!
NARU'S TREA-SURE!
IT'S FINE, JUST FINE.
KEEP YER HANDS OFF IT!

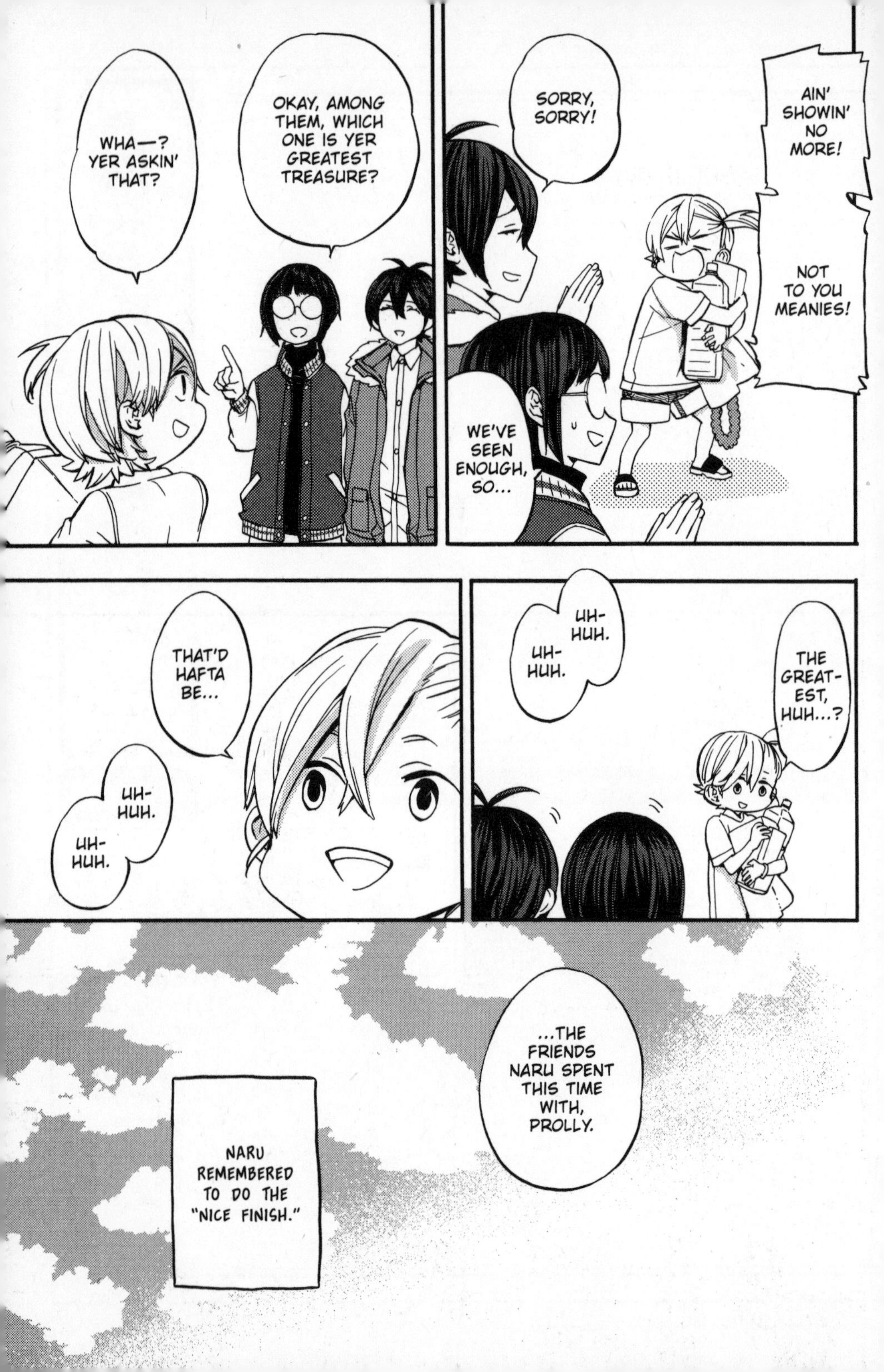

AIN' SHOWIN' NO MORE!
NOT TO YOU MEANIES!
SORRY, SORRY!
WE'VE SEEN ENOUGH, SO...
OKAY, AMONG THEM, WHICH ONE IS YER GREATEST TREASURE?
WHA—? YER ASKIN' THAT?
THE GREAT-EST, HUH...?
UH-HUH.
UH-HUH.
THAT'D HAFTA BE...
UH-HUH.
UH-HUH.
...THE FRIENDS NARU SPENT THIS TIME WITH, PROLLY.
NARU REMEMBERED TO DO THE "NICE FINISH."

BARAKAMON NEWS

Vol. 510

BARAKAMON Café, Now Open for a Limited Time!!

Everyone, thank you very much for buying Volume 17 of *BARAKAMON*! Thanks to your warm support, a *BARAKAMON* café is currently open in Tokyo's Ikebukuro! At the café, in addition to the delicious and fun menu, you can find exclusive merchandise on sale, such as a Café-Book including a manga specially drawn by Yoshino-sensei! We've also prepared things such as bonus perks for café visitors, so please be sure to stop by!

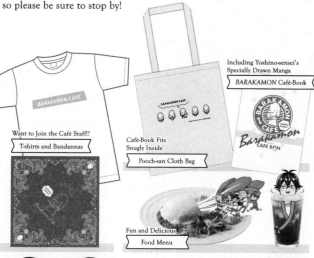

BARAKAMON CAFE
Including Yoshino-sensei's Specially Drawn Manga
BARAKAMON Café-Book
Want to Join the Café Staff!?
T-shirts and Bandannas
Café-Book Fits Snugly Inside
Pooch-san Cloth Bag
Fun and Delicious
Food Menu

2018 6.12 TUE ▶ 7.29 SUN

You can make your reservation here, as well as find menu and merchandise information!!

BARAKAMON Café Official Site ▶ https://barakamon-café.com

BARAKAMON Hijacks *Monthly Shonen Gangan*'s July Issue with a Cover, Lead Position, and Dbl-Pack-ins!!

Specially Drawn!
Overlapping Book Cover
Dbl-Pack-ins
Luncheon Mat
You Can Read the Next Chapter After This Volume!

The July issue of *Monthly Shonen Gangan*, which goes on sale the same day as this volume, features *BARAKAMON* on the cover, in the lead position with color pages, and dbl-pack-ins! It includes a specially drawn book cover you can use over this volume, as well as a refreshing luncheon mat, so please make sure to get a copy!

Please note the items on this page were only available in Japan.

<Approved for Third-Class Mail> Vol. 510 BARAKAMON

Next Volume— The Conclusion.

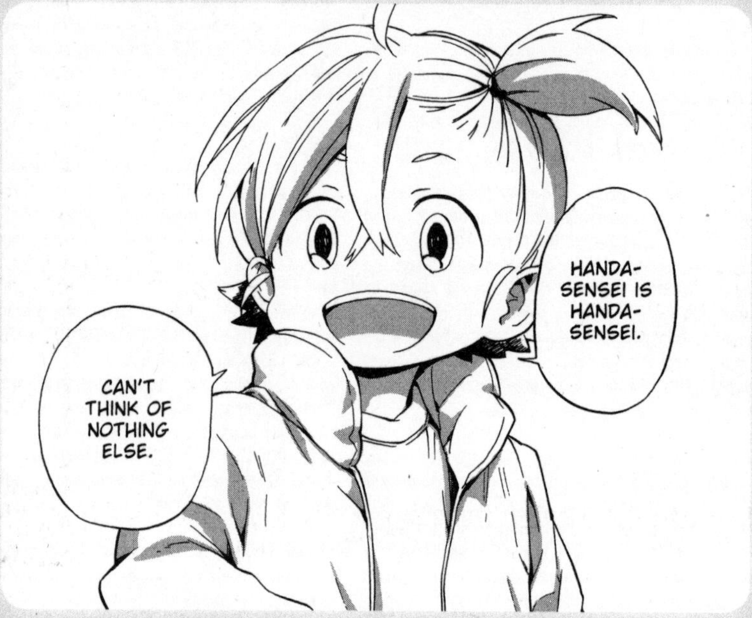
HANDA-SENSEI IS HANDA-SENSEI.
CAN'T THINK OF NOTHING ELSE.

Don't miss Volume 18 of *BARAKAMON*!

COMMON HONORIFICS

no honorific: Indicates familiarity or closeness; if used without permission or reason, addressing someone in this manner would constitute an insult.

-san: The Japanese equivalent of Mr./Mrs./Miss. If a situation calls for politeness, this is the fail-safe honorific.

-sama: Conveys great respect; may also indicate that the social status of the speaker is lower than that of the addressee.

-kun: Used most often when referring to boys, this indicates affection or familiarity. Occasionally used by older men among their peers, but it may also be used by anyone referring to a person of lower standing.

-chan: An affectionate honorific indicating familiarity used mostly in reference to girls; also used in reference to cute persons or animals of either gender.

-sensei: A Japanese term of respect commonly used for teachers, but can also refer to doctors, writers, and artists.

Calligraphy: Japanese calligraphy has a long history and tradition, with roots stemming from ancient China. One of the traditions carried over was the Chinese expression of the "Four Treasures," which refers to the brush, ink, paper, and inkstone used in calligraphy. Traditionally, an inkstick—solidified ink—is ground against an inkstone filled with water in order to produce ink with which to write. This time-consuming process helped to teach patience, which is important in the art of calligraphy. However, modern advances have developed a bottled liquid ink, commonly used by beginners and within the Japanese school system.

Gotou Dialect: Many of the villagers, especially the elderly ones, are actually speaking the local Gotou dialect in the original Japanese. This dialect is reflected in the English translation with some of the grammar elements of older Southern American English to give it a more rustic, rural coastal feel without making it too hard to read. (It's not meant to replicate any particular American accent exactly.) This approach is similar to how dialect is made accessible in Japanese media, including *Barakamon*, because a complete dialect with all of its different vocabulary would be practically incomprehensible to most Tokyo residents.

Yen: 100 yen is roughly equal to one US dollar.

INSIDE COVER

Salute and **kanpai** are the Italian and Japanese equivalents of "cheers," respectively.

Shochu is a Japanese liquor distilled from a variety of possible ingredients (sweet potato here), much like vodka or brandy.

Flower-viewing is a popular Japanese spring pastime, where people gather in groups to sit among the cherry blossom trees while they're in bloom. It also tends to be an occasion for eating and drinking heavily.

PAGE 33

"In spring, one sleeps a sleep that...": Miwa's quoting the proverb *Shunmin akatsuki wo oboezu*, which means "In spring, one sleeps a sleep that knows no dawn."

PAGE 50

"Callie? But neither one's calico...": The original Japanese had the suggested catlike name be Mike ("mee-keh"), which means "tortoise shell pattern."

PAGE 74

Let's Stay in the Countryside!: *Inaka ni Tomarou!* was a weekly travel series that ran on TV Tokyo from 2003—2010.

PAGE 79

"Akio-P!": "Name-P," with the "P" standing for "Producer," is a naming style that was originally used in the gaming/software world, such as in iDOLM@STER and Vocaloid, as well as on the Japanese video site Niconico, but has become more generally known and used since then.

PAGE 98

Yuna and Akio realized the "creepy lady" they'd seen was the nice woman who made their food right after they heard her nickname, **Panchi**, because it refers to her *panchi-paama* ("punch-perm") curly hairstyle that is usually associated with gangster-type men.

PAGE 127

Drop-off is a fishing term for the area where a coastal seabed, lake bed, etc., shifts abruptly from shallow to deep. Fish tend to gather at such places because it's easy to find food while still being close to deep water for escape. The Japanese term, shiome, has a slightly different meaning: a visible line on the water surface that indicates a boundary between two different water masses. Since shallow and deep water are effectively different water masses, "drop-off" and *shiome* are equivalent for fishing purposes. So look for a subtle line next time you're out fishing!

A **yaen**, with two "squid jig poles" linked together to serve as a sort of spear, doesn't seem to be used much in squid fishing outside Japan; usually, the spiked prongs are on the lure itself, or a single pole with prongs is used as the site to attach the actual baitfish.

PAGE 142

The brand name **YOSHINO** (the creator's name!) is most likely referring to SHIMANO, a company which is best known for cycling components but also manufactures fishing tackle and accessories like Headmaster is wearing. The name of his rod, "YOSHINO Eging Rod Extend Fermata," is probably referring to SHIMANO's Sephia XTUNE line of rods, and the name of his reel, GRAVITY 4000G, is probably a reference to SHIMANO's GRAPPLER line of reels.

PAGE 150

Ucc: The actual coffee brand name is "Ucc," with the logo entirely in roman letters; here, they substituted in the Japanese *hiragana* symbol for "u".

ON17

Satsuki Yoshino

Translation/Adaptation: Krista Shipley, Karie Shipley
Lettering: Lys Blakeslee

Barakamon Vol. 17 © 2018 Satsuki Yoshino SQUARE ENIX CO., LTD. First
published in Japan in 2018 by SQUARE ENIX CO., LTD. English translation
rights arranged with SQUARE ENIX CO., LTD. and Yen Press, LLC through
Tuttle-Mori Agency, Inc.

English translation © 2019 by SQUARE ENIX CO., LTD.

Yen Press
1290 Avenue of the Americas
New York, NY 10104

Visit us at yenpress.com
facebook.com/yenpress
twitter.com/yenpress
yenpress.tumblr.com
instagram.com/yenpress

First Yen Press Edition: February 2019

Yen Press is an imprint of Yen Press, LLC.
The Yen Press name and logo are trademarks of Yen Press, LLC.

Library of Congress Control Number: 2015296448

ISBNs: 978-1-9753-0304-4 (paperback)
       978-1-9753-0305-1 (ebook)

10 9 8 7 6 5 4 3 2 1

WOR

Printed in the United States of America